WRITING THE AMERICAN CLASSICS

Art is the path of the creator to his work.

—Emerson, "The Poet"

WRITING THE AMERICAN CLASSICS

EDITED BY

James Barbour and Tom Quirk

The University of North Carolina Press

Chapel Hill and London

© 1990 The University of North Carolina Press
All rights reserved

Library of Congress Cataloging-in-Publication Data

Writing the American classics / edited by James Barbour and Tom Quirk.
    p. cm.
    Includes bibliographical references.
    ISBN 0-8078-1896-8 (alk. paper) ISBN 0-8078-4280-x (pbk. : alk. paper)
    1. American literature—History and criticism. 2. Authors,
American—Biography. 3. Canon (Literature). 4. Authorship.
I. Barbour, James, 1933– . II. Quirk, Tom, 1946– .
PS88.W7 1990
813'.509—dc20   89-16648
                                         CIP

The paper in this book meets the guidelines for permanence and durability of the Committee on Production Guidelines for Book Longevity of the Council on Library Resources.

Passages from John Bennett's "Ishmael at His First Cutting-In," in *The Struck Leviathan,* © 1952 by the University of Missouri Press, are used by permission.

Passages from the manuscript of *The Sun Also Rises* by Ernest Hemingway are used by permission of The Ernest Hemingway Foundation.

Passages from the papers of Richard Wright are used by permission of Ellen Wright.

A version of Keneth Kinnamon's essay appears as the Introduction to his *New Essays on Native Son.* © 1990 by Cambridge University Press.

An extract from the letter of John Steinbeck to Wanda Van Brunt, 22 February 1949, © 1990 by Elaine A. Steinbeck, is used by permission of McIntosh and Otis, Inc.

The John Steinbeck–Wanda Van Brunt correspondence is quoted with permission of the Steinbeck Research Center, San Jose State University Library, San Jose, California.

The John Steinbeck–Paul Caswell correspondence is quoted with permission of the Steinbeck Archives, Steinbeck Library, Salinas, California.

Manufactured in the United States of America
94 93 92 91 90   5 4 3 2 1

IN MEMORY OF LEON HOWARD
FRIEND, TEACHER, SCHOLAR

Contents

JAMES BARBOUR AND TOM QUIRK

Introduction

At the Academy of Fine Arts in Florence Michelangelo's *David* stands
at the end of the gallery. As one approaches this masterpiece of Renaissance sculpture, one passes the *Prigioni*, or "Slaves." These are
four unfinished pieces commissioned for the funeral monument of
Pope Julius II, a project that was begun again and again for some
thirty years before it was finally abandoned. The *Prigioni* now serve as
muted introduction to the *David*—figures unreleased from the stone
yet suggestive of the forms they would have taken had circumstance
conspired in their favor. And in the distance stands the masterwork,
the *David*, serene and accomplished.

In a sense this collection of essays is meant to convey this sort of
approach to certain masterpieces of American literature. For these are
the stories of stories. They describe the genesis and circumstance of
several important American books—how they were conceived and
reconceived; how they were created and how discovered; how, often,
an author's ambitions enlarged as the project grew in the imagination
and therefore forever outran achievement in a way that made many
writers believe their finished works, works we accept as classics, to be
failures. This was the case with William Faulkner's *The Sound and the
Fury*. For it was not until he believed that the doors of publication were
closed to him that he began to write for himself and attempted to tell
the story of Caddy Compson four times over and from four different
perspectives. Each time, he thought he had failed to tell her story
properly. If Faulkner believed that his novel was ultimately a failure,
still it was written during a "matchless time," when the resources of
talent and energy converged and conspired to produce a book for
which he always had a special fondness. The same was true for F. Scott
Fitzgerald, who kept extending the deadline for completion of *Tender
Is the Night* until the writing occupied nearly a decade of the writer's
short life and the book had changed and matured in ways that paralleled the author's own artistic and emotional growth. What had begun
as the story of a young man who would kill his mother in a drunken
rage altered its course several times before it took the form of its
publication in 1934. By that time his wife, Zelda, had had her own

mental breakdown and Scott could finally fictionalize the experience of his own marriage. In a way, though, *Tender Is the Night* was not finished even then, for he was convinced that the novel needed dramatic restructuring. "DO YOU THINK THAT ONCE PUBLISHED A BOOK IS FOREVER CRYSTALIZED" he wrote Bennett Cerf, and he began to reformulate a book that in a sense had grown up alongside of him.

These are only two of the more familiar instances of works of the imagination that took the strange and interesting paths of their creators and enlisted the best efforts and sometimes obsessive commitments of talented writers who were moved to create more out of inner necessity than practical obligation. In this collection Sally Wolff and David Minter tell the story of the composition of *The Sound and the Fury*, and Scott Donaldson that of *Tender Is the Night*, but it seems to be rather characteristic of America's greatest books that they were born out of a context of personal or commercial failure. So great was his disappointment with his own lack of literary success that Faulkner once complained he might quit the literary business and go to work to earn his living. The profits for *Tender Is the Night* did not discharge Fitzgerald's debts to his publishers; Herman Melville complained in the midst of composing *Moby-Dick* that "dollars damned him" and prevented him from writing the sort of book he desired; and Henry Thoreau, who had paid the publishing costs for *A Week on the Concord and Merrimack Rivers*, owed the printer money and had some seven hundred unsold copies of his book to serve as fateful warning for his next work, *Walden*. Yet Melville became so involved in his book that it took him an additional year to complete it; and Thoreau labored seven years on *Walden*, as it evolved from a lecture about his life at the pond to a satire of his culture and eventually to a meditative and introspective account of his "real" rather than his "actual" life.

The shifting interests and involvement of a writer with his or her material accordingly requires amendment and reconciliation of the text in ways that refuse logic, pattern, or neatness. The ship's carpenter on the *Pequod* may speak for any number of American authors who sought to fashion and refashion, mend, repair, and enlarge upon the material of the imagination:

> I don't like this cobbling sort of business—I don't like it at all. . . . I like to take in hand none but clean, virgin, fair-and-square mathematical jobs, something that regularly begins at the beginning, and is at the middle when midway, and comes to an end at the conclusion; not a cobbler's job, that's at an end in the middle, and at the beginning at the end.

But the composition of so many of America's most interesting books proves that the ways of the imagination are more often than not a cobbler's business in one way or another. Willa Cather built her *Professor's House* around the high mesa of the Tom Outland story; Twain removed the raft chapter from *Huckleberry Finn* and put it into *Life on the Mississippi* and made several late and seemingly unnecessary insertions into the completed manuscript; and Benjamin Franklin reorganized and made major additions to his autobiography in the long and curious course of its composition at the same time that he was writing the story of a life that, as he well knew, only death could complete.

The essays in this volume attempt to trace the contours of the genesis and composition of several major works in American literature. This is a collection of genetic-biographical essays about how certain American texts came to be. But the contributors are not simply interested in tracing the compositional histories of these works but in identifying, as well, the unique resources of the creative imagination as it encounters and searches for its material—as it in a sense discovers its story in the telling. Melville, for example, in writing the cetology chapters of *Moby-Dick*, discovered the symbolic qualities of his white whale, one of the most potent symbols in all of American literature. Twain discovered in his creation of Huckleberry Finn and Jim an unsuspected dignity, even nobility of character, that he was unable to assign them consciously but, through the commands of his own imaginative vision, dramatized so authentically that generation after generation of readers have been proud of Huck for choosing hell above his own self-interest and have been willing to go there with him. And Hemingway's running commentary in the notebooks in which he composed *The Sun Also Rises* reveals the shifting focus of his story as he searched for the hero of his book. What began in the desire to write a book about bullfighting quickly shifted to a short story and then gradually evolved into a full-fledged novel. In the process Hemingway mastered his craft and, at the same time, told a story replete with a spiritual suggestiveness that he could not have anticipated at the beginning.

The cobbling business of the literary imagination uncovers unguessed dramatic opportunities and reconciles or combines sometimes trivial or pedestrian preoccupations in a way that transcends narrow desires for public favor or commercial success. Often a writer will defer to the practical judgment of publishers and editors. Richard Wright removed the portions of *Native Son* that portrayed the sexually charged nature of his young central character, and Twain deleted parts of *Life on the Mississippi* that revealed his intense anti-Southern feelings, though he was able to smuggle some of that feeling into *Huckleberry Finn*. But the impetus of the creative imagination issues its own mysterious appeal nevertheless, and it is that mystery that a study of the compositional history of a text seeks to reveal.

In *East of Eden* John Steinbeck attempted to write a book that would "contain all in the world I know [about writing] and it must have everything in it of which I am capable." So concerned was he with matters of invention while he was composing this most ambitious novel that the writing process itself became a metaphor for the book. He kept a daily record of his progress in a series of letters that eventually would be published as *Journal of a Novel.* This "journal" provides fascinating access to the creative process as it spreads beyond the accumulating pages of his manuscript—the author "invents" the environment for his inventing, constructing a special writing table and paperweight and giving over several pages in his journal to a sort of metaphysics of the selection of proper pencils. Cather's *Professor's House*, as James Woodress shows, had its beginnings in the experience of visiting the ancient cliff dwellings in Mesa Verde National Park. Her immediate response was to write a story she would call "The Blue Mesa." But it was not until several years later that she could complete the tale that would eventually be called "Tom Outland's Story," and that story, in turn, became a centerpiece to be framed by the story of Godfrey St. Peter and fashioned into one of her most moving and disturbing novels. What began in rather ordinary ambition became over the course of time an interesting problem of form that she solved with a literary sophistication that nevertheless preserved the original feeling of encountering the cliff dwellings of an ancient people. And Wright combined in *Native Son* what he knew from his own life of the experience of young black men in the South and North with convictions about class struggle that he had acquired through his contact with the Communist party in a way that made Bigger Thomas representative of the victimization of black and white alike.

The essays in this volume record the efforts of the imagination to address and master the matter before it; this is the path of the creator we have attempted to present. We wish to take the reader through that period or process when the figure is finally conceptualized and lifted out of the marble that surrounds it. That process is an adventure of the mind and heart, capable of venturing in the undiscovered country of the imagination and retrieving some portion of its own awareness and discovery. These essays are written for a common reader—someone simply interested in our cultural history and the creation of our literature in ordinary and actively human ways. Such an interest is typically prior to interpretation or theory. It derives from a curiosity, and sometimes an awe, about how such and such a work came to exist—what motivated its creation, informed its vision, urged its completion. For many it is just that sort of interest that brought us to love our authors and our books as lavish, surprising, sometimes reckless, and often entrancing feats of the imagination made by engaged human beings who have passed on to us something of that vital involvement and energy in their works.

In a sense these stories are twice-told tales and as such are not meant primarily for the specialist. The cumulative discoveries of innumerable scholars have enabled the contributors to render the histories of the subjects with accuracy and measured judgment, but the essays were written for the student who is in the process of learning the history of books and for the teacher, still a student, in search of knowledge about the creator and the created. Nevertheless there is much that is new in these essays that may interest and inform the specialist as well. Many of the contributors have given fresh attention to the manuscripts and extratextual evidence that inform an account of the composition of their chosen texts. Some have inspected newly discovered material or have given a fuller account of the relevance of extant evidence to the genesis of a certain work. Still others have demonstrated the interrelated concerns of other works published by the same author or have given a completer account of the biographical circumstance that motivated or engendered a text. All have contributed in some way to a fuller understanding of the unique circumstances of composition and special features of the individual imagination as it sought to realize itself in literary creation. And to the extent that genetic inquiry is a species of criticism (though that is not its primary function) it possesses a certain explanatory power over works of imagination. All of the essays here in some fashion, and to a greater or lesser degree, provide new and convincing interpretations of these texts.

Perhaps a word is in order concerning the title of our volume. By the term "classic" we mean nothing more than that the subjects of this collection of essays have found a permanent place in our literary canon. They are books that are read and reread, in the classroom and out, and have continued to interest several generations of readers. The works we have selected for discussion were chosen not on the basis of some exclusive cultural or aesthetic privilege but because the stories of their composition are interesting and existing evidence allows those stories to be told. No doubt the canonical status of any book may be challenged for any number of reasons, but the word "classic" may be applied without much hesitation to all but two of the titles discussed here. Cather's *Professor's House* may not enjoy the long-standing and wide acceptance of *My Ántonia* or *Death Comes for the Archbishop*, but its artistic poise and originality assure it a continuing power to interest all manner of readers, and its acceptance as a classic seems a sure eventuality. Likewise Steinbeck's *East of Eden* may never preempt the importance of *Grapes of Wrath*, but it was intended to be the author's great achievement. If it failed, finally, it was a classic failure and serves as an example of a book for which the creator seemed willing to fabricate everything but was unable to transform his fabrication into greatness. Even so, Cather and Steinbeck have always had a popular following and their books, including *The Professor's House* and *East of Eden*, have continued to be read. They have found their place in our literature without the necessary authorization or endorsement of the literary establishment. The stories of their composition will not necessarily reform opinion, but they may serve to make them more completely ours.

More than the European writer, Stephen Spender observes in *Love-Hate Relations: English and American Sensibilities*, the American writer *"exists"* in his or her fiction and poetry: "One feels, reading Melville, Whitman and Hemingway, that the writer's subjective consciousness permeates the object created. It may be for this reason that the biography of American writers seems so much more relevant to understanding their works than does that of English ones. The more one knows about these Americans the better one understands the subjectivity conveyed." What may be said of the biographies of American writers may also be said of America's books. These essays are the biographies of books; they seek to show how the figures of the imagination were released from the intractable solidity of their subject matter through artistic craft and emotional commitment. If they also serve to increase a reader's understanding of our literature, both as formally constituted texts and as literary creations, so much the better.

WRITING THE AMERICAN CLASSICS

J. A. LEO LEMAY

Lockean Realities and Olympian Perspectives: The Writing of Franklin's *Autobiography*

Beginnings and endings are the two most important places in the structure of most literary works of any length, for they typically introduce the most important aspects of the speaker and the work's fictive world and conclude with invaluable clues for its interpretation, assessment, and achievement. Tracing the genesis of a book with an exceptionally complicated and fascinating compositional history such as Benjamin Franklin's *Autobiography* repays our efforts by disclosing a conscious literary artistry that the author sometimes took pains to conceal and a structural design that might be mistaken for carelessness or indifference. Autobiographies necessarily possess a structure that combines a strong progressive movement (the sequential life story), a dialectical urge (the present position and knowledge of the writer/subject versus the earlier position and comparative ignorance of the subject/writer), a cyclical movement (always returning from the past time being described to the present and back again to the past), and a final failure. Not only is the narrative always returning from the present to the supposed recollection of a particular time in the past, but the narrative also continually drives forward and gains upon the present which, in its turn, continually advances. Though the life story approaches ever closer to the present, it can never reach it, for only the writer's death will stop the remorseless attenuation of the present into the future. And though a major denouement may provide an opportunity for a closure, every reader knows that change (from a state of holiness, happiness, despair, poverty, wealth, fame, sinfulness, failure, or success) is an inherent part of life. Death alone provides the closure for an autobiographer—providing, of course, that the life proves interesting to the end. The writer's attempt to record his own life is thus necessarily doomed to, at best, partial completion. So every autobiography attempts, by its form if not its content, to triumph over time and death—Franklin, like all great autobiographers, realized the nature of the attempt and its necessary failure.

1

Franklin was a consummate literary artist who paid special attention to the *Autobiography*'s opening and to its several closures, though he twice (at the end of Part 1 and the end of Part 3) concluded the story of his life on a note, not of finality, but of future possibility. This essay is devoted primarily to the opening and the several endings of the book.[1] And since a detailed examination of the process of composing the *Autobiography* reveals a major addition (and reorganization) within the work, I have also attempted to explain why Franklin made the addition.

I. The Basic Facts

Franklin wrote the *Autobiography* over an eighteen-year period, in three countries.[2] The *Autobiography* can be said to have four parts. The text itself justifies the division into Parts 1, 2, and 3; the history of composition and publication reveals a fourth part. In composing the *Autobiography*, Franklin wrote on folio sheets, folded once to make four pages, and folded again to make a crease lengthwise down the middle of the page. He then would write on only one-half of the width of a page, leaving the other column (to the creaseline) blank for possible additions or revisions. He began the *Autobiography* in England. Part 1 (87 manuscript pages) was written in 1771, while Franklin, aged sixty-five, vacationed at the home of Jonathan Shipley, Bishop of St. Asaph. Franklin stayed at Twyford, the bishop's country estate, for two weeks, from Tuesday, 30 July, to Tuesday, 13 August. He spent his days, as he later reminisced to the bishop, doing "a little Scribbling in your Garden study."[3] He also wrote the outline of the *Autobiography* at this time.

The *Autobiography* is mainly chronological, and Part 1 brings the story of his life down to 1731, concluding with his marriage to Deborah Read and his "first project of a public nature" (*A*, 72), founding the Library Company of Philadelphia. The outline, however, comes down to the time that Franklin began writing (1771) and concludes with "My character. Costs me nothing to be civil to inferiors, a good deal to be submissive to superiors &c. &c." (*A*, 205.25–27).[4] Evidently Franklin intended to round off the *Autobiography* by discussing his personality.

Thirteen years later, Franklin, now aged seventy-eight, wrote Part 2 (17 manuscript pages) in Passy, France. In 1784 he had been living in Passy as minister to France for eight years. He had concluded his major business in France (bringing France into the American Revolutionary War against England and, later, making a peace treaty between the United States and England). He was now waiting for

Thomas Jefferson to replace him as minister before returning to America. Part 2, the most famous section of the *Autobiography*, does not advance the chronological story of Franklin's life. It seemingly repeats the same topic that had finished Part 1 in 1771 (the founding of the Library Company of Philadelphia); briefly takes up his religion; and spends almost all of its pages on Franklin's "bold and arduous Project of arriving at moral Perfection" (*A*, 78).

Part 3 (119 manuscript pages), longer than all the other parts of the book combined, was written four years later, beginning in August 1788. Franklin had returned to Philadelphia in 1785 but had been busy as president of the Pennsylvania Assembly (in effect, governor of Pennsylvania) and as a member of the Constitutional Convention until 1788. Part 3 tells of his life from 1731 to 1757, when he arrived in London on his first Pennsylvania Agency. He sent copies of the first three parts to Benjamin Vaughan in England (2 November 1789) and to Louis Le Veillard in France (13 November 1789).[5] But we know from letters in October 1788 that he had completed most of Part 3 a year earlier, for he reported to the Duke de La Rochefoucauld on 22 October 1788 that he had brought his "personal History . . . down to my fiftieth year" (*NCE*, 205) and to Benjamin Vaughan on 24 October 1788 that "the history of my life" was "now in the year 1756, just before I was sent to England" (*NCE*, 205–6).

Changes in the ink and the handwriting enable us to guess that in 1788 he wrote as far as the account of his assembly messages against Governor Denny (*A*, 157.33 [ms. p. 197*]).[6] It would therefore at first seem that only seventeen additional pages (157.33–166.13 [ms. pp. 197*–213]) were written after October 1788. But the handwriting, ink, and paper all show that he actually wrote an additional section of the manuscript (11 manuscript pages) after October 1788 and inserted it in an earlier section of Part 3 (121.34–129.33 [ms. pp. 156–66]).

Part 4 (8 manuscript pages) was also written in Philadelphia, sometime after he sent off copies of the first three parts in October 1789. Franklin died on 17 April 1790, at age eighty-four, so Part 4 must have been written within a five-month period, while Franklin was eighty-three or eighty-four. Part 4 brings the story of his life from his arrival in England in 1757 down to his successful negotiations against the Penns in 1760. By the time of his death, Franklin had been suffering from kidney stones for more than a decade, and the last manuscript page of the *Autobiography* is written in a slanting, feeble hand that suggests he was writing while sitting in bed, suffering.

II. Beginning the *Autobiography*

The form of the *Autobiography*'s opening deliberately resembles a letter, with a heading (the date and place "Twyford, at the Bishop of St Asaph's 1771") and a salutation ("Dear Son"). The letter addresses his son, William Franklin, who in 1771 was at least forty years old.[7] William Franklin had been the royal governor of New Jersey for nearly nine years and was probably the most adroit and successful royal governor in the colonies. But the "Son" to whom the *Autobiography* is addressed is presumably an adolescent or young adult, aged, say, twelve to twenty-five, who can learn the lessons ("the conducing Means" [*A*, 1]) that the *Autobiography* will teach. As Abel James wrote Franklin after reading Part 1, such writings are of "vast importance" in providing models and guides for youths (*NCE*, 58). Benjamin Vaughan also thought the *Autobiography* would be useful in "the forming of future great men" (*NCE*, 59), and Franklin himself wrote to Vaughan that he especially selected the contents with a "view to benefit the young reader" (*NCE*, 206). But the successful governor William Franklin was already formed. He was not a youth and would hardly benefit from the *Autobiography*. The book was not written for him.

Besides, Franklin was writing an autobiography, a whole book, not a letter. After all, he drew up an outline for the *Autobiography* that brings his life story down to 1771. Furthermore, he begins with his 1758 visit to Ecton and Banbury in Northamptonshire, where he and William examined the church records and gravestones. Some of the genealogical data survive in William Franklin's hand (*Papers*, 8:119). Unless Franklin believed that his son was an idiot, there would be no point in telling William about the information and anecdotes they learned together. William knew them as well as Franklin. Further, we know from other sources that a number of the anecdotes Franklin relates in the *Autobiography* were old favorites, told to various friends throughout his life (*NCE*, 207–11). Surely William Franklin knew many of them. Common sense as well as various bits of evidence testify that the opening words of the *Autobiography*, "Dear Son," are a fiction. The *Autobiography* was not really meant as a letter (or a book!) addressed to William Franklin. Why, then, does Franklin pretend it is?[8]

He had at least three good reasons. First, "Dear Son" as the opening of a book signals a book's genre and contents. Conduct books—that great genre that flourished when society was changing from a feudal, rural order composed largely of peasants and aristocrats into an urban, modern one, with a rising middle class—typically began with the salutation "Dear Son."[9] Conduct books introduced a new society. They taught individuals how to behave in the transformed conditions. Franklin's *Autobiography* belongs in the genre—but it is the most radical conduct book, for it portrays a world without distinct social classes, without fixity, without absolute values. It portrays a world where the individual chooses what to do, what to become, where to live, and what to believe. It is radically different from the stable, class-conscious, hierarchical worlds portrayed by Franklin's contemporaries Samuel Richardson, Henry Fielding, and Tobias Smollett, as well as from the God-centered universe portrayed by his American contemporary Jonathan Edwards. In its implications, the fictive world of Benjamin Franklin's *Autobiography* is frighteningly new, different, and fundamentally insecure, a world where the individual must constantly create whatever reality lies underneath the perpetually shifting appearances.[10]

Second, the salutation attests to the truthfulness, the normalcy, the ordinariness, the commonplaceness, and the reality of the *Autobiography*'s fictive world. The second sentence says, "You may remember the Enqueries I made among the Remains of my Relations when you were with me in England" (1). What could be more ordinary? What better testimony to the truth could one have? And what could be less pretentious, less self-important, less ridiculous, than the straightforwardness of that statement? After all, the besetting sin of autobiography as a genre is the exaggerated self-importance of the writer. The self-deluding pride of mankind was a favorite Franklin theme. He was well aware that most autobiographers finally appeared to be foolishly vain figures. Every litterateur of Franklin's day knew the lesson of the wonderful mock autobiography by Alexander Pope and John Gay, "Memoirs of P. P., Clerk of This Parish," which claimed that an autobiography "might justly be entitled, *The Importance of a Man to Himself*."[11] Franklin's salutation "Dear Son" was the first of many efforts to make the persona of the *Autobiography* seem to be truthful, normal, ordinary, commonplace, real, and reasonably modest—even though Franklin in cynical moods thought that vanity was essential to a person's life and happiness. The point of view, or perspective, that Franklin here establishes has important literary and philosophical implications. His usual perspective affirms that though society is (or should be) fluid, that though absolute verities seem not to exist, and that though people are (or should be) free to create themselves, nevertheless the dense texture of time and place, of circumstances and events, constitutes all the reality that is necessary for the individual to function in the world. But even this minimum security is occasionally satirized. Franklin sometimes undercuts the commonsensical assurance that the Lockean world of appearance is sufficient and is all that we can really know by emphasizing a dichotomy between appearance and reality (*A*, 60, 68, 90). He also sometimes rises to an Olympian point of view.

Third, and perhaps most important, through his salutation Franklin achieves a warm and intimate tone. The reader *is* (or rather *is put in the place of*) Franklin's son. The writer and the reader have a relationship of support and trust, of teaching, learning, and love. They have shared experiences and exist in a continuing state of mutual love and respect. (See the references to *we* in *A*, 3 and 4.) *You* occurs repeatedly in Part 1 of the *Autobiography*: for example, 1 (five times), 3 (twice), 4 (twice), 8, 24 (twice), 51 (three times), 58, and 63. *You* is simultaneously the reader and William Franklin. Franklin dropped this fiction after Part 2 of the *Autobiography*, and when he wrote Part 3, he added at the end of Part 1 an explanation of the change: "Thus far was written with the simple Intention of gratifying the supposed Curiosity of my Son; what follows being . . ." (*A*, 72). Then he struck out "simple" and inserted "express'd in the Beginning" after "Intention." Then he canceled all after "Intention," so that the revised account read: "Thus far was written with the Intention expressed in the Beginning & therefore contains several little family Anecdotes of no Importance to others. What follows was written many years after in compliance with the Advice contained in these Letters, and accordingly intended for the Publick. The Affairs of the Revolution occasion'd the Interruption."

In the canceled phrase Franklin admitted ("the *supposed* curiosity of my Son" [my emphasis]) that the salutation and references to his son, "you," were all a fiction, and he conceded that the rest of the *Autobiography*, "intended for the public," would be more formal. Too bad; for the fiction of the letter to his son added a complexity to the relationship between author and reader that he abandoned in the rest of the book (with an important exception at the end of Part 2). In fact, Franklin certainly appreciated the effect of this fiction—and the holograph manuscript reveals that he added to the effect late in the composition of Part 3 (1789).

The content of the heading or dateline is unusual. In a normal heading of a letter in the eighteenth century or today a specific date is almost always given, but the place is often omitted. Franklin's heading, however, is printed in most texts as "Twyford, at the Bishop of St Asaph's, 1771." (Of course, the identifying phrase "at the Bishop of St Asaph's" after "Twyford" would have been superfluous if the *Autobiography* were really addressed to William Franklin, who knew quite well that Twyford was the bishop's home.) Franklin emphasizes the place, rather than the time, of composition. He probably had two reasons for doing so. First, he did not remember the exact time—and he even, at first, wrote down the wrong year. The *Genetic Text* reveals that Franklin at first wrote "1770" and then wrote a heavy "1" over the "0." In fact, the heading was an afterthought, added in 1789 (see *A*, 218, note for 1.1–3). The second reason to emphasize the place (and to include it at all) was to commemorate Franklin's old friend Jonathan Shipley, Bishop of St. Asaph, who had died the year before this addition was made and who had, in the Revolutionary period, abandoned the possibility of further promotion in the Church of England in order to support Franklin and the American cause. The key point, however, for our purpose is that the deliberate addition of the heading in 1789 strengthens the impression that the *Autobiography* was originally meant to be a letter addressed to his son—and the late date that Franklin added to the heading is one more bit of evidence that the letter form was a carefully contrived fiction.

Carl Van Doren suggested that during his first day's composition Franklin wrote as far as his parents' epitaph. The conjecture seems likely, partly because the epitaph (*A*, 9–10) concludes two full sheets of writing (eight pages), and would have been a logical place to stop. The following words, at the beginning of the third sheet (page 9 of the holograph manuscript), also seem to suggest that a break and some reflection have occurred: "By my rambling digressions I perceive my self to be grown old. I used to write more methodically" (*A*, 10). Van Doren suggested that "this was probably when he thought of the need for an outline."[12] I agree, especially since, as Van Doren pointed out, the first topic in the outline ("My writing") is taken up soon afterward (*A*, 12), and since none of the information in the first ten manuscript pages of the *Autobiography* is represented by topics in the outline. But after manuscript page 12, almost every paragraph in Part 1 of the *Autobiography* has a corresponding topic in the outline.

Reading over the first day's composition also evidently made Franklin dissatisfied with the *Autobiography*'s beginning, and he therefore made a long addition after the second sentence of the opening (and still later added a clause to the second sentence). The addition takes up two full columns in manuscript pages 1 and 2. It is by far the longest addition in the columns originally left blank. The long addition gives the *Autobiography* a much fuller beginning, explaining at length why Franklin supposedly wrote the book.

Franklin gives five reasons for writing the *Autobiography*, but most of them are fictions. The first reason in the addition amplifies the reason briefly expressed in the first two sentences. He is going to provide William Franklin with a number of family anecdotes. The second reason gives his fundamental purpose. In a long compound, complex sentence, he writes that his *Autobiography* is to be a conduct book: "the conducing Means I made use of . . . my posterity may like to know, as they may find some of them suitable to their own Situations, and therefore fit to be imitated." The deliberate statement reinforces the purpose implicit in the salutation "Dear Son," but the *Autobiography* differs from most conduct books because it focuses on the means to achieve an end, rather than upon the end to be achieved.[13]

Franklin does say something about ends, though goals or ends are deliberately subordinated to means. The first dependent clause ("Having emerg'd from the Poverty & Obscurity in which I was born and bred, to a State of Affluence and some Degree of Reputation in the World") brings up the popular themes of the American Dream, both the economic, or rags-to-riches, theme (about which Franklin actually says very little) and the theme of obscurity to fame (or nebulousness to identity)—an archetypal recapitulation of every human being's development.[14] The second dependent clause ("and having gone so far thro' Life with a considerable share of Felicity") brings up that common goal in life, happiness. The ends or goals mentioned, then, are wealth, fame, and happiness—though each is qualified. These ends could be considered a third reason for writing the book.

The fourth reason is to relive his life. Franklin explains that the closest he could come to reliving his life was remembering it, "and to make that Recollection as durable as possible, the putting it down in writing" (2). Of course this is not really an important reason for writing the *Autobiography*. Writing is hard work, not the gratification that remembering might be. Here Franklin struck the first of his postures as a dotish old man. "Hereby, too, I shall indulge the Inclination so natural in old Men, to be talking of themselves and their own past Actions, and I shall indulge it, without being troublesome to others who thro' respect to Age might think themselves oblig'd to give me a Hearing, since this may be read or not as any one pleases." This is simply cant. Old people may like to talk about themselves, but the sustained discipline of writing a book is entirely different from rambling reminiscences. And Franklin, at age sixty-five, was hardly a garrulous old man. He was the most famous American in the world and the most famous living scientist. He was among the greatest writers of the age. He was the agent for Pennsylvania, Georgia, New Jersey, and Massachusetts to Britain. He was the leading spokesman for America in Europe, and he was among the most influential persons of his day. Almost anyone in the world would have been honored and flattered to hear Franklin's reminiscences. Franklin's posture jokes about old people and calls for the reader to join him in the joke, and at the same time it distances the author and asks the reader to regard the persona with bemused sympathy.

The fifth and final reason Franklin gives for writing the book is, "perhaps I shall a good deal gratify my own vanity." Again, absolute cant. He could gratify his vanity by visiting any one of several dozen London coffee shops. There, he would be the center of attention of an admiring circle. Writing alone in a garden was hardly a way to gratify his vanity. It did, however, introduce the theme of vanity (one of the major themes in the book) and it also directly confronted that primary sin of the autobiographer—unconscious vanity and overweening partiality to oneself. Franklin immediately makes an acute observation that strikes us with a shock of recognition: "Indeed I scarce ever heard or saw the introductory Words, *Without Vanity I May Say*, &c. &c. but some vain thing immediately follow'd." He proceeds to another (and, in this case, a rather cynical) perception—"Most People dislike Vanity in others whatever Share they have of it themselves"—before turning the tables on all the old commonplace ideas of vanity: "but I give it fair Quarter wherever I meet with it, being persuaded that it is often productive of Good to the Possessor & to others that are within his Sphere of Action" (*A*, 2).

How is that? What does he mean? That sentence dumbfounds the reader. Suddenly Franklin has transformed the discussion of his ostensible reasons for writing his *Autobiography* into a philosophical consideration of the nature of humanity and human motivation. After two *aperçus* into the omnipresence of vanity in human beings, he seems to justify vanity, positing it as a major cause of beneficence. The last sentence in this added paragraph takes the unexpected argument a step further. Toying with the idea of the usefulness of vanity, Franklin almost sacrilegiously makes the presence of vanity an occasion for thanking God. In traditional Christian thought, one must fight against the presence of pride (the first deadly sin) in oneself. But the consummate irony is that Franklin describes vanity as "among the other Comforts of Life" (*A*, 2). He has gradually changed the perspective from the ordinary and commonplace to a cosmic view of the situation of human beings. Life, he implies, would be unbearable if blinding vanity did not make people the center of their own universes. From some demigod's viewpoint, vanity is indeed a comfort of human life. The Olympian perspective also suggests another—higher and truer—reality than the world of appearances.

Reading over the opening sometime within the next two weeks, Franklin added a brief paragraph to it, thanking God for the "Happiness of my past life." Religion was to be another major subject of the *Autobiography*. (In one of the few repetitions in the *Autobiography*, Franklin twice lists the points of his deistic creed [*A*, 76, 92].) But he added the paragraph in an attempt to forestall the criticism that he was irreligious. Indeed, it probably occurred to him that his last sentence might offend some Christians. Franklin was infamous among his friends for his religious opinions, which he took up and dropped without any consistency, although he mainly was, or pretended to be, a deist.[15] Despite this final addition to the opening, the main criticism of the *Autobiography* from its first appearance to the present has been that it (or Franklin) is not sufficiently Christian.[16]

The transformed and expanded opening of the *Autobiography* gives it a deliberate and formal introduction, a series of supposed explanations for writing the book, and (in the closing sentences of the first paragraph) an extraordinary sophistication and subtlety. Besides introducing several of the book's major themes, it prepares the reader for some of the tones of humor, irony, familiarity, and abstruse thought that will recur throughout. It also introduces two important postures of the persona: first, the trusted sage giving advice (presumably to his son); and second—a persona that partially burlesques the first—a fond, foolish old man who loves to ramble on about himself and his past. For the close reader, these self-contradictory postures playfully anticipate the elusive nature of reality that is a major subject of the *Autobiography*. Above all, the additions to and revisions of the original opening two sentences give a full sense of a beginning to a long and complex work of art.

III. The Additions in Part 3

One surprising and interesting fact that emerges about the composition of the *Autobiography* from a detailed examination of the paper, foliation, and handwriting is that manuscript pages 156–66 (*A*, 121.38–129.34) were written after manuscript pages 167–97* (129.35–157.33).[17] The inserted pages contain an account of the founding of the Pennsylvania Hospital (*A*, 121–23), the Reverend Gilbert Tennent's subscription for a new building for Philadelphia's Second Presbyterian Church (123–24), Franklin's projects for keeping the streets clean and for paving them (124–25), his design for streetlights (125–26), his proposal to Dr. John Fothergill for cleaning and keeping clean the streets of London and Westminster (126–29), and his concluding paragraph justifying attention to "these trifling Matters" (129). Only two of these six topics appear in the outline: "Project of Hospital my share in it. Its success" (*A*, 204.16–17), and "Project for paving the city" (204.27–28). They are separated by more than fifteen topics, and the latter comes immediately before the topic concluding Part 3 of the *Autobiography*, "I am sent to England" (204.28). Indeed, Franklin's bill for paving the streets was evidently not taken up in the Pennsylvania assembly until

3 March 1758—more than a year after he had left for England. Chronologically it belongs at the very end of Part 3 or in Part 4. Of course, Franklin did not meet Dr. Fothergill until he was in England, and the proposal probably was made sometime after the end of Part 4. Why then, one may wonder, did Franklin introduce these additional topics? Why are they out of chronological order? And why would he put them all together—so that they seemed, even to him, to demand an apology for dwelling upon such minor matters?

The long addition accomplishes two related purposes. First, it reinforces the persona that he especially wanted to present himself as achieving, *amicus humani generis*, a friend to humankind.[18] Friendly contemporaries like John Winthrop and Edmund Burke bestowed this epithet on him.[19] Franklin viewed the *amicus humani generis* as the highest type of human being and the one most deserving fame, and wanted to present himself in this way.[20] The added section allows him to praise his contemporaries who carried through beneficent designs: Dr. Thomas Bond, the Reverend Gilbert Tennent, John Clifton, and especially Dr. John Fothergill, "who was among the best men I have known, and a great Promoter of useful Projects" (*A*, 126). Gathering together this group of projectors and projects makes them stand out. They create a more forceful impression than if they were simply introduced in the *Autobiography* at different places in their correct chronological order. And when Franklin concludes the series with that high praise for Fothergill, the astute reader realizes that Franklin is not only presenting Fothergill as a friend to mankind but also praising himself. Fothergill, a double for Franklin, is but the shadowy type; the real antitype, the truly "great Promoter of useful Projects," is Franklin.

Second, the addition makes Franklin's achievements more human and thus more approachable as models. He wrote the *Autobiography* as a kind of conduct book, with himself as an example of what (and, in some instances, what not) to do. But who could hope to attain his eminence as a politician, statesman, scientist, or writer? Franklin's achievements resulted from a combination of great genius and extraordinary application. They were beyond the realm of most people's potential. The projects related in this addition, however, were relatively modest, and some were perhaps even trivial. But they were the kinds of achievements most people might attain. Unlike Franklin's more famous accomplishments, these provided realistic models. They proved that even the most ordinary citizens (like the otherwise unknown John Clifton) could make a difference in their neighbors' lives.

Finally, too, the addition showed that Franklin was not above such "trifling Matters," and that ordinary and mundane affairs were important to the quality of life. These two purposes, especially the latter, explain why Franklin changed his original intention from "Here bring in an Account of my electrical Fame." Instead, he later canceled "electrical Fame" and added "Part in establishing the Hospital . . ." (*A*, 121.34–35). He therefore allowed the story of the "Rise and Progress of my Philosophical Reputation" (*A*, 152) to remain in its place near the end of Part 3 (152–56) and concentrated in this long addition on comparatively humdrum though useful projects.

IV. Closure in the *Autobiography*

Franklin deliberately concluded the *Autobiography* three times—when he finished Part 1, Part 2, and Part 3. The only time he stopped when he did not deliberately end a book was when he stopped writing Part 4, which of course is the actual end. There he did not even put in the period to conclude the last sentence.

In a way, no autobiography can ever be complete, for the complete story of an individual's life includes his death. Franklin's outline is mainly chronological, with many topical notes; when he wrote it in 1771, he brought the list of topics down to that date, with notes on his character concluding the topics. The form of the book as originally projected in the outline is not what he wrote in 1771. When he took up the outline again in 1784, he added a list of topics covering his life between 1771 and 1778, concluding with "To France, Treaty &c." The continuation of the outline (*A*, 205.30–35) is simply a series of chronological and topical notes without any suggestion of a conclusion.

The closure of Part 1. When he stopped writing Part 1 in 1771, Franklin had to return to London, where he knew he would once again be caught up in an extraordinarily busy routine and would not soon have another chance to take up the *Autobiography*. Indeed, he might never be able to return to it. He hoped to, however, and he added a marginal note for the next topic, "My Manner of acting to engage People in this and future undertakings" (*A*, 72).

The foliation of the paper containing the holograph manuscript provides evidence concerning Franklin's intention in 1771. All the writing was done on folio sheets (each folded to make four pages) through manuscript page 84. Then he took up a single leaf (one half of a folio sheet, containing only two pages). Evidently he planned to conclude his writing within two pages. (The alternative, but unlikely, explanation is that he had used up all the full sheets of paper on hand and only had leaves left.) The last full sheet (ms. pp. 81–84) describes his hardships and gradual success as an independent printer in Philadelphia. At the very end of page 84, he introduces the next topic, his marriage to Deborah Read. He probably thought he could deal with this topic in one page and with the following topic, the Library Company, in one more page. (These two topics appear in sequence in the outline [A, 203.27].) After all, this would take Franklin completely through his youth and early manhood, through all his most formative years, and would see him established well in life with a wife, a business, and his first public project.

But Franklin was not quite finished when he exhausted the space on manuscript page 86 with "This was the Mother of all the N American Subscription Libraries now so numerous." He wrote "It" and then took up another leaf (not another full sheet) and finished the sentence: "is become a great thing itself, and continually increasing." He added a dash or flourish—a symbol that he often employed at rhetorical conclusions in his manuscripts.[21] Evidently he intended, if only for a second, to end at that point. But he was not satisfied with that closing, and so he added another sentence about the significance of the libraries: "These Libraries have improved the general Conversation of the Americans, made the common Tradesmen & Farmers as intelligent as most Gentlemen from other Countries, and perhaps have contributed in some degree to the Stand so generally made throughout the colonies in Defence of their Privileges." These words conclude Book 1. The final sentence opens up the focus and provides a definite sense of an ending. Franklin has shifted his perspective from the nitty-gritty details and particular circumstances (which characterize the usual point of view in the *Autobiography* and are part of the sense of texture and dense Lockean reality the book conveys)[22] to a time-spanning and world-spanning view recalling the Stamp Act and subsequent and ever-growing tensions between America and England. Though the story of his life has only been brought down to his twenty-fifth year, 1731, the references in the final sentence bring the situation down to the present (1771) and to the great, unresolved, and ever more threatening conflict.

The last sentence is also a fitting closure because of the explicit and implicit attitudes and philosophy it conveys. Franklin begins by implying that Americans have benefited from the libraries and that the improvement is reflected in their "general conversation." The attitude underlying this statement implies that the majority of people will "improve" in ideas and learning if they have the opportunity. It conveys an egalitarian and a positive, even optimistic, view of humanity. Second, he says that the libraries have made the "common Tradesmen & Farmers as intelligent as most Gentlemen from other Countries." The statement is patriotic, anti-aristocratic, and obviously egalitarian.

The use of the word *intelligent* is especially interesting, for its primary meaning is not knowledge of books and ideas (listed only third in the unabridged *Oxford English Dictionary*) but instead "having the faculty of understanding." Franklin, a literary genius sensitive to denotations as well as connotations of words, seems to be asserting that there is no difference between "common Tradesmen & Farmers" in America and "most Gentlemen" in other countries. As mentioned above, the America that Franklin portrayed in the *Autobiography* was classless. The reality, of course, was different. In America, as in England and Europe, the social structure was hierarchical. Gentlemen sent for laborers and craftsmen (including printers like Franklin) when they had business for them. Ordinary people were automatically supposed to defer to gentlemen (to step, for example, off a narrow paved path into the mud when they met). But times were changing, especially in America—and even more so in the imagination of Franklin. Wealth and family had been attacked and discredited as the basis for social distinction. What remained for most thoughtful students of social organization in the eighteenth century was not just acquired ability, but a profound difference in the degree of ability. The faculty of intelligence was supposed to distinguish the upper from the lower classes.[23]

Franklin, however, attacks the distinction. There is no difference in ability, in fundamental intelligence, he says, between the "common Tradesmen & Farmers" and "most Gentlemen." The basis of social hierarchy is thereby annihilated. Furthermore, he implies that America is the land of democracy and achieved opportunity because the "common" Americans have reached the intellectual level achieved by "most Gentlemen" in England or Europe. And this difference between Americans and the English reminds him of their political differences and of the Americans' revolutionary stand from the time of the Stamp Act to the present, "in Defence of their Privileges." The sentence also suggests that republican principles are synonymous with knowledge. Learning will naturally convince the student that the rights and liberties (or "Privileges") of the people are fundamental principles that must be defended and upheld. Learning, Franklin ultimately implies, will necessarily lead to belief in a democracy.

Thus the conclusion of Part 1 achieves the sense of an ending not only by enlarging the perspective from a confined, limited, Lockean reality in place and time to a global perspective, but also by making the final sentence resound with meanings, significance, and implications. Had Franklin never been able to return to the *Autobiography*, Part 1 alone would have survived as a consummate work of art. Many students have thought that Part 1 is the best and most entertaining portion of the *Autobiography*, and that everything thereafter is anticlimactic. Of course, the first editions of the *Autobiography* printed only Part 1. What is most surprising, however, is that the popular edition of the *Autobiography* until the end of the nineteenth century continued to be Part 1, with the addition of Henry Stuber's continuation.[24] William Temple Franklin's edition (1818) of the first three parts simply did not compete.[25]

The closure of Part 2. Part 2 even more admirably concludes the *Autobiography*. Part 2 begins with an introduction—the letters of Abel James and Benjamin Vaughan—saying why Franklin should write an autobiography and what its contents should be. James, in Philadelphia, had read Part 1 and therefore knew the themes and the approach that Franklin had already taken (*A*, 182–84). He retained the manuscript of Part 1 and the original outline, but in the spring or early summer of 1782 wrote Franklin urging him to go on with the *Autobiography* and enclosing a copy of the outline made by his clerk Henry Drinker. Franklin then sent James's letter and the outline to his disciple Benjamin Vaughan, asking Vaughan's advice. Vaughan's literary ability and intimate knowledge of Franklin enabled him to write a much more detailed list of reasons why Franklin should continue the *Autobiography*, which he thought should be published in conjunction with Franklin's long-projected work, "The Art of Virtue" (*A*, 186, 188, 189; *NCE*, 223–26). Vaughan's letter probably influenced the contents of Part 2, for it presents a modified version of the "Art of Virtue." Part 2, however, ends with the topic that Franklin originally meant to use as the conclusion of the book, "My character" (*A*, 205.25)—the last topic in the original outline of the *Autobiography*, though he omitted the one detail that he listed under that general topic in the outline ("Costs me nothing to be civil to inferiors, a good deal to be submissive to superiors").

Part 1 had brought the outline down to the topics "Marry. Library erected." Franklin says in the second paragraph of Part 2 that he does not recall whether he gave "an Account . . . of the means I used to establish the Philadelphia public Library" (*A*, 73). Although he partially repeats the account of establishing the Library Company at the beginning of Part 2, what he now focuses upon is the "means" he used. That was in fact to be the next topic he would take up if he ever returned to writing the book, for his marginal self-reminder at the end of Part 1 was "My Manner of acting to engage People in this and future Undertakings" (72).

The subsequent entries in the outline are pertinent. After "Library erected," the following fourteen entries appear:

Manner of conducting the Project. Its plan and Utility. Children. Almanack. The Use I made of it. Great Industry. Constant Study. Fathers Remark and Advice upon Diligence. Carolina Partnership. Learn French and
German. Journey to Boston after 10 years. Affection of my Brother. His
Death and leaving me his Son. Art of Virtue. (*A*, 203.27–33)

Part 2 takes up the first two topics, skips the next three ("Children.
Almanack. The Use I made of it."), takes up the topics "Great Industry" (*A*, 75.21), "Constant Study" (75.17), "Fathers Remark and Advice upon Diligence" (75.28), skips the next five topics, and takes up
his religion (76–78) as an introduction to the modified version of his
"Art of Virtue."[26] As described in his 1760 letter to Lord Kames, the
projected work on virtue would focus upon the means to achieve the
desired ends, and he held up to scorn the Apostles' "ineffectual
charity" in exhorting "the Hungry, the Cold, and the Naked, *be ye fed,
be ye warmed, be ye clothed*, without shewing them how they should get
Food, Fire, or Clothing" (*NCE*, 224). Franklin repeated the same criticism in discussing the "Art of Virtue" in the *Autobiography* (*A*, 88–89).

As Franklin talks about the "Art of Virtue" that he had meant
someday to write, he is actually then presenting it—in terms of the
story of his own efforts at self-transformation, his "bold and arduous
Project of arriving at moral Perfection" (*A*, 78). Of course the list of
thirteen virtues leads into a consideration of his own character, beginning with his attempt to achieve "Order" (87). He strove valiantly but
concluded that with respect to Order he was "incorrigible" (87). After
writing a general consideration of his character in terms of the virtues
(and the "imperfect state" [88] he attained), he turns to that favorite
subject, vanity or pride, to conclude the topic.

The ending of Part 2 provides an artful closure for the *Autobiography*. Unlike Part 1, the physical manuscript gives no indication of his
intention, for it consists of five full sheets (ms. pp. 88–104), and
Franklin finished writing near the bottom of the first page of sheet 5
(*A*, xxvii). The final paragraph, consisting of five sentences, reads:

> In reality there is perhaps no one of our natural Passions so hard to
> subdue as *Pride*. Disguise it, struggle with it, beat it down, stifle it, mortify
> it as much as one pleases, it is still alive, and will every now and then peep
> out and show itself. You will see it perhaps often in this History. For even if
> I could conceive that I had compleatly overcome it, I should probably be
> proud of my Humility. (*A*, 90–91)

Once again, Franklin steps back from his ordinary perspective, the
factual, limited viewpoint of everyday experience, to a more philosophical and distanced perspective. The first two sentences deal with
"our natural passions," that is, the general passions of humankind,

and the point of view is that of a demigod, someone scornful of the struggles of humanity. Then Franklin turns the table on himself and makes the reader the demigod—one who will see the writer Franklin inadvertently revealing his own vanity. In the final sentence he drives home the point that vanity is an innate human quality with a witticism ostensibly against himself, but really, of course, recurring to an Olympian perspective that views his own actions, as well as humanity's in general, with irony—and some scorn.[27]

Although the prevailing structure of the *Autobiography* is that of simple sequential chronological progress, the conclusion of Part 2 also suggests a cyclic structure. The topic of vanity or pride recalls the beginning of the *Autobiography*, in particular the conclusion of the first paragraph, where Franklin gave as one reason for writing the book that it would gratify his "own vanity." That echo of the earlier passage on vanity, which also splendidly achieved an Olympian perspective of "Vanity among the other Comforts of Life" (*A*, 2), seems absolutely suitable as a conclusion to a discussion of his character, for he began the book with an account of the characters of his ancestors. (For example, of his father he wrote, "I think you may like to know something of his Person & Character" [8].) Thus there is a touch of the cyclic round of human life, with various generations striving and failing to escape from the imprisoning effects of their humanity and vanity. Although only implicit in this and several other passages of the *Autobiography*, the interrelation of vanity, human limitation, and cyclic repetition is explicit in Franklin's great bagatelles of a few years earlier, "The Ephemera."[28]

The diction at the end of Part 2 also suggests a cyclic structure, a return to the book's opening: the direct address *You* in the sentence "You will see it perhaps often in this History." *You* of course is the reader. But the opening established the primary supposed reader as Franklin's son William. William Franklin, not the reader, has been the supposed referent for "you" as it was used throughout Part 1. Franklin's disclaimer about the audience of the *Autobiography* at the end of Part 1 (his statement that the latter parts were "intended for the publick" rather than for his son [72]), was, as I pointed out above, actually not written until 1788. Part 2, therefore, at the time Franklin finished it in 1784, still pretended that the primary referent for *You* was William Franklin. Thus "You" recalls the opening salutation of the *Autobiography*, "Dear Son."

With these two echoes of the opening of the *Autobiography* to jog the reader's memory, the book achieves a quite finished form, for it has indeed told a considerable story (through the formative years to the means whereby Franklin was able to achieve whatever he had accomplished in life), and thus it recurs back to the opening in still other ways, by fulfilling his hope in the beginning to present "the conducing means I made use of" (*A*, 1), and by, in the telling of the story, "living" his "Life over again" (2). With such echoes of the beginning, the cycle returns from the conclusion of Part 2 to the beginning of Part 1 and returns again to the conclusion in a constantly turning wheel. Structurally, Part 2 has the book's most aesthetically satisfying ending.

The closure of Part 3. Part 3 takes the story of Franklin's life down to 1757. In the outline, the topic concluding Part 3 is "I am sent to England" (*A*, 204.28). It is followed by a large closing bracket, evidently Franklin's sign that he had come this far in his list of topics. The final words of Part 3, indented in a paragraph to themselves, are "We arrived in London the 27th of July 1757." There is no note in the manuscript for the next topic, perhaps because this sentence itself begins the London period in Franklin's life, which (with a two-year hiatus back in Philadelphia, 1762–64) was to continue until 1775. Certainly the normal perspective of Lockean reality, the factual, ordinary basis of the *Autobiography* does not change.

But in Franklin's life story the arrival in London marks the beginning of another set of friends, another set of routines and memberships in different organizations (with the club of Honest Whigs replacing the Junto as his favorite), and another set of political concerns. The outline makes these new starts obvious. Here are the next ten topics:

Negotiation there. Canada delenda est. My Pamphlet. Its reception and Effect. Projects drawn from me concerning the Conquest. Acquaintance made and their services to me Mrs..S.., Mr Small. Sir John P. Mr. Wood. Sargent Strahan and others. Their Characters. (*A*, 204.28–32)

The only topic that directly continues the earlier story is the first, the negotiations with the Pennsylvania Proprietors over the issue of taxing their property. The other topics either concern new acquaintances or new political questions that begin to anticipate the causes of the American Revolution. Franklin's arrival in England was a logical place for him to stop, and he did so. He sent copies of the *Autobiography* to his friends: one copy to France and another to England. His biographers all agree that this point represents a major break in his life. It begins a new chapter (or even a new volume) in every biography I have examined.[29]

Rhetorically, the ending of Part 3 is inferior to the earlier two endings, but it certainly is a logical closure. Even rhetorically, it does have one interesting characteristic. It strongly suggests that more is to come—that, in the words of Henry David Thoreau, Franklin had "several more lives to live."[30] It completed one phase of his life, and just put him on the brink of beginning another. The end of one life and the beginning of another is not without appeal as a suitable closure, though one does miss the rhetorical portentousness of, say, Thoreau's last line: "The sun is but a morning star."

The closure of Part 4. Having attempted to justify three closures in the *Autobiography*, why not attempt to justify the last—the ending of Part 4, the actual end of the book? After all, the next topic in the outline, "Negotiation there," continues the story of Pennsylvania's politics, and Part 4, though brief, does provide a conclusion for that topic. But Part 4 begins with Franklin's dramatic introduction to the opinions of England's key politician, Lord Granville, President of the Privy Council. Franklin reports that "his Lordship's Conversation having a little alarm'd me as to what might be the Sentiments of the Court concerning us, I wrote it down as soon as I return'd to my lodgings" (*A*, 167). He then places Granville's views in 1757 in perspective, contrasting them with what he thought were the former attitudes of the House of Commons in 1744 and its future attitudes in 1765. This topic looks forward to the Stamp Act and the Revolution. As it is not present in the outline, it may be that in 1771 Franklin saw no reason to include that alarming and memorable scene, whereas the American Revolution made the conversation seem more significant. The interview with Granville prepares the way for more to follow. Those plans, however, were canceled by Franklin's death on 17 April 1790. But perhaps I have underestimated Franklin's art. Perhaps the absence of the period (that commonest symbol of closure) at the end (?) of the final sentence of Part 4 was deliberate. After all, every possible reader knew that important events followed.

Notes

1. Most essays on the *Autobiography*'s structure have argued that the different times and places when and where Franklin composed the book resulted in different purposes and personae becoming more important in the four different parts. I agree but emphasize that Parts 2, 3, and 4 *supplement* what has already been presented in Part 1, and that they do not radically change the nature of the book or its major themes. With the important exception of Part 2, they mainly continue Franklin's life story. Important studies of the structure are Sayre, "The Worldly Franklin and the Provincial Critics"; Levin, "*The Autobiography*: The Puritan Experimenter"; Aldridge, "Form and Substance"; Sappenfield, *A Sweet Instruction*; and Dawson, "Franklin's 'Memoirs' in 1784."

2. This summary is based upon evidence printed in *The Autobiography of Benjamin Franklin: A Genetic Text*, ed. Lemay and Zall, xix–xxxiii. Unless otherwise noted, all page references are to this edition (cited as *A* in the text), which shows all cancellations, revisions, and additions. Line numbers have been cited as well in references to notes in the outline (202–5). The only previous essay especially focusing upon the significance of the manuscript revisions in the *Autobiography* is Zall's "Portrait of the Autobiographer as an Old Artificer."

3. *Papers of Benjamin Franklin*, ed. Labaree, Willcox, et al. (hereafter *Papers*), 22:200.

4. Two topics ("Farce of perpetl. Motion" and "Writing for Jersey Assembly") in the outline as it existed in 1771 were added out of chronological order at the end (see *A*, 210, notes for 205.28, 205.29).

5. *Franklin's Autobiography: A Norton Critical Edition*, ed. Lemay and Zall (hereafter *NCE*), 207.

6. Because Franklin carelessly repeated the numbering of ms. pp. 191–200, the second series of ms. pp. 191–200 is distinguished by an asterisk in the *Genetic Text*.

7. His date of birth is unknown but is usually given as 1731, no doubt so that he might seem to be the legitimate son of Benjamin and Deborah Read Franklin. But he was illegitimate and was probably born in 1729. See *Papers*, 3:474n.

8. More briefly and without citing any evidence from the holograph manuscript of the *Autobiography*, I argued in "Benjamin Franklin," 238–39, that the letter device was a fiction.

9. See, for example, Wright, *Advice to a Son*.

10. Aspects of this theme have been discussed by Ward, "Who Was Benjamin Franklin?" (reprinted in *NCE*, 325–35); Cawelti, *Apostles of the Self-Made Man*, 9–24; Ketcham, "Benjamin Franklin: *Autobiography*"; and Lemay, "Benjamin Franklin, Universal Genius," *The Renaissance Man in the Eighteenth Century* (pertinent section reprinted in *NCE*, 349–60).

11. *Prose Works of Pope*, ed. Cowler, 2:109. Captain John Knox says, "Accounts of Transactions, in which the Writer has borne any part, are generally drawn with so evident a design of making him 'The hero of the Tale,' that they have been called in the just severity of wit, 'The Histories of Man's Importance in his own Eyes.' " An Historical Journal of the Campaigns in North America, 2 vols. (London, 1779), 1:v. The best-known reference to the "Memoirs of P. P." and to its moral occurs in the first paragraph of Nathaniel Hawthorne's "Custom House" sketch, prefatory to *The Scarlet Letter*.

12. Van Doren in *Franklin's Autobiographical Writings*, 210.

13. One of the earliest and best reactions to D. H. Lawrence's hostile chapter on Franklin in *Studies in Classic American Literature* (1923; reprinted in *NCE*, 289–99), Schneider's "Significance of Franklin's Moral Philosophy" emphasizes that Franklin is primarily concerned with an ethics of means rather than ends and also maintains that Franklin perceived that moral distinctions have no basis in the absolute but are relative to a human point of view.

14. For an analysis see my "Franklin's *Autobiography* and the American Dream," reprinted in *NCE*, 349–60.

15. William Robertson, historian and principal of the University of Edinburgh, wrote to William Strahan in 1765 concerning Franklin's recommendation of Ezra Stiles for a doctorate in divinity: "For my Own part I have implicit confidence in his Recommendation even of a Doctor of Divinity though Theology I believe is of all the Sciences the only one in which I suspect he is not

perfectly sound." *Papers* 12:69–70. Aldridge, *Benjamin Franklin and Nature's God*, provides an extended analysis of Franklin's religious thought.

16. See Richard Price's letter to Franklin of May 1790 (written after reading the first three parts of the *Autobiography*), and the editorial comments in *NCE*, 241–43, 249, 258–59, 270–71. Ironically, a recent criticism is that he was not entirely atheistic—see *NCE*, 279.

17. For the evidence see *A*, xxvii, xxxiii, and 241 (textual note for 121.34–37).

18. Humphreys, " 'The Friend of Mankind,' " supplies some contexts for the topos in the eighteenth century. Adair's *Fame and the Founding Fathers*, 3–26, is also pertinent.

19. Writing to the Reverend Richard Price on 10 April 1775, John Winthrop called Franklin the "Friend of Liberty, of America and Mankind." *Correspondence of Richard Price*, ed. Thomas and Peach, 1:204. In a letter to Franklin on 15 August 1781 Burke called him "the lover of his species" and on 28 February 1782, "the friend of mankind." *Writings of Franklin*, ed. Smyth, 8:318, 320.

20. Before editing the *Genetic Text*, I presented a number of reasons for believing that Franklin regarded the *amicus humani generis* as the type of person most deserving fame and that he presented himself as a friend to mankind in the *Autobiography*. The fact that this long passage was written later and inserted into the *Autobiography* strengthens that contention. See Lemay, "Benjamin Franklin," 241–43.

21. For an examination of Franklin's uses of dashes in composition see *A*, 252–53.

22. Lynen, *The Design of the Present*, 90, has shrewdly contrasted the usual perspective of Franklin's *Autobiography* ("a view qualified and limited to just that portion of reality which appears within the self's horizon") with that of Jonathan Edwards's "eternal point of view" in his "Personal Narrative."

23. Franklin printed numerous proverbs in *Poor Richard* attacking wealth and family as bases for social distinction. Though early in his life Franklin (like almost everyone in his day) had assumed that blacks were inferior in intelligence to whites, he had changed his mind before 17 December 1763 (*Papers*, 10:395–96). In a letter to Lord Shelburne, Benjamin Vaughan explained Franklin's radical attitudes toward class differences: "He thinks that the lower people are as we see them, because oppressed; and then their situation in point of manners, becomes the reason for oppressing them." *NCE*, 219. Franklin's position is thus more democratic and more radical than Jefferson's advocacy of a natural "aristoi" in his letter to John Adams of 28 October 1813. Jefferson, *Writings*, ed. Peterson, 1304–10. For some traditions of "natural aristocracy" see the index of Harrington, *Political Works*, ed. Pocock, s.v. "Aristocracy, natural."

24. The young Philadelphia litterateur Dr. Henry Stuber began writing a biographical account of Franklin for the *Universal Asylum and Columbian Magazine* shortly after Franklin's death. It appeared monthly from May 1790 through June 1791. When the Robinsons in London printed a retranslation of the unrevised Part 1 of Franklin's *Autobiography* back into English, they supplemented Part 1 with Stuber's biography from the *Universal Asylum*. This mishmash remained the best-known and most frequently reprinted version until the late nineteenth century, when John Bigelow's 1868 edition gradually superseded the Robinsons' 1793 edition. See *A*, li–liii.

25. Ford, *Franklin Bibliography*, nos. 437–546 and 387ff. See also *A*, li.

26. Dawson, "Franklin's 'Memoirs' in 1784," 287, 289, has argued that "Parts I and II together comprise the only completed, unitary form the 'Memoirs' have ever possessed." In maintaining that Franklin deliberately concluded the *Autobiography* at the end of Part 2, he also commented upon the reordering of the topics of the outline: "To serve the moral purpose of Part II, other topics were advanced from the places assigned them in the 'Notes.' Thus, the discussion of the 'Art of Virtue' was brought ahead of a half-dozen other outline entries, and the importance of Franklin's reception on October 1, 1768, 'King of Denmark invites me to Dinner. Recollect my Father's Proverb,' was moved forward some thirty-seven years from its originally intended position." Although Franklin entered the latter notes in the outline at their correct chronological position (*A*, 205.16–17), he nevertheless intended to introduce his "Father's Remark and Advice upon Diligence" (203.29–30) at this chronological point.

27. Dawson, "Franklin's 'Memoirs' in 1784," 290, observed: "Not incidentally, this self-depreciating ending turns upon the same irony with which Franklin gives their point to many of the bagatelles he wrote in these Passy years, and this neatly fashioned closure is a unique mark of division in a book whose other parts break off abruptly." I might add that throughout his life Franklin made ironic turns upon the persona in ending his essays. Lemay, *The Canon of Benjamin Franklin*, 79.

28. For an analysis see Lemay, "Benjamin Franklin," 234–38.

29. See Van Doren, *Franklin*, 269–70; Parton, *Life and Times of Franklin*, 2:338; McMaster, *Franklin as a Man of Letters*, 167–68; Fleming, *The Man Who Dared the Lightning*, 69–70; Hawke, *Franklin*, 161–62; and Wright, *Franklin of Philadelphia*, 110.

30. Thoreau, *Walden*, ed. Shanley, 323.

Works Cited

Adair, Douglass. *Fame and the Founding Fathers.* Edited by Trevor Colbourn. New York: W. W. Norton, 1974.

Aldridge, Alfred Owen. *Benjamin Franklin and Nature's God.* Durham: Duke University Press, 1967.

———. "Form and Substance in Franklin's Autobiography." In *Essays on American Literature in Honor of Jay B. Hubbell*, edited by Clarence Gohdes, 47–62. Durham: Duke University Press, 1967.

Cawelti, John G. *Apostles of the Self-Made Man.* Chicago: University of Chicago Press, 1965.

Dawson, Hugh J. "Franklin's 'Memoirs' in 1784: The Design of the Autobiography, Parts I and II." *Early American Literature* 12 (1978): 286–93.

Fleming, Thomas. *The Man Who Dared the Lightning.* New York: W. M. Morrow, 1971.

Ford, Paul Leicester. *Franklin Bibliography: A List of Books Written by, or Relating to Benjamin Franklin.* Brooklyn, N.Y.: n.p., 1889.

Franklin, Benjamin. *The Autobiography of Benjamin Franklin: A Genetic Text.* Edited by J. A. Leo Lemay and P. M. Zall. Knoxville: The University of Tennessee Press, 1981.

_____. *Benjamin Franklin's Autobiographical Writings*. Edited by Carl Van Doren. New York: Viking Press, 1945.

_____. *Benjamin Franklin's Autobiography: A Norton Critical Edition*. Edited by J. A. Leo Lemay and P. M. Zall. New York: W. W. Norton, 1986.

_____. *Papers of Benjamin Franklin*. Edited by Leonard W. Labaree, William B. Willcox, et al. New Haven: Yale University Press, 1959–.

_____. *The Writings of Benjamin Franklin*. Edited by Albert Henry Smyth. 10 vols. 1907. Reprinted. New York: Haskell House, 1970.

Harrington, James. *The Political Works of James Harrington*. Edited by J. G. A. Pocock. Cambridge: Cambridge University Press, 1977.

Hawke, David Freeman. *Franklin*. New York: Harper & Row, 1976.

Humphreys, A. R. " 'The Friend of Mankind' (1700–60)—An Aspect of Eighteenth-Century Sensibility." *Review of English Studies* 24 (1948): 203–18.

Jefferson, Thomas. *Thomas Jefferson: Writings*. Edited by Merrill D. Peterson. New York: Library of America, 1984.

Ketcham, Ralph L. "Benjamin Franklin: *Autobiography*." In *Landmarks of American Writing*, edited by Hennig Cohen, 20–31. New York: Basic Books, 1969.

Knox, John. *An Historical Journal of the Campaigns in North America*. 2 vols. London, 1779.

Lawrence, D. H. *Studies in Classic American Literature*. New York: T. Seltzer, 1923.

Lemay, J. A. Leo. "Benjamin Franklin." In *Major Writers of Early American Literature*, edited by Everett Emerson, 205–43. Madison: University of Wisconsin Press, 1972.

_____. "Benjamin Franklin, Universal Genius." In *The Renaissance Man in the Eighteenth Century*, 1–44. Los Angeles: William Andrews Clark Memorial Library, 1978.

_____. *The Canon of Benjamin Franklin 1722–1776: New Attributions and Reconsiderations*. Newark: University of Delaware Press, 1986.

Levin, David. "*The Autobiography of Benjamin Franklin*: The Puritan Experimenter in Life and Art." *Yale Review* 53 (1963): 258–75.

Lynen, John F. *The Design of the Present: Essays on Time and Form in American Literature*. New Haven: Yale University Press, 1969.

McMaster, John B. *Benjamin Franklin as a Man of Letters*. Boston: Houghton Mifflin, 1887.

Parton, James. *Life and Times of Benjamin Franklin*. 2 vols. Boston: Ticknor & Fields, 1867.

Pope, Alexander. *The Prose Works of Alexander Pope*. Edited by Rosemary Cowler. 2 vols. Hamden, Conn.: Archon Books, 1986.

Price, Richard. *The Correspondence of Richard Price*. Edited by D. O. Thomas and Bernard Peach. 2 vols. Durham: Duke University Press, 1963.

Sappenfield, James A. *A Sweet Instruction: Franklin's Journalism as a Literary Apprenticeship*. Carbondale: Southern Illinois University Press, 1973.

Sayre, Robert Freeman. "The Worldly Franklin and the Provincial Critics." *Texas Studies in Literature and Language* 4 (1963): 512–24.

Schneider, Herbert W. "The Significance of Benjamin Franklin's Moral Philosophy." Columbia University Department of Philosophy, *Studies in the History of Ideas* 2 (1925): 291–312.

Thoreau, Henry David. *Walden*. Edited by J. Lyndon Shanley. Princeton: Princeton University Press, 1971.

Van Doren, Carl. *Benjamin Franklin*. New York: Viking Press, 1938.

Ward, John William. "Who Was Benjamin Franklin?" *American Scholar* 32 (1963): 541–53.

Wright, Esmond. *Franklin of Philadelphia*. Cambridge: Harvard University Press, 1986.

Wright, Louis B., ed. *Advice to a Son: Precepts of Lord Burghley, Sir Walter Raleigh, and Francis Osborne*. Ithaca: Cornell University Press, 1962.

Zall, P. M. "A Portrait of the Autobiographer as an Old Artificer." In *The Oldest Revolutionary*, edited by J. A. Leo Lemay, 53–65. Philadelphia: University of Pennsylvania Press, 1976.

JAMES BARBOUR

"All My Books Are Botches":
Melville's Struggle with *The Whale*

On 1 June 1851, as his book was "in its flurry," Herman Melville informed his Berkshire neighbor Nathaniel Hawthorne that he was going to New York to bury himself in a third-story room and slave on his "Whale" as it was "driving through the press." Then appraising his situation and his art, Melville confided that he could no longer find the tranquility in which one ought to write: financial circumstances dictated that he write popular fiction, an act that he could not altogether bring himself to do. The result was both personally and artistically disastrous:

> Dollars damn me; and the malicious Devil is forever grinning in upon me, holding the door ajar. My dear Sir, a presentiment is on me,—I shall at last be worn out and perish, like an old nutmeg-grater, grated to pieces by the constant attrition of the wood, that is, the nutmeg. What I feel most moved to write, that is banned,—it will not pay. Yet, altogether, write the *other* way I cannot. So the product is a final hash, and all my books are botches. (*Letters*, 128)[1]

Six months after having committed himself to his genius and, as a result, having transformed a pedestrian whaling story into the great American novel of the nineteenth century, Melville concluded that his book was a failure. He had been unable to bring the disparate parts of his novel together; hence it was a "final hash." He also knew that he had, in the final months of writing *Moby-Dick*, looked too deeply into the dark nature of existence and had spoken unacceptable truths to a conventional world. The experience of writing *Moby-Dick* was unalterable: Melville believed as an artist that he had written himself away from his audience and was inevitably doomed to neglect and silence.

I

This history of *Moby-Dick* begins properly in the summer of 1849, when in the space of four months Melville wrote two novels.[2] The first was the "beggarly" *Redburn* (1849), which he described as a "nursery tale" based on his first experience at sea on a merchant ship to Liverpool; the other was *White-Jacket* (1850), a narrative loosely patterned on his return home from the Pacific seven years before on a man-of-war.

When Melville returned from his youthful adventures in the South Pacific and decided to make his living as a professional writer, he proposed to keep to a schedule of publishing a novel a year, a rate that he hoped would provide for himself and his family. His writing of *Typee* (1846) and *Omoo* (1847), extravagant accounts of his jumping ship, falling in with the Typees, a cannibal tribe, and his escape and subsequent wanderings in the Pacific, kept to this schedule. But as an author Melville was growing intellectually during this period, borrowing books that excited his imagination from the library of his friend Evert Duyckinck, editor of the *Literary World*, a journal that published his reviews and articles; Melville was diving into a world of ideas. (He later wrote to Hawthorne, "Until I was twenty-five, I had no development at all. From my twenty-fifth year I date my life. Three weeks have scarcely passed, at any time between then and now, that I have not unfolded within myself" [*Letters*, 130].) Inflamed with the works of Spenser, Burton, Browne, and the German romances, Melville changed his new work *Mardi* (1849) into a philosophical and political allegory. He was writing the type of book he wanted to write—he would later characterize them as "books that fail"—but the effort took him almost two years. *Mardi* was panned by reviewers and sold poorly. The lesson was too obvious: to support his growing family he must write more simply and quickly. He repented of his misadventure, at least temporarily, by doubling his efforts in the summer of 1849, but it brought no joy. *Redburn* and *White-Jacket* were, as he described them to his father-in-law, Judge Lemuel Shaw, "two jobs, which I have done for money—being forced to it, as other men are to sawing wood" (*Letters*, 91). The conflict in his art was to repeat itself a year later, when Melville, concluding a fanciful but somewhat typical whaling adventure, was to rewrite the story by consciously committing himself to his genius and to failure.

In the winter of 1849 Melville sailed to England to secure a favorable contract for *White-Jacket*. He arrived home on the *Independence* on 1 February 1850 to begin the most crucial eighteen months of his life. Melville typically wrote his early novels in a semi-autobiographical mode—all but *Mardi* were founded on his personal experience—so, predictably, for his sixth novel he turned to his own early adventures. On 3 January 1841, at the age of twenty-one, he had sailed from New Bedford on the whaler *Acushnet* bound for the South Pacific; this experience would provide the basis for the novel he would eventually call *Moby-Dick*.

Melville's progress with the book is recorded in two letters. The first, to Richard H. Dana, Jr., on 1 May 1850, describes the work.

About the "whaling voyage"—I am half way in the work, & am very glad that your suggestion so jumps with mine. It will be a strange sort of book, tho', I fear; blubber is blubber you know; tho' you may get oil out of it, the poetry runs as hard as sap from a frozen maple tree;—& to cook the thing up, one must needs throw in a little fancy, which from the nature of the thing, must be ungainly as gambols of the whales themselves. Yet I mean to give the truth of the thing, spite of this. (*Letters*, 108)

Two months later, on 27 June, Melville wrote to his English publisher, Richard Bentley, anticipating completion of the book in the fall and further describing it as "a romance of adventure, founded upon certain wild legends in the Southern Sperm Whale Fisheries, and illustrated by the author's own personal experience, of two years & more, as a harpooneer" (*Letters*, 109).

Melville claimed that the work was based on his experience as a harpooner (a claim repeated by Ishmael in "The Affidavit" [chapter 45]), but he had spent at most six months as a harpooner, if that.[3] The story more likely was fashioned from Melville's experience as a common seaman on the *Acushnet* and combined with events taken from his whaling sources;[4] the narrative frame was borrowed from J. Ross Browne's *Etchings of a Whaling Cruise*, which Melville had reviewed for the *Literary World* on 6 March 1847. Browne's story tells of a greenhorn sailor who along with a traveling companion is gulled by an innkeeper; he sails with a brooding "Captain A——," who has his differences with the first mate; Browne's ship sails around the Cape of Good Hope, as does *Moby-Dick*'s Pequod (the *Acushnet* rounded Cape Horn); and *Etchings* includes scenes of the captain's appearance before the quarterdeck, the first lowering, the trying-out process, and a dream yarn. And despite his romantic account of the whale fisheries, Melville no doubt told of the often brutal conditions on board whaling ships (the "truth of the thing" he promised to Dana). Melville describes his work in progress as a "whaling voyage" and a "romance of adventure" that takes place in the fisheries—no particular whale is mentioned. But a year later he refers to the book as "The Whale," the title given to the English edition.

Melville's steady progress on the novel allowed him to return to the Berkshires in July to visit his cousin Robert and his aunt Mary with an eye toward moving his wife, Elizabeth, and his son, Malcolm, to the country. While touring the countryside with his cousin, he concocted the idea of having a party in August for the literary lights of the Berkshires, to which he invited, among others, Oliver Wendell Holmes, his Lenox neighbor Nathaniel Hawthorne, Hawthorne's publisher, James T. Fields, and his New York friends Evert Duyckinck and Cornelius Matthews. In the midst of the planned activities Duyckinck had the opportunity to look at Melville's manuscript and wrote to his brother George on 7 August, "Melville has a new book mostly done— a romantic, fanciful & literal & most enjoyable presentment of the Whale Fishery—something quite new."[5]

Two days before, the group had climbed Monument Mountain, where Melville walked to the end of a projecting rock and pretended to pull on imaginary rigging as Hawthorne looked for the great carbuncle. James T. Fields in *Yesterday with Authors* (Boston, 1878) remembered the remainder of the day:

> In the afternoon . . . we made our way, with merry shouts and laughter, through the Ice-Glen. Hawthorne was among the most enterprising of the merrymakers; and being in the dark much of the time, he ventured to call out lustily and pretend that certain destruction was inevitable to all of us. After this extemporaneous jollity, we dined together at Mr. Dudley Field's in Stockbridge, and Hawthorne rayed out in a sparkling and unwonted manner. I remember the conversation at table chiefly ran on the physical differences between the present American and English men. Hawthorne stoutly taking part in favor of the American.[6]

The meeting with Hawthorne and the evening's conversation deeply affected Melville. His aunt Mary had recently given him a copy of Hawthorne's *Mosses from an Old Manse*, and Melville, immediately after meeting Hawthorne, read the tales and was profoundly moved by them. He found in Hawthorne a "shock of recognition" that prompted him to write a review, "Hawthorne and His Mosses," that Duyckinck printed in successive issues of the *Literary World* (17 and 24 August 1850).[7] Melville found in Hawthorne "that blackness . . . that so fixes and fascinates me":

> this great power of blackness in him derives its force from its appeals to that Calvinistic sense of Inner Depravity and Original Sin, from whose visitations, in some shape or other, no deeply thinking mind is always and wholly free. For, in certain moods, no man can weigh this world, without throwing in something, somehow like Original Sin, to strike the uneven balance. (*NCE*, 540–41)

Melville also found a similar blackness in Shakespeare, whom he had been reading recently:

> But it is those deep far-away things in him; those occasional flashings-forth of the intuitive Truth in him; those short, quick probings at the very axis of reality:—these are the things that make Shakespeare, Shakespeare. Through the mouths of the dark characters of Hamlet, Timon, Lear, and Iago, he craftily says, or sometimes insinuates the things, which we feel to

be so terrifically true, that it were all but madness for any good man, in his own proper character, to utter, or even hint of them. Tormented into desperation, Lear the frantic King tears off the mask, and speaks the sane madness of vital truth. (*NCE*, 541–42)

The conversation at the party comparing American and English men must have been in Melville's mind, for he imaginatively placed Shakespeare in modern times in America. "There are," he reasoned, "minds that have gone as far as Shakespeare into the universe. And hardly a mortal man, who, at some time or other, has not felt as great thoughts in him as any you will find in Hamlet." Shakespeare, he believed, was not unapproachable: "Believe me, my friends, that men not very much inferior to Shakespeare, are this day being born on the banks of the Ohio" (*NCE*, 543).

Melville then ponders the conditions that would allow for an American Shakespeare. He would be a novelist and he would need— and the metaphor indicates whom Melville has in mind—"plenty of sea-room to tell the Truth in" (*NCE*, 544). This latter-day Shakespeare would create new forms and a new language: "it is better to fail in originality, than to succeed in imitation. . . . Failure is the true test of greatness" (*NCE*, 545). Melville closes with a portrait of Hawthorne that expresses "the temper of his mind,—that lasting temper of all true, candid men—a seeker, not a finder yet":

A man now entered, in neglected attire, with the aspect of a thinker, but somewhat too rough-hewn and brawny for a scholar. His face was full of sturdy vigor, with some finer and keener attribute beneath; though harsh at first, it was tempered with the flow of a large, warm heart, which had force enough to heat his powerful intellect through and through. He advanced to the Intelligencer, and looked at him with a glance of such stern sincerity, that perhaps few secrets were beyond its scope.
"I seek for Truth," said he. (*NCE* 547–48)

The description, as one would expect, is of Melville, not Hawthorne.[8] Melville had called himself forth from the wilderness of American literature to write the great American novel. He stated the requirements and challenged his own genius. Hawthorne was simply the "resonator" that allowed him to write his way in.[9] Melville continued during the next year to read his own thoughts into Hawthorne's writing.

Hawthorne had, in Melville's words, dropped "germinous seeds into my soul" (*NCE*, 548), but the sproutings would have to wait, for Melville had not forgotten the painful lesson of writing "books that fail." In the months that followed he moved his family into a new home outside Pittsfield. In October he was sawing and hammering and moving furniture, and he continued working on his whaling adventure, writing cetological chapters for the narrative. Melville habitually inserted factual material into completed manuscripts. This was his intention when, in late April, he checked out William Scoresby's *Arctic Regions* and *History and Description of the Northern Whale Fisheries* from the New York Society Library and ordered Thomas Beale's *Natural History of the Sperm Whale* from Putnam's—at this time he was halfway through his book, according to his letter to Dana, and evidently thinking about adding informational ballast.

The cetological chapters occupied Melville throughout the remainder of 1850. From Carlyle's *Sartor Resartus*, which he borrowed from the well-stocked library of Duyckinck, Melville learned how to transform Scoresby's dull, sermonic tome into burlesqued sources. And he was working Beale's *Natural History*, his main cetological source, into the manuscript, enlarging his novel and writing with ease and excitement. His letter of 13 December to Duyckinck recounts his work day:

> My own breakfast over, I go to my workroom & light my fire—then spread my M.S.S. on the table—take one business squint at it, & fall to with a will. At 2½ P.M. I hear a preconcerted knock at my door, which (by request) continues till I rise & go to the door, which serves to wean me effectively from my writing, however interested I may be. . . . Can you send me about fifty fast-writing youths, with an easy style & not averse to polishing their labors? If you can, I wish you would, because since I have been here I have planned about that number of future works & can't find enough time to think about them separately. (*Letters*, 117)

On 16 December he was composing "The Fountain" (chapter 85), a chapter that provides the precise date of its composing and indicates that he was still working at the cetology: "thousands of hunters should have been close by the fountain of the whale, watching those sprinklings and spoutings—that all this should be, and yet, that down to this blessed minute (fifteen and a quarter minutes past one o'clock P.M. of this sixteenth day of December, A.D. 1850), it should still remain a problem . . ." (*M-D*, 370). At Christmas he left his books behind and joined his wife and their son in Boston, where they had gone to spend the holidays with her father. While he was there the judge checked Scoresby out of the Boston Atheneum for him.[10] Melville was still laboring at the cetology.

But the whale sank Melville's book. The evidence for this lies in the cetological chapters themselves. The whale grew from whale to Whale to WHALE. Ishmael, our cetological expert who personally has seen the whale, prefaces his dissertation by classifying the whale bibliographically and begins his presentation by reviewing man's efforts at capturing the whale pictorially and concludes by discussing its skeletal remains; between the signs of the cetacean and its remains, he describes in exhaustive detail the whale from the outside in and from top to bottom—head to flukes, blubbery blanket to penis—but the living whale, as he readily admits, continues to escape him. Of painted likenesses, "you must needs conclude that the great Leviathan is that one creature in the world which must remain unpainted to the last" (M-D, 264), and of his bones, "How vain and foolish, then, thought I, for timid untravelled man to try to comprehend aright this wondrous whale by merely poring over his dead attenuated skeleton" (M-D, 453). The whale, like life itself, resists man's intellectual efforts and remains a mystery: it is too huge, too vital, too transcendentally other for man's reductive intelligence to "capture" it. The whale is the symbol of that which is beyond man's intellectual and imaginative reach, beyond art and language. And by dedicating himself to the pursuit of the ungraspable beast, Melville was consciously committing himself to a foredefeated venture.

In "Ishmael: At His First Cutting-In" the poet John Bennett evokes the wonder of the animal:

In God's name, who can see the Whale entire?
Who name him in his great entirety?
Preponderant, that flesh whelmed my sight!

My quarrel with God is that He gave me less
Of eye and tongue than I find needful here.[11]

Ishmael, when he comes at last to "The Tail" (chapter 86) and concludes with his cetological efforts, in exasperation offers the only meaningful and truthful comparison: the whale, like God, exists beyond our ability to know.

The more I consider this mighty tail, the more do I deplore my inability to express it. At times there are gestures in it, which, though they would well grace the hand of man, remain wholly inexplicable. In an extensive herd, so remarkable, occasionally, are these mystic gestures that I have heard hunters who have declared them akin to Free-Mason signs and symbols. . . . Dissect him how I may, then, I go skin deep; I know him not, and never will. But if I know not even the tail of this whale, how understand his head? much more, how comprehend his face, when face he has none? Thou shalt see my back parts, my tail, he seems to say, but my face shall not be seen. But I cannot completely make out his back parts; and hint what he will about his face, I say again he has no face. (M-D, 378–79)

In declaring that if he could not know the tail, then how could he possibly understand the face, Ishmael undoubtedly had in mind the passage from *Exodus* (33:20, 23) in which God declared to Moses, "Thou canst not see my face: for there shall no man see me, and live. . . . And I will take away mine hands, and thou shalt see my back parts: but my face shall not be seen."

In writing about the whale, Melville had gone from cetology to theology and had arrived at the hieroglyph that God used as a self-symbol of his otherness in speaking to Job out of the whirlwind: "Canst thou draw out leviathan with an hook? or his tongue with a cord which thou lettest down? . . . Who can discover the face of his garment: or who can come to him with his double bridle? Who can open the doors of his face? his teeth are terrible round him. . . . Upon earth there is not his like, who is made without fear. He beholdeth all high things: he is king over all the children of pride" (*Job* 41:1, 13–14, 33–34).

When Melville concluded the cetology he knew that the whale had whelmed his little "whaling voyage." Ishmael jokingly anticipates the changes in the book that the whale has wrought: "One often hears of writers that rise and swell with their subject, though it may seem but an ordinary one. How, then, with me, writing of this Leviathan? Unconsciously my chirography expands into placard capitals. Give me a condor's quill! Give me Vesuvius' crater for an inkstand! . . . so magnifying, is the virtue of a large and liberal theme! We expand to its bulk. To produce a mighty book, you must choose a mighty theme. No great and enduring volume can ever be written on the flea, though many there be who have tried it" (*M-D*, 456). Melville must now create a protagonist equal in stature to the whale. The germinous seeds of August had sprouted.

II

In the early months of 1851 Melville was writing something new and exciting. Previously playful and generous in his letters to Duyckinck, he was now consciously brusque in declining to write for Duyckinck or to send him a daguerreotype for "Our Portrait Gallery" of *Holden's Magazine* (*Letters*, 120–21, 12 February). He fictionalized Duyckinck's request in his next novel, *Pierre* (1852), where his young author-hero is approached by the joint editor of *Captain Kidd Monthly*, who attempts to shanghai him and "his mug" for the next issue: " 'Look you, my good fellow,' said he [Pierre], submitting to his impartial inspection a determinately double fist,—'drop my arm now—or I'll drop you. To the devil with you and your Daguerreotype!' " (*P*, 254).[12]

Pierre's naive literary adventures in New York City—his attempt to transform himself from a precious minor poet into a major writer by bringing "new, or at least miserably neglected Truth to the world"

(*P*, 283) and his absolute failure—have been recognized as Melville's ironic and burlesque fictionalizing of the final stages of his writing of *Moby-Dick* and the novel's rejection. (Poor Pierre is denounced as a fraud by his publishers, Steel, Flint & Asbestos.) But the whole of *Pierre* is better interpreted as an extended allegory of Melville's year-and-a-half struggle with his "Whale." Exhausted after writing *Moby-Dick*, he turned immediately to a story that he described early on as a "rural bowl of milk."[13] But full of himself and his momentous decision to throw himself upon his genius and write something new and great and American, Melville soon externalized the experience and told his own story.

Pierre begins as a bucolic tale of Pierre Glendenning and his blonde fiancée, Lucy Tartan, but Pierre spies the dark-haired Isabel and is soon convinced that she is his half-sister, daughter of his deceased father's brief passionate romance. She is foreign, strange, and beautiful. Pierre has seen her image in the foliage of a primeval pine tree and recognizes in her a resemblance to the chair-portrait of his father that captured a momentary heightened look of ecstasy on his father's face. Isabel's mysterious history has been told to her by a guitar that automatically sings to her of her past. Pierre decides to protect Isabel and defy convention by running away to New York City to live with her there in a charade marriage. Pierre's imperious and unforgiving mother dies from the shock of his decision. Cut off from the family fortune, Pierre attempts to make his way in the world as an author who will write of hitherto forbidden truths. Lucy joins the pair in the city and attempts to help them by selling portrait sketches. Pierre, however, is beyond help when his manuscript is rejected. He rashly kills his double, his impeccably correct cousin Glendenning Stanley, and is arrested and taken to the Tombs where he, Isabel, and Lucy die together.

Lucy and Isabel represent opposing artistic forces in Melville's life. Lucy is literal representation (the portrait artist) that catches the surface of life and is conventionally acceptable. Isabel is strange and mysterious: she represents the subconscious and the nonverbal (the guitar that is "her mother" and tells her story). Pierre also intuits a deep and strong relationship between himself and Isabel; he has foreshadowings of it in nature (the pine tree) and in the "chair-portrait" of his father that his mother despises. But Isabel is also unacceptable because of her illegitimacy. Pierre's mother, who embodies convention, will accept Lucy because she is no threat to her relationship with her son, but Isabel is anathema. The young women represent the choice that confronted Melville as an author when he was writing *Moby-Dick*.

In his famous introduction to the Hendricks House edition of

Pierre, Henry A. Murray discusses their significance. Lucy is, as her name suggests, "light": "Lucy is a serene conserver, who lives, enjoys, promotes, and ministers to the reasonable values of her society; she represents the inherited, cultivated, civilized virtues of the land."[14] Isabel, on the other hand, is "the personification of Pierre's unconsciousness."[15] "When we first met her," Murray reminds us, "she was almost wholly passive, undifferentiated, existing in utter darkness and without hope, a deep well of potentialities for both good and evil. She is the unconscious mind, she-who-must-be-brought-to-light, she-who-must-be-shaped. What she becomes depends on how she is treated."[16] He is correct in observing that Pierre's

path of deliverance and growth lies here. If he can resurrect Isabel from the dead, he himself will be reborn with a solidly founded fortitude.

What Isabel has done for Pierre is beyond reckoning. She has called forth unifying and fructifying sacrificial love, by means of which he can shed the outworn cloak of his past self and reach a new, deeply rooted, broader state of being. She has stirred his unconscious so profoundly that within a few weeks the frivolous author of "The Tear" and "The Tropical Summer" will be transformed into the audacious writer of a "mature work." Isabel, in other words, has converted fancy into imagination. She is not a child-bearing woman but *la femme inspiratrice*. "Sun or dew, thou fertilisest me!" Pierre says to her. In the evening she will play her mystic guitar till Pierre feels "chapter after chapter born of its wonderful suggestiveness."[17]

Lucy and Isabel, then, are the dichotomies that confronted Melville in finishing his whaling romance: to choose to write acceptable and popular romances and, consequently, to prosper, or to elect to listen to the deeper whisperings of his genius that intuited the truths that he felt "to be so terrifically true." Melville, like his little author, selected Isabel, darkness, and the unknown, aware that the decision would force his growth as a writer but his death as a popular romancer. Pierre's exclamation about Isabel—"thou fertilisest me!"—echoes Melville's earlier announcement that Hawthorne had dropped "germinous seeds" into his soul.[18] The consequences of Melville's decision to plunge into Ahabian truths is dramatically realized in Pierre's slaying his double, dealing death to himself. Melville, the aspiring American Shakespeare, willed to kill Melville, the popular writer, by rewriting *Moby-Dick*.

The revision of the book in the early months of 1851 focused on Ahab. In the ferment it was Shakespeare who showed him the way. Melville read in Coleridge's famous essay on *Hamlet* that "one of Shakespeare's modes of creating character is to conceive any one intellectual or moral faculty in morbid excess, and then to place himself

. . . thus mutilated or diseased, under given circumstances." Melville made the reference apparent by writing of Ahab, "For all men tragically great are made so through a certain morbidness. Be sure of this, O young ambition, all mortal greatness is but disease."[19] Melville's monomaniacal captain ranted like an Elizabethan, and like Lear he "tears off the mask and speaks the sane madness of vital truth," and in "The Quarter-Deck" (chapter 36) proclaims that "if man will strike," he must "strike through the mask" (M-D, 164). Ahab's appearances frequently occur in chapters with dramatic stage settings (principally chapters 36–40 and 119–22). And as Lear has his fool, so Ahab has Pip, his craven-crazed cabin boy. But the "Ahab world is closer to Macbeth than to Lear. In it the supernatural is accepted": both characters are deluded and given false security through unfulfillable prophecy, and both share a waking hell that has destroyed sleep.[20]

Melville brilliantly adapted his literary sources to his own purposes. It was not Shakespeare's tragic heroes, however, who gave Melville the direction for his captain's revised quest; rather it was Carlyle's *Sartor Resartus* from whom he again borrowed. Carlyle's hero, the philosophical Teufelsdröckh, was depicted as sailing off on his own isolated quest in search of truth: "Quitting the common Fleet of herring-busses and whalers, where indeed his leeward, laggard condition was painful enough, he desperately steers off, on a course of his own, by a sextant and compass of his own." So Ahab leaves the eminently sensible captain of the *Samuel Enderby* (chapter 100), who declines to pursue the white whale that has taken his arm, and in the concluding segment of *Moby-Dick* (chapter 106 through the "Epilogue") Ahab duplicates Teufelsdröckh's metaphorical acts by destroying his sextant (chapter 118) and creating a compass of his own (chapter 124).[21]

Late in February Melville asked his father-in-law to acquire a copy of Owen Chase's *Narrative* for him. Apparently Melville was contemplating changes in the conclusion of his story and wanted to have Chase's book before him. He had read Chase's account of the sinking of the *Essex* by a sperm whale when sailing on the *Acushnet* in 1841 and had mentioned the affair in "The Affidavit" (chapter 45).[22] Clues to the change Melville made in the story are found in the foreshadowings in the early narrative, in which the characters were to die separately: Queequeg was to take "a last long dive" (anticipated in chapter 13), and Pip preceded the others in death.[23] Sometime that spring Melville decided that the crew of the *Pequod* should be joined in death, so he bundled the piecemeal deaths together and ushered them into eternity with one cataclysmic event.

Evidence of Melville's work on *Moby-Dick* is recorded in a series of letters that he wrote to Hawthorne in the spring and summer of 1851. It is significant that Hawthorne—the source of Melville's inspired decision to write a great, truthful book and his conduit to Shakespeare—should replace Duyckinck as Melville's confidant, for the shift represents a transference of his allegiance from the practical and commercial world of editors and publishing that Duyckinck represented to the private world of genius and artistic inspiration that Melville attributed to Hawthorne. In mid-April, as Melville was working with Chase's *Narrative*, he wrote another "review" of Hawthorne's work. Again it revealed more of Melville than of Hawthorne. Melville had received a copy of *The House of the Seven Gables* on 11 April and had quickly read it. In a letter praising Hawthorne's book, he describes Clifford Pyncheon as "full of an awful truth throughout. He is conceived in the finest, truest spirit. He is no caricature. He is Clifford" (*Letters*, 124). Readers of Hawthorne's novel will remember Clifford as the soul who is too timid to run away from home. Melville is talking about himself and his own book again. This is apparent when he lauds Hawthorne.

> We think that into no recorded mind has the intense feeling of the visable [*sic*] truth ever entered more deeply than into this man's. By visable truth, we mean the apprehension of the absolute condition of present things as they strike the eye of the man who fears them not, though they do their worst to him,—the man who, like Russia or the British Empire, declares himself a sovereign nature (in himself) amid the powers of heaven, hell, and earth. He may perish; but so long as he exists he insists upon treating with all Powers upon an equal basis. If any of those other Powers choose to withhold certain secrets, let them; that does not impair my sovereignty in myself; that does not make me tributary. And perhaps, after all, there is *no* secret. We incline to think that the Problem of the Universe is like the Freemason's mighty secret, so terrible to all children. It turns out, at last, to consist in a triangle, a mallet, and an apron,—nothing more! We incline to think that God cannot explain His own secrets, and that he would like a little information upon certain points Himself. . . .
>
> There is the grand truth about Nathaniel Hawthorne. He says NO! in thunder; but the Devil himself cannot make him say *yes*. (*Letters*, 124–25)

The passage reverberates with Ahab's dramatic speech in "The Candles" (chapter 119), where in Shakespearean tones he asserts his individual sovereignty:

> I now know thee, thou clear spirit, and I now know that thy right worship is defiance. To neither love nor reverence wilt thou be kind; and e'en for hate thou canst but kill; and all are killed. No fearless fool now fronts thee. I own thy speechless, placeless power; but to the last gasp of my earthquake life will dispute its unconditional, unintegral mastery in me. In the

midst of the personified impersonal, a personality stands here. Though but a point at best; whenceso'er I came; whereso'er I go; yet while I earthly live, the queenly personality lives in me, and feels her royal rights. (*M-D*, 507)

Ahab in his proud defiance and his heretical assertions stands astride the narrative. By April the White Whale had met his foe.

Of her husband's work at this time Elizabeth later recalled that he worked on his book uninterruptedly: "Wrote White Whale or Moby Dick under unfavorable circumstances—would sit at his desk all day not eating any thing till four or five oclock then ride to the village after dark."[24] Young Pierre, Melville's fictional counterpart, sits in his room: "He will not be called to; he will not be stirred. Sometimes the intent ear of Isabel in the next room, overhears the alternate silence, and then the long lonely scratch of his pen. It is, as if she heard the busy claw of some midnight mole in the ground. . . . Here surely is a wonderful stillness of eight hours and a half, repeated day after day. In the heart of such silence, surely something is at work. Is it creation or destruction?" (*P*, 304).

It was an inspired creation, but it was also draining Melville of his creative energy. On 1 June he could foresee the end, and it was now that he informed Hawthorne of his plans to go to New York and slave over the 'Whale' while it was in press" (*Letters*, 128). The romance of the whale fisheries had been changed in the frenzy of spring into the more recognizable "Whale" that Melville was going to "take . . . by the jaw" and "finish . . . up in some fashion or other" (*Letters*, 129). He concludes the letter by reflecting on his writing of the book and what the recent years have meant in terms of his personal growth:

> I have come to regard this matter of Fame as the most transparent of all vanities. I read Solomon more and more, and every time see deeper and deeper and unspeakable meanings in him. I did not think of Fame, a year ago, as I do now. My development has been all within a few years past. I am like one of those seeds taken out of the Egyptian Pyramids, which, after being three thousand years a seed and nothing but a seed, being planted in English soil, it developed itself, grew to greenness, and then fell to mould. So I. Until I was twenty-five, I had no development at all. From my twenty-fifth year I date my life. Three weeks have scarcely passed, at any time between then and now, that I have not unfolded within myself. But I feel that I am now come to the inmost leaf of the bulb, and that shortly the flower must fall to the mould. (*Letters*, 130)

Melville apologizes for going on about himself too much, but with an awareness that in writing to Hawthorne he has persisted in revealing himself: "—I talk all about myself, and this is selfishness and egotism. Granted. But how help it? I am writing to you; I know little about you, but something about myself. So I write about myself,—at least, to you" (*Letters*, 129).

His writing was drawing to a close at the end of June, his Herculean labor nearly over. He was, as he wrote to Hawthorne again on 29 June, working on his house and his book: "I have been building some shanties of houses (connected with the old one) and likewise some shanties of chapters and essays" (*Letters*, 132). He was joining the original romance to the new creation, writing philosophical chapters to harmonize the tone of the book, and preserving parts of the original where they would fit. The carpenter of the *Pequod*, also an artist-maker who has to make a life buoy out of Queequeg's coffin, and thus fashion one thing out of another, speaks for Melville in his task of rewriting *Moby-Dick*.

> I don't like this cobbling sort of business—I don't like it at all; it's undignified; it's not my place. Let tinkers' brats do tinkering; we are their betters. I like to take in hand none but clean, virgin, fair-and-square mathematical jobs, something that regularly begins at the beginning, and is at the middle when midway, and comes to an end at the conclusion; not a cobbler's job, that's at an end in the middle, and at the beginning at the end. (*M-D*, 525)

After threatening to visit Hawthorne ("I am going to treat myself to a ride. . . . Have ready a bottle of brandy, because I always feel like drinking that heroic drink when we talk of ontological heroics together"), Melville reveals the motto of his book: "The tail is not yet cooked—though the hell-fire in which the whole book is broiled might not unreasonably have cooked it all ere this. This is the book's motto (the secret one),—Ego non baptiso te in nomine—but make out the rest yourself" (*Letters*, 133). Melville was recognizing the two sources of his inspiration—Hawthorne and Shakespeare—that had carried him through his six-month revision, for in the seventh volume of his Shakespeare (the volume containing *Lear*, *Othello*, and *Hamlet*) he recorded the motto in full:

> Ego non baptizo te in nomine Patris et
> Filii et Spiritus Sancti—sed in nomine
> Diaboli. —madness is undefinable—
> It & right reasons extremes of one,
> —not the (black art) Goetic but Theurgic magic—
> seeks converse with the Intelligence, Power, the Angel.[25]

Melville had in rewriting the book fallen into Ahab's mad but brilliant mind, had explored the inexplicable malevolence of life, and had thrust through the mask into the vacancies beyond. He had, as he later confessed to Hawthorne, "written a wicked book"; but he had spoken the truth and thus felt "spotless as the lamb" (*Letters*, 142).

Melville's fit was over. He wrote to his English publisher, Bentley, on 20 July that the closing sheets of his new work were passing through the press and could be forwarded in two or three weeks. If Melville's account in *Pierre* is at all factual, his proofing was at best haphazard: "As every evening, after his day's writing was done, the proofs of the beginning of his work came home for correction, Isabel would read them to him. They were replete with errors; but preoccupied by the thronging, and undiluted, pure imaginings of things, he became impatient of such minute, gnat-like torments; he randomly corrected the worst, and let the rest go" (*P*, 340).

On 10 September the proof sheets of his new work *The Whale* were sent to England, a year and a month after it was said to be "mostly done." Shortly afterward he changed the title for the American edition to *Moby-Dick* and dedicated the book to Nathaniel Hawthorne "in token of my admiration for his genius." Melville had paid his debts.

He had written better than he knew. He had produced a great and prophetic book. On 14 August the *Acushnet*, the model for the gothic *Pequod*, was wrecked on St. Lawrence Island. Four days later the *Ann Alexander* of New Bedford was rammed and sunk by a whale. A similar fate was to visit his novel.

III

George R. Stewart observes of Melville's compositional habits that

he did not plan a book carefully to begin with or even think it through in his mind. In addition to *Moby-Dick*, others of his books start in one direction and then shift. . . .

If a writer is unable to think his book through at first trial, he may also be unable to think it through at second trial or at third. Thus we may conceive of Melville—his creative imagination always outrunning his critical judgment and his technical skill—having first one idea and writing rapidly and vigorously a book of that sort. But a new idea comes and takes possession of him. He decides to discard much that he has already written, revise the rest, and write much anew.[26]

This is confirmed by Melville's writer Lombardo in *Mardi*—a book subject to the same compositional detours and repairs that occurred in *Moby-Dick*—when he speaks of writing his great *Kostanza*: "When Lombardo set about his work, he knew not what it would become. He did not build himself in with plans; he wrote right on; and so doing, got deeper and deeper into himself; and like a resolute traveller, plunging through baffling woods, at last was rewarded for his toils."[27]

When Melville had time to create a book—not hurriedly scribble "two jobs" as he did with *Redburn* and *White-Jacket*—his imagination responded to what he had written, and the work literally grew out of itself. Frequently he also planned to write informational material in the later stages of composition to be interpolated into the manuscript: first the adventure story and then the facts. In writing *Typee* he added a "bulk of new matter" consisting principally of three chapters: 20, 21, and 27.[28] In *Omoo*, his second novel, he inserted material originally intended for *Typee*, interpolated late chapters into the manuscript, and in the second half of the book presented material from his sources "in straight descriptive blocks. Some of it he reported as his own observations; some he said was told to him by native informants. . . . Often he took his material . . . without changes."[29] *Mardi* was more extensively revised, for the book evolved from an autobiographical account of his Pacific travels into a philosophical allegory involving discussions about religion, philosophy, and the ideal state. When news of the European upheavals of 1848 reached New York, Melville added on twenty-three chapters of political allegory. The study of how Melville cobbled his books is as interesting as the study of their composition.

Moby-Dick was written in three distinct periods of composition: the original story of the whale fisheries, which was mostly done by August 1850; the cetological chapters that were added to the narrative in the remaining months of 1850; and the revision begun early in 1851 under the influence of Shakespeare. Harrison Hayford is undoubtedly correct in asserting that the pages of *Moby-Dick* "were not necessarily written, by any means, in the order in which they now stand," but that "it is possible to distinguish various parts of the book as written earlier or later in the course of its composition."[30] Every chapter cannot be assigned a period of composition, but the manner in which Melville generally "made" his book can be reconstructed.

Scholars who have examined the composition agree that the land chapters (1–22) are part of the early narrative. They are different in style and atmosphere (realistic and colloquial) and in the function of the characters (Bulkington is destined for a larger role, and Ishmael and Queequeg will be presumably more involved in the action); the chapters point toward very different conflicts and events than those that occur on board the *Pequod*.[31] The initial chapters, however, did not escape some revision. For in rewriting the novel and in eliminating certain characters and shifting the roles for others, Melville returned to the land chapters and patched them to match, as much as possible, the remainder of the narrative. Thus these chapters demonstrate unnecessary duplication, with two sailings (from New Bedford and Nantucket) and two sidekicks for the narrator (Queequeg replacing Bulkington, who is "hidden out" when the *Pequod* sails [chapter

23]).[32] Melville's penchant for duplication is evident again in the dramatic chapters of the novel.

Additional early chapters may be determined by assigning dates to events and references in the book. The dated material does not determine, with one exception, the exact time of composition; instead it offers a date prior to which the material could not have been written and a general period of composition, assuming the composition followed the events within a period of months. The dated chapters are as follows:

1. "Cistern and Buckets" (chapter 78) compares the fall of one of the harpooners into the whale's head with the collapse of Table Rock into the Niagara, an event that occurred on 25 June 1850.

2. "The Affidavit" (chapter 45) echoes the phrase in Melville's letter to Bentley, 27 June 1850, in which he cites his two years' experience as a harpooner.

3. "Heads and Tails" (chapter 90) retells an anecdote that Melville read in the *Literary World* of 29 June.

4. "The Jereboam" (chapter 71) refers to the Niskayuna Shakers, a bit of information Melville gleaned from *A Summary View*, a history of the Shakers that he purchased on 21 July while making the agricultural tour with his cousin Robert.

5. "A Bower in the Arsacides" (chapter 102) describes the skeleton of the whale as a "wonderful sight. The wood [growing through it] was green as mosses of the Icy Glen," the spot that Melville and his guests visited on 5 August.

6. "Ambergris" (chapter 92) compares the stench rising from the hold of a Greenland whaler to the smell arising from "excavating an old city graveyard, for the foundation of a Lying-In Hospital." The old cemetery in Pittsfield was excavated to make room for the new hospital, which was dedicated on 8 September.

7. "The Fountain" (chapter 85) refers to "this blessed minute (fifteen and a quarter minutes past one o'clock P.M. of this sixteenth day of December, A.D. 1850)."

The land chapters and the dated chapters offer the scattered skeletal remains of the early narrative. (See figure 1.) The post-August dates confirm that Melville was indeed writing cetological chapters during this period: "A Bower in the Arsacides" (chapter 102), "Ambergris" (chapter 92), and "The Fountain" (chapter 85) belong to the cetology.

The early narrative may also be located by tracing Melville's use of Beale's *Natural History*, his primary cetological source. He requested a copy of Beale when he was halfway through his whaling adventure, and the book arrived 10 July. But Melville traveled with his cousin for a week, then moved his family to the Berkshires and entertained his literary friends in the weeks that followed, so the "mostly done"

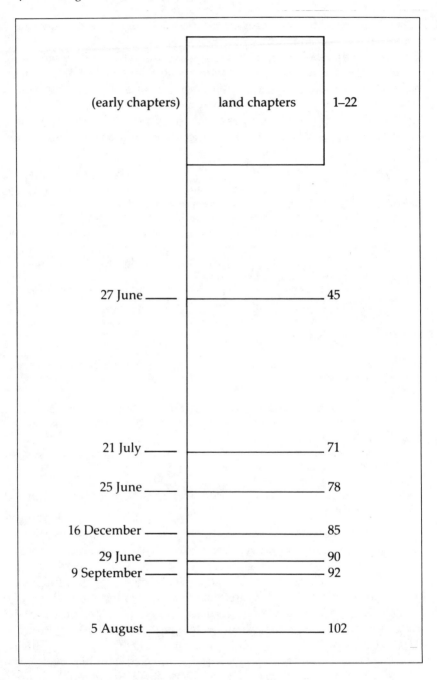

Figure 1. The dated chapters in *Moby-Dick*

manuscript that Duyckinck read could hardly have contained material from Beale, material that apparently was incorporated into the manuscript in the months after August. These references do not appear with any frequency until chapter 55; they are integral to chapters 55 through 92 and appear again in a cluster of continuous cetological chapters from 102 through 105.[33] The Beale chapters lead to the cetological center of the novel—chapters that were conceived and planned as part of the original whaling adventure. Melville had intended for the early story to have a loose structure—very much like that of *Typee*, *Omoo*, and *Mardi*—that could be opened up in places and into which chapters and portions of chapters of late composition could be inserted. To this end he wrote two types of cetological chapters: "loose chapters" that could be inserted anyplace in the manuscript and "fast chapters" that were fastened onto the existing narrative. The "loose chapters" include "Cetology" (32), which offers the bibliographical classification of whales, and two clusters: the first (chapters 55–57) anticipates the descriptive anatomical chapters by offering artistic representations of the whale, and the latter (chapters 102–5) considers the skeletal remains of the whale. The "fast chapters" begin when the *Pequod* captures a whale and belong to a narrative sequence commencing with "The Line" (60) and concluding with "Ambergris" (92). These chapters contain the dated references—except for "The Affidavit" (45), which is itself a "loose chapter"—and thus locate the vestigial remains of the whaling romance in the revised novel. (See figure 2.) It is of interest that this section contains almost nothing of Ahab and nothing of Moby Dick; rather they focus on the mates, particularly Stubb, and on Ishmael and Queequeg.

The portion of *Moby-Dick* that belongs to the period of revision can be traced most readily through Melville's references and allusions to Shakespeare. Many of the chapters are dramatic vignettes with stage settings. These occur with great frequency in chapters 26–29, 36–42, and 106 through "Epilogue," and also in the individual chapters 94 and 99.[34] Melville's structural doubling, evident in the "loose" cetological chapters, is apparent in the dramatic chapters 36–40 and 119–22. In contrast to the early whaling adventure chapters, the revised segments feature Ahab and his increasingly mad quest for Moby Dick.

What, then, of the further remains of the original narrative? It is likely that Melville told what remained of that story in "The *Town-Ho's* Story" (chapter 54). Ishmael perhaps hints of the origin of the chapter by stating at the beginning that it is a twice-told tale: "for my humor's sake, I shall preserve the style in which I once narrated it" (*M-D*, 243). The fate of the *Town-Ho* picks up many of the narrative lines antici-

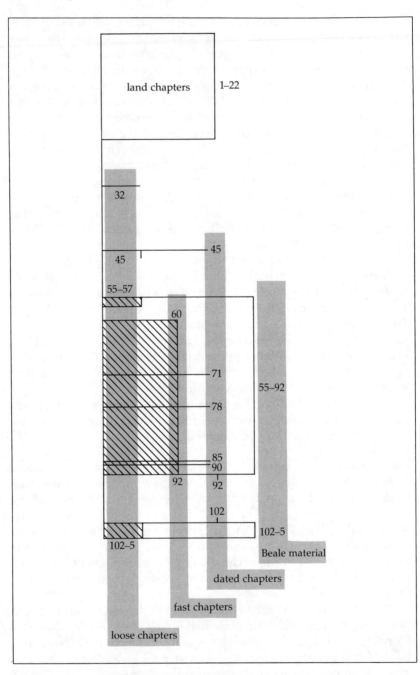

Figure 2. Loose and fast cetological chapters in *Moby-Dick*

pated in the land chapters of *Moby-Dick*, foreshadowings that are never fulfilled in the novel.[35]

Harrison Hayford has suggested the missing connection between the two stories.[36] In "Merry Christmas" (chapter 23) Bildad bids a doleful farewell to his friend and fellow owner Peleg; then, inexplicably, they leave the ship together. Originally, perhaps, Peleg—a peg-legged Peleg—stayed on the ship as mate and part owner. Peleg was the original Radney, mate and part owner of the *Town-Ho*, who struggles with Steelkilt, the original Bulkington. But Radney as Peleg tears off after Moby Dick, the whale that demasted him, and is killed; the *Town-Ho*, already leaking and crippled, limps into port. Peleg's continuing presence in the original story would account for Ishmael's anticipation of further kicks he would receive on the voyage (it is Peleg's kicking him in part that prompts the remark), and Peleg's confrontation with Ahab would account for Ahab's remark to Starbuck that the mate is always "pratting about owner's rights." Starbuck probably replaced Peleg once the *Pequod* put to sea. Of course more than one character may have tried on the leg in the revision, for Stubb's name suggests a stump and he too is associated with kicking, although he is wisely advised against it in a dream (chapter 31). Ahab, however, was finally given the leg as a belated Christmas gift sometime in early 1851.[37]

Another revision occurs in "The Castaway" (chapter 93). Pip, the cabin boy, originally preceded the others in death (chapter 27, American edition).[38] When Pip jumps into the ocean in "The Castaway" and is left behind, he sinks to the bottom and drowns. In the revision, however, Melville rescues Pip from his watery grave; he miraculously appears on the deck of the *Pequod*, insane from having sat on the bottom of the ocean and having witnessed the great truth of God's indifference—he saw the foot of the Weaver God on the treadle of the loom, mindlessly weaving creation's garments. Pip is brought back in the Shakespeare-inspired revision to play the Fool to Ahab's Lear.

The original narrative preserved in the middle section of *Moby-Dick* is bracketed by "The *Town-Ho*'s Story" (chapter 54), into which Melville deposits the conclusion of the early novel, and by "The Castaway" (chapter 93), which marks the point at which Melville departs from the original and begins to write a new conclusion. The final "loose" cetological cluster (chapters 102–5) is followed by Ahab's receiving a new leg (chapter 106), perhaps symbolic in Melville's mind of the revised novel itself. The rewritten chapters and the new conclusion follow. (See figure 3.)

Some chapters show an early revision ("Queen Mab" [31] is a prime candidate); others were probably in the original but were sub-

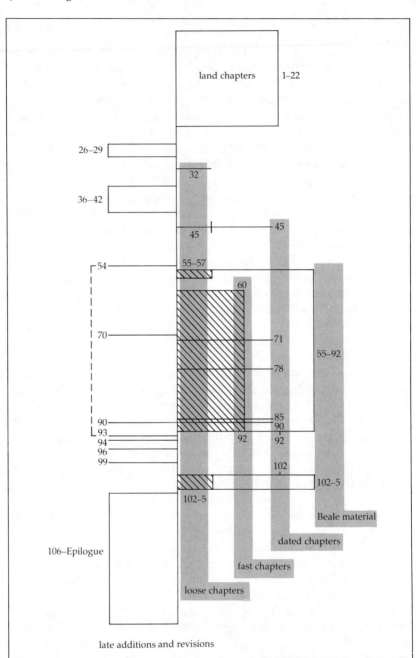

Figure 3. Late additions and revisions in *Moby-Dick*, with framing chapters for the early narrative (chapters 54 and 93)

ject to a later revision ("The Try-Works" [96] was modeled after a scene in Browne's *Etchings* and apparently reworked after Melville turned to Ahab's dark perception). Other chapters were written in the spring and inserted into the manuscript ("The Sphinx" [70] and "The Doubloon" [99]), while some were broken off and added to ("The Mat-Maker" [47], "Ahab's Boat and Crew—Fedallah" [50], and "A Squeeze of the Hand" [94]). Some of these no doubt were the shanties Melville was building and attaching to the manuscript in the late spring and summer. And in arranging the novel Melville stitched the longer sections together with transitions fashioned from chapters of both early and late composition. Still, try as one may to reconstruct Melville's "Whale," Ishmael wisely cautions that merely the fragments have been recovered, for only "in the heart of quickest perils; only when within the eddyings of his angry flukes; only on the profound unbounded sea, can the fully invested whale be truly and livingly found out" (*M-D*, 453–54). We have found no more than the smallest part of the vertebrae. "Thus we see how the spine of even the hugest of living things tapers off at last into simple child's play" (*M-D*, 454).

IV

Ishmael concludes his consideration of the whale by announcing that "the eternal whale will still survive, and rearing upon the topmost crest of the equatorial flood, spout his frothed defiance to the skies" (*M-D*, 462). Such optimism seemed misplaced with regard to *Moby-Dick*. Melville's book was to plunge in his own lifetime, not to rise until the twentieth century. But in resigning himself in rewriting *Moby-Dick* to failure in his own time, Melville achieved the kind of success that comes when genius is true to its own perception and design. He wrote honestly, and his success came late and endured.

The reviews of *Moby-Dick* were generally unkind. The book was light years ahead of its time. Duyckinck, who admired the unrevised narrative, delivered the cruelest cut when he pronounced the final product to be an "intellectual chowder."[39] At first *Moby-Dick* sold poorly and then not at all. Harper and Brothers reported an initial sale of 1,535 copies; two months later another 471 copies were sold. Then it was over: orders dribbled in over the next quarter century (only two copies were purchased in 1876), and the book went out of print in America in 1887 with a total sale of 3,180 copies.[40] Melville's response was to rage at his publishers and his audience in *Pierre* and then lapse into increasing silence. His final short stories are replete with symbols of communications gone awry: a rotted mailbox, the Dead Letter Office, mute and isolated figures. In 1857 he published *The Confidence-Man*, his last novel. Perhaps the Old Jokester was playing his last and best joke, for Melville's new publisher, Dix, Edwards, and Company, went bankrupt. Melville read the signs and quit writing fiction. Thirty-four years later he died. His passing was scarcely noticed except to observe that he was the author of *Typee*, his first and most popular book. Melville's premonition, confessed to Hawthorne, had come true: he would be remembered as "a man who lived among the cannibals" (*Letters*, 130).

Moby-Dick surfaced again in the Melville revival that began in 1919. In our time only Woody Allen's Zelig has not read it. The book was too insane for its day; it needed the bedlam of modern times. *Moby-Dick* speaks to the contemporary reader. Melville intuited Freudian notions of the human personality, and he understood that the perceiver truly creates reality and then tumbles into his own projections. But at the heart of *Moby-Dick* is the struggle between ego and community personified in the death-seeking Ahab and the companion-seeking Ishmael. In a world of despair Ishmael, the balanced man, has learned to live with a horror, to cure himself of his alienation, and to find in the midst of the mad, thrashing world of wounded whales and the men that surround him the still, quiet center of his soul. Ishmael asks us to relish the quiet enjoyments, to squeeze hands all around and save ourselves by sharing and caring, while simultaneously Ahab sails away from Ishmael's intelligence into the darkness of his own mind, asserting his enormous ego against history and circumstances. Modern man, like cannibal old Ahab, persists in sharkishly consuming himself, a fact confirmed by man's ravaging of his environment and by the events and the political machinery of the twentieth century that he has constructed. Ahabian man has gained the absolute power to pull on the pillars of the temple and bring the world crashing down upon him. In *The Great American Novel* Philip Roth burlesques but does not exaggerate the apocalyptic conclusion of *Moby-Dick*:

> Today some clever publisher would probably bring out *Moby-Dick* as one of those "How To Do It" books, provided he left off the catastrophic conclusion, or appended it under the title, "And How Not To." . . . Only read your daily papers, fans—every day news of another stream, another town, another species biting the dust. Wait, very soon now whole continents will be canceled out like stamps. Whonk, Africa! Whonk, Asia! Whonk, Europa! Whonk, North, whonk, South, America! And, oh, don't try hiding. Antarctica—*whonk* you too! And that will be it, fans, as far as the landmass goes. A brand new ballgame.[41]

It is to the awesome insanity of our century that Melville speaks. His failure was that of the prophet in his own time. History has been catching up with him and his book ever since.

Notes

1. *Letters of Herman Melville*, ed. Davis and Gilman (cited hereafter as *Letters*).

2. The following books and articles offer an examination of the compositional history of *Moby-Dick*: Howard, "Melville's Struggle"; Olson, *Call Me Ishmael*; Vincent, *Trying-Out*; Howard, "Second Growth" in *Melville*, 150–79; Stewart, "Two *Moby-Dicks*"; Barbour, "Composition of *Moby-Dick*"; Barbour, "*Town-Ho*'s Story"; Barbour and Howard, "Carlyle and the Conclusion"; Hayford, "Unnecessary Duplicates"; Quirk, "More on the Composition"; Howard, *Unfolding of "Moby-Dick"*. Recently an extensive summary of the history and a listing of the sources has been compiled in "Historical Note" in Melville, *Moby-Dick*, ed. Hayford, Parker, and Tanselle, 618–89. Quotations from *Moby-Dick* in this essay are taken from this edition and cited hereafter as *M-D*.

3. During his South Pacific wanderings, Melville could only have served as a harpooner on the *Charles and Henry*, but he was probably hired on as a boat steerer (Howard, *Melville*, 63–64).

4. Other than Browne's *Etchings*, Melville also used Frederick D. Bennett's *Narrative of a Whaling Voyage Round the Globe* (1840), Rev. Henry T. Cheever's *The Whale and His Captors* (1850), and Frederick Allyn Olmstead's *Incidents of a Whaling Voyage* (1841).

5. Leyda, *Melville Log*, 1:385.

6. Ibid., 1:384.

7. Reprinted in Melville, *Moby-Dick* (Norton Critical Editions), 535–51. Quotations from "Hawthorne and His Mosses" are taken from this edition and cited hereafter as *NCE*.

8. Miller in *Melville*, 38, offers the following description of Hawthorne: he had a "magnificent high forehead, thinning hair, a long, ascetic face; the mouth was delicate and sensitive, the chin receding. The attire—the black coat, the high collar, the silken cravat—set off the fragile countenance. The tokens of middle age did not conceal the beauty—no other word will do—of that face which in youth and early manhood had almost a virginal delicacy."

9. The word "resonator" is taken from Charles Olson, who said he would serve as "resonator" for Merton Sealts, Jr.—that is, "a target" for his letters, " 'to feel yr way in,' as he put it, adding that sometimes letters are 'a more organic way to arrive at form, than outlines or plans.' " Sealts, "Olson, Melville," 182.

10. Leyda, *Melville Log*, 1:279.

11. Bennett, "Ishmael."

12. Melville, *Pierre*, ed. Hayford, Parker, and Tanselle. All quotations are taken from this edition and cited hereafter as *P*.

13. Howard, *Melville*, 183.

14. Murray, "Introduction," xc.

15. Ibid., lii.

16. Ibid., lxxxviii–lxxxix.

17. Ibid., liii.

18. Other parallels should be pointed out. For example, Isabel lives in a "small . . . red farm house" much like the little red cottage that Hawthorne occupied outside Lenox, and her image has been sketched by the foliage of a pine tree just as the outline of the whale has been spied in "masses of rock" and traced out in "the starry heavens" (*P*, 110; *M-D*, 270-71).

19. Howard, *Melville*, 165.
20. The quoted comment is from Olson, *Call Me Ishmael*, 53.
21. For a complete discussion see Barbour and Howard, "Carlyle and the Conclusion."
22. Heffernan, *Stove by a Whale*, reprints the *Narrative* with Melville's annotations and markings.
23. The American edition of *Moby-Dick*, for which Melville did not revise the proof sheets, reads, "not many of them [the crew] ever came back. Black little Pip—he never did—oh, no!—he went before. Poor Alabama boy" (chapter 27). See Tanselle, "Discussions," 852–53.
24. Leyda, *Melville Log*, 1:412.
25. Olson, *Call Me Ishmael*, 52.
26. Stewart, "Two *Moby-Dicks*," 447.
27. The quotation is taken from Davis, *Melville's "Mardi,"* 94.
28. For the composition of *Typee* see Howard, "Historical Note," 277–302.
29. See Roper, "Historical Note," 319–44.
30. Hayford, "Unnecessary Duplicates," 149.
31. Stewart, "Two *Moby-Dicks*," 420–26.
32. Hayford in "Unnecessary Duplicates" has a brilliant and complete discussion of the duplication in the land chapters.
33. Howard in *Unfolding of "Moby-Dick"* lists sixteen chapters in the sequence from 55 through 92 as being derived from Beale.
34. The influence of Shakespeare is thoroughly documented in Long, "The Hidden Sun."
35. See Vincent, *The Trying-Out*, and Barbour, "*Town-Ho's* Story."
36. Hayford, "Unnecessary Duplicates."
37. Quirk, "More on the Composition."
38. Melville had the book set and stereotyped at his own expense. In making revisions in the text he felt free to make whatever changes he wanted in the proof sheets bound for England, because they would be reset for the English edition. But the American edition was already plated, and he would have to pay for whatever changes he made. Errors, therefore, appear in the American edition that were corrected in the English.
39. Melville, *Moby-Dick* (NCE), 613.
40. Thirty-five additional calf copies may be added to these figures, but fifteen of them were sold at cloth prices. Sales figures are derived from Tanselle, "Sales of Melville's Books."
41. Roth, *Great American Novel*, 44.

Works Cited

Barbour, James. "The Composition of *Moby-Dick*." *American Literature* 47 (November 1975): 343–60.

———. "The *Town-Ho's* Story: Melville's Original Whale." *ESQ* [*Emerson Society Quarterly*] 21, no. 2 (1975): 111–15.

Barbour, James, and Leon Howard. "Carlyle and the Conclusion of *Moby-Dick*." *New England Quarterly* 49 (June 1976): 214–24.

Bennett, John. "Ishmael: His First Cutting-In." In Bennett, *The Struck Leviathan: Poems on "Moby-Dick,"* 39. Columbia: University of Missouri Press, 1952.

Davis, Merrell R. *Melville's "Mardi": A Chartless Voyage.* New Haven: Yale University Press, 1952.

Hayford, Harrison. "Unnecessary Duplicates." In *New Perspectives on Melville,* edited by Faith Pullin, 128–61. Kent, Oh.: Kent State University Press, 1978.

Hayford, Harrison, Hershel Parker, and G. Thomas Tanselle. "Historical Note." Sections II–VI. In Melville, *Moby-Dick,* edited by Hayford, Parker, and Tanselle, 618–89.

Heffernan, Thomas Farel. *Stove by a Whale: Owen Chase and the "Essex."* Middleton, Conn.: Wesleyan University Press, 1981.

Howard, Leon. *Herman Melville.* Berkeley and Los Angeles: University of California Press, 1951.

———. "Historical Note." In Herman Melville, *Typee,* edited by Harrison Hayford, Hershel Parker, and G. Thomas Tanselle, 277–302. Evanston: Northwestern University Press and The Newberry Library, 1968.

———. "Melville's Struggle with the Angel." *Modern Language Quarterly* 1 (June 1940): 196–205.

———. *The Unfolding of "Moby-Dick": Seven Essays in Evidence.* Edited by James Barbour and Thomas Quirk. Glassboro, N.J.: Melville Society, 1987.

Leyda, Jay. *The Melville Log.* 2 vols. New York: Harcourt, Brace, 1951.

Long, Raymond. "The Hidden Sun: A Study of the Influence of Shakespeare on the Creative Imagination of Herman Melville." Ph.D. dissertation, University of California, Los Angeles, 1965.

Melville, Herman. "Hawthorne and His Mosses." In *Moby-Dick,* edited by Harrison Hayford and Hershel Parker, 535–51. Norton Critical Edition. New York: W. W. Norton, 1967.

———. *The Letters of Herman Melville.* Edited by Merrell R. Davis and William H. Gilman. New Haven: Yale University Press, 1960.

———. *Moby-Dick.* Edited by Harrison Hayford, Hershel Parker, and G. Thomas Tanselle. Evanston: Northwestern University Press and The Newberry Library, 1988.

———. *Pierre.* Edited by Harrison Hayford, Hershel Parker, and G. Thomas Tanselle. Evanston: Northwestern University Press and The Newberry Library, 1971.

Miller, Edwin Haviland. *Melville.* New York: George Braziller, 1975.

Murray, Henry A. "Introduction." In Herman Melville, *Pierre,* pp. xiii–ciii. New York: Hendricks House, 1962.

Olson, Charles. *Call Me Ishmael.* New York: Reynall & Hitchcock, 1947.

Quirk, Thomas. "More on the Composition of *Moby-Dick*: Leon Howard Shows Us Ahab's Leg." *Melville Society Extracts* 46 (May 1981): 6–7.

Roper, Gordon. "Historical Note." In Herman Melville, *Omoo,* edited by Harrison Hayford, Hershel Parker, and G. Thomas Tanselle, 319–44. Evanston: Northwestern University Press and The Newberry Library, 1968.

Roth, Philip. *The Great American Novel.* New York: Penguin, 1986.

Sealts, Merton M., Jr. "Olson, Melville, and the *New Republic*." *Contemporary Literature* 22 (Spring 1981): 167–86.

Stewart, George R. "The Two *Moby-Dicks*." *American Literature* 25 (January 1954): 417–48.

Tanselle, G. Thomas. "Discussions of Adopted Readings." In Melville, *Moby-Dick*, edited by Hayford, Parker, and Tanselle, 809–906.

———. "The Sales of Melville's Books." *Harvard Library Bulletin* 18 (April 1969): 195–214.

Vincent, Howard P. *The Trying-Out of Moby-Dick*. Boston: Houghton Mifflin, 1949.

ROBERT SATTELMEYER

The Remaking of *Walden*

By late 1848 and early 1849 the literary component of the "private business" that Henry Thoreau had gone to Walden Pond to transact seemed finally about to begin yielding a return on his investment. Since he had left his cabin in September 1847, after a stay of just over two years, Thoreau had been working alternately on two books that he had begun there. The first was *A Week on the Concord and Merrimack Rivers*, a compendium of his early works and a tribute to his late brother John woven into the narrative of a boating and hiking expedition they had taken in 1839. Like its successor, *A Week* was the product of a long gestation—almost ten years elapsed between the experience on which it was based and the publication of the book. The second, called *Walden, or Life in the Woods*, treated his experiment at the pond and contained as a counterpoint an ambitiously conceived indictment of American and particularly New England materialist values. Now, some eighteen months later, *A Week* was finally finished and *Walden*, Thoreau thought, was also close to completion. He approached publishers with this two-book package, and after W. D. Ticknor offered to publish *Walden* but required him to underwrite the printing of *A Week* at a cost of $450, Thoreau finally arranged with James Munroe to publish *A Week* and to follow it up with *Walden*. He would still have to guarantee the cost of producing *A Week*, but Munroe at least did not require payment in advance, offering to let Thoreau repay the costs from the sales of the book.[1]

As a relatively unknown young American author, Thoreau could probably not expect to improve these terms. Ralph Waldo Emerson, who had played a large and generous part in fostering Thoreau's literary career during the preceding decade, had advised him to take the risk, assuring him that his book would find readers on both sides of the Atlantic.[2] And Thoreau had good reasons to believe that *Walden* would improve upon whatever success his first book might have. Its subject matter was more timely, lively, and controversial than *A Week*'s (Ticknor had, after all, agreed to publish it at his own expense without seeing a completed manuscript). More important, Thoreau was currently riding the crest of a small wave of celebrity for his Walden experiment and a series of lectures drawn from the *Walden* manuscript in progress that he was delivering in lyceums around New England. Between November 1848 and the following April he lectured twice in Concord, once each in Gloucester, Massachusetts, and Portland, Maine, twice in Salem, and three times in Worcester, and declined an invitation to Bangor, Maine, because details of the trip could not be worked out. Horace Greeley's *New York Tribune* ran a favorable editorial on his lectures and the experiment on which they were based that provoked letters from readers, was reprinted, and even prompted a flattering account of Thoreau in his hometown paper, the Concord *Yeoman's Gazette.*[3] The last item is perhaps the most notable, for the townspeople had generally regarded Thoreau, the Harvard-educated son of a respectable middle-class family, whose only apparent occupations were occasional stints of manual labor and loafing around the local woods and streams, with a mixture of puzzlement and scorn. Until now, the only time he had attracted the town's attention was in 1844 when, while cooking a mess of fish on one of his outings, he had inadvertently started a fire that burned several hundred acres of woods.

But he could afford to ignore the cries of "burnt woods!" that occasionally still echoed after him in the streets of Concord, for his literary career seemed finally about to blossom on several fronts. His long essay "Ktaadn, and the Maine Woods" had been running in *Sartain's Union Magazine* from July through November 1848, and early in 1849 Elizabeth Peabody asked him for an essay version of "Resistance to Civil Government" (later to become famous as "Civil Disobedience") for a volume entitled *Aesthetic Papers* that she was editing. When he replied to her request, on 5 April, he was in the midst of writing out printer's copy for *A Week*, and the tone of his answer suggests a harried but, one suspects, secretly pleased young writer, who must have been happy to have this kind of problem for a change: "I have so much writing to do at present, with the printers in the rear of me, that I have almost no time left, but for bodily exercise; however, I will send you the article in question before the end of next week."[4] The culmination of this intense burst of literary activity, he thought, would be *Walden*. He had revised the book during the last year, polishing but expanding only slightly the version he had written at the pond in 1846–47, and though it was still addressed to a New England lecture audience (with references to "hearers" instead of "readers"), Thoreau considered it close enough to completion to initiate negotiations for its publication and to begin to mark the manuscript for a printer.[5]

But "literary contracts are little binding," as he had prophetically written in the first draft of *Walden* (a remark he later canceled), and a

number of circumstances were even then developing that would subvert his plans to publish *Walden* on the heels of *A Week*. His literary
fortunes, his friendships, his domestic relations, his characteristic
pursuits, and even his notion of his proper literary métier were to be
transformed during the next year; and the book that he thought of as
nearing completion would undergo an even more startling metamor-
phosis over the next five years, doubling in size, radically changing its
structure, and shifting in subtle but profound ways the themes of its
earliest versions before it finally saw print in the summer of 1854. The
transformation, though dramatic, was natural and inevitable, for the
book was an expression of the life, Thoreau's attempt to fulfill his own
first requirement of a writer and render a simple and sincere account
of himself. This task, as he knew, paradoxically rendered him liable to
the charge of obscurity, for it was his real and not merely his actual life
that he must attempt to represent. As his relations changed over the
years, as his reflections on his life at the pond deepened, as his
interest in nature became at once more passionate and more professional, and as his sense of his literary vocation developed in response
to early disappointments, the book evolved along with the author
until it became less a simple history of his life at Walden alternating
with a critique of contemporary culture, and more the sum of his
histories simultaneously present in a text at once fabular, mythic,
scientific, and even scriptural in its dimensions.

The most obvious factor affecting Thoreau's plans for his second
book was the fate of his first. *A Week* received little publicity, had
mixed reviews, and sold hardly at all—only about two hundred copies
out of an edition of a thousand. Thoreau found himself liable for about
$300 in manufacturing costs (nearly a year's ordinary wages for him)
with no prospects of being able to pay them from sales, and he finally
ended up, as is well known, with the more than seven hundred
unsold copies swelling the shelves of his own small personal library.
Clearly, he could not undertake to publish another book on his own
account under these circumstances (it took him about four years to
pay off Munroe), and publishers were unlikely to regard him as a
good candidate to risk their own money on at this time.

An even more disturbing implication of *A Week*'s lack of success,
however, was that Thoreau would have to rethink his notions of a
literary career in the light of economic and cultural realities. He had
devoted a decade of his life to literary labors, and at the end of it he
found himself deeply in debt and in no danger of becoming a household word. So like virtually all his contemporaries among the serious

writers of antebellum America, he found that the public was unlikely to make it worth his while to produce his best work, and that if he would continue to write he would have to alter both his strategies and his tactics.

At the same time, developments in his personal life seemed to urge him away from old habits and old relationships and prompt him in the direction of new pursuits that would lend themselves to an altered conception of his literary task. His long apprenticeship to Emerson was drawing to a close, signaled by a quarrel of some bitterness that followed upon Emerson's return from Europe in the summer of 1848: Thoreau was disenchanted with his mentor's newfound worldliness and willingness to reside in what Emerson termed in "Experience" the "mid-world"; and the older man had come home with a solid sense of English progress and culture that made his young Concord friend's various renunciations seem paltry and parochial. He found Thoreau's solitary pursuit of nature ultimately leading only to "want and madness."[6] After *A Week* was published, Emerson brought their disagreement to a head by criticizing the book and refusing to review it. In response, Thoreau filled many pages of his fragmentary journal for 1849 with anguished reflections on the breakup of their friendship.[7]

Partly in response to this quarrel, no doubt, Thoreau devoted more and more of his own energy to precisely that nature study that his former patron found so unrewarding. Until this period his interest in nature had been strong but somewhat amateurish—largely appreciative and conventional but neither detailed nor systematic. The first version of *Walden*, for example, either did not contain or contained in only embryonic stages many passages of natural history that readers tend to regard as central to the book—the battle of the ants in "Brute Neighbors," the extended descriptions of Walden and neighboring ponds in "The Ponds," or the account of thawing sand and clay that marks the climax of "Spring." But 1849 found Thoreau beginning to adopt both a much more intense and much more professional attitude toward the study of nature. In a rudimentary way he began to sketch out for himself a life's work in the field.

His newfound dedication to nature study did not arise solely out of stubbornness or as a compensation for the loss of friendship, however. Certainly it represented an attempt to systematize the Transcendentalist quest for direct contact with divinity through nature, and in this sense it signals a maturity of purpose and constitutes a logical development of the enthusiasm of his earlier years. The great difficulty with the sort of experience of divinity that Emerson had described in *Nature*—when one becomes a transparent eyeball through which the currents of the Universal Being circulate—was that such an experience was by its nature both transient and unpredictable. It could not be depended upon to recur. Thoreau began to see that a constant and studied application of his energy to the observation of nature could, on the other hand, lead both to real knowledge and a steady elevation of his life through a kind of continual drenching in the reality that lay behind nature.

He was guided and inspired in this endeavor by the example of Louis Agassiz, America's most eminent natural scientist, with whom he began to correspond and for whom he collected specimens beginning in 1847. Agassiz was an indefatigable fieldworker and taxonomist, but his thought was also deeply tinctured by the German *Naturphilosophie* he had been exposed to in his youth, and he never abandoned his fundamental belief that thought and spirit and law were anterior to their expression in nature. At about the same time, Thoreau read and took notes on Samuel Taylor Coleridge's *Hints toward the Formation of a More Comprehensive Theory of Life*, a treatise on the use of natural history as a means to the discovery of underlying laws of creation.[8] He began to teach himself taxonomy and to acquire standard botanical and zoological reference works, and he settled into the third floor of his family's new house, which became a sort of combination bedroom, study, and museum for his growing collections of specimens. All these developments conspired to transform him, by 1850, into a budding natural historian who saw his life's work unfolding before him in the fields and on the streams of his native village. He had become a serious walker too, extending his excursions to "some new hill or pond or wood many miles distant" nearly every day, and his life was beginning to settle into the routine of morning writing and afternoon walks that would continue for the rest of his active life.[9]

And though he continued to develop new literary projects, the bulk of Thoreau's writing was now taking place in his journal. At about the same time that he began to extend and regularize his walks, he also began to keep his journal much more systematically than previously and to fill its entries with detailed descriptions of natural phenomena. He was not shifting from the writing of books to keeping a private journal merely because his literary ambitions had met with little fulfillment; he was discovering an appropriate medium for his new interest in nature, one that allowed him to replicate in the journal, as it were, the sequentiality, the randomness, and the endless iteration of nature and to inscribe himself into the process.[10] He made it into a distinctive vehicle for his purposes, hypothesizing an ideal reader and composing long entries, often several days' worth at a time, from notes that he had gathered during recent walks—using the convenient but finally fictional "dailiness" of the form to create the spontaneity and immediacy he always strove for. The new journal would play a major role in the revision of *Walden* over the next several years and would, as we shall see, become a part of the creation of that work in very complex ways.

In 1850, then, Thoreau had a manuscript of *Walden* that only inchoately reflected what he had learned at the pond, that did not embody the new directions his life was taking, and that was in any event probably unsalable. So he ceased thinking of the manuscript as finished, or nearly so. Perhaps he was temporarily soured on book publishing after his experience with *A Week*, but probably he was also awaiting such developments as his new modes of life and writing would bring. He did not let the book lie fallow, for he drafted into the journal passages of reflection on his life in the woods that were clearly intended for the manuscript and that were eventually added in later revisions.[11] But apparently he did not begin to revise the manuscript as a whole until sometime in 1852. Then he began energetically to work on *Walden* again, adding new material and revising previous drafts in four distinguishable stages, not counting his final fair copy for the printer, between 1852 and 1854.[12] Thus, although there are seven identifiable manuscript drafts (or, more precisely, partial drafts) of *Walden*, ranging from 1846 to 1854, its composition mainly took place in two phases. The first stage includes the first draft written at Walden in 1846–47, along with the second and third drafts that were written nearly together in 1848–49 and that primarily polish material in the first draft. The second stage consists of the four successive partial drafts written between 1852 and the book's publication in 1854.

The extant *Walden* manuscript material provides an almost embarrassing richness of evidence for assessing the genesis of the book—a situation that has its pitfalls as well as its advantages. Since J. Lyndon Shanley's milestone study, *The Making of "Walden"* (1957), students of the book have known that the 628 leaves of *Walden* manuscript in the Huntington Library actually constitute seven distinct drafts. Assembling clues furnished by differences in paper, ink color, and handwriting, matching pagination and continuous text from one leaf to another, and studying the incorporation of interlined revisions, Shanley was able not only to reconstruct the first draft of *Walden* but also to organize the surviving leaves of the manuscript into the six subsequent drafts that preceded the final one, the one presumably lost because it was not returned to Thoreau by the printer. This is a situation virtually unmatched in the annals of American literature, for no other recognized classic of our culture survives in as many significant prepublication versions: few books, of course, go through as complex a gestation process, and fewer still are the writers who scrupulously save their early drafts.

This very abundance of evidence, however, poses some difficulties. The most obvious one, perhaps, is that all this material makes it much easier to say *how* Thoreau wrote and rewrote his book than to determine *what* the revision adds up to in terms of the completed book and the life that called it forth. Indeed, with such a history, one wonders whether the book as published ought to be regarded as "finished" at all, or whether it might not be more accurate to view it as one more unfolding and provisional stage in Thoreau's account of himself. A more practical problem engendered by the wealth of manuscript material is that its very abundance creates a deceptive impression of completeness. It does not necessarily follow that the drafts that survive are identical to the versions that Thoreau successively composed: he may very well, for example, have only preserved portions of later drafts that significantly altered or expanded earlier versions. Likewise, at least two of the drafts (the second and the fourth) stop well short of the end of the book. Thoreau may indeed have stopped at these points, but he may also have gone on, discarding for any number of reasons the latter portions. Additionally there may have been intervening drafts that have not survived because they were incorporated into later versions. All this is hypothetical, of course, but the fact remains that the most that can accurately be said is that the seven partial drafts (not one of which is complete, as missing page numbers indicate), along with various passages in the journal, constitute the surviving evidence of Thoreau's work on *Walden*.

But probably the greatest hazard the *Walden* manuscripts pose is that their very abundance and variety make categorizing and generalizing the revisions extremely difficult. So many different kinds of revision exist that it becomes virtually impossible to characterize them succinctly: the alteration of single words, the modification of sentence structure, the reordering of paragraphs, the deletion of sentences and paragraphs, the growth by gradual accretion of a particular passage, the introduction of wholly new passages, the introduction of new chapters, and the reordering of chapters within the whole—and all perhaps taking place within a single version. Further complicating this situation is the fact that the final version incorporates the earlier versions in a very complex manner, not superseding them (as, say, Melville's final draft of *Moby-Dick* appears to have done to the first version) but subtly transforming them while often leaving individual passages relatively intact.

All the foregoing is intended to introduce a note of caution and provisionality about such general inferences as may be drawn, but I do not wish to sound like the man in Pudd'nhead Wilson's calendar who complained because his coal had too many prehistoric toads in it. The critic must finally rejoice that the documents marking the stages in the growth of Thoreau's masterpiece are so plentiful, however he or she may wish that some of them could be ignored from time to time. Although there are doubtless subtle stages of growth that could be traced through virtually every year between 1845, when Thoreau began to write entries in the journal that were clearly designed for some literary work based on his life at the pond, and 1854, when the book was finally published, the most dramatic story involves the remaking of the book that took place during the second phase of composition between 1852 and 1854. Thoreau's conception of the work greatly enlarged and matured during these years, and if some of the portions that were added during this phase conflict with assertions made in the earlier versions, it is a mark of Thoreau's maturity as a writer and a thinker that he allowed such inconsistencies to stand. Much of the richness of the book ultimately derives, I believe, from Thoreau's incorporation of reflections from the intervening years that are allowed to stand alongside accounts of his life that he actually wrote at the pond, so that *Walden* is at once both retrospective and dramatic. It embodies a summing but not a summing up of experience. I do not believe this effect was the result of a conscious design on Thoreau's part, but rather that it came about with a certain organic inevitability from the writer's steadfast application to his task during a period of artistic and intellectual growth.

At the same time, of course, Thoreau was highly self-conscious about the process of revision, and *Walden*, moreover, like so many other American books, calls attention to itself as a deliberately composed text. It begins with an allusion (itself added in a late revision) to the very process of composition that I have been discussing: "When I wrote the following pages, or rather the bulk of them, I lived alone, in the woods." This seemingly straightforward reference to the immediate contextual circumstances of the book introduces us immediately by means of a characteristic wordplay to the writer's awareness of the difference between his immediate and his later, mediated vision: only the "bulk" or gross proportions of the book may be said to have been composed at the pond.

The greatest difference between the 1846–49 versions and the 1852–54 versions is that the second half of the book is much more extensively developed in the later versions. Shanley summarized the difference between the first draft and the published version as follows:

It [the first draft] represents various parts of *Walden* very unevenly. It contains approximately 70 per cent of the first half—"Economy" through

"The Bean Field"; a little less than 30 per cent of "The Village" through "Higher Laws" [chapters 8–11]; less than 50 per cent of "Brute Neighbors" through "Spring" [chapters 12–17]; and none of "Conclusion." Likewise, the second and third versions, written in 1848–1849, consist essentially of a recopying with some revision of the first two-thirds of the first draft, carrying the story only through the material of the sixth chapter, "Visitors."[13]

Obviously these early versions were composed with a lecture audience in mind, and they may in fact have been used by Thoreau as his lecture manuscript itself—a large mass of material that was not divided into chapters but that could easily be broken up to suit the number and length of his speaking engagements. The fact that a greater proportion of this early material survives in the finished form of the first half of the book than in the second half means that the early chapters of *Walden* are much more closely tied to Thoreau's original design and purposes than the later chapters. These, in turn, he wrote for the most part with a book in mind, and they tend more than the first chapters to reflect his interests and concerns during the 1850s.

In reading the book, then, one responds to and follows not only the temporal structure of the Walden experience (the two years of Thoreau's life compressed into a single annual cycle from one spring to the next) but also and perhaps more subliminally the larger development of the narrator over the course of a decade of spiritual and intellectual growth. The effect is not one of "before" and "after," or of two different accounts of the growth of a mind such as one finds in the early and late versions of Wordsworth's *Prelude*, but rather of an earlier self subsumed but still present, as it were, within the later. Nevertheless some of the principal differences between the earlier and later versions of *Walden*, and to some extent the first and second halves of the book, may be described.

The early chapters, particularly "Economy" and "Where I Lived, And What I Lived For," betray their lineage as lecture material in a number of ways, the most obvious of which is their rhetorically high profile: they are more satiric, hyperbolic, confrontational, and full of invective than the later chapters. "I should not presume to talk so much about myself and my affairs as I shall in this lecture," the first version of *Walden* begins, "if very particular and personal inquiries had not been made concerning my mode of life." Beginning with this sardonic acknowledgment of those who had minded his business for him, Thoreau launches a counterattack against the "mean and sneaking lives" his contemporaries lived.[14] And, as he makes clear in an early journal draft of this lecture from the winter of 1845–46, he was particularly concerned to say something about his audience's "outward condition or circumstances in this world."[15] *Walden* was thus at first quite narrowly and parochially conceived: it was not until the post-1852 revisions that the phrase "Addressed to My Townsmen" was dropped from Thoreau's working title. The account of his own life in this version serves as an example that contrasts with the misapplication of force in most lives, but it is not a story whose deeper implications are fathomed. In fact, in the first draft his account of himself ends quite lamely—"Thus was my first year's life in the woods completed"—for clearly Thoreau did not yet realize what the experience signified for himself, however much he was aware of its exemplary potential for his contemporaries.[16]

The early versions and early chapters are also more outer-directed because they were largely conceived and executed during the height of Thoreau's interest in reform during the mid- to late 1840s. He had composed a lecture on reform and reformers during this period, written about reformers in *A Week*, and of course written "Resistance to Civil Government" in response to his night in jail in 1845. The 1840s were a millennial decade generally, and reform movements, ranging in seriousness from abolitionism to Sylvester Graham's advocacy of male chastity and a high-fiber diet, were pandemic in American culture. Within Transcendentalism itself there was a lively debate over reform, and the movement had spawned experimental communities at Brook Farm and Fruitlands. Responding to this climate, Thoreau conceived of his life at Walden at first as a kind of experimental community of one that could serve as a counterexample not only to the unawakened among his townspeople but also to the false reforms and reformers of his age. His earliest journal entries at Walden during the summer of 1845 blend accounts of his life with a critique of contemporary values and culture, and the first draft already contains an indictment of foolish philanthropy and false reforms.[17] Although he continued to be interested in the problem of reforming the reformers and would add much to this section of "Economy" through the various versions, by the early 1850s Thoreau's concern with social and political issues, like that of the nation at large, was increasingly focused on slavery, its extension, and the enforcement of the Fugitive Slave Law. These issues did not lend themselves to treatment in his manuscript in progress, and they would not culminate for him until the addresses he would deliver on John Brown after the Harper's Ferry raid in 1859. He would develop the book as a whole along quite different lines, be less insistent upon addressing the outward condition of humanity, and come to regard his experience at Walden less as an example to misguided reformers and more as a personal quest involving doubt and uncertainty as well as discovery.

The clearest indication of this change may be seen in the character of the narrator and his rhetoric in the second half of the book, the portion that was mostly written after 1852. From "The Ponds" on, the book is more introspective, meditative, and descriptive and contains relatively few passages of sustained satire. When there is a brief return to the themes of "Economy," as in the account of the Irishman John Field and his family in "Baker Farm," Thoreau's criticism is muted by sympathy, and the family is presented in such homely detail and with such particularity that, like their chickens, they become too humanized to roast well. Beginning with its namesake chapter, the pond itself becomes a major character, and Thoreau appears to have been pacified by its waters. In contrast to his stance in the early chapters, like Ishmael in *Moby-Dick* he no longer seems to have a maddened hand and splintered heart turned against the wolfish world; like Ishmael, too, he turns instead to a journey in which meditation and water are wedded and which has as its aim the discovery of the ungraspable phantom of life—even if he has to be content with less exotic surroundings and pursuits: traveling a good deal in Concord, having for a soothing savage Alek Therien the woodchopper, and fishing for pouts on Walden Pond.

The major mark of the book's altered conception in the post-1852 expansions is the extent to which Thoreau developed and amplified the seasonal cycle that undergirds the structure of *Walden*. Shanley describes, for example, the changes made in this aspect of the book during the fifth version, written during late 1852 and early 1853:

> The greatest growth in Thoreau's conception of *Walden* resulted, however, from his seeing how he might fill out his account of the progress of the seasons and describe the changes they had brought in his daily affairs and thoughts; by doing so, he would express more adequately the richness and the completeness of his experience. He had to develop particularly the fall and part of the winter. He did so by greatly enlarging "Brute Neighbors," by developing "House-Warming" for the first time, and by completing "Winter Visitors"; he also made significant though smaller additions to "Winter Animals" and "The Pond in Winter." There was so much new material in version V that Thoreau was not able simply to insert it in previous copy as he had done with most of the new material in IV. He had to make fresh copy of practically all of "The Ponds," "Higher Laws," "Brute Neighbors," "House-Warming," "Former Inhabitants; and Winter Visitors," and "The Pond in Winter."[18]

The cumulative effect of these additions was to alter the focus of the book radically. In the early versions the critique of American culture dominated ("Economy" and "Where I Lived, and What I

Lived For" still make up nearly a third of the finished book, and represented an even larger proportion in the early drafts), in which the story of Thoreau's own life served, as we have already seen, as a counterpoint. The cyclical pattern of the year was relatively unimportant. Now, however, with the annual cycle developed and amplified, there exists for the first time a "story" with a kind of plot: the journey or quest of the narrator passing through various changes marked by the progress of the seasons and advancing toward some kind of self-knowledge. The book begins to acquire mythic and archetypal dimensions and, in the relative deemphasis of social criticism attendant upon the expansion of these other elements, becomes less topical and more universal in its reference.

Doubtless the addition of material about fall, winter, and the second spring contributes to verisimilitude and to a felt sense of the passage of a year. There is a satisfying structural coherence about this pattern as realized in the finished book, a kind of harmonic or tonic closure felt in arriving once more at spring. At the same time, however, this is a relatively simple, unsophisticated, and not particularly novel structure. The same pattern may be said to inform the *Farmer's Almanac*. Nor is the discovery of the seasonal cycle itself what is most important. Critics have occasionally pointed to a journal entry for 18 April 1852, in which Thoreau announces "For the first time I perceive this spring that the year is a circle," as marking such an insight and signaling a new design for *Walden* (*J*, 3:438).[19] But surely Richard Lebeaux is correct to point out that "more likely, he was indicating that this was the first time *this spring* that he had seen the year as a circle."[20] For a naturalist to observe for the first time at age thirty-five that the year is a circle is equivalent to a hydrologist's discovering that water runs downhill. As Robert D. Richardson, Jr., has recently observed, with several decades of critical explications of the seasonal structure in mind, "We have made too much of the seasonal structure of *Walden*, too easily assuming that the book's message is to accept the seasonal cycle of nature as final wisdom. Such a view, essentially objective, conservative, and tragic, is not at last what Thoreau wanted or taught."[21]

Thoreau developed the seasonal emphasis of *Walden* not because it was the logical structure for his book but because he was interested in the seasons of his own life and because he came to believe, as he put it in the fall of 1857, "These regular phenomena of the seasons get at last to be—they were *at first* of course—simply and plainly phenomena or phases of my life. The seasons and all their changes are in me." He concluded this entry by remarking "The perfect correspondence of Nature to man, so that he is at home in her!" (*J*, 10:127).[22] The remaking of *Walden* in large part involves an effort to tell the truth of the first proposition by following out the artistic implications of the second—the "perfect correspondence" by which nature's seasons express our own.

It was the need to probe the meaning of his Walden experience, to come to terms with the great event in his life, and by writing to relive and recapture that experience, rather than discovering that the year is a circle, that stimulated Thoreau to begin expanding his manuscript in 1852. In January—the tenth anniversary of his brother John's death and very close to the time he began working on the manuscript again— he asked himself in the journal:

> But why I changed? why I left the woods? I do not think that I can tell. I have often wished myself back. I do not know any better how I ever came to go there. Perhaps it is none of my business, even if it is yours. . . . I must say that I do not know what made me leave the pond. I left it as unaccountably as I went to it. To speak sincerely, I went there because I had got ready to go; I left it for the same reason. (*J*, 3:214, 216)

Two days later, on 24 January, he admonished himself to take up his pen in the service of fathoming such mysteries at the same time that he lamented his own inability to recapture the glorious past:

> If thou art a writer, write as if thy time were short, for it is indeed short at the longest. Improve each occasion when thy soul is reached. Drain the cup of inspiration to its last dregs. Fear no intemperance in that, for the years will come when otherwise thou wilt regret opportunities unimproved. The spring will not last forever. These fertile and expanding seasons of thy life, when the rain reaches thy root, when thy vigor shoots, when thy flower is budding, shall be fewer and farther between. Again I say, remember thy Creator in the days of thy youth. . . . Why did I not use my eyes when I stood on Pisgah? Now I hear those strains but seldom. My rhythmical mood does not endure. I cannot draw from it and return to it in my thought as to a well all the evening or the morning. I cannot dip my pen in it. I cannot work the vein, it is so fine and volatile. Ah, sweet, ineffable reminiscences! (*J*, 3:221–22)

This despondency, a recurring nightmare of the Romantics, who most feared that they might cease to feel, was only temporary, but it points toward the complex of emotions that led Thoreau to reconceive *Walden*. Uncertainty about his motives for going to and leaving the pond dogged him, and he felt that he must answer those questions for himself through his writing, even though he temporarily doubted his ability to work the vein. He must create an account of his former experience that would satisfy the demands of imagination and memory, rather like the speaker of Frost's "The Road Not Taken," who really knows that there was no perceptible difference between the two paths at the time but also knows that he must invent a story that will account for the distance he has traveled and also link himself with his own past: "I shall be telling this with a sigh / Somewhere ages and ages hence."

So the new work on *Walden* primarily expanded the later sections of the book that describe autumn, winter, and the second spring, a seasonal epoch in which mature affirmation comes only after a long probation and after having faced doubt, anxiety, and even evil in both the self and nature. At the same time, it needs to be kept in mind that much of this pattern is implicit, as Thoreau tends to editorialize less and to write less explicitly about himself in these sections, depending more on the "perfect correspondence" between man and nature to endow his descriptions of natural phenomena with human significance.

Something of an exception to this pattern of implicitness, and an exception that may serve by its expository nature as a convenient example of the altered tone of Thoreau's thinking, is the chapter "Higher Laws," most of which was added, apparently, during the fourth through the seventh versions. It had started out as a treatise on fishing and hunting, leading to a discussion of diet and advocating vegetarianism on both economic and philosophical grounds. In this respect it was consistent with the emphasis on reform and the subject matter of the early versions. Until the sixth version, in fact, it carried the title "Animal Food."[23] But the original tension in the chapter— Thoreau's genuine ambivalence about hunting and especially fishing—is eventually cast into the shade in later versions by a more serious conflict between "animal" and "spiritual": "We are conscious of an animal in us, which awakens in proportion as our higher nature slumbers" (W, 219).[24] This conflict most dramatically expressed itself for Thoreau over the issues of what he termed chastity and sensuality. Whatever the efficient cause of this concern, he was troubled by his own inability to master this side of his nature. He cannot speak of these topics, he fears, without betraying his own impurity. In the fifth version he canceled an even more revealing sentence: "I do not know how it is with other men, but I find it very difficult to be chaste."[25] These fears, obviously arising out of personal experience of some kind, lead to the pronouncement that "Nature is hard to be overcome, but she must be overcome" (W, 221), a statement that seems hopelessly in conflict with the narrator's stance toward nature elsewhere.

This assertion may be reconcilable with Thoreau's attitude toward nature in other passages, but the tension is really central to the completed book, I think, and a sign of maturity on Thoreau's part, a recognition that nature and the human self in which it is reflected have depths heretofore unplumbed but needing to be faced. Thoreau's apprehensions about purity and chastity, while they may appear only quaint or priggish to a twentieth-century audience, represent an acknowledgment by him of a part of his nature more basic (and base) than he had previously seen. Something of this recognition carried over and expressed itself in his revisions of other portions of *Walden*, in the course of which he was able to develop this line of thought in more positive ways.

The realization that his own as well as external nature possessed such subterranean dimensions could be exhilarating as well as disquieting. It carried Thoreau some distance toward a theory of the unconscious and led him to speculate on the extent to which intellectual and creative activity was dependent upon functions of the mind that lay below the threshold of conscious thought. Characteristically, he expressed this insight in terms of a correspondence between man and nature, in a journal entry in 1851, just before beginning his major reworking of *Walden*. Having read the botanist Asa Gray's description of how a plant grows upward toward the light and simultaneously downward, he observed:

> So the mind develops from the first in two opposite directions: upwards to expand in the light and air; and downwards avoiding the light to form the root. One half is aerial, the other subterranean. The mind is not well balanced and firmly planted, like the oak, which has not as much root as branch, whose roots like those of the white pine are slight and near the surface. One half of the mind's development must still be root,—in the embryonic state, in the womb of nature, more unborn than at first. For each successive new idea or bud, a new rootlet in the earth. The growing man penetrates yet deeper by his roots into the womb of things. The infant is comparatively near the surface, just covered from the light; but the man sends down a tap-root to the centre of things. (*J*, 2:203)

The most dramatic application of this perspective in *Walden* is Thoreau's radical revision and amplification of the climactic sand foliage passages in "Spring" during the last versions, where this "truly *grotesque*" (that is, coming from underground) vegetation manifests the generative and creative forces of nature, however visceral or excremental its appearance (*W*, 305). Thoreau had reached an earlier stage of understanding the beneficial potential of such threatening and disturbing natural forces on his first trip to the Maine wilderness in 1846, when he came in contact on Mount Katahdin with a kind of nature that threatened to extinguish rather than heighten consciousness and when he had also faced the fact that here "one could no longer accuse institutions and society, but must front the true source of evil" (that is, the self).[26] This knowledge in turn had already led him to express in the first draft of *Walden*, composed the following year, a theory of the necessity of wild nature to the human psyche that incorporated the essentially ungraspable nature of nature as a positive fact: "At the same time that we are in earnest to explore and learn all things, we require that all things be mysterious and unexplorable, that land and sea be infinitely wild, unsurveyed and unfathomed by us because unfathomable. We can never have enough of Nature" (*W*, 317–18).[27]

Paradoxically, that we can never have enough of nature and that nature must also be overcome are but different expressions of the same fact, the complexity of our own nature that grows upward and downward at the same time. There is a womb of nature and an answering womb—dark, unconscious, and powerful—in the mind. Ultimately Thoreau renders nature more complexly in the later versions of *Walden* because he sees human nature more complexly, starting with his own. Accounts of natural phenomena convey little of what Thoreau termed in *A Week* "the mealy-mouthed enthusiasm of the lover of Nature." To the fourth version, for example, he added the account of the battle of the ants to "Brute Neighbors," unflinchingly observing—even under a microscope—the "internecine war" in nature that was going on underfoot. And the owls in "Sounds," which in the first versions stood rather conventionally and melodramatically for the "fallen souls that once in human shape night-walked the earth," come to suggest by the fourth version "a vast and undeveloped nature which men have not recognized. They represent the stark twilight and unsatisfied thoughts which all have." As one might almost predict, the last phrase originally read "which I have."[28]

The expansion of the fall and winter chapters of the manuscript during the second stage of composition thus created a strong counterpoint to and eventual transformation of the dominant spring imagery of *Walden*. The new proportions suggest, of course, that Thoreau became increasingly concerned with his own awakening and less obsessed with waking up his neighbors. They also suggest, at the level of seasonal change in the narrator, that the second spring is of a different order of magnitude than and not merely a repetition of the first, and comes as a result of his having sent down his "tap-root into the centre of things." By doing so, he succeeds himself, the self that like an infant was "comparatively near the surface" in understanding the phenomena of his own life.

The second spring is a kind of second growth intimately related and akin to the second growth of autumn itself, a time when fruits mature and seeds ripen. Thoreau had not earned the affirmations of the "Conclusion" (the last chapter to be written) until he had achieved the mature growth depicted in "The Ponds" through "Spring." This phase of *Walden*, in which autumnal imagery abounds, points toward the predominantly autumnal atmosphere of Thoreau's later essays: the close of "Walking," say, or the whole of "Wild Apples" and "Autumnal Tints." He had arrived at an autumnal phase in his own life, in which the fruit of his earlier experiences at Walden had matured, experiences that enjoy a kind of second spring in his imaginative recreation of them in the book. The questions he had begun his revision by asking ("But why I left the woods?") he could now answer: "I left the woods for as good a reason as I went there. . . ." (*W*, 323). Thoreau largely effaced from the final text the fact that this affirmation arose out of a profound experience of self-doubt and even disgust (such as we glimpse in "Higher Laws"), but it is evident in the manuscript, in which the following aside to the passage just quoted is preserved:

> If the reader think that I am vainglorious, and set myself above others, I assure him that I could tell a pitiful story respecting myself as well as him if my spirits held out, could encourage him with a sufficient list of failures, and flow humbly as the gutters. I think worse of myself than he is likely to think of me, and better too, being better acquainted with the man. Finally, I will tell him this secret, if he will not abuse my confidence—I put the best face on the matter.[29]

Nevertheless the fable of *Walden*, he thought, expressing his mature vision (and contained in miniature in the story of the Artist of Kouroo in the "Conclusion"), had a lasting quality that would make up for early disappointments and self-doubts. He believed himself to be, in the best and most nearly literal sense of the term, a late-bloomer, and he confided as much to his journal in April 1854, while reading proof for *Walden*:

> Some poets mature early and die young. Their fruits have a delicious flavor like strawberries, but do not keep till fall or winter. Others are slower in coming to their growth. Their fruits may be less delicious, but are a more lasting food and are so hardened by the sun of summer and the coolness of autumn that they keep sound over winter. The first are June-eatings, early but soon withering; the last are russets, which last till June again. (*J*, 6:190–91)

Besides the emphasis on the seasons and the corresponding story of individual growth, the most important major change between the early and later versions of *Walden* lies in the more learned and scientific cast of the later additions and revisions. The maturity of the final version is not a matter of age and self-knowledge alone, but of knowledge of the world. It takes the form of a theory of nature, which, as Emerson had said in his first book, *Nature*, was the aim of all science. In the finished version of *Walden* Thoreau is a scientist; not a scientist in precisely the sense we assume the term to mean today, but a scientist nevertheless, one who believed that the results of his investigations into nature expressed actual and not merely "poetic" truth. "Spring"—and especially the climactic account of thawing sand and clay in the railroad cut—contains not only the apogee of Thoreau's personal growth and rebirth but also the conclusion of his scientific investigation of the laws that underlie natural phenomena. The fact that these two investigations culminate together does not mean that one is a "symbol" of the other but rather that, for Thoreau, there really was a "perfect correspondence of Nature to man" that it was his mission to describe.

Thoreau's development as a natural scientist during the years of *Walden's* second growth was coincident, however, with his more general development as a reader and thinker. He had always possessed something of a scholarly cast of mind, and since college he had kept a series of commonplace books in which he recorded passages from his reading. But like his journal-keeping, after 1850 this note-taking became more detailed and regular, and over the years his store of learning found its way into the *Walden* manuscript in hundreds of quotations from and allusions to his reading.[30] These additions were spread throughout the manuscript, so that the consistently high level of allusiveness becomes a persistent textural and even thematic element of the entire book, deepening its level of reference, mitigating the parochial nature of its subject matter, and extending its appeal, by implication, to a much broader audience than the "my townsmen" of the original subtitle.

Walden as revised invokes, in other words, a world of other texts sacred and profane, familiar and arcane, learned and popular. One of the most engaging or the most irritating traits of the narrator (depending upon whether one is reading the book for the fifth time or attempting to get through it for the first time) is his propensity to cite examples and authorities. (Like both *Moby-Dick* and *Huckleberry Finn* among its peers in nineteenth-century American literature, *Walden* engages the issue of "authorities" in partly playful and partly serious ways, out of the American writer's long-standing anxiety about his or her indigenous culture coupled with defiance of more established cultural traditions.) We are told, among innumerable bits of arcane knowledge, how long the ancients considered it proper to trim one's fingernails, house construction techniques of native Americans in New England, how the Romans made bread, how long the Vishnu Purana stipulates one must wait for a guest, and how a Tartar described the dispatching of an enemy. Thoreau added many of these specific allusions and most of the extended quotations from source material in later versions. In part this process marks the change from a lecture-centered to a book-centered conception, but it also reflects Thoreau's growing tendency to ground his work in concrete observation and precise reference and anticipates the sort of detailed scholarly approach to subjects that would become more common for him during the 1850s. In *Walden* these allusions work as part of the retrospective urge of the book that complements the immediacy of the material actually composed at the pond; they constitute a "re-search" impulse that broadens the implications of particular episodes and connects the activities described to the wider human community both past and present.

In this context Thoreau's scientific expansions to *Walden* are a subset of these pervasive amplifications drawn from reading and observation. On a more fundamental level, however, the more scientific cast of the revised book, with its emphasis on the careful and detailed description of such central phenomena as the pond itself, the habits of various animals—now identified by genus and species as well as popular name—the Walden ice, and above all the thawing sand and clay of the railroad embankment, reflects Thoreau's commitment to natural history studies (along with writing, of course) as his principal life's work. Until quite recently at any rate, it has been the custom to derogate Thoreau's abilities as a scientist, as though his unfitness in this field were a necessary precondition to taking him seriously as an artist. But whatever the actual merits of his scientific work, it is clear that he regarded his studies seriously, and equally clear that he had a good grasp of contemporary theoretical controversies in the natural sciences during the years before Darwin's *Origin of Species* (1859) signaled the triumph of a paradigm that has held sway ever since.[31] Certainly he was not doing "normal" science from a post-Darwinian perspective; he was, however, operating according to scientific traditions and theoretical orientations quite viable in his own day, and it is from this perspective that his natural history studies in *Walden* (as well as his post-*Walden* essays in this field) are best understood.

Basic to Thoreau's methodology as a naturalist is an emphasis on perception and the centrality of the observer, features which today of course tend to relegate natural history to the status of "soft" science if it is considered a scientific discipline at all. He inherited this emphasis from Goethe, who was the founding father, so to speak, of the German school of *Naturphilosophie* from which Thoreau drew much of his theoretical orientation and whose most distinguished practitioner in America was Louis Agassiz. For Thoreau the perceiving consciousness was not a "personality" that distorted the accuracy of observation but a necessary component of the equation by which phenomena could be understood and rendered meaningful. In order to write "The Ponds," for instance, one of the key chapters of *Walden*, he worked for several years observing Walden under different conditions, making excursions for that specific purpose and writing up his observations in the journal for eventual incorporation into the book. The portrait that eventually emerged emphasized the purity of the pond and the myriad ways that any natural fact, carefully and accurately perceived, dissolves the difference between perceiver and perceived: "A lake is the landscape's most beautiful and expressive feature. It is earth's eye; looking into which the beholder measures the depth of his own nature" (W, 186). This statement is not finally a geologic anthropomorphism, or even a literary conceit, but an expression of the belief that the study of nature is ultimately the study of the self, for it is only after many years of observation that this relationship suggests itself (this particular passage first appeared in the sixth version).

Thoreau's descriptions of the ponds are largely about the process of perception itself, emphasizing that what we see when we look at a body of water is its surface and a boundary where two elements meet. The results of observation here depend upon the position of the observer relative to the object observed—a kind of perceptual relativity that points out (as relativity theory in physics also does) the illusory nature of absolute measurement. Walden is "a perfect forest mirror" that registers all change and all life on its surface, above its surface, and even below its surface, while at the same time continually changing color itself depending on conditions both known and unknown. The picture of the pond is a series of partial perceptions, each stressing the vantage point of the perceiver as a major component. In the four paragraphs that constitute the central description of Walden Pond itself, for example, we find the following markers of place: "You may see from a boat," "I have in my mind's eye," "Standing on the smooth sandy beach," "When you invert your head," "From a hilltop," and "on such a height as this, overlooking the pond" (W, 185–87). The final perspective in this section, a paragraph that first appears in the fifth version, takes us in imagination to a still higher vantage point and demonstrates concretely how the seen proves the unseen:

> A field of water betrays the spirit that is in the air. It is continually receiving new life and motion from above. It is intermediate in its nature between land and sky. On land only the grass and trees wave, but the water itself is rippled by the wind. I see where the breeze dashes across it by the streaks or flakes of light. We shall, perhaps, look down thus on the surface of air at length, and mark where a still subtler spirit sweeps over it. (W, 188–89)

Characteristically, Thoreau begins by emphasizing a key word—"field"—that operates, like nature itself, at several levels simultaneously, suggesting a range of meanings from the most obvious (an open expanse) to progressively more complex suggestions of the relation between the observer and what is observed: a field as that which is bounded (field of vision); a field as the subject of study or calling (as in his "half-cultivated field" in "The Bean Field"); and as a space upon which something is drawn or projected. The surface of the pond is more interesting and significant for the meaning it may transmit than for any significance which may be said to reside in it intrinsically. Both nature and the language with which the poet describes it are, as Emerson said in "The Poet," vehicular and transitive.

If "The Ponds" stresses methodology and the importance of the observer, "Spring" emphasizes results. The famous passages describing the sand foliage that effloresces on the railroad cut—sure evidence of a spring that "precedes the green and flowery spring"—announce the discovery of a law in nature, a discovery that coincides with Thoreau's own second spring. His perception, rightly trained and furnished once more with several years' careful study of the phenomenon, is able to anticipate spring and discern the operation of fundamental principles of generation and creativity in nature, while at the same time discovering the operation of the same power in himself. It needs to be stressed that the thawing sandbank is not intended by Thoreau as a figurative equivalent of his own awakening but rather as evidence of the operation of a law that animates both nature and man.

Like the descriptions of the ponds, Thoreau's account of the sand foliage was the product of several years of observation and evolution in his thought. In the first version the phenomenon elicits only a brief mention as one of the signs of spring:

> As I go back and forth over the rail-road through the deep cut I have seen where the clayey sand *like lava* had flowed down when it thawed and as it streamed it assumed the forms of vegetation, of vines and stout pulpy leaves—unaccountably interesting and beautiful—as if its course were so to speak a diagonal between fluids & solids—and it were hesitating whether to stream in to a river, or into vegetation—for vegetation too is such a stream as a river, only of a slower current.[32]

By the final version this account had grown to more than 1,500 words, and what was at first "unaccountably interesting and beautiful" came eventually to illustrate no less than "the principle of all the operations of Nature," the underlying ur-phenomenon of the leaf, which metamorphoses from the lowest and presumably inorganic forms of matter upward to higher life forms until "the very globe continually transcends and translates itself, and becomes winged in its orbit" (W, 308, 307). Thoreau was composing material for this section in the journal right up until *Walden* went to press. He added the climactic phrase "There is nothing inorganic," as well as the longer passage quoted below, in an entry for 5 February 1854. This conclusion is less a private testimony of faith than a challenge to prevailing scientific paradigms:

> The earth is not a mere fragment of dead history, stratum upon stratum like the leaves of a book, to be studied by geologists and antiquaries chiefly, but living poetry like the leaves of a tree, which precede flowers and fruit,—not a fossil earth, but a living earth; compared with whose great central life all animal and vegetable life is merely parasitic. (W, 309)

Here, translating and metamorphosing the figure of the leaf, he contrasts his discovery of the creative force working through nature to both the older eighteenth-century argument from design, which discovered evidence of creation at some former date, and the developing orthodoxy of positivist science, which sees all nature ultimately as matter capable of being broken down and analyzed. To say that the earth is "living poetry" is not merely to make a figure of speech but to express a conviction that the same power that animates the poet's creativity works through and animates nature as well. Thoreau did not think of himself as making a statement that was poetically true only. One of his key revisions in this section of "Spring" was to alter his conception of the agency behind this power. In an early version he had felt himself to be standing "in the studio of an artist" when witnessing this phenomenon, but in the final version he stands "in the *laboratory* of the Artist who made the world and me" (emphasis added).[33] This fusion of the perspective of the scientist and the artist reflects Thoreau's stubborn resistance to the notion of there being two truths—one imaginative and one scientific—and likewise reflects the extent to which the climactic insights of *Walden* owe their origin to his own absorption in the natural sciences during the book's second growth.

Walden ultimately invalidates the apology Thoreau once offered for his attempt to fuse life and art—"My life has been the poem I would have writ / But I could not both live and utter it." His response to changes in himself as well as in his outward circumstances during the 1850s, along with his newfound commitments to the journal and his natural history studies, helped him to deepen and enrich the story of his life at the pond far beyond its expression in the book he wanted to publish in 1849. At the same time, the formal elements of *Walden*— its architectonics, its style, the relation of its parts to the whole— ought not to be considered as fixed or final in the version that Thoreau published in 1854. Its form no less than its content was dictated by his life, and had he delayed publishing it still further the book would doubtless have continued to evolve along with him. His revisions were not directed toward filling out or realizing a design that he kept before him but toward incorporating stages of growth within the design that already existed. *Walden* is, in this respect, an archetypal Romantic text, like *Leaves of Grass*, that developed as its author developed and that preserves experience while continually reinterpreting it.

The sense of proportion that the completed book conveys is less the result of conscious artifice than of the integrity and the single-mindedness of the endeavor that produced it. Largely as a result of vestiges of the looser and more associative structure of the original lectures, many of its proportions are in fact quite awkward (the length of "Economy" compared with the chapters that follow, for example), and many of its transitions, such as from "Where I Lived" to "Reading," are rather arbitrary. But Thoreau's vision as expressed in his revisions was finally coherent (if not always consistent), his attention to detail at the level of words, sentences, and paragraphs superb, and the resulting whole has a finish certainly more evident now than when it was published: it took nearly a hundred years for *Walden* to achieve canonical status in American literature.

Such a trajectory of fame would of course have pleased Thoreau, for it fitted his own conception of his life and work as late-blooming. And like many of his contemporaries—especially Whitman, Melville, and Dickinson—he found himself more or less consciously writing to posterity and aware that an audience for his writing had yet to be created. A true work, he thought, turning as usual a necessity into a virtue, would reveal its proportions and its integrity over time, and come to enjoy, like the bug that emerged from the apple-tree table in the concluding fable of *Walden*, its perfect summer life at last. A year before he went to live at the pond, and fully ten years before *Walden* would be published, he concluded an essay on Homer, Ossian, and Chaucer with a meditation that might have described his hopes for his own best account of his life:

> There is a soberness in a rough aspect, as of unhewn granite, which addresses a depth in us, but a polished surface hits only the ball of the eye. The true finish is the work of time and the use to which a thing is put. The elements are still polishing the pyramids. Art may varnish and gild, but it can do no more. A work of genius is rough-hewn from the first, because it anticipates the lapse of time, and has an ingrained polish, which still appears when fragments are broken off, an essential quality of its substance. Its beauty is at the same time its strength, and it breaks with a

lustre. . . . it will have to speak to posterity, traversing these deserts, through the ruin of its outmost walls, by the grandeur and beauty of its proportions.[34]

Notes

1. See Johnson, "Historical Introduction," 469–70.
2. Emerson to Thoreau, 2 December 1847, *Correspondence of Thoreau*, ed. Harding and Bode, 195. Hereafter cited as *Correspondence*.
3. Harding, *Days of Thoreau*, 236–42.
4. *Correspondence*, 242.
5. The surviving portions of the *Walden* manuscript are housed at the Henry E. Huntington Library and designated HM 924. The two-stage second draft of *Walden*, labeled as versions "II" and "III" by Shanley in *The Making of "Walden,"* 27–30, contains pencil interlineations in Thoreau's hand indicating, for example, places where extra space should be set between lines.
6. Emerson, *Journals and Miscellaneous Notebooks*, 10:345.
7. Johnson, "Historical Introduction," 478–79; see also Sattelmeyer, " 'When He Became My Enemy.' "
8. Sattelmeyer and Hocks, "Thoreau and Coleridge's *Theory of Life*."
9. To H. G. O. Blake, 20 November 1849, *Correspondence*, 250–51.
10. See Cameron's provocative study of Thoreau's journal, *Writing Nature*.
11. Rossi, " 'Laboratory of the Artist,' " 8–9, points out that Thoreau continued to compose passages for *Walden* during this time: evidence from his use marks in and indexes to the manuscript of the journal suggest that he transferred these passages to a draft in progress.
12. See Shanley, *The Making of "Walden,"* 30–32; Clapper, "The Development of *Walden*," 31–32; see also Adams and Ross, "The Endings of *Walden*," in *Revising Mythologies*, 165–92, which appeared while this essay was in press.
13. Shanley, *The Making of "Walden,"* 94; see also Clapper, "The Development of *Walden*," 30.
14. Shanley, *The Making of "Walden,"* 105, 108.
15. *Journal 2: 1842–1848*, 187.
16. Shanley, *The Making of "Walden,"* 208.
17. See ibid., 133–37.
18. Ibid., 67.
19. *Journal*, 3:438. Subsequent references to this edition are cited parenthetically in the text.
20. Lebeaux, *Thoreau's Seasons*, 159.
21. Richardson, *Thoreau*, 310.
22. The importance of this passage is pointed out by Lebeaux, in *Thoreau's Seasons*, 293; I am also indebted in the following passages on the seasons of *Walden* to Lebeaux's discussion of the issue in chapter 5 "Second Spring," 151–97.
23. Clapper, "The Development of *Walden*," 566.
24. *Walden*, ed. Shanley, 219. Subsequent references to this edition are cited parenthetically in the text.
25. Clapper, "The Development of *Walden*," 588.
26. Thoreau, "Ktaadn, and the Maine Woods," in *The Maine Woods*, ed. Moldenhauer, 16.

27. Shanley, *The Making of "Walden,"* 207.
28. Clapper, "The Development of *Walden*," 361–64.
29. Ibid., 854.
30. See Sattelmeyer, *Thoreau's Reading,* 75–77.
31. See ibid., 78–92; also Hildebidle, *Thoreau*; Howarth, *The Book of Concord*, 190–211; and Rossi, " 'Laboratory of the Artist,' " esp. 151–201. I am especially indebted to Rossi's discussion of Thoreau's knowledge of contemporary science and his analysis of the sand foliage passages in "Spring."
32. Shanley, *The Making of "Walden,"* 204.
33. *Walden*, 306; see Rossi, " 'Laboratory of the Artist,' " 200.
34. "Homer. Ossian. Chaucer.," in *Early Essays and Miscellanies*, ed. Moldenhauer, Moser, and Kern, 173.

Works Cited

Adams, Stephen, and Donald A. Ross. *Revising Mythologies: The Composition of Thorerau's Major Works*. Charlottesville: University Press of Virginia, 1988.

Cameron, Sharon. *Writing Nature*. New York: Oxford University Press, 1985.

Clapper, Ronald A. "The Development of *Walden*: A Genetic Text." Ph.D. dissertation, University of California, Los Angeles, 1967.

Emerson, Ralph Waldo. *The Journals and Miscellaneous Notebooks of Ralph Waldo Emerson*. Edited by William H. Gilman, et al. 16 vols. Cambridge: Harvard University Press, 1960–82.

Harding, Walter. *The Days of Henry Thoreau*. New York: Alfred A. Knopf, 1965.

Hildebidle, John. *Thoreau: A Naturalist's Liberty*. Cambridge: Harvard University Press, 1984.

Howarth, William L. *The Book of Concord*. New York: Viking Press, 1982.

Johnson, Linck C. "Historical Introduction." In Henry D. Thoreau, *A Week on the Concord and Merrimack Rivers*, edited by Carl F. Hovde, William L. Howarth, and Elizabeth Hall Witherell, 433–500. Princeton: Princeton University Press, 1980.

Lebeaux, Richard. *Thoreau's Seasons*. Amherst: University of Massachusetts Press, 1984.

Richardson, Robert D., Jr. *Thoreau: A Life of the Mind*. Berkeley and Los Angeles: University of California Press, 1986.

Rossi, William J. " 'Laboratory of the Artist': Henry D. Thoreau's Literary and Scientific Use of the *Journal*, 1848–1854." Ph.D. dissertation, University of Minnesota, 1986.

Sattelmeyer, Robert. *Thoreau's Reading*. Princeton: Princeton University Press, 1988.

————. " 'When He Became My Enemy': Emerson and Thoreau, 1848–49." *New England Quarterly* 62 (1989): 187–204.

Sattelmeyer, Robert, and Richard A. Hocks. "Thoreau and Coleridge's *Theory of Life*." In *Studies in the American Renaissance 1985*, edited by

Joel Myerson, 269–84. Charlottesville: University Press of Virginia, 1985.

Shanley, J. Lyndon. *The Making of "Walden."* Chicago: University of Chicago Press, 1957.

Thoreau, Henry D. *The Correspondence of Henry David Thoreau.* Edited by Walter Harding and Carl Bode. New York: New York University Press, 1958.

_____. *Early Essays and Miscellanies.* Edited by Joseph J. Moldenhauer and Edwin Moser, with Alexander Kern. Princeton: Princeton University Press, 1975.

_____. *The Journal of Henry D. Thoreau.* Edited by Bradford Torrey and Francis H. Allen. 14 vols. Boston: Houghton Mifflin, 1949.

_____. *Journal 2: 1842–1848.* Edited by Robert Sattelmeyer. Princeton: Princeton University Press, 1984.

_____. *The Maine Woods.* Edited by Joseph J. Moldenhauer. Princeton: Princeton University Press, 1972.

_____. *Walden.* Edited by J. Lyndon Shanley. Princeton: Princeton University Press, 1971.

TOM QUIRK

Nobility out of Tatters:
The Writing of *Huckleberry Finn*

Willa Cather once wrote, "There is a time in a writer's development when his 'life line' and the line of his personal endeavor meet."[1] For her, the intersection of these two lines occurred when she wrote her first significant novel, *O Pioneers!* (1913). The writing of this novel produced in her the excitement that comes from writing out of one's "deepest experience" and "inner feeling,"[2] and her course was directed by the "thing by which our feet find the road on a dark night, accounting of themselves for roots and stones which we have never noticed by day."[3] These remarks are as true for Mark Twain as they were for Cather herself; and whether he knew it or not, the lines of his familiar experience and his literary ambition converged sometime in July 1876, when he began to write the book he would eventually name *Adventures of Huckleberry Finn*.

Cather's personal endeavor was distinctly artistic, and she had committed herself to the high calling of art at least twenty years before she achieved in *O Pioneers!* the sort of satisfaction that allowed her to say that she had hit the "home pasture" at last. Twain's literary development was more haphazard. He once remarked that his life consisted of a series of apprenticeships and that he was surprised to discover, at the age of thirty-seven, that he had become a "literary person." Only four years after this revelation he embarked on the writing of "Huck Finn's Autobiography" (as he had described it in a letter to W. D. Howells),[4] the book that has secured for him the reputation as something significantly more than a mere "literary person." And part of the mystery of *Huckleberry Finn* is how Twain's achievement in this book outran his qualifications to write it. But Twain too was guided by some "thing" within him, though he seems often to have lost his way. At times, in fact, he wanted to abandon the journey altogether. But he did not, and the result was a book that transmuted fact and experience into memorable fiction.

"No more beautiful or instructive example of the artist's dilemma, of the source of his passions, and how, if ever, he must lovingly resolve them, is available to us than this passion of Mark Twain, resolved in *Huckleberry Finn*."⁵ So wrote another Midwestern novelist, Wright Morris. Artistic development and maturity, Morris insisted, demand more than the acquisition of literary technique; they require, as well, the recognition of the contingency of fact and the permanence of fiction. The edges of fact and fiction sometimes blurred for Twain, but in *Huckleberry Finn*, "in one moment of vision, a state of hallowed reminiscence, he seemed to grasp the distinction," and "his genius flowed into it."⁶ What we know of the composition of *Huckleberry Finn* suggests not a single moment of vision, however, but several. Nevertheless, a general statement about the relation of fact to fiction Morris once made in an essay has an appropriateness to Mark Twain's relation to his book:

> We are, indeed, cunning and inscrutable creatures, mad for facts that we must turn into fiction to possess. If it's about man, it's about fiction, and the better the fiction, the more it's about. The worse the fiction, the less we have of the facts of life. If we are to be more rather than less human—one of our many stimulating options—we will turn from what we see around us, and attend to the promptings within us. The imagination made us human, but *being* human, becoming more human, is a greater burden than we imagined. We have no choice but to imagine ourselves more human than we are.⁷

The facts of the composition of *Huckleberry Finn* tell us something about the fiction that is the novel. And one of the things they tell us is that Mark Twain, mainly through his identification with Huck, imagined himself more completely human than he probably was himself, and in doing so provided his readers with the same opportunity.

I

In a sense we know both too much and too little about the making of *Huckleberry Finn*. The extant evidence for its composition is of several sorts. The single most important piece of evidence is a holograph manuscript now housed in the Buffalo Public Library. This manuscript represents approximately three-fifths of the novel and consists of most of chapter 12, all of chapters 13 and 14, and chapters 22 through the concluding chapter 43, all written in Twain's beautifully clear hand. Extant too is a draft of Twain's parody of the Hamlet soliloquy, presumably inserted into chapter 21 sometime after that chapter was written. And there is the familiar "raft chapter" extracted from the novel and included in *Life on the Mississippi* (1883), and now, in the Iowa-California edition of the novel, restored to chapter 16. There are as well letters and other sorts of testimony related to *Huckleberry Finn*, and there are various references to the book in Twain's notebooks. Finally, there are the "Working Notes" for the novel, which Bernard DeVoto divided into three distinct groups and which are particularly significant in reconstructing the composition of the novel. These notes record ideas for future episodes, reminders about what he had already written, and notations about the vernacular speech of his characters. We know as well that at least one typescript of the novel was made in two stages and that this served as the printer's copy for the first edition. Howells had the first two-fifths retyped because it was so cluttered with revisions, including some of Howells's own markings. The holograph of that portion of the manuscript of the novel was probably destroyed after that typescript was completed, and no portion of the typescript itself has survived.

On the basis of most of this evidence (not all of it was available to him), DeVoto speculated that *Huckleberry Finn* was composed in two distinct stages.[8] Chapters 1 through 16 (minus the interpolated *Walter Scott* episode and the King Solomon debate) were written in the summer of 1876, for Twain wrote Howells on 9 August that he had written about 400 manuscript pages in a month and was only partly satisfied by the result and had decided to pigeonhole or burn the novel when it was complete. The remainder, claimed DeVoto, was written in an eruptive burst of inspiration in 1883. We do know, at any rate, that on 1 September 1883 Twain wrote his English publisher that he had just finished the book.

DeVoto's account of the composition of *Huckleberry Finn* was based upon a conscientious inspection of available evidence, and it placed special emphasis on the effect that Twain's Mississippi River trip in 1882 had in revitalizing the author's interest in the pigeonholed manuscript of Huck's adventures. Twain made this trip to gather first-hand reacquaintance with life along the river in order to complete *Life on the Mississippi*, a book which had its origin in the simple reminiscence he published as "Old Times on the Mississippi" in 1875. For DeVoto and others, the real beneficiary of this trip was not his river book, however, but *Huckleberry Finn*. DeVoto had divided the working notes into three distinct groups (A, B, and C), but he assumed that all of these notes for continuing the Huck manuscript were written after that trip and offered evidence that Twain had at last discovered the "true purpose" of the book he had abandoned six years earlier. In the remaining chapters Twain would "exhibit the rich variety of life in the great central valley," a variety that included in its diverse effects the chicanery and venality of the king and duke, the senseless cruelty of the Bricksville loafers, and the stupid and violent attachment to clannish pride of the feuding Grangerfords and Shepherdsons.[9] Such was the prevailing view of the making of *Huckleberry Finn* through most of the 1940s and 1950s, until Walter Blair challenged that view in 1958 with his essay "When Was 'Huckleberry Finn' Written?"[10]

The Working Notes for *Huckleberry Finn* were written in a variety of ink colors and on different kinds of paper. Taking his cue from DeVoto that a study of the kinds of paper and ink Twain used between 1876 and 1884 might yield useful information about the dates of composition of these notes, Blair undertook an exhaustive and impressive investigation of Twain's writing materials during that period. He surveyed more than 400 of Twain's letters, 26 of his manuscripts, and all the notebook entries he made during these years. He found that Twain used pencils, typewriters, and at least five kinds of ink; he noted the many kinds and sizes of paper that the author used in letters, notes, and manuscripts. This massive array of evidence of Twain's writing habits is dizzying in its variety and complexity—sometimes Twain used two kinds of paper in a single letter, and a manuscript of any length might contain a half a dozen kinds. But Blair was nevertheless able to discern a pattern in the evidence that he collected, one that enabled him to date the working notes and, in turn, to plot the development of the novel over those seven years.

The violet ink used in Group A of the working notes was particularly significant because Blair discovered that with only a few exceptions Twain used this color ink sporadically between 1876 and 1880 and only when he was at Hartford, and more importantly that he ceased to use it altogether after the fall of 1880. Blair's conclusion, of course, was that these notes were written before the summer of 1880 and, therefore, that DeVoto was wrong in claiming they were written when Twain was "fresh" from his river trip in 1882.[11]

A more precise dating of Twain's working notes enabled Blair to reconsider other available evidence (including the internal evidence provided by the notes themselves) in a new light and to offer the convincing hypothesis that *Huckleberry Finn* was written in at least four rather than two stages. The first stage occurred in the summer of 1876. At that time Twain wrote the first sixteen chapters (excluding the *Walter Scott* and King Solomon episodes), or up to that point in chapter 16 where the steamboat smashes through the raft. Then, sometime in 1879–80, he resumed the manuscript. Huck had survived the smashup and had climbed ashore to be a witness to the stupidity and needless violence of the Shepherdson-Grangerford feud. Evidently he paused halfway through this episode to write the first set of working notes for the continuation of Huck's adventures, for one of the notes indicates a belated decision to resurrect the raft and to continue the river voyage of Huck and Jim: "Back a little, CHANGE—raft only *crippled* by steamer."[12]

At some period or periods between 1880 and June 1883, Twain wrote chapters 19 and 20 and most of 21, the chapters that introduce the king and the duke and dramatize their various con games. Later, probably in March 1883, he wrote the Hamlet soliloquy and inserted it into the already completed chapter 21. At some time after that, Twain wrote the Group C notes. The following summer he completed the novel in a final explosive burst of creative inspiration or, perhaps, of simple determination to finish a book that had begun so long before. In any event Twain was so productive that he confessed to Howells in a letter dated 22 August 1883 that he himself could not believe how much he had written in so short a time.[13] Blair speculates that Twain wrote two Bricksville chapters, the Wilks chapters, and the *Walter Scott* episode (part of chapter 12 and all of chapter 13) before he carried his narrative to its conclusion. Apparently the King Solomon debate was written separately (the manuscript shows that he numbered those pages 1–17 and then renumbered them to conform with the pagination of the manuscript).[14] It seems likely that this debate represents Twain's final contribution to the novel that had begun seven years earlier.

Blair's account of when *Huckleberry Finn* was written is so thoroughgoing and his conclusions so meticulously intelligent that for thirty years it has withstood the minute scrutiny of scholars and critics (including those involved in the Mark Twain Project specifically engaged in accumulating new evidence about the book). His conclusions about the stages of composition have remained pretty much intact and unchallenged. Still, charting the stages of composition of the book was but preliminary to determining its genesis as an imaginative creation. Having plotted in its essential outlines the genetic history of *Adventures of Huckleberry Finn*, Blair made it possible to give a fuller and more comprehensible story of the making of this American classic. If some of the customary beliefs about the book had to be abandoned, other hypotheses about the novel and its author might be plausibly asserted. Moreover, *Huckleberry Finn* could be more accurately placed within the full range of Twain's interests and activities during the seven-year period of its growth.

Mark Twain was a man of many enthusiasms and as many angers. He was a man so easily diverted, so constantly and busily employed in so many projects, that one is reminded of an acrobat who spins a dozen plates atop as many sticks—rushing back and forth between and among the plates to keep them spinning while starting yet another that will further scatter his attention. Blair's scholarly adventures in tracing the chronology of *Huckleberry Finn* led him to trace as well the several forces that shaped it. This he did in his "biography of a book," *Mark Twain and Huck Finn* (1960). It was a study every bit as complex and as instructive, though in a different way, as sifting through the evidence of composition, but it gave a human and circumstantial coherence to the process he had identified mostly on the basis of physical evidence.

It would be pointless to give a comprehensive survey of Blair's findings in *Mark Twain and Huck Finn*. He offers there a detailed account of Twain's activities between 1874 and 1884—an account of his reading and writings, his business affairs, his political attitudes, and his family situation. Blair chose to give greater emphasis to Twain's immediate circumstance than to the remembered experiences of his childhood in Hannibal or his pilot years on the Mississippi, because he considered the ways the author modified youthful recollection and reminiscence according to his present state of mind more important in determining how such a book came to be.

One of the conclusions Blair had drawn in "When Was *Huckleberry Finn* Written?" after determining that the first group of the working notes was written before Twain's river trip in 1882 was that Twain did not need to revisit the places of his youth in order to revitalize his imagination. He was capable in this book, as he had been in others of his writings, of "generating within himself, without external stimuli, the power to summon to his memories vivid recollections of times past and to give them form and meaning."[15] A consideration of Twain's immediate situation and state of mind disclosed as well that such vivid remembrance was spurred by his immediate present, for which the fiction served as satisfactory expression, compensation, or resolution.

II

Mark Twain and Huck Finn makes concretely and amply clear what Bernard DeVoto had also noted—namely, that *Huckleberry Finn* had its origins and peculiar motivation in a certain sort of romantic escapism. The world was too much with Twain in the early to mid-1870s. He had tried, since his marriage in 1870, to accommodate what he took to be Livy's desires for his reform but had eventually rebelled. If he had taken up wickedness again, he did so with the overly tender conscience of a backslider; and he now pretty much confined his smoking to his study and kept his cussing out of earshot. He consumed his three old-fashioneds a day with a punctuality that might support his claim that they were good for his digestion. Twain had, like Huck in *Tom Sawyer*, decided "to smoke private and cuss private, and crowd through or bust."[16]

But other things were troubling him as well. His family and

friends had been plagued by illness or death, and financial worries made his recently completed Hartford mansion seem as much an excess as a comfort. It was at any rate not a citadel, for the Clemenses had constant visitors, some of them invited, and Twain was bothered by the burden of his enormous correspondence. He was overworked by his diversions and diverted from his work in a way that made his literary output seem depleted or inconsequential. Added to this was the fact that he had turned forty in November 1875. His friend John Hay had told him that forty was the "zenith" of a man's life, the time when one was on the "top of the hill," but Twain may have felt he was already over it.[17] He was at least weary and pestered and frustrated, and it was in this state of mind that he allowed himself to dwell on Huck Finn's autobiography.

Twain had resisted Howells's urgings that he carry Tom Sawyer's story into his adulthood, and he observed in a letter on 5 July 1875 that such a book would have to be autobiographical. But he promised that by and by he would "take a boy of twelve & run him on through life (in the first person)."[18] This impulse may have combined with another he had indulged in a final, probably discarded chapter of *Tom Sawyer*, which recorded in some detail Huck's miserable and cramped life at the Widow Douglass's. The opening chapter of *Huckleberry Finn* may in fact be a rewritten version of that discarded chapter from Huck's point of view, and even as he was reading proof for *Tom Sawyer* at Quarry Farm, overlooking Elmira, in the summer of 1876, Twain had begun to fulfill his promise to his readers at the conclusion of that book to "take up the story of the younger ones again and see what sort of men and women they turned out to be."[19] If this is so, he must have realized almost immediately that he could not take Huck into his maturity. That summer he wrote some 400 manuscript pages (by his mistaken reckoning he was halfway through the novel), and though it was crowded with incident his hero had aged only a few months. More importantly, he must have recognized at some level that he could better ease his own adult worries and youthful longings and speak his own dissatisfactions in the vernacular idiom of a boy who as yet had had no childhood of his own.

Quarry Farm provided the seclusion he needed to finish reading proof for *Tom Sawyer*. It provided as well the occasion and opportunity for Twain to contemplate Huck's character as he appeared in that book and to develop the suggestiveness he found there in his new novel. Huck resisted the widow's efforts to civilize him in ways that resembled Twain's own rebellion and that could be characterized as simple, boyish mischief. Huck had promised Tom in the earlier book that he would endure the widow's pestering and would stick with her so long

as he could join in the high adventures Tom's proposed gang of robbers promised. But in the autobiographical story Huck is as disappointed by Tom's lies about magic and elephants and A-rabs as he had
been by the widow's talk about Providence and prayer, and he likens
Tom's boasts and deeds to Sunday school.

The appearance of Pap imposed a new and all too real set of
circumstances on Huck. He manfully rebelled against his father (including going to school just to spite him), but after his abduction and
subsequent confinement in Pap's cabin he found that it "was lazy and
jolly, laying off comfortable all day, smoking and fishing, and no
books nor study" (*HF*, 30).[20] However, when Pap got too handy with
the hickory, and when he threatened to "stow" Huck in some distant
hiding place, Huck plotted his own escape. Jackson's Island was a
better retreat, but it was lonesome too, and when Twain introduced
the slave Jim as a companion and the raft and the river as their home
he had found an ideal image for lightening the load of frustrations that
bore down upon him.

But the reintroduction of Jim committed the author to a different
kind of narrative. Unlike his persona's companion the "Reverend" in
"Some Rambling Notes of an Idle Excursion" (1877), or Harris in *A
Tramp Abroad* (1880)—both modeled after Twain's friend, the minister
Joseph Twichell—Jim resisted the role of straight man and butt for
pranks. Though Jim had appeared as a comic figure in the opening
chapters, the seriousness of his situation as a runaway slave forced
upon his creator an immediate awareness of the complexity of his
circumstance and character that only slowly dawned on Huck, and
was sometimes forgotten by Twain himself.

When Huck and Tom played their tricks on the sleeping Jim in
chapter 2, their joke had no grave consequences and in fact provided
for a certain burlesque treatment. But Huck's prank with the dead
rattlesnake in chapter 10 is potentially lethal and makes Huck sorry
enough to make sure Jim does not find out that the snakebite is his
fault. In chapter 15 Huck plays a second trick on him by convincing
Jim that he merely dreamed that they had been separated in the fog.
Again the joke backfires, for when he discloses the trick in order to
have his laugh, Jim gives him a tongue-lashing that so affects Huck
that he "humbles himself to a nigger."

Jim's situation provided a rationale for the two to drift along
nights, idle away the time, and stay clear of people. But Jim's escape
was fundamentally more serious than Huck's, and more serious than
Mark Twain's own desire to escape. For Jim could endure Miss Watson's rough treatment and her constant "pecking" at him; he could
even endure, as we later learn, the enforced separation from his

family. But the fearful prospect of being sold down the river was something he could not bear.

Twain's identification with his little hero enabled him to vent his feelings of constraint and frustration and to relieve symbolically the pressures that seemed to be hemming him in. But providing Huck with a runaway slave as companion meant that Twain was dragging along with him a portion of his own troubled conscience in a way that had social and personal implications. It forced upon Huck a sense of the "real" that the merely aggravating sham and pretense of the world at large could not, and presented him with a moral dilemma that a boy could not comprehend intellectually but might mysteriously solve emotionally. It also committed Huck to a course of action that was in absolute defiance of everything he took to be moral and correct. This he did when he cleverly deceived the slave traders in chapter 16 and was to do again more dramatically in chapter 31 when he had his crisis of conscience and decided to go to hell rather than turn Jim in.

But the introduction of Jim had other effects upon Twain's fiction as well. If it qualified and corrected the impulse toward a simple romantic escapism, Jim's various protective gestures gave to Huck an innocence and sense of belonging that a place under the widow's roof or in Tom's band of robbers could not. Jim's presence enfolded Huck in what Kenneth Burke would call a "preforensic circle"—an atmosphere of familiar attachment and mutual trust that some may prefer to call family but that is at any rate happily free of the necessity to be on the lookout for double dealing and masquerade.[21] The very qualities— canniness and deviousness—that Huck acquired in fending for himself, and that make him a precocious expert in the ways of the world, are at the same time obstacles to a recognizable childhood. Only by degrees does Huck learn how to respond to Jim's affection and care.

Twain well recognized that the idyllic existence of their life on the raft was a fragile and precarious one, and if he at first indulged in a romantic escapism in fashioning his story and in establishing an image of perfect freedom, it soon became the sort of honorable romanticism and escapism Wallace Stevens identified as the foundation of artistic creation. In "The Noble Rider and the Sound of Words," Stevens remarks that "the pressure of reality is, I think, the determining factor in the artistic character of an era and, as well, the determining factor in the artistic character of an individual. The resistance to this pressure or its evasion in the case of individuals of extraordinary imagination cancels the pressure so far as those individuals are concerned."[22] Such evasiveness is not to be condemned, for the art that issues out of it enriches the world and sets out to express the human soul. And if this is true, Stevens asks, "how is it possible to condemn escapism?": "The poetic process is psychologically an escapist process. The chatter about escapism is, to my way of thinking, merely common cant. My own remarks about resisting or evading the pressure of reality mean escapism, if analyzed. Escapism has a pejorative sense which it cannot be supposed that I include in the sense in which I use the word. The pejorative sense applies where the poet is not attached to reality, where the imagination does not adhere to reality, which, for my part, I regard as fundamental."[23]

Twain's attachment to reality—not only the reality of his own immediate circumstance and the remembered evocations of his youth, but of the possibilities of his created characters and the cultural and political realities of life in the Mississippi valley "forty or fifty years ago"—and his attendant resistance to the pressures of that same reality invested his fiction with a form that transcended the narrowly personal and provincial character that impelled it. The humor at the very center of the book and the laughter it provokes, as James M. Cox has observed, is itself a "relief from responsibility,"[24] but it is also Twain's artistic manner and his own peculiar form of resistance to the pressures of reality. It was not flight from fact, but a resistance to, even an evasion of the pressure of fact that prompted Twain's fiction, and this quality makes Morris's observation about the "beautiful example" of the writer's dilemma as it was eventually resolved in *Huckleberry Finn* especially acute. For Huck stands as a palpable fiction whose very existence is determined by the dogged recalcitrance of the world as it is. Or, as Roy Harvey Pearce once noted, Huck forever exists "not as an actuality but as a possibility" in a way that led Pearce to define him as the ideal type expressed in the phrase of Wallace Stevens, an "impossible possible philosopher's man."[25]

It is not likely that Twain's involvement in *Huckleberry Finn* occurred to him in anything like these terms. But his attachment to the reality of the world Huck lived and breathed in, a world Twain knew from his own experience, forced upon him in chapter 16 a decision about the narrative direction his book would take. Twain's personal experience superbly outfitted him to recall in vivid detail life along the Mississippi, all the way to New Orleans if necessary. It constituted a reservoir of memory that might be given fictional form. But his familiarity with the Ohio River (Jim's road to freedom) was insufficient to sustain his story. At any rate he let his heroes slip past Cairo in the fog and was now presented with the narrative difficulty of taking a runaway slave ever deeper into the South. In evident frustration with this dilemma Twain had a steamboat run over the raft, and it is at that point that he pigeonholed the manuscript.

Huck and Jim attribute their misfortune in missing the Ohio to the evil effect of the rattlesnake skin. And in a paragraph just previous to the smashup Huck addresses the reader on this point: "Anybody that don't believe yet, that it's foolishness to handle a snake-skin, after all that that snake-skin done for us, will believe it now, if they read on and see what more it done for us" (*HF*, 130). This paragraph was probably inserted at some stage of revision, because had Twain envisioned their future mishaps he would not have broken off his story at this point. The paragraph also allays any fears the reader might have that Jim might have died in the accident, for no further mention of Jim is made until Huck is reunited with him in the middle of chapter 18. But wrecking the raft was a gesture symbolic of Twain's own frustration with the way his story was developing, and it is by no means clear that he intended at this time to resurrect either the raft or Jim. Certainly the easiest way out of his dilemma was to get rid of Jim altogether. He could drown him or let him find his freedom or otherwise dispose of a character that was an encumbrance to Huck and his creator alike. Huck could have acquired a new companion and continued his drift downstream in a way that would have allowed Twain, through Huck, to survey Southern manners and customs with greater latitude and freedom. These were some of Twain's options, but he did not choose to exercise them.

As Henry Nash Smith observes, Twain was constantly discovering meanings in his narrative as he went along and inventing the technical methods to explore them. The gestation of *Huckleberry Finn* reveals a "dialectical interplay" in Twain, a process in which "the reach of his imagination imposed a constant strain on his technical resources, and innovations of method in turn opened up new vistas before his imagination."[26] He did not, in any event, follow the path of least resistance in developing his story, and the paradoxical situation of having a runaway slave escape into the deep South stretched his imagination to the end of its tether. Or, as Twain himself would have said, his "tank" had run dry by the end of that summer, and it would be another three years before it had sufficiently filled for him to take up his story once again.

III

When Twain did return to Huck's autobiography, sometime in 1879–80, a new set of circumstances defined his state of mind, and evidently he began the boy's new adventures with little thought about reviving the romantic image of a pair of lazy drifters on the Mississippi. When Huck "clum" ashore after the accident on the river, he did not pause to ponder Jim's fate or to grieve his possible death. Apparently Twain was anxious to involve Huck in the new dramatic conflicts that had inspired him to return to the novel, and it was not until he was well into the feud chapters that he stopped to record his first set of working notes and there decided that the raft should only be damaged, not destroyed. In short, Twain had other things on his mind, and he resurrected his little hero to give voice to his own mature convictions.

Some three years intervened between the time Twain dropped the *Huck* manuscript and the time he picked it up again. During those years he had toured Germany, France, and Italy and had published an imaginative autobiographical account of his travels as *A Tramp Abroad*; and by 1880 he had written a good deal of the novel he would call *The Prince and the Pauper* (1882). In both books he was working out powerful, antagonistic feelings about elitist culture and aristocratic pretense.

Early in 1879 he wrote Howells that he wished he could give the "sharp satires on European life" his friend had mentioned, but he was in no mood for satire: "A man can't write successful satire except he be in a calm, judicial good-humor; whereas I *hate* travel, and I *hate* hotels, and I *hate* the opera, and I *hate* the old masters. In truth I don't ever seem to be in a good enough humor with ANYthing to satirize it; no, I want to stand up before it & *curse* it, and foam at the mouth."[27] Nevertheless he employed in *A Tramp Abroad* a satirical device adequate to his anger and sufficiently muted to preserve his humor. By adopting a persona who was rather more apt to question his own feelings of astonishment or revulsion when confronted by senseless or violent European customs (as, for example, the student duels in Germany) than to express his contempt for the customs themselves, Twain developed a satirical strategy that he would use in the feud chapters of *Huckleberry Finn*. And in *The Prince and the Pauper* he found that he could satisfy his immediate impulse toward strong satire without risking adverse reaction by making his subject historically remote. As early as 1872 Twain had wanted to write a satire of English institutions, but his subsequent travels to England had softened him toward the British. His reading in English history reawakened his anger, however, and the result was a book that expressed his deepest dissatisfactions and at the same time could be advertised as "A Tale for Young People of All Ages."

Both of these fictional strategies entered into *Huckleberry Finn* when he began the Grangerford-Shepherdson chapters. Twain's sardonic response toward the verse of the "Sweet Singer of Michigan," Julia A. Moore, found an outlet in Huck's undoubting admiration for

Emmeline Grangerford's poetic gifts. The same is true of Huck's description of the Grangerford house itself (which may have been written as early as 1876). And Twain's own mordantly satirical purposes were only thinly disguised by Huck's uncomprehending curiosity about the origin and nature of the feud itself. Huck's naiveté adequately conveyed the author's solid contempt for such timid and senseless attachment to prejudice. In Huck's eyes the tribes of Shepherdson and Grangerford are a "handsome lot of quality" (*HF*, 144) whose possessions and sentiments alike participate in an order of cultivation and gentility quite beyond his understanding. In Twain's, they both epitomize the sham and pretense that Twain (now an ardent Republican) had come to localize in the South and yet represent, more generally, an American version of the aristocracy that, through his recent reading about the French Revolution, Twain had come to despise to the extent that he might be described (as he in fact did describe himself a few years later) as a "Sansculotte."[28]

As Michael Davitt Bell has observed, Huck Finn exists as both a literary character and a literary device, and to collapse this distinction often results in unnecessary critical confusions because the same character is often made to serve different artistic purposes.[29] Throughout most of the feud chapters Twain used Huck as a satirical device designed to establish his own strong feelings through his narrator's naive reactions. But when Huck, in clipped and defensive understatement, reported on his reaction to Buck Grangerford's killing, Twain was dramatizing the traumatic effects of violence on his created character.

By the end of chapter 18, however, he had reinstalled Huck and Jim on the raft, where things were once again "free and easy and comfortable." He opened the next chapter with his lyrical description of how they put in the time on the river. These evocations of idyllic drift, as Walter Blair points out, could have been written at almost any time during the period from 1880 to 1883. For whenever he was vexed by the pressures of reality, Twain allowed his imagination to dwell on the possibilities of escape and seclusion. But during most of the second phase of composition he had been more aggressively ironic in his treatment of the bugbears of his imagination: aristocratic values, cloying sentimentality, and unnecessary violence.

This sort of control over his material signals a shift in Twain's creative process as it developed alongside the accumulating pages of the manuscript. In the first phase of composition he had found the means to project his own complex feelings of frustration into his created character in a way that required only the simplest explanation of their causes. A whippoorwill's song might convey his loneliness, and a stiff collar or the widow's "pecking," his feelings of repression. But when he returned to the manuscript Twain had bigger fish to fry, and the result was that though he still identified with him, he absorbed Huck into himself rather than the other way round. He made his young vernacular hero serve the mature purposes of his creator. In a word, Twain's manner and motivation had progressed from those of an escapist writer to those of a professionally skillful one, one whose imaginative impulses were the same but whose technical means were more rational and whose artistic effects more calculated.

This same imaginative process obtained when he wrote the king and duke chapters, though the motivating circumstances had changed. In 1881 Twain hired his nephew, Charles Webster, as his business agent. Webster tackled the job with a dramatic energy and aggressiveness that may have inclined him to invent tasks (and get results) over and above the regular duties of a financial manager. But there was no doubt that Twain needed such a manager, for his finances were always complicated and his extravagant expenditures and investments in the early 1880s bordered on caprice. Twain's financial worries were legitimate enough, but Webster added to his uncle's anxiousness by convincing him that he was being cheated right and left by scoundrels and con men. Webster had a questionable knack for discovering cheats, and Twain, constitutionally suspicious anyway, was easily persuaded that he was being defrauded. Something of this suspiciousness went into the creation of his famous rascals, the king and the duke, whose diverse talents as confidence men adequately symbolized the various cheats, from plumbers to publishers, that Twain was convinced were attempting to hoodwink him. And by having these characters adopt titles of royalty Twain could continue his burlesque of aristocratic values.

The king and duke are composite figures, partly inspired by Twain's "recollection vaults" (*HF*, 178) and partly by present acquaintance. As he had done in the feud chapters, in fashioning his homespun picaros he also drew upon the reading in Southwestern humorists he was doing for the volume that would eventually appear as *Mark Twain's Library of Humor* (1888). The king and duke were so characterized by humbug, chicanery, and pretense that they became objects of contempt and figures of fun. But as fictional devices this pair provided their creator with a double opportunity. He could satirize *in them* such despicable or laughable qualities as false eloquence, venality, backbiting, deception, or invented claims to privilege; and he could satirize *through them* the ignorant, credulous, or sentimental victims who were their prey.

Twain's rogues also solved a narrative problem for the author: for they enabled him to continue to move Huck and Jim further downstream. They effectively commandeered the raft and, by printing up a reward poster for Jim, devised a way to travel daytime and make temporary excursions onshore to ply their trade. This, in turn, provided Huck with the opportunity to describe loathesome backwater behavior and to witness the Boggs shooting. By 1880 Twain had begun to develop a general bitterness that he would succinctly express as a larger contempt for the "damned human race," and by freeing Huck to wander about town and observe the manners and customs of a representative cross section of humanity Twain's scorn could be delivered broadcast.

IV

In his rendering of the Bricksville loafers and the Boggs shooting in chapter 21 Twain had already begun to dramatize his disdain of the common man and woman. When he settled down in Elmira in June 1883 to finish his book, he began with Colonel Sherburn's verbal attack on the mob. Twain had prepared his readers for a lynching and had several times in his working notes made references to such a scene. But he had also conveyed more subtly in chapter 21 his distrust of the mob, and by the time he came to write chapter 22, his contempt for the crowd outstripped his contempt for the Southern aristocrat.[30] Colonel Sherburn, who had lived in the North and had been raised in the South, spoke the author's own convictions about the cowardice of the "average" man in a way that made him as much a hero in chapter 22 as he had been a villain in chapter 21.

Life on the Mississippi and *Huckleberry Finn* had a cross-pollinating effect upon one another. The Huck manuscript provided germs for development of certain portions of *Life on the Mississippi*, and Twain had lifted the raft episode from it and put it in chapter 3 of his "standard" work on the Mississippi. In turn, Twain's return to the river in 1882 and his writing about the modern South had stimulated certain youthful memories that might pay dividends in *Huck*. But nostalgia had combined with outrage, and Twain had excised from *Life on the Mississippi* two chapters of strident social criticism and had generally toned down his more virulent attacks upon the South. The intensity of his anti-Southern feeling remained, however, and in fact may have been exacerbated by this same restraint. In any event the author allowed Sherburn, rather than Huck, to speak his contempt in the scene that began the last phase of composition of the novel.

Twain soon resumed Huck's persona, however, and his methods of satire become more familiar. He concluded the chapter with Huck at the circus, where he worries over the drunken bareback rider. The comedy of this episode was meant to comment upon the seriousness of the Boggs episode in the previous chapter and is one of the more conspicuous examples of satirical pairings of incidents that occur throughout the book. But the development of the circus scene as a counterstatement to the Boggs episode points to the workmanlike attitude Twain brought to his book that summer.

By 1883 *Adventures of Huckleberry Finn* had become a commercial venture, and it is difficult to tell whether inspiration or simple determination supplied the kind of motivation that allowed Twain to produce so many pages of manuscript so quickly and, by his own account, so effortlessly.[31] He had been disappointed by the sales of *The Prince and the Pauper* and *Life on the Mississippi* and, soon after he finished *Huck*, decided to publish the book himself under the imprint of Chas. L. Webster & Co. The last phase of composition betrays something of the practical attitude of a professional novelist intent on finishing a book in which he had invested considerable time and energy. At any rate Twain pushed toward his conclusion and most days found the going easy.

In the last half of *Huckleberry Finn* the author was able to make the most of his invention. He had recorded in his working notes a few episodes he wanted to develop (the circus rider incident and the obscene Royal Nonesuch were included, but fortunately Twain's desire to have Huck and Jim and Tom explore the countryside on an elephant remained unfulfilled), and he had made elaborate notes for the evasion scene. But this second half is remarkable for its relative lack of incident. The improvisations of the Wilks funeral and the evasion at least are stretched to the point of artificiality and seem to have less to do with resolving the inner tensions of the author than with delivering broad and popular comedy. These episodes had been prepared for in advance, and the notes show that the evasion had been planned with a good deal of calculation. But the notes also show that Twain carefully reread the portion of the manuscript that he had already completed, and the most interesting and memorable events are those that drew upon the emotional attitudes he had established in the earlier portions and now contemplated and probed for their implications.

The proletarian sympathies Twain had acquired a few years before persisted, despite his distrust of the mob, and they became localized and found a certain focus in his attitude toward Jim. Twain's last group of working notes reveal an interest in developing Jim's character more fully. He twice reminded himself that Jim has a wife and two children and anticipated the moment in chapter 23 where Jim grieves because he believes he will never see his family again and, in turn, recalls his unintended cruelty to his infant daughter, whom he discovered to be deaf and dumb. Jim's mourning makes Huck believe that Jim "cared just as much for his people as white folks does for theirn. It don't seem natural, but I reckon it's so" (HF, 201). This incident immediately follows, and therefore comments on, Huck's description of the conduct of "Henry the Eight," who used to marry a new wife every day and "chop her head off" the next morning. And it comments as well on the feigned deaf and dumbness of the King in the next chapter.

Twain also wrote in his working notes: "Back yonder, Huck reads & tells about monarchies & kings &c. So Jim stares when he learns the rank of these 2."[32] Again, Twain was preparing to use Jim's reaction rather than Huck's as the vehicle for his satire, and the "back yonder" became the interpolated chapter 14, where Huck describes the "style" kings and dukes put on. The only king Jim is familiar with is King Solomon, whom he "knows by de back" (HF, 95). Solomon's apparent insensitivity regarding the child he was going to chop in two derives, so Jim believes, from the way he was "raised" and his circumstance. A man, such as Jim, "dat's got on'y one er two chillen" cannot afford to be wasteful of them, but Solomon, who has some "five million," may treat them as expendable items of property.

This debate apparently satisfied the author's intention rather telegraphically recorded in another note—"Solomon with child by de hine laig."[33] And Huck and Jim's debate about why a Frenchman "doan talk like a man" (which concludes the chapter) probably derived from a stray remark Twain had written at the end of chapter 20: "I found Jim had been trying to get [the king] to talk French, so he could hear what it was like" (HF, 176).

Chapter 14 was written separately, and probably after Twain had taken his story through "Chapter the Last." In any event it not only prepares the reader for Jim's reaction to the king and duke but gives to a slave a native intelligence, a righteous indignation, and a vernacular eloquence that had not been fully dramatized before. Moreover, Jim can get riled by the example of Solomon as a man who seemingly treats his children and wives as chattels, and who would rather live in the confusion of a "bo'd'n house" than, as Jim believes a truly wise man would, "buil' a biler-factry" (HF, 94). Jim's reaction to Solomon is the reaction of a slave to the Southern mentality, which immorally prefers the chaos of a "harem" of kept servants to sensible industrialization.

If chapter 14 was written out of the felt necessity to add to the picture Twain had drawn of Jim, Huck's recollection of Jim's self-sacrifice and affection in chapter 31 offers a consolidated picture of Jim's generosity of spirit:

> [I] got to thinking over our trip down the river; and I see Jim before me, all the time, in the day, and in the night-time, sometimes moonlight, some-times storms, and we a floating along, talking and singing, and laughing. But somehow I couldn't seem to strike no places to harden me against him, but only the other kind. I'd see him standing my watch on top of his'n, stead of calling me—so I could go on sleeping; and see him how glad he was when I come back out of the fog; and when I come to him again in the swamp, up there where the feud was; and such-like times; and would always call me honey, and pet me, and do everything he could think of for me, and how good he always was; and at last I struck the time I saved him by telling the men we had small-pox aboard, and he was so grateful, and said I was the best friend old Jim ever had in the world, and the *only* one he's got now (*HF,* 269–70).

It is this catalog of recollections that decides Huck on going to hell rather than turn Jim in. One can easily imagine that (as he studied the completed portion of the manuscript, and as the working notes to some extent reveal) Twain similarly recollected the accumulated examples of Jim's humanity and generosity of spirit and discovered in him a fit emblem for the best there is in the common lot, one for whom one might even risk everlasting fire. In this sense Jim plays a role analogous to the peasant Gerasim in Tolstoy's *The Death of Ivan Ilych*—a figure of such warm and authentic sympathies that in the midst of misery and doubt he inspires a mystical faith in human possibility and, by his example, urges a revaluation of conventional political pieties.

In the tangle of contrived narrative improbabilities Huck's decision to go to hell stands out as the most improbable event of all. For it gathers together in a single dramatic moment the implications of the fiction Twain was creating and runs absolutely counter to what he believed to be the incontestable facts of the world. But unlike those improbable details and incidents designed to prolong or resolve dramatic conflicts—such as the broken arm of William Wilks, the mystery of the tattoo, the appearance of Tom Sawyer with his ever proliferating plans for the evasion, or the implausible guilty conscience of the widow that resulted in her freeing Jim before her death—Huck's decision to go to hell is not mere contrivance. Rather it is a fiction that affirms a certain faith in the possibility of human freedom and nobility and runs counter to Twain's announced cynicism.

By the time the author settled down to finish his novel in the summer of 1883, he had formed a set of generalized convictions and had embraced the deterministic philosophic position he had articulated a few months earlier in "What Is Happiness?"—a paper he had delivered at the Monday Evening Club. The conclusions he drew in this lecture, he later recalled, were straightforward and absolute: there is no such thing as personal merit; man is merely a "machine automatically functioning"; "no man ever does a duty for duty's sake"; "there is no such thing as free will and no such thing as self-sacrifice."[34] Some years before Twain had privately recorded similar beliefs in the margins of his copy of W. E. H. Lecky's *History of European Morals*, and his subsequent reading and experience had only fortified those convictions. Twain's philosophic opinions had to some extent always been present in *Huck*, but in this last phase of composition they entered into the novel at some expense to narrative credibility.

In *Life on the Mississippi* Twain had recalled the emotional quality of youth as "a time when the happenings of life were not the natural and logical results of great general laws, but of special orders, and were freighted with very precise and distinct purposes—partly punitive in intent, partly admonitory; and usually local in application."[35] At odd moments Twain had abandoned this quality in the last half of the novel and allowed Huck to speak with a latitude of experience and moral authority beyond his years and beyond his immediate interests. He permitted him to conclude on the cruelty of the "human race" and make comments about the "average" man or woman (something Colonel Sherburn could do more plausibly because he had traveled in the North and lived in the South and had acquired the cynicism of age and experience); and he had had Huck make such observations as "kings is kings" or "Take them all around, they're a mighty ornery lot. It's the way they're raised" (*HF*, 200).

One could not say that Huck had become worldly wise or jaded, but his commentary sometimes tends toward general observation at the expense of local assertion. The qualities of stupefaction and surprise that he had before displayed and that served as satirical strategy are frequently shifted onto Jim, and the particularity of experience is too often reserved for the purely technical virtuosity of the humbug of the duke and dauphin or the childish pranks of the evasion.

Everything Twain rationally thought to be true militated against Jim's recorded self-sacrifice and Huck's dramatic decision to help him to freedom. But these were fictions that mysteriously commanded belief, and they were latent in the emotional attitudes Twain had established in earlier portions of the novel. Twain himself recalled, in

1895, that Huck's first bout with his conscience in chapter 16 represented a contest between a "sound heart" and a "deformed conscience" and that "conscience suffers defeat."[36] Huck's white lie to the slave traders in that chapter suggested the more affecting decision in chapter 31, and the latter is more powerful because Huck actively chooses what he takes to be an everlasting damnation in the "bad place" Miss Watson had so vividly described to him.

The evasion chapters undoubtedly compromise the purity of Huck's purpose, but they do not entirely overthrow it. And Twain may have anticipated the erosion of Huck's moral dignity in those chapters where Tom Sawyer superintends their high-jinks. In any event he seems to have written the interpolated *Walter Scott* episode just before he began the Phelps chapters. DeVoto suggested that the primary motivation for inserting this episode was to provide Huck with the history books he reads to Jim.[37] This may be so, but it would have been much simpler to have included those books with the "truck" they took off the floating house in chapter 9. Blair argues, more plausibly, that Twain had his eye out for opportunities to repeat "motifs with variations" and that this scene of a real robber gang provided a dramatic parallel to Tom Sawyer's gang of robbers in chapter 3.[38] Certainly the name of the steamboat evokes an image of the romanticism so characteristic of Tom. But the same episode also provides a parallel to the evasion scene, and with a significant variation.

Huck himself invites the comparison when he rebukes Jim's hesitancy to board the wreck and reminds him that Tom would never miss the chance for such an adventure. When they find that they are trapped on the *Walter Scott* with real murderers, however, Huck instantly recognizes that this is no time for "sentimentering" (*HF*, 86). After he and Jim escape in the gang's boat, Huck begins to worry about the men and to hatch a plot that will get them out of their scrape. His resolution and plan are acted out with efficiency and dispatch and are happily free of the romantic impulse. This scene provides a dramatic contrast to the evasion episode. Huck may call the experience an "adventure," but his natural sympathy for the other Jim (the murderer Jim Turner) and his practical attempt to rescue him and the others demonstrate Huck's native decisiveness, uncorrupted by the influence of Tom Sawyer. The evasion in its way is as "mixed-up en splendid" (*HF*, 340) as Jim says it is, but Twain had to some extent preserved the purity of Huck's sound heart by dramatizing his reaction to the moral emergency aboard the *Walter Scott*.

The final two chapters of *Huckleberry Finn* hastily tie up the loose ends of Twain's narrative. Jim learns that he had been set free in Miss Watson's will two months earlier. The mystery of Tom's cooperation in

Jim's rescue is explained by the fact that he thought it great fun to set a free nigger free. And Huck learns that Pap was the dead man aboard the floating house. The end of *Huckleberry Finn* is inexcusably happy— Jim owns himself, Huck is rid of Pap and free to use his six thousand dollars to sponsor a new adventure in the Indian Territory, and the bullet Tom received in the leg is now proudly worn around his neck for all the world to see. But Twain concluded on the same note of resistance to the pressures of civilization that had been in the book from the beginning, and by having Huck light out for the Territory ahead of his comrades, he promised his readers and committed himself to a continuation of their adventures in another book.

For the next seven months Twain worked on several projects and may have actually begun to write his promised sequel in *Tom and Huck among the Indians*; at least he did some reading for it. But much of his time was spent preparing his manuscript for publication. He made many revisions and did some rewriting, nearly always with an artistic intent rather than out of deference to contemporary literary taste or personal squeamishness, and by mid-April 1884 mailed off the manuscript. He carefully supervised E. W. Kemble's illustrations for the book and Webster's promotional campaign to sell it by subscription, and he embarked on a lecture tour with George Washington Cable, in part as an effort to promote sales of the book. He also had to put up with the aggravation of the technical problems of supplying his book with a heliotype of a bust of himself as a frontispiece[39] and the obscene joke of some mischief-maker who had defaced the plate of Kemble's illustration of Huck standing before Aunt Sally and Uncle Silas. But at last the book was complete. It was published in England and Canada in December 1884 and in the United States the following February.

V

The seven years' genesis of *Huckleberry Finn* eventuated in a book that was more hopeful than its happy ending might suggest. For it made potent, and in a thoroughly original and unstarched idiom, a drama of human possibility that transcended its narrowly human origins. "Give us a new work of genius of any kind," wrote Willa Cather in an open letter in defense of "escapism" in literature, "and if it is alive, and fired with some more vital feeling than contempt, you will see how automatically the old and false makes itself air before the new and true."[40] *Huck Finn* is brimming with contempt, or at least feelings of anger and frustration, but it is also alive with the feeling and the fiction of human possibility.

The novel made vivid an original image, or several images really, of nobility in tatters: The absurd image of Jim in a dress forgoing his chance for freedom in order to nurse his wounded tormentor, Tom Sawyer. Of Huck sitting in a wigwam choosing between everlasting and everlasting. Or of Huck and Jim together, forming what Twain once called a "community of misfortune,"[41] floating down the Mississippi River on a hot summer night. And there is some evidence that Twain wanted to highlight those same qualities.

Three of Twain's most significant revisions, as Blair has pointed out, signal the final emphasis the author wanted to give to his book. He trimmed the excessively rhetorical eloquence from Colonel Sherburn's speech and made it more colloquial and therefore more local and authentic. He supplemented the scene of Jim's homesickness with the passages that disclose the man's sense of regret for the way he had treated his daughter. And he added enough to Huck's struggle with his conscience to rid the scene of any tinge of burlesque and to give it the sort of memorable emphasis it has in the printed book.

The attempt to establish such nobility on so slight and improbable a foundation as the adventures of a barely literate and necessarily suspicious boy provided Twain with (to borrow the language of Henry James) "as interesting and as beautiful a difficulty as you could wish."[42] The difficulties were unsought, however, and the solutions were sometimes improvised or finessed. And there are gaps in the narrative logic of the book big enough to throw a dog through. But the novel is sustained by its rendering of life rather than by a formal narrative coherence, and the manifold impulses that produced it call into question the desire of critics to find a unified intention or an artistic wholeness in works of the imagination. The enduring interest of the book derives from its quiet affirmations rather than its satire, however brilliant.

"There is no element more conspicuously absent from contemporary poetry than nobility," observed Wallace Stevens in a passage that has a special relevance to *Huckleberry Finn*:

> There is no element that poets have sought after, more curiously and more piously, certain of its obscure existence. Its voice is one of the inarticulate voices which it is their business to overhear and to record. The nobility of rhetoric is, of course, a lifeless nobility. . . . For the sensitive poet, conscious of negations, nothing is more difficult than the affirmations of nobility and yet there is nothing that he requires of himself more persistently, since in them and in their kind, alone, are to be found those sanctions that are the reasons for his being and for that occasional ecstasy, or ecstatic freedom of the mind, which is his special privilege.[43]

That Twain's cynicism and skepticism made him supremely "conscious of negations" is a familiar truth. That he experienced in the writing of his masterpiece an "occasional ecstasy, or ecstatic freedom of mind," scarcely less so. Something of that ecstasy must have derived from the satisfaction that came from finding, in the tangle of his material and the meanness he knew to be the world, the room to affirm as well as condemn. For Wallace Stevens, and one may suppose for Twain as well, the capacity to affirm nobility as a permanent fiction forever at odds with the contingency of fact has less to do with artistic freedom than it does with the power of the imagination over events. "It is the violence from within that protects us from a violence from without. It is the imagination pressing back against the pressure of reality. It seems, in the last analysis, to have something to do with our self-preservation; and that, no doubt, is why the expression of it, the sound of its words, helps us to live our lives."[44]

In the making of *Huckleberry Finn*, and virtually from the beginning, Twain had resisted the pressures of reality by the efforts of his imagination and in a voice he eventually made his own. Nothing about the book commanded Twain's more minute attention than the sounds of its words. His working notes disclose how exactingly he had overheard and recorded the otherwise inarticulate voices of his created characters, and even if we did not have Twain's "Explanatory" to tell us that the book is a vernacular tour de force, the novel itself shows how absolutely he earned the evident pride he took in its language. But the language of the novel, the angle of its vision, the ample reach of its imagining, did more than retrieve the life of the Mississippi valley, now a hundred and fifty years past. In part, the achievement of the *Adventures of Huckleberry Finn* is revealed in its creative vision, for it showed how completely Twain might imagine things as bad as they can be, and better than they are. The book provided its author, as it has its readers, with a means to resist the pressures from without. It is a novel that, finally, may have to do with something as improbable as self-preservation.

Notes

1. Cather, "Preface" to *Alexander's Bridge*, vi.
2. Ibid.
3. Ibid., ix.
4. *Twain–Howells Letters*, 1:144.
5. Morris, *The Territory Ahead*, 88.
6. Ibid., 84.
7. Morris, "If Fiction Is So Smart, Why Are We So Stupid?" 182.
8. See DeVoto, "Noon and the Dark," in *Mark Twain at Work*, 45–82.

9. Ibid., 69.

10. This essay, as any essay having to do with the composition of *Huckleberry Finn* must be, is deeply indebted to the work of Walter Blair. The indebtedness here is extensive enough to omit elaborate documentation; unless otherwise indicated, discussion of the physical evidence of composition, the state of the author's mind at the time of writing, and the several influences on the book derive in some measure from Blair's "When Was *Huckleberry Finn* Written?" or *Mark Twain and Huck Finn*. A more recent and succinct accounting of the composition is Blair's "Introduction" to *Huckleberry Finn*, ed. Blair and Fisher.

From the substantial body of scholarship and criticism related in some way to the composition of *Huckleberry Finn* the following might be profitably consulted as well: Budd, "Introduction" to the facsimile edition of the manuscript of *Huckleberry Finn*; Ensor, "The Contributions of Charles Webster and Albert Bigelow Paine to *Huckleberry Finn*"; Krause, "Twain's Method and Theory of Composition"; Pauly, "Directed Readings"; and Smith, *Mark Twain*, 113–37. More recently Victor Fischer has determined, on the basis of evidence too intricate and complicated to go into here, that the composition of the feud chapters and the chapters that introduce the king and duke may have not occurred in distinct phases, for it appears that Twain was working on the Huck manuscript intermittently throughout the period between 1879 and 1883. Fischer has not yet published his findings, however, and it would be unfitting to anticipate the conclusions he may draw from his research.

11. The complete working notes are published in DeVoto, *Mark Twain at Work*, 63–78, passim, and in Blair and Fischer's edition of *Huckleberry Finn*, 711–61. Blair made still other refinements on DeVoto's interpretation of the working notes. Group B of the notes consists of only two manuscript pages. Blair concluded, on the basis of the kind of paper used, that B-1 also belongs to the period when Twain wrote Group A. Page B-2 was written separately and probably belonged to a series of notations the author made while he was going through the portion of the manuscript written in 1876, for the notes include references to page numbers in the now lost manuscript. Hence page B-2 probably also belongs to the period when Twain wrote Group A. Blair agreed with DeVoto that Group C was likely written in the summer of 1883. This last group includes reminders about what Twain had already written and suggestions for possible narrative development, only a few of which are realized in the novel.

12. DeVoto, *Mark Twain at Work*, 67.

13. *Twain–Howells Letters*, 1:438.

14. I have given a conjectural account of the significance of this episode in " 'Learning a Nigger to Argue.' "

15. Blair, "When Was *Huckleberry Finn* Written?" 24.

16. *Tom Sawyer*, ed. Gerber and Baender, 259.

17. Reported in Blair, *Mark Twain and Huck Finn*, 88.

18. *Twain–Howells Letters*, 1:92.

19. *Tom Sawyer*, ed. Gerber and Baender, 260.

20. *Huckleberry Finn*, ed. Blair and Fischer, 30. Cited hereafter as *HF*.

21. Burke uses the term in *Attitudes toward History*, 209, and elsewhere. He discusses the same concept under the label "inner circle" in "The Relation Between Literature and Science." A passage in that essay is coincidentally

pertinent to my later discussion of Twain's shift from an escapist writer to one who discovered he could embody more abstract thought in a work of regionalism: "The inner circle is essentially the childhood level of experience. Such a thought makes one realize the special appeal that 'regionalism' may have for the poetic mind. For regionalism tends simply to *extend* the perspective of intimacy and immediacy that one gets in childhood. In childhood one does not think by concepts. . . . The poet is happiest in handling material of this sort. In his scrupulous childhood, he evolves a structure of meanings, all highly intimate and personalized. And as he confronts 'new matter,' the abstract, impersonal, political, and economic matter of adult experience, his earlier integration is threatened. Some poets, when encountering this threat, tend to 'freeze' at the earlier intimate level. They continue perfecting their personalized perspective, simply ignoring the matter that lies outside its circle. I think that we get in uncritical forms of regionalism an aspect of this tendency. Whatever abstractness in the outer critical-conceptual circle they cannot humanize, they reject" (166–67). The integrations of childhood and adult experience in *Huckleberry Finn* prove that Twain did not "freeze" in the creation of his book, though the same integration may have cost him a certain narrative credibility.

22. Stevens, "The Noble Rider and the Sound of Words," 22–23.

23. Ibid., 30–31.

24. Cox, *Mark Twain: The Fate of Humor*, 44.

25. Pearce, "Yours Truly, Huck Finn," 323.

26. Smith, *Mark Twain*, 113.

27. *Twain–Howells Letters*, 1:248–49.

28. Ibid., 2:595.

29. See Bell, "Mark Twain, 'Realism,' and *Huckleberry Finn*," 50.

30. For a discussion of the significance of the crowd in *Huckleberry Finn* see Mills, *The Crowd in American Literature*, 66–75.

31. In August 1883 Twain wrote Howells how delicious his productivity was, confessing that "nothing is half so good as literature hooked on a Sunday on the sly" (*Twain–Howells Letters*, 1:438).

32. DeVoto, *Mark Twain at Work*, 75.

33. Ibid.

34. Quoted in Blair, *Mark Twain and Huck Finn*, 337.

35. *Life on the Mississippi*, 19:434.

36. Quoted in Blair, *Mark Twain and Huck Finn*, 143.

37. DeVoto, *Mark Twain at Work*, 62.

38. Blair, *Mark Twain and Huck Finn*, 347.

39. For an account of Twain's decision to include this heliotype and the possible reasons for it see Budd, " 'A Noble Roman Aspect.' "

40. Cather, "Escapism," 26.

41. Quoted in Blair, *Mark Twain and Huck Finn*, 143.

42. James, "Preface" to the New York edition of *Portrait of a Lady*, 51.

43. Stevens, "The Noble Rider and the Sound of Words," 35.

44. Ibid., 36.

Works Cited

Bell, Michael Davitt. "Mark Twain, 'Realism,' and *Huckleberry Finn*." In *New Essays on Huckleberry Finn*, edited by Louis J. Budd, 35–59. Cambridge: Cambridge University Press, 1985.
Blair, Walter. "Introduction." In Twain, *Adventures of Huckleberry Finn*, ed. Blair and Fischer, xiii–l.
_____. *Mark Twain and Huck Finn*. Berkeley and Los Angeles: University of California Press, 1960.
_____. "When Was *Huckleberry Finn* Written?" *American Literature* 30 (March 1958): 1–25.
Budd, Louis J. "Introduction." In Mark Twain, *Adventures of Huckleberry Finn*, facsimile of the manuscript, 2 vols., 1:ix-xx. Detroit: Gale Research, 1983.
_____. " 'A Noble Roman Aspect' of *Adventures of Huckleberry Finn*." In *One Hundred Years of Huckleberry Finn: The Boy, His Book, and American Culture*, edited by Robert Sattelmeyer and J. Donald Crowley, 26–40. Columbia: University of Missouri Press, 1985.
Burke, Kenneth. *Attitudes toward History*. Boston: Beacon Press, 1959.
_____. "The Relation between Literature and Science." In *The Writer in a Changing World* (Second American Writers' Congress), edited by Henry Hart, 158–71. New York: Equinox Cooperative Press, 1937.
Cather, Willa. "Escapism: A Letter to the *Commonweal*." In *Willa Cather on Writing: Critical Studies on Writing as an Art*, 18–29. New York: Alfred A. Knopf, 1949.
_____. "Preface." In *Alexander's Bridge*, v–ix. Boston and New York: Houghton Mifflin, 1922.
Cox, James M. *Mark Twain: The Fate of Humor*. Princeton: Princeton University Press, 1966.
DeVoto, Bernard. *Mark Twain at Work*. Cambridge: Harvard University Press, 1942.
Ensor, Allison. "The Contributions of Charles Webster and Albert Bigelow Paine to *Huckleberry Finn*." *American Literature* 40 (May 1968): 222–27.
James, Henry. "Preface" to the New York edition of *Portrait of a Lady*. In Henry James, *The Art of the Novel: Critical Prefaces*, 40–58. New York: Charles Scribner's Sons, 1962.
Krause, Sydney. "Twain's Method and Theory of Composition." *Modern Philology* 56 (February 1959): 167–77.
Mills, Nicolas. *The Crowd in American Literature*. Baton Rouge: Louisiana State University Press, 1986.
Morris, Wright. "If Fiction Is So Smart, Why Are We So Stupid?" In Wright Morris, *About Fiction: Reverent Reflections on the Nature of Fiction with Irreverent Observations on Writers, Readers, and Other Abuses*, 180–82. New York: Harper & Row, 1975.
_____. *The Territory Ahead*. Lincoln: University of Nebraska Press, 1978.

Pauly, Thomas. "Directed Readings: The Contents Tables in *Huckleberry Finn*." *Proof* 3 (1973): 63–68.

Pearce, Roy Harvey. "Yours Truly, Huck Finn." In *One Hundred Years of Huckleberry Finn: The Boy, His Book, and American Culture*, edited by Robert Sattelmeyer and J. Donald Crowley, 313–24. Columbia: University of Missouri Press, 1985.

Quirk, Tom. " 'Learning a Nigger to Argue': Quitting *Huckleberry Finn*." *American Literary Realism* 20 (Fall 1987): 18–33.

Smith, Henry Nash. *Mark Twain: The Development of a Writer*. New York: Atheneum, 1967.

Stevens, Wallace. "The Noble Rider and the Sound of Words." In Wallace Stevens, *The Necessary Angel: Essays on Reality and Imagination*, 1–36. New York: Vintage Books, 1951.

Twain, Mark. *Adventures of Huckleberry Finn*. Edited by Walter Blair and Victor Fischer. *The Works of Mark Twain*, vol. 8. Berkeley and Los Angeles: University of California Press (in cooperation with the University of Iowa), 1988.

———. *The Adventures of Tom Sawyer*. Foreword and notes by John Gerber. Text established by Paul Baender. Berkeley and Los Angeles: University of California Press, 1980.

———. *Life on the Mississippi*. Vol. 19, *The Writings of Mark Twain*. New York: Gabriel Wells, 1923.

———. *Mark Twain–Howells Letters: The Correspondence of Samuel L. Clemens and William D. Howells, 1872–1890*. Edited by Henry Nash Smith and William M. Gibson. 2 vols. Cambridge: Harvard University Press, 1960.

JAMES WOODRESS

The Composition of *The Professor's House*

While the reviews of *A Lost Lady* were still appearing, Willa Cather plunged into the writing of her next novel, *The Professor's House*. According to her long-time friend and companion Edith Lewis, she returned from a six-months' trip to Europe in 1923 with the idea for the novel in mind. She never explained how she happened to invent the character of Godfrey St. Peter and his story of midlife crisis, but "Tom Outland's Story," the long self-contained tale that Cather inserted in the middle of the novel, already had been written. Its genesis lay eight years in the past, the year 1915, when she and Lewis had taken a trip to Mesa Verde National Park.

The sight of the ancient cliff dwellings in the park had worked powerfully on her imagination, and the following year she planned a work of fiction to be called "The Blue Mesa." She again visited the Southwest in the summer of 1916, and later when she stopped off to see her family in Red Cloud, Nebraska, before returning to her home in New York, she began writing "The Blue Mesa." She put in perhaps two months working on it but found the materials intractable and put the manuscript aside. The experience at Mesa Verde was too fresh and vivid to use immediately. Her literary method required that her emotions be recollected in tranquility, and she never was able to create with authenticity fiction from data worked up contemporaneously. In addition, she returned to New York in the fall of 1916 with the idea in mind for *My Ántonia* and for the next two years was occupied with that novel. She then went on to write her World War I novel, *One of Ours*, and *A Lost Lady* before going back to the material inspired by the Southwest. It was probably in the summer of 1922, when Cather first visited Grand Manan Island in the Bay of Fundy, that she got out "The Blue Mesa" and completed it as "Tom Outland's Story."

Thus when she actually began writing *The Professor's House*, a bit over one-quarter of the novel was in her portfolio and ready to use. What she needed was to build a novel around the story. The winter of 1923–24 was a productive period, and in addition to working on *The Professor's House* Cather was able to take time off to plan an edition of

Sarah Orne Jewett's best stories for Houghton Mifflin to keep a promise she once had made. But at the same time, she was becoming a highly visible novelist and finding it difficult to preserve her privacy. *One of Ours* had been a best-seller and had won the Pulitzer Prize; *A Lost Lady* had been both a critical and a financial success. She was deluged with invitations to speak at schools and colleges and for the first time hired a secretary to handle her correspondence, turn down unwanted engagements, and head off people who wanted to take up her time.

In March 1924 she knocked off writing for a week to entertain Frieda and D. H. Lawrence, who passed through New York on their way to Mabel Dodge Luhan's ranch in New Mexico. She enjoyed the Lawrences enormously but so exhausted herself doing all the things she had planned for them that she had to go to a resort in the Pocono Mountains in Pennsylvania to rest. She returned in time to attend Robert Frost's fiftieth birthday dinner at the Brevoort Hotel at the end of March. Then in April and May she got back to her novel, and in June, when she again went west to Red Cloud, she took the unfinished manuscript with her. Later that summer in the cottage she rented at Whale Cove on Grand Manan Island she resumed work on *The Professor's House* and on 7 September wrote a friend that she was nearly half finished with the first draft. She was then in high spirits, surrounded by wild woods and wild weather, the ambience she loved. The tempests in the Bay of Fundy pleased her, and after her usual three-hour stint of writing in the mornings, she walked along the deserted cliffs overlooking the sea, rain or shine. By the end of September the autumn fogs began rolling in and she packed up to go south. She stopped off in Jaffrey, New Hampshire, where she had been going since 1916 for a few weeks nearly every fall. By the middle of October she was back in her apartment on Bank Street in Greenwich Village and pushing hard to finish *The Professor's House*. She took along part of the manuscript when she again went to Red Cloud for Christmas, leaving it in Chicago with her old friend Irene Weisz to read. She must have completed the novel soon after she returned to New York in January.

Between the time she finished *The Professor's House* and its publication day in September she had time for several other projects. The first was her edition of Jewett's stories, for which she wrote an introduction, and when Houghton Mifflin brought out the collection the next year she was pleased with it. Her new publisher, Alfred Knopf, to whom she had switched in 1921, persuaded her to write three introductions and an essay for his in-house manual, *The Borzoi*, during these months before her new novel came out. She introduced Defoe's *Fortunate Mistress*, Gertrude Hall's *Wagnerian Romances*, and Stephen Crane's *Wounds in the Rain*. The essay was on Katherine Mansfield.

When spring came to Greenwich Village, Cather was ready to begin her annual travels, first going north to Maine in May, then west to Nebraska, Arizona, and New Mexico in June. The trip to Maine was to take part in a centennial celebration of the Bowdoin class of 1825, which had included Hawthorne and Longfellow. She went not to honor Hawthorne and Longfellow, she said, but to express her gratitude to the college for having awarded an honorary degree to her former friend and role model Jewett. Bowdoin's two famous sons, she explained, had the credits to graduate, but the college did not have to give Jewett a degree.

In mid-June Cather and Lewis were settled at the San Gabriel Ranch near Española, New Mexico, and there Cather finished reading proof on *The Professor's House*. The serialized version of the novel was already appearing in *Collier's*. In July the two women visited Mabel Dodge Luhan at Taos and stayed in the Pink House, where the Lawrences had lived the previous summer. While she was there Cather went to see the Lawrences, who then were living on the ranch Mabel had given Lawrence in exchange for the manuscript of *Sons and Lovers*. After leaving Taos Cather and Lewis went to Santa Fe, where they found a large accumulation of mail forwarded from New York. There was an astonishing number of letters from solemn professors and hard-boiled publishers, as Cather put it, telling her that "Tom Outland's Story" had given them a pulse.

In August Lewis returned to New York and Cather traveled north to Denver, where she rented an apartment and entertained her brother Roscoe and his three daughters from Wyoming, as well as her mother and sister Elsie, who came on from Nebraska. Then she returned east by way of Red Cloud, where she spent two weeks before continuing on to New York. She stayed only three days before going up to New Hampshire for her usual visit to the Shattuck Inn at Jaffrey. New York was more hideous than ever, and again she said she was soon going to leave the city for good. She was back on Bank Street by the end of October. By this time most of the reviews of her new novel had appeared, and she was surprised at how good they were. *The Professor's House*, she wrote Dorothy Canfield Fisher, was certainly not her favorite among her books. She also had gotten Knopf into something of a bind by switching from her western subjects. She was like an old wild turkey who forsakes the feeding ground as soon as there are signs of people, which in her case meant readers and book-buyers.

In this novel Cather left her Nebraska locale for a fictitious university town named Hamilton on the shores of Lake Michigan not far from Chicago. Her protagonist, Godfrey St. Peter, is a professor whose field of specialization is Spanish colonial history. He has recently completed his life's work, a multivolume history, *The Spanish Adventurers in North America*, which has won an important prize and a handsome sum of money. His wife has used the prize money to build a new house and finally move out of the cramped rented place they have lived in for many years. The professor cannot bring himself to leave the old house, especially the attic study where he wrote his books and the formal French garden he has created outside. He insists on paying the rent and continuing to use his old study.

Book 1 ("The Family") develops the character of the professor and his relationship with Lillian his wife, his daughters Kathleen and Rosamond, and their husbands Scott McGregor and Louis Marsellus. The reader learns that the professor, who is at the peak of his professional career, is strangely discontented with life and reluctant to face the future. He spends more and more of his time reliving the past. For a long while his marriage has been a loveless union, and his relationship with Rosamond is unhappy. She has been corrupted by the wealth of her husband Louie, a somewhat abrasive Jewish entrepreneur. St. Peter still is close to Kathleen, his younger daughter, but she is married to a dissatisfied newspaperman who is too good for his job. The reader also discovers that the professor mourns the loss of the one truly gifted student he ever had, Tom Outland, who had been killed in World War I.

Book 2 ("Tom Outland's Story") is a seventy-page story-within-a-story. It is the record of Tom's life before arriving at the professor's house nearly twenty years earlier. This is the tale inspired by Cather's visit to Mesa Verde ten years before. It is an account of Tom's discovery of the cliff city high up under the rim of the Blue Mesa and his exploration of the ruins with his cowboy companion Roddy Blake. Tom and Roddy work all summer among the cliff dwellings, excavating, collecting, cataloging; then Tom goes to Washington in the winter to announce the discovery to the director of the Smithsonian Institution. In Washington he meets with monumental indifference and after six frustrating months returns to New Mexico only to find that his partner has sold the artifacts to a German archeologist. Tom is angry and crushed by this event and quarrels with Roddy, who then disappears. Tom hides himself in the cliff dwellings for the summer, undergoes a spiritual rebirth, begins to educate himself, and then with money from a summer's work on the railroad goes to college.

The novel concludes with a brief final book called "The Professor," which takes place in the late summer and early fall. The professor has stayed home while Louie and Rosamond have taken Mrs. St. Peter to Europe. Louie tried to persuade his father-in-law to go, but St. Peter begged off. As the fall term begins, the professor has no heart for his lectures. He feels a premonition of death and wants to be alone. His family is about to return from Europe, and he does not see how he can go on living with them. He lies down to take a nap in his attic study, and while he is sleeping, a storm comes up, the window blows shut, and his gas stove goes out. The old sewing woman Augusta, who has come to get the keys to the new house, arrives just in time to save him from asphyxiation. On his couch recovering, he realizes that his temporary unconsciousness has been beneficial: "He had let something go—and it was gone; something very precious, that he could not consciously have relinquished, probably" (*PH*, 282).[1] His family would not realize that he was no longer the same man, but he now could face the future with fortitude. Cather too experienced something like this psychic annihilation in the period before writing the novel. She wrote in the front of a presentation copy to Robert Frost that "this is really a story of 'letting go with the heart.' "[2]

There is no evidence that Cather realized how much autobiography she was putting into the novel. When Dorothy Canfield Fisher joked about her writing a middle-aged story, she admitted she had; doesn't everyone have a middle-aged mood sometimes? she replied. At the same time she called the novel a nasty, grim little tale and wondered why it seemed to be selling better than any of her books so far. She had had one reaction from a friend when she tried out the manuscript on Irene Weisz the previous winter, and she was pleased that Irene got the really fierce feeling that lay behind the rather dry and impersonal manner of the telling. She may have known subconsciously that she was revealing a good deal of herself and for that reason tried to cover her tracks by creating a male protagonist and setting the novel in Michigan. Nothing can hide the spiritual malaise of Professor St. Peter/Willa Cather, however, from anyone in adequate command of her personal history and public statements.

Lillian St. Peter says to her husband midway in the novel: "You are not old enough for the pose you take. . . . Two years ago you were an impetuous young man. Now you save yourself in everything. . . . all at once you begin shutting yourself away from everybody. . . . I can't see any change in your face, though I watch you closely. It's in your mind, in your mood. Something has come over you" (*PH*, 162–63). The professor replies that he really doesn't know what's wrong with him: "It's the feeling that I've put a great deal behind me, where I can't go back to it again—and I don't really wish to go back. . . . And now I seem to be tremendously tired." He concludes by saying: "I'll get my second wind" (163–64). One cannot read this passage without remembering Cather's statement made eleven years later (1936) that the world broke in two for her about 1922. The professor does get his second wind after his near death, though life in the future will be a diminished thing. Cather weathered this midlife crisis and continued writing novels, but the resolution of the problem, which for the professor occurs in one dramatic episode at the end of the story, took place undramatically for his creator as a slow process of adjustment extending over several years.

The autobiographical parallels between Cather and St. Peter are striking. The same age as Cather, the professor was born on a farm on the shores of Lake Michigan, which has for him the same emotional pull that the mountains of the Shenandoah Valley had for Cather. He had a strong-willed Protestant mother, a gentle father, and a patriarchal grandfather, all of which Cather had. When he was eight, his parents dragged him out to the wheatlands of Kansas, as Cather's parents had taken her to Nebraska, and "St. Peter nearly died of it" (*PH*, 30). As an adult he went back to the region of his childhood for his professional career, just as Cather went east. After he had been teaching a number of years, he conceived his plan for a great historical work and then devoted fifteen years of his life to writing it. "All the while that he was working so fiercely by night, he was earning his living during the day," as Cather earned her living as journalist and teacher while she wrote fiction in her spare time. "St. Peter had managed for years to live two lives. . . . But he had burned his candle at both ends to some purpose—he had got what he wanted" (28–29). The first three volumes of his history made no stir at all, just as Cather's first three books, *April Twilights*, *The Troll Garden*, and *Alexander's Bridge*, brought her little acclaim. With the professor's fourth volume (for Cather it was *O Pioneers!*) he began to attract attention; with the fifth and sixth (for Cather, *The Song of the Lark* and *My Ántonia*) he began to be well known; and with the last two volumes (for Cather, *One of Ours* and *A Lost Lady*) he achieved an international reputation. These parallels leave out only *Youth and the Bright Medusa*, which contains all reprinted stories. Then the professor won the Oxford Prize for History, which brought him five thousand pounds. Cather's Pulitzer Prize was a modest sum, but her royalties from Knopf the year before writing *The Professor's House* were close to the equivalent of five thousand pounds.

The autobiographical similarities go much deeper than these rather obvious correspondences. The large preoccupation with houses in the novel has a considerable relevance to one aspect of Cather's life. Leaving a place she had lived and put down roots in was for her a painful experience freely acknowledged in her letters and interviews. The removal from Willow Shade, her spacious and comfortable childhood home in Virginia, had been a wrenching blow. Her departure for college from the cramped little house in Red Cloud, Nebraska, was perhaps less traumatic, but she returned to it often in her affections and in her fiction. The loss of the McClung house in Pittsburgh, where she had lived during her years as a high school teacher, was the most shattering experience of all. That house not only had been her home, but it also had been her refuge even after moving to New York. It was there too that she had worked in a sewing room/study at the top of the house, as the professor does in her novel. When the professor refuses to leave the old house and his study, it is not hard to believe that Cather was giving her fictional character an option that she herself had not enjoyed. The house had been sold after old Judge McClung died and Cather's dearest friend Isabelle McClung got married. The professor's reluctance to move is best explained in terms of Cather's deep feelings, and it also may explain why Cather never left New York, even though she often threatened to.

Besides the biographical significance of houses, their use in the novel structures its disparate parts. What seems to some readers a disjoined work with a long self-contained story inserted in the middle gains unity through houses as subject and symbol. In Book 1 the new house Mrs. St. Peter has built is no place the professor can feel at home in. Although it is comfortable and modern, it does not suit his personality and temperament, and he wants no part of it. He does eat and sleep there but spends much of his time in the old place, in the garden and high up in the attic study. Also the house that Rosamond and Louie are building is patterned after a Norwegian manor, which the professor thinks is unsuitable and inappropriate on the shores of Lake Michigan. In contrast to these houses are the cliff dwellings of the Blue Mesa. When Tom Outland discovers the silent city in Book 2, he is enraptured by the houses the ancient people have built. Their beauty arises from the harmony of their surroundings; form follows function in their design and construction. Tom's spirits soar as he sits among the ruins high over the canyon, as though suspended in air. The houses of the people who once lived on the mesa symbolize for him a life perfectly adapted to the environment, a stark contrast to the ugly office buildings filled with faceless government workers that he sees when he visits Washington. In the final book of her novel Cather completes her house symbolism in a dark mood. As the professor lies on his couch in his study almost wishing for death, he has a vision of the grave as one's final house. He quotes from Longfellow's translation of the Anglo-Saxon poem "The Grave":

For thee a house was built
Ere thou wast born
For thee a mould was made
Ere thou of woman camest. (*PH*, 272)[3]

Many people apparently asked Cather about the unusual structure of the novel, but she never bothered to reply until Pat Knopf, in whose education she took a great interest, posed the question. She wrote him explaining what she was trying to do, and he showed the letter to Burgess Johnson, his English professor at Union College, who asked and received permission to publish it in the College English Association's newsletter. "When I wrote *The Professor's House*," she said, "I wished to try two experiments in form. The first is the device often used by the early French and Spanish novelists; that of inserting the *Nouvelle* into the *Roman*."[4] This, of course, she already had done to a lesser extent in her earlier novels. The second experiment, which interested her more, was something a little vague, she said, but was "very much akin to the arrangement followed in sonatas in which the academic sonata form was handled somewhat freely."[5] By this musical analogy she seems to have meant only the use of the three-part sonata form with the different parts providing contrast.

There was more to it than this, however, and she went on to explain: "Just before I began the book I had seen, in Paris, an exhibition of old and modern Dutch paintings. In many of them the scene presented was a living-room warmly furnished, or a kitchen full of food and coppers. But in most of the interiors, whether drawing-room or kitchen, there was a square window, open, through which one saw the masts of ships, or a stretch of grey sea." She purposely overfilled the professor's house with stuffy new things, "American proprieties, clothes, furs, petty ambitions, quivering jealousies—until one got rather stifled. Then I wanted to open the square window and let in the fresh air that blew off the Blue Mesa." In this section she presented Tom Outland, who had a fine disregard for all the trivialities that encumbered the lives of the other characters. This interesting explanation may have helped readers in 1940, but today the novel's organization scarcely bothers anyone. Cather told Johnson that she thought the unusual structure was sufficiently bound together in two ways: first, the professor's life with Tom Outland was just as real and vivid to him as his life with his family, and second, Tom was constantly in the professor's house during his student life. Tom and the atmosphere he brought with him really became a part of the old house that the professor could not altogether leave.

Although *The Professor's House* is Cather's most revealing novel for the biographer, there is a great deal more to it than a story that works out personal problems. It is a rich, complex novel, a major accomplishment. There is so much in it to tease the imagination that it generates a steady stream of critical attention. Only *My Ántonia*, *A Lost Lady*, and *Death Comes for the Archbishop* can rival it for exegesis. It may be that a novel with a professor as protagonist has special interest for academics, who write most of the criticism, but the novel is full of ambiguities that invite explication. Cather realized that she had provided plenty of opportunity for critical scrutiny when she wrote Fisher that the reviewers seemed to think her novel a crossword puzzle. E. K. Brown, Cather's first biographer, thought the main theme of the novel was the professor's unconscious preparation for death symbolized through the various houses described in the story.[6] Leon Edel, who completed Brown's biography, made an independent psychoanalytic interpretation of St. Peter. He related the professor's inability to move from the old house to Cather's childhood insecurity and need for maternal protection. Houses symbolized wombs, and the professor's sense of loss revealed Cather's devastation over Isabelle McClung's marriage. Louis Marsellus was a fictional projection of Isabelle's husband, Jan Hambourg.[7] David Stouck read the novel as a powerful piece of social criticism, a satire on twentieth-century materialism.[8] Susan Rosowski saw *The Professor's House* as a "book of dreams," also a "watershed book" in Cather's canon. "In redeeming St. Peter's original self by dreams, Cather shifted the terms of identity from individuality developed empirically—through experience—to that which lies beneath experience and which is, therefore, protected from the vicissitudes of time."[9] To Doris Grumbach it seemed clear that "the professor's problem lies in his late and blinding realization that the life he had been leading, the life of father and husband, is, and always had been, a false one for him, that his existence within these roles is no longer bearable and that death is preferable to living any longer in the stifling, elaborately furnished and *false* (for him) house of women and marriage."[10] All of these readings and others are provocative and insightful, and the novel will continue to receive new analyses.

There are two major themes running through the novel, one personal, the other public. Although there is a great similarity between Cather and her professor, Godfrey St. Peter is also everyman. His problem is the problem of every thinking person: how does one live in a world of change? How does one face the future when the old verities have been blown away, and the world has entered a new era of chaos and uncertainty? No one can evade the issues that this book raises. For Cather it was the world of the Twenties, the postwar Jazz Age, but the problem persists in any period: the chaos following

World War II or the present uncertainties under the threat of nuclear holocaust. This is the personal equation that St. Peter must try to solve for himself. The public theme of the novel is a strong indictment of materialism. As Cather became richer and richer and America wallowed in prosperity in the years before the stock market crash in 1929, she became increasingly preoccupied with the corrupting power of money. This theme is nothing new in her work, for it appears as early as *O Pioneers!* But here it is woven into the fabric in the entire novel.

At the outset of the story the professor is confronted with the new house his wife has built with his prize money. After years of struggle in writing his history it has come to this ostentatious display of conspicuous consumption. His wife asks him: "Is there something you would rather have done with that money than to have built a house with it?" He says no, but "if with that cheque I could have bought back the fun I had writing my history, you'd never have got your house" (*PH*, 33). As the professor thinks about his daughters, he is even more depressed over the effect money has had on them. Tom Outland, that incorruptible youth, had left behind him, in the professor's opinion, a disastrous legacy. He had become a scientist and inventor and had willed to his fiancée Rosamond the patent for a revolutionary new aircraft engine. After Tom's death in the war Louis Marsellus had married Rosamond and as a sharp businessman had turned the patent into a fortune. The money has poisoned the relationship between Kathleen and Rosamond. The younger daughter is jealous of her sister's wealth, and the elder has become hard, grasping, mercenary. When Augusta, the sewing woman, loses her life savings in a bad investment, Rosamond refuses to help her, and after St. Peter accompanies Rosamond to Chicago to select furniture for her new house, he returns exhausted by the experience. He tells Lillian: "It turned out to be rather an orgy of acquisition. . . . She was like Napoleon looting the Italian palaces" (154).

The professor sits in his old sewing room study beside the dressmaker's dummies he has refused to let Augusta remove. They remind him of Tom's college days, when his daughters were young: "Oh, there had been fine times in this old house then; family festivals and hospitalities, little girls dancing in and out, Augusta coming and going, gay dresses hanging in his study at night. . . . When a man had lovely children in his house, fragrant and happy, full of pretty fancies and generous impulses, why couldn't he keep them? Was there no way but Medea's, he wondered" (*PH*, 125–26). On another occasion, after he has observed the hostility between his daughters, "two faces at once rose in the shadows outside the yellow circle of his lamp; the handsome face of his older daughter, surrounded by violet-dappled fur, with a cruel upper lip and scornful half-closed eyes, as she had approached her car that afternoon before she saw him; and Kathleen, her square little chin set so fiercely, her white cheeks actually becoming green under her swollen eyes" (89–90). He goes to the window and looks towards the physics building, where Tom had worked in his laboratory: "A sharp pain clutched his heart. Was it for this the light in Outland's laboratory used to burn so far into the night!" (90).

The corrupting power of money extends beyond the professor's family. It also seduces his colleagues, even Robert Crane, St. Peter's staunchest ally over the years in the battle to keep the state legislature and the board of regents from turning the university into a trade school. Crane, a dedicated scientist, had been Tom Outland's teacher and had helped him with his invention. After Louie parlays Tom's invention into a fortune, Crane wants a cut of the wealth. The professor does not think this an unreasonable desire, but he is saddened to see his colleague diverted from his passion for science by a greedy wife and her loud-mouthed lawyer brother, who want to sue Louie. The professor feels that Louie, if properly approached, would be generous. Everything comes to money in the end, Roddy Blake had told Tom Outland after selling the artifacts to the German archeologist, and St. Peter in his depressed state probably would have agreed. It pained him to admit that even he, whose tastes were simple and unpretentious, had been able to live the life of a scholar amid adequate creature comforts because his wife had a little money of her own.

Godfrey St. Peter, one of Cather's most complex and enigmatic characters, emerges from the novel as a credible, three-dimensional, flawed human being. We see him from all angles—in his relations with his wife, daughters, sons-in-law, colleagues, students, Augusta the sewing woman, and especially Tom Outland. He has not been a great success as a husband, although he and Lillian live together in harmony after having raised their daughters. Love has gone out of the marriage years before the story opens. Both Tom Outland and the professor's inability to give himself to his family have come between them. Another of Cather's divided personalities, he has for years isolated himself in his study working on his history and living a lonely life of the mind. His students and family have had to make do with only half of him. He is a Hawthornesque character whose mind has developed at the expense of his heart.

But Cather does not overly accentuate his failings. Though he is an elitist who takes refuge in his French garden and his study, he recognizes social obligations. He gets along with his two sons-in-law without approving completely of either: Scott McGregor, who wastes his talents writing good-cheer pieces for his newspaper, and Louis Marsellus, who is insensitive and aggressive though good-natured and public-spirited. Nor has he ever shortchanged his students, though he thinks most of them dull clods. He loved youth; it kindled him: "If there was one eager eye, one doubting, critical mind, one lively curiosity in a whole lecture-room full of commonplace boys and girls, he was its servant" (PH, 28).

We catch a glimpse of the professor in his classroom at the end of one of his lectures. In response to a student's question he is thinking out loud about science, art, and religion. "No, Miller, I don't think much of science as a phase of human development. It has given us a lot of ingenious toys; they take our attention away from the real problems, of course, and since the problems are insoluble, I suppose we ought to be grateful for distraction" (PH, 67–68). Science has not given us any richer pleasures, as the Renaissance did, nor any new sins. "Indeed, it takes away the sins of the world." In olden days, when men and women crowded into the great cathedrals of Europe, each one was a principal "in a gorgeous drama with God, glittering angels on one side and the shadows of evil coming and going on the other." Life was then a rich thing. The professor goes on to say that it makes us happy to surround our creature needs and bodily instincts with as much pomp and circumstance as possible. "Art and religion (they are the same thing in the end, of course) have given man the only happiness he has ever had" (69). St. Peter ends the hour: "You might tell me next week, Miller, what you think science has done for us, besides making us very comfortable."

While the professor goes through his midlife crisis, he lives much in his memories. In one scene he recalls his young days in France, when he lived with the Thierault family in Versailles as tutor to their boys, who became closer to him than his own brothers. He remembers those golden days with intense nostalgia. In another scene the professor and his wife attend a performance of *Mignon* in Chicago, an opera he remembers hearing repeatedly in his student days in Paris. The music he loves: it is the expression of youth. When the soprano sings "Connais-tu—le pays," it stirs him deeply "like the odours of early spring"; it recalls "the time of sweet, impersonal emotions." He turns to Lillian: "It's been a mistake, our having a family and writing histories and getting middle-aged. We should have been picturesquely shipwrecked together when we were young." Lillian agrees but quickly adds: "One must go on living, Godfrey" (PH, 93–94).

The final scene of memory occurs late in the novel before the professor's near asphyxiation. In his reverie the boy the professor had left many years before in Kansas returns to him, "The original, unmodified Godfrey St. Peter" (*PH*, 263). It seems now to the professor that "life with this Kansas boy, little as there had been of it, was the realest of his lives." This boy was not a scholar. "He was a primitive. He was only interested in earth and woods and water. Wherever sun sunned and rain rained and snow snowed, wherever life sprouted and decayed, places were alike to him. . . . He seemed to be at the root of the matter; Desire under all desires, Truth under all truths. He seemed to know, among other things, that he was solitary and must always be so" (264–65). In this important passage the professor strips away the external trappings of his life. What is left is the essential, autonomous human being. He is now ready with the help of the slammed window and blown-out stove to go on with his life, to learn to "live without delight" (282). It is a bleak, unsentimental ending that reflects Cather's mood in 1925.

It is significant that at the end of the novel it is old Augusta who saves the professor. She is solid, real, a woman whose life has been spent serving others, a pious Catholic who asks little of the world. "Augusta, he reflected, had always been a corrective, a remedial influence. . . . Augusta was like the taste of bitter herbs; she was the bloomless side of life that he had always run away from,—yet when he had to face it, he found that it wasn't altogether repugnant." She was unsentimental, practical, and he would rather have her with him at that moment than anyone else. There was "a world full of Augustas with whom one was outward bound" (*PH*, 280–81).

"Tom Outland's Story," which has been greatly admired by readers and reprinted as a separate tale, is generally regarded as one of the two or three best stories in Cather's canon. It is about the same length as "Coming, Aphrodite!" or "Uncle Valentine," about sixteen thousand words. Cather herself thought it was a good piece of narrative. The title character is particularly engaging—youthful, energetic, full of idealism, talented. Whereas the professor reflects Cather's thoughts and feelings at the age of fifty-three, Tom Outland is her youthful other self. Nowhere does Cather display better her ability to evoke the past and surround it with an aura of romance. The real account of finding the lost civilization of Mesa Verde, the springboard for this tale, is an exciting adventure, but Cather adds a great deal to the story she heard from Dick Wetherill's brother when she visited Mancos in 1915.[11] She makes it a story of youthful idealism and defeat. Not only is Tom frustrated in his efforts to preserve the relics of the cliff dwellings as a national treasure by the indifference of official Washington and Roddy Blake's lack of understanding, but he also goes off, like Claude Wheeler in *One of Ours*, to fight and die in World War I. But before his final defeat he lives a rich though brief life.

There are wonderful moments in this story that reflect Cather's delight in the Southwest. She answered from Santa Fe a fan letter praising *The Professor's House* while it was still running in *Collier's* by saying that neither years nor miles could ever lessen the pull or the excitement this country had for her. When Tom goes back to the mesa after Roddy Blake has sold the artifacts and departed, he comes to a clear realization of his experience in finding the lost city: "The excitement of my first discovery was a very pale feeling compared to this one. For me the mesa was no longer an adventure, but a religious emotion" (*PH*, 251). Cather must have experienced similar emotions in 1915, during the hours she and Lewis sat on a rock a thousand feet below the cliff city, waiting to be rescued after they had gotten lost in Soda Canyon. The memory of those moments went into Tom's diary, which the professor edits while his wife, daughter, and sons-in-law are traveling in Europe: "The grey sage-brush and the blue-grey rock around me were already in shadow, but high above me the canyon walls were dyed flame-colour with the sunset, and the Cliff City lay in a gold haze against its dark cavern. In a few minutes it, too, was grey, and only the rim-rock at the top held the red light. When that was gone, I could still see the copper glow in the piñons along the edge of the top ledges. The arc of sky over the canyon was silvery blue, with its pale yellow moon, and presently stars shivered into it, like crystals dropped into perfectly clear water" (250).

Tom's death, which had occurred a decade before the story opens, was an irreparable blow to the professor. Tom had appeared one day out of nowhere while he was writing his history and had grown closer to him than a younger brother. They were inseparable companions; they traveled together in the Southwest; they had a community of interest and understanding that bound them tightly. So close were they that Lillian was jealous of Tom. "In a lifetime of teaching, I've encountered just one remarkable mind," he tells his daughter (PH, 62). But the memory of Tom lives on, and throughout the novel he is a powerful presence. His legacy, a scientific invention that like King Midas turns everything into gold, is the crowning irony.

Although Cather never told anyone where she got the idea for Tom Outland and the professor, the germ of the relationship between Tom and St. Peter goes back at least to her years as a high school teacher in Pittsburgh. One of her early pieces of apprentice fiction is a short story called "The Professor's Commencement," which she published in the *New England Magazine* in 1902. This is one of the tales she wanted forgotten after she became a novelist, and intrinsically it is unimportant. She made almost no use of her experiences as a high school teacher of English in her fiction ("Paul's Case" being a notable exception), but in "The Professor's Commencement," which is mostly about the retirement of Emerson Graves after teaching literature for thirty years to the sons and daughters of Pittsburgh's working class, there is this arresting passage:

> the desire had come upon him to bring some message of repose and peace to the youth of this work-driven, joyless people, to cry the name of beauty so loud that the roar of the mills could not drown it. Then the reward of his first labors had come in the person of his one and only genius; his restless, incorrigible pupil with the gentle eyes and manner of a girl, at once timid and utterly reckless, who had seen even as Graves saw; who had suffered a little, sung a little, struck with true lyric note, and died wretchedly at three-and-twenty in his master's arms, the victim of a tragedy as old as the world and as grim as Samson, the Israelite's.[12]

It seems clear from this excerpt that the seed from which *The Professor's House* ultimately grew lay dormant in Cather's mind for some thirteen years until the wind and the sun of the blue mesa breathed life into it.

Even before this happened, however, Cather created another, though quite different, professor-student relationship in her first novel, *Alexander's Bridge* (1912). There Professor Lucius Wilson, who teaches psychology in a western university, is the former teacher of Bartley Alexander, a famous bridge builder at the time the novel opens. Wilson comes to Boston to visit Bartley and his wife at the outset of the novel; but he is only a minor character who serves as a Jamesian *ficelle*, or confidant, to help Cather tell the tragic tale of her bridge builder. Although Bartley had been Wilson's student, albeit an indifferent one, and his friend, he was neither protégé nor surrogate son, as Tom Outland was to St. Peter. In fact, Wilson had thought Bartley had a fatal flaw in his moral nature, though he was enormously interesting and stimulating to observe.

In yet another and more important way *Alexander's Bridge* looks ahead to *The Professor's House*. The character of Alexander himself foreshadows the creation of Godfrey St. Peter. Cather was fascinated by characters who were divided against themselves, and a good many such may be found throughout her fiction. She herself was a divided personality during the years that she was managing editor of *McClure's Magazine*, conducting by day the affairs of the leading muckraking journal in the country and trying by night to become a successful writer of fiction. At the age of forty-three Bartley Alexander goes through a midlife crisis, just as Cather later did, and as St. Peter does. Bartley yearns to recapture his lost youth and struggles unsuccessfully to reconcile desire and possibility. Cather gives him a melodramatic death when his new bridge collapses and he drowns in the St. Lawrence River. Thirteen years later Cather gives St. Peter a much more likely conclusion to his midlife crisis by having him learn to live without delight.

There are further interesting parallels between Alexander and St. Peter in their nostalgic memories of youth. Late in *Alexander's Bridge* Bartley rushes to Canada in response to a telegram warning him that his bridge is showing dangerous signs of stress. As he passes through New England on the train, he catches a fleeting glimpse of a group of boys sitting about a campfire by a river. This view casts his mind back to the days when he also was a boy camping by a western river, just as St. Peter too, late in *The Professor's House*, reflects at length on the boy he left behind in Kansas and thinks that perhaps his life then was the most real of his lives. At another point in both novels, the protagonists recall their student days in Paris. In *Alexander's Bridge* Bartley remembers walking with Hilda, his youthful love, who gave an old woman flowers, while he gave her a franc. The old woman looked at them in despair, for it was not their flowers or money she wanted but their youth. In *The Professor's House* St. Peter recalls buying a bouquet from a young family of street vendors and trying to give it to one of a group of passing schoolgirls; but just as he was putting out his hand, a chaperoning nun flapped up like a black crow and stopped him. These passages in the two novels are close to mirror images of each other.

Cather's literary method usually drew on memories from her own past. This is true of all of her Nebraska novels populated by immigrant women like Alexandra Bergson in *O Pioneers!* and Ántonia Shimerda in *My Ántonia* or friends of childhood like Marion Forrester in *A Lost Lady*. Young Thea Kronborg in *The Song of the Lark* is young Willa Cather growing up in Red Cloud; the heroine of *Lucy Gayheart* was suggested by someone Cather knew when she was a child; *Sapphira and the Slave Girl* draws on her earliest memories of Virginia. Even *Death Comes for the Archbishop* owes much to Cather's discovery of the Southwest in 1912. Thus it is not surprising to find in Professor St. Peter an avatar of Professor Emerson Graves and Bartley Alexander.

The reviews of *The Professor's House* are a motley collection ranging from ecstatic praise to complete rejection. The favorable ones far outnumber the unfavorable, but neither those who liked the novel nor those who disliked it could agree on their reasons. James Ford in the *Literary Digest* hailed the book as the best Cather had yet written.[13] He found the professor a great characterization and "Tom Outland's Story" the most thrilling account he had ever read of a dead-and-gone civilization. On the other hand the *New York Times* reviewer called the book a catastrophe.[14] The first book of the novel was "ingeniously invented and admirably carried along as far as it goes. It stops in mid-channel. Book the second is an amateurish essay in archeological adventure. It is flat, stale and unprofitable. Book the third finds Miss Cather far beyond her philosophical depth." Henry S. Canby, who was to become one of Cather's friends, reviewed the novel for the newly founded *Saturday Review of Literature*.[15] He was one of the few reviewers who saw beneath the surface the real story of the "slow discovery by Professor St. Peter—of himself." He was more interested in this novel than Cather's others because "the soul, after all, is the greatest subject for art." The experimental structure of the novel bothered many critics even when they thought the performance on the whole superior. The most perceptive critics, however, would have agreed with R. C. Kennedy in the *New Statesman*: "There is no formal shape to the whole; and yet it has the very accent of truth. It would be difficult to convey, without seeming to exaggerate, the ease and precision with which fine inexplicable shades of mood and emotion are rendered."[16]

For Schuyler Ashley in the *Kansas City Star* the professor was "indubitably the most valuable attainment of Willa Cather's new novel. To create such a man, talented, whimsical without eccentricity, and innately attractive; to make him credible and complete is a substantial accomplishment."[17] This reviewer, however, thought Cather was very hard on her own sex, surrounding the professor as she did with a worldly wife, a greedy elder daughter, and a jealous younger one. He quoted St. Peter's comment about Euripides, who went to live in a cave by the sea in his old age: "It seems that houses had become insupportable to him. I wonder whether it was because he had observed women so closely all his life?" (*PH*, 156).

During Cather's lifetime readers and critics never rated *The Professor's House* among her best novels. *My Ántonia*, *A Lost Lady*, and *Death Comes for the Archbishop* all were considered important works, as indeed they are, but *The Professor's House* was relegated to a lower status. Cather herself agreed with this estimate and thought *My Ántonia* and *Death Comes for the Archbishop* were her most enduring works. Since her death, however, *The Professor's House* has taken its place among the other three, and each year all four books generate a large amount of critical exegesis. No longer are the stories of Godfrey St. Peter and Tom Outland neglected or forgotten, and the novel's selection for this collection of essays suggests that it is going to have a long life and an ever-increasing number of enthusiastic readers.

Notes

1. Cather, *The Professor's House* (New York: Alfred A. Knopf, 1925), 282. All quotations are from this edition, cited as *PH* in the text.

2. Sergeant, *Cather*, 215.

3. As she often did, Cather quoted from memory a little inaccurately. The correct text: "For thee was a house built / Ere thou wast born, / For thee was a mould meant / Ere thou of mother camest."

4. Cather, *Cather on Writing*, 30.

5. Ibid., 31.

6. Brown, *Cather*, 237–47.

7. Edel, *Literary Biography*, 91–122 (*The Stuff of Dreams*, 219–40).

8. Stouck, *Cather's Imagination*, 96–106.

9. Rosowski, *The Voyage Perilous*, 130, 142.

10. Grumbach, "The Small Room," 337.

11. For a thorough investigation of the discovery of Mesa Verde, the Wetherills' relations with the Smithsonian Institution, and Cather's use of this material, see Harrell, " 'We Contacted Smithsonian.' "

12. Cather, *Collected Short Fiction*, 290.

13. Ford, "The Professor's House."

14. "The Professor's House," *New York Times Book Review*, 6 September 1925, 8.

15. Canby, "The Professor's House."

16. Kennedy, "The Professor's House."

17. Ashley, "The Professor's House."

Works Cited

Ashley, Schuyler. "The Professor's House." *Kansas City Star*, 3 October 1925.

Brown, E. K. *Willa Cather: A Critical Biography*. Lincoln: University of Nebraska Press, 1987.

Canby, H. S. "The Professor's House." *Saturday Review of Literature*, 26 September 1925, 151.

Cather, Willa. *Collected Short Fiction, 1892–1912*. Edited by Virginia Faulkner. Lincoln: University of Nebraska Press, 1965.

———. *The Professor's House*. New York: Alfred A. Knopf, 1925.

———. *Willa Cather on Writing: Studies in Writing as an Art*. Foreword by Stephen Tennant. New York: A. A. Knopf, 1962.

Edel, Leon. *Literary Biography*. Garden City, N.Y.: Doubleday Anchor Books, 1959. Revised ed. in Edel, *The Stuff of Dreams*. New York: Harper & Row, 1982.

Ford, James. "The Professor's House." *Literary Digest International Book Review*, November 1925, 775.

Grumbach, Doris. "A Study of the Small Room in *The Professor's House*." *Women's Studies* 11, no. 3 (1984): 327–45.

Harrell, David. " 'We Contacted Smithsonian': The Wetherills at Mesa Verde." *New Mexico Historical Review* 62 (July 1987): 229–48.

Kennedy, R. C. "The Professor's House." *New Statesman*, 19 December 1925, 306.

"The Professor's House." *New York Times Book Review*, 6 September 1925, 28.

Rosowski, Susan. *The Voyage Perilous: Willa Cather's Romanticism*. Lincoln:

University of Nebraska Press, 1986.

Sergeant, Elizabeth Shepley. *Willa Cather: A Memoir*. Lincoln: University of Nebraska Press, 1967.

Stouck, David. *Willa Cather's Imagination*. Lincoln: University of Nebraska Press, 1975.

WILLIAM BALASSI

Hemingway's Greatest Iceberg:
The Composition of *The Sun Also Rises*

If a writer of prose knows enough about what he is writing about he may omit things that he knows and the reader, if the writer is writing truly enough, will have a feeling of those things as strongly as though the writer had stated them.

—Death in the Afternoon, *192*

In an interview with George Plimpton published in 1958 Ernest Hemingway said, "If it is any use to know it, I always try to write on the principle of the iceberg. There is seven eighths of it under water for every part that shows. Anything you know you can eliminate and it only strengthens your iceberg. It is the part that doesn't show."[1] Nowhere did Hemingway so thoroughly or so daringly apply this technique than in the composition of *The Sun Also Rises*, either leaving things out as he wrote or excising them in revision. The result is a richly textured but elusive story that has been plagued by misreadings since its publication in 1926.

Now that the manuscript is available to scholars, however, it is possible to retrace Hemingway's steps as he created his first novel. We see him starting with a short story about actual people that focuses on his own disturbing emotions generated by the recent fiesta in Pamplona. We see his notes to himself and his changes of direction as he fictionalizes names and events and works out where his story will go and how it will get there. We see him approaching the novel as a series of one-day writing tasks, almost as though he were writing a connected series of short stories. We see him experimenting with form and technique, creating a complex, multilayered novel. And by comparing the manuscript with the published text, we see how effectively he applied his iceberg theory and the impressive degree to which the first draft corresponds, word for word, with the published novel. Altogether, the manuscript of *The Sun Also Rises* reveals the remarkable story of how Ernest Hemingway wrote his first novel.

I

In 1925 Hemingway was a twenty-six-year-old transplanted Midwesterner living in Paris. He had long since abandoned the conventional morality of his family and upper-middle-class community of Oak Park, Illinois, but he retained a number of Midwestern traits, including a love of strenuous activity, a belief in work as a moral value, and a need for a system to live by.[2] He was also, according to Archibald MacLeish, "one of the most human and spiritually powerful creatures" he had ever known, able to persuade people to do things they otherwise never would do: box, fish, go on walking tours, attend bullfights, accompany him on vacation, drink his drinks, and adopt his enthusiasms.[3] In return he provided camaraderie and excitement. But he was inordinately thin-skinned, sensitive to real or imagined slights, and he all too often lashed out with shocking vindictiveness against the perceived disloyalty of former friends.

When he was eighteen Hemingway entered World War I as a Red Cross ambulance driver in Italy. Six weeks later, while delivering chocolate and cigarettes to Italian soldiers in the forward trenches, he was nearly killed by shrapnel from an exploding Austrian shell. He spent the next six months in a Milan hospital where he fell in love with and became engaged to his nurse, Agnes von Kurowsky. Two months after his return to Oak Park in January 1919, however, she jilted him to become engaged to someone else. Two years later, after a courtship conducted largely by correspondence, he married a shy, sheltered girl from St. Louis, Hadley Richardson. By 1925 they had a son and a strained marriage.

Hemingway had been a journalist since 1917, first as a cub reporter for the *Kansas City Star* (1917–18), then, successively, as a feature writer for the *Toronto Star* (1920), a copywriter for the trade journal of the Cooperative Society of America (1920–21), European correspondent for the *Toronto Star* and occasionally for Hearst's International News Service (1922–23), and finally a reporter in Canada for the *Toronto Star* (1923). At the end of 1923, however, he gave up journalism to pursue serious writing full time.

Since 1922 he had been studying the craft of writing under the tutelage of Ezra Pound and Gertrude Stein. When he was not writing, he was voraciously reading the masters and the best of his contemporaries. Sylvia Beach, owner of the Paris bookstore Shakespeare and Company, called him her best customer; and in *Hemingway's Reading, 1910–1940* Michael Reynolds claims that "Hemingway's reading was more important to his art and to his life than Coleridge's was to his."[4] In 1923 he published the first of two slim volumes, *Three Stories and Ten*

Poems, which included "Up in Michigan," "Out of Season" (one of his first "iceberg" experiments), and his Sherwood Anderson story, "My Old Man," and followed it in 1924 with *in our time*, which consisted of eighteen brief prose experiments in tone and diction. Then during the first seven months of 1924 he wrote an impressive series of stories, most of which focused on Nick Adams and carried his young hero from his childhood in "Indian Camp," through a brief love affair, into the war and his wounding, and to his return home in "Big Two-Hearted River." These stories, together with the vignettes, formed the basis of his first full-length book, *In Our Time*, which was to be published in the fall of 1925 by Boni and Liveright.

This is how things stood in late June of 1925 when Hemingway left for Spain. Spain in general and bullfighting in particular held special meaning for him. Spain was "healthy," easily "the best country in Europe," the only one left "that hasn't been shot to pieces"; and the bullring was "the only remaining place where valor and art can combine for success."[5] He was profoundly moved by the spectacle of the bullfight: "It isn't just brutal like they always told us. It's a great tragedy—and the most beautiful thing I've ever seen and takes more guts and skill and guts again than anything possibly could. It's just like having a ringside seat at the war with nothing going to happen to you."[6]

In 1925 Hemingway was making his third annual pilgrimage to the Fiesta de San Fermin in Pamplona. This fiesta was particularly suited to his personality and needs. It matched his large-mannered enthusiasm, tested his courage, and challenged his endurance. It provided ceremony and excitement, nourished his physical and spiritual appetites, and produced some of the best bullfights in Spain. Altogether it was a fitting way each year to observe the anniversary of his wounding on 8 July 1918.

When he first started coming to the fiesta, before tourists overran it in 1925, it was wonderfully exotic. Each July peasants throughout Navarre packed themselves within the ancient city for a nonstop week of religious and secular festivities: processions, masses, Basque sports, entertainments, music, moonlight dances in festive regional costumes, fireworks, and Pamplona's unique spectacle of the running of the bulls followed by the "amateurs." Each morning at 5:45 musicians marched through the streets, arousing the festivalers, who crowded along the fenced-off, nine-hundred-yard course from the corrals to the bullring to watch the brave and foolhardy test their courage by running the route in front of the onrushing bulls scheduled for that afternoon's *corrida*. The festivities continued in the bullring as amateur bullfighters, Hemingway and his friends among them, joined the runners in testing their skill and courage with the bulls while hundreds of musicians, each playing his own tune, added to the cacophony of sounds and sights. Afterwards everyone headed for the streets and cafés of the town to celebrate and await the afternoon's bullfight. The fiesta was a week-long, nonstop party that could be very good or very bad. Hemingway knew both kinds.

In 1924 the fiesta had been a huge success. Hemingway had invited his cronies—Chink Dorman-Smith, John Dos Passos, Donald Ogden Stewart, George O'Neil, and Bill Bird (along with Bird's wife, Sally, and his own wife, Hadley)—and his enthusiasm was contagious.[7] The revelers threw themselves into the fiesta, singing and dancing in the streets, entering the ring to take part in the "amateurs," attending afternoon bullfights, drinking much, and sleeping little. A few days after the fiesta Hemingway wrote to Ezra Pound, "Having been bitched financially and in a literary way by my friends I take great and unintellectual pleasure in the immediate triumphs of the bull ring with their reward in ovations, Alcoholism, being pointed out on the street, general respect and other things Literary guys have to wait until they are 89 years old to get."[8]

For the 1924 fiesta Hemingway, the gamesmaster, had chosen the players well, but for the 1925 fiesta he assembled a disastrous combination. Donald Ogden Stewart, who attended both fiestas, contrasted the two:

> The first is the one I remember with the most pleasure. It was a masculine time. Things were great. Pamplona was ours. No one else had discovered it. I have nothing but the most satisfying memories of that trip. It was vintage Hemingway. It was a happy time. And then the lovers came along. On that second trip Duff Twysden and Harold Loeb were busily playing their roles as Brett Ashley and Robert Cohn, and Pat Guthrie was there as Mike Campbell. It wasn't just that a woman was along. Hem's wife, Hadley, and Sally, Bill Bird's wife, were with us on the first trip. It wasn't that. But by the second trip everything had changed somehow. Harold was having this affair with Duff; Duff was supposedly engaged to Pat and there seemed to be something between Hem and Duff. I don't mean physically, but something. . . . The lovers and their tensions dominated the second trip. It was good for the book of course, but not for the people.[9]

II

When Hemingway went to Pamplona in 1925, he was gathering material not for a novel but for a book about bullfighting.[10] But by a week after the fiesta he was shaping the events into a short story that used the names of his companions. He wrote this story quickly: 4,700 words in two or three days, an unusually fast pace for him.[11] It was one of his better stories, but he never published it because it soon became part of something larger.

In this ironic tale the narrator, called "Hem," tells the story of how he endangered the career and possibly the life of a promising young bullfighter by exposing him to the very temptations from which he was to protect him. Hem is caught between two worlds. He resides in Paris among expatriates whose belief in values had been shattered by the Great War, yet he himself is devoted to the world of *afición* with its passionate love of bullfighting, its spiritual and even mystical overtones, and its unstated code of behavior. However, unlike Quintana, the hotel owner whose passion is pure and whose obligations are clear, Hem finds his emotions complicated by sexuality, drunkenness, and contradictory rules of behavior, which cause him to doubt whether he truly has *afición*. Perhaps he is, after all, more like the other expatriates than he would like to admit. It is from this painful perspective of still-new self-awareness that he tells his story.

Manuscript evidence suggests that Hemingway paused four times while writing this story, dividing the text into five writing sessions.[12] The first focuses on the sensational nineteen-year-old bullfighter, "Niño de la Palma" (whose name Hemingway used for his title), and on his susceptibility to the temptations that accompany success in the bullring.[13] After watching him, Hem and Quintana agree that Niño is "the best torero we had seen, [with] the finest and purest style and the most authority in the ring" (193.4).[14] They are genuinely excited to be witnessing the emergence of a bullfighter "as rare as Caruso" (193.4). They know that he must be protected and brought along slowly if he is to reach his enormous potential, but when Niño, apparently drunk, is mistakenly carted into Hem and Hadley's room at six in the morning, it is evident that keeping him from temptation will be difficult.

The second session shifts the attention to the narrator, who is angered because this year the fiesta has become fashionable due to the return to the bullring of the great Juan Belmonte. Even the American ambassador has shown up. And with him is "Mrs. Carleton," "a cute little short one" with "lovely sunburnt color" hair, "capable of taking any man away after he has passed a certain age" (193.6–7).[15] A growing crowd gathers around the car of the "cunningly stupid" ambassador, who remains inside waiting to be officially welcomed by local dignitaries who either do not know or do not care about his arrival (193.6). Eventually the others in the narrator's group—"Duff," "Don," "Bill," "Pat," and "Hadley"—talk Hem into helping out.[16] Quickly taking charge, Hem sends a policeman for the mayor and makes reservations for the ambassador at the "other Hotel," desiring as little contact with him as possible (193.8). Then he talks to the "lively" Mrs. Carleton who "worship[s]" bullfighters, has apparently had an affair with at least one, and indicates a desire to meet Niño (193.8–9). Though Hem despises this kind of person, he nevertheless finds her sexually attractive: "She had been turning all this . . . ⌊ sex appeal on ⌊ me all the time we were talking and of course . . . ⌊ you are never ⌊ immune at the time" (193.10).[17] After the mayor arrives, looking embarrassed, Hem returns to his group at the restaurant.

In the third writing session, Hemingway briefly described that afternoon's bullfight that, like so much of the fiesta, promised much but proved disastrous, not only because the bulls refused to charge, making them unpredictable and dangerous, but also because people such as the ambassador and his group made Hem "feel sick" (193.13). The next day at the fiesta it is raining, and Hem's group despondently drink absinthe, watching the skies drizzle and the town fill up with outsiders come to see Belmonte. By the time they return to the hotel, they are "pretty tight" (193.17).

Hem then meets Quintana, who looks worried because he has been asked to convey a supper invitation to Niño from the ambassador. Both men know that Niño must be kept away from Mrs. Carleton, and so, with Hem's approval, Quintana decides not to deliver the invitation. This excites their *aficionado* passions because they have protected Niño from "people [who] would wreck him to make a nymphomaniacs [*sic*] holiday" (193.19). But Hem specifically differentiates their responses: "I was a little tight and Quintana was impassioned. As a matter of fact I was impassioned too. . . . [We] felt we'd each met some one who knew life and other drunk feelings. Only Quintana wasn't drunk. It was only me who was drunk" (193.19). Such pointed contrast suggests that something about Hem's response is troubling him.

In the fourth session Hem then joins the others in the hotel's restaurant where they are having a boisterous, drunken time. Sitting at the next table is Niño, who invites Hem to have some wine with him and a bullfight critic from Madrid. Eventually Duff calls over to their table and, without taking her eyes off Niño, asks Hem to introduce his friend. At this point, Hem should have done something to keep Niño away not only from Duff, who represents the same threat as Mrs. Carleton, but also from the rest of the group, who if anything pose more of a threat to Niño than the ambassador's group do. But, like Jake, who later will not refuse Brett's request to meet Pedro Romero, Hem does not refuse Duff's request. The fourth session ends as Niño and the bullfight critic stand up to be introduced.

In the final session of the story Niño comes over to their table, is given a large glass of cognac, and finds himself barraged with drunken non sequiturs, such as Pat's insistence that Hem "Tell him bulls have no balls" and "Tell him Duff wants to see him put on those green pants" (193.26). The climax occurs as Quintana walks into the restaurant and sees Niño with a large glass of cognac in his hand, sitting between Hem and two women in evening dresses at a table full of drunks. Without even a nod Quintana walks out, disgusted and dismayed that Hem would be sitting in the middle of it all, doing nothing, this man with *afición*, who only an hour before had been so moved at having protected Niño from similar circumstances. Hem comments, "All of a sudden I realized how funny it was" (193.27).

It may be that Hemingway originally intended to conclude the story at this point; such an ending would certainly have been appropriate for this ironic tale. Instead, however, he extended the story by shifting the focus to the expatriates. After Quintana leaves, Hem interrupts what undoubtedly would have been an insulting toast by Pat and enables Niño to exit gracefully. Duff then comments on Niño's good looks and—picking up on Pat's earlier line—agrees that she would indeed love to see him get into his tight-fitting clothes. Pat criticizes Hem for having interrupted him and, declaring that he wants to settle things, suddenly begins to verbally assault not Hem but "Harold." The fact that this is the first reference to the model for Robert Cohn suggests the new direction Hemingway was taking. Pat is engaged to Duff and is understandably angry at Harold, who the month before had had an affair with Duff. He demands that Harold leave, but Harold just sits there, refusing to go and seeming to enjoy everything that has to do with "his affair with a lady of title" (193.30). As Pat lunges toward Harold, Hem grabs him and tells him that he can't fight there in the hotel. The story ends as Pat is stumbling on the stair, Harold is putting his glasses back on, and—if Hem remembers correctly—Hadley and Duff are talking about their mothers.

The conflicts in this story suggest that Hemingway's real subject is not so much the potential corruption of Niño as the turmoil within Hem as he unsuccessfully tries to resolve the tensions and contradictory values between the *afición* world he prefers and the expatriate world he inhabits. In the published novel, though some of this material remains, its significance can be easily overlooked, for it is embedded within the larger story; in the Scribner's text, for instance, the moment in the restaurant when Montoya sees Pedro Romero drinking with Jake's group appears as part of the rising action leading to Jake's betrayal of *afición* for Brett's sake. But as Michael Reynolds has pointed out, it is from that Jamesian "special moment" in the restaurant that the story evolved.[18] That special moment when Hem's *afición* is called into question is the real beginning of *The Sun Also Rises*.

III

On 23 July Hemingway opened a blue-covered notebook and wrote "page 38—Niño de la Palma / continued from loose sheets" (I.2).[19] Soon, however, it would no longer be Niño's story. During the next five sessions Hemingway transformed the manuscript from a nonfiction short story about the fiesta to a clearly fictionalized novel about "Jake," "Duff," and "Gerald Cohn." That transformation started within the first sentences of the notebook.

"That was the kind of crowd we were," he began, "a fine lot," followed by several examples: "Don was the best of the lot and he was on a hilarious drunk and thought every body else was and became angry if they were not. Duff had [been somebody once and] something once, she still had a certain wonderful vitality. . ." (I.2).[20] These sentences suggest that Hemingway planned to characterize each of the expatriates in order to show—as he put it several pages later— "what a fine crowd we were, what a good crowd for a nineteen year old kid to get in with" (I.6–7), but when he got to Duff, something happened, and the record of what that "something" was may be contained in the first sentence he wrote about her.

He began by referring to her as someone already relegated to the past: "Duff had [been somebody once and] something once." Perhaps like Jake later in the manuscript, Hem is implying that he is "pretty well through with Duff" (IV.42). But then Hemingway inserted a clause that brought her right back into the present and, in the process, changed the course of what he was writing: "she still had a certain wonderful vitality." Like the word "lively" he had used to describe Mrs. Carleton, "vitality" suggests the sexual nature of Hem's attraction. Hemingway apparently intended to summarize her as "the typical Montparnasse drunk" and go on to the next expatriate, but the interjected clause about her "vitality" altered the direction of the sentence, and he found himself either unwilling or unable to summarize her in a single statement. For the rest of that session and all of the next, he wrote about her.[21] By the time he tried to return to the original pattern with the words "There were two others," the story he was telling had changed so much that he crossed out this line and chose an altogether different approach (I.7). As Jake later observed, Niño "never really had a chance to be the hero" (II.7). Duff was the reason. It is also worth noting that while other characters were soon to receive fictionalized names, she remained "Duff" throughout the manuscript.

We are told that Duff can only "command her will enough" to pose during the early afternoons, when she sits for portraits by second- and third-rate painters (I.2). At one time she had been painted by all "the first rate painters," but that was "long ago" (I.3). She is living in Paris "like an outcast," waiting for a divorce from her second husband, who during the war had commanded a destroyer in the North Sea, which turned him into a violent alcoholic (I.2). When he found out that Duff did not love him, he tried to kill her. He has custody of their son and refuses to grant a divorce, though he has agreed to a separation.

In the next session Hemingway focused on Duff's relationship with Pat. One day she offered to go away with him "because Pat was lonely and sick and as she said 'one of us, obviously a good chap'" (I.4). They left that afternoon for the Continent, and when they reached Paris they stopped at a hotel with "only one room free," and that one happened to have a double bed. Pat, who we later find out is Duff's cousin, offered to go to another hotel, but Duff said, "No. Why not," and so began their relationship (I.4).

With the aid of her "then very strong will," she "cured" Pat of "various habits" that she "did not think a man should have" (I.4).[22] Pat is "an undischarged bankrupt . . . quite a serious thing in England" (I.4). He is "charming . . . nice . . . weak" and usually well behaved, except when he is very drunk, at which times he becomes "objectionable" and "embarrassing" (I.4–5). They spend their time drinking and waiting for Pat's weekly allowance, which is always late and therefore always already spent. Duff sleeps until early afternoon, occasionally poses for portraits, and drinks heavily every day from four until two in the morning. Each day is "a replica of the day before," differing only according to whether Pat has behaved well or not (I.5). But unlike Pat, no matter how much Duff drinks—and she drinks more than he does—she "never los[es] her form" (I.6). She does, however, shut the world out in three stages. First she stops speaking, then she stop seeing, and finally she stops hearing, though she always manages to be pleasant to anyone greeting her, "but in reality she ⌐ neither ⌐ heard nor saw anything" (I.6). With this image of vacancy Hemingway completed her portrait. But though Duff is "the typical Montparnasse drunk" leading an aimless, decadent life, Hem is nevertheless attracted to her, and it is this dominating physical attraction that will eventually lead to the narrator's betrayal of *afición* for her sake.

Hemingway then skipped a line and wrote: "I dont not know why I have put all this down. It may mix up the story. . ." (I.6). The double negative, though perhaps nothing more than a slip of the pen or an uncorrected change from the contraction to two words, occurred at a particularly important time and seems to say that Hemingway both did and did not know why he had "put all this down." After all, if his purpose was to show how bad Duff was for Niño, the details of her marriages and how she spends her days went far beyond what was necessary. But perhaps he already knew that the story had moved in a new direction and that Duff's biography had "mix[ed] up the story." However, he was not yet ready to accept the change, and so he instead reiterated his original purpose: "I wanted to show you what a fine crowd we were, what a good crowd for a nineteen year old kid to get in with," and then he probably ended the session by setting up a return to the original pattern: "There were two others" (I.6–7).

But between sessions he made a major decision. Abandoning his plan to write about the "two others," he instead started to fictionalize names and events. It may be that he had begun to see the lines of an emerging story, one that would make use of a love relationship between the narrator and Duff as a means of extending and intensifying the conflicts established in the opening story.[23] Whatever the reason, something had changed, and he was now writing a novel.

The first to receive a fictionalized name was "Hem."[24] Initially he was "Rafael," then briefly "Ernest," before becoming "Jacob" (I.8). Jake was named for a favorite uncle who bought lavish Christmas gifts and led what seemed to the boy a romantic life filled with interdicted pleasures such as smoking, gambling, drinking, and other vices he was too young to be told about. When this "fondly" remembered uncle died, Jake, still a young boy, attended his funeral (I.7). Throughout most of the ceremony he could not see his uncle anywhere, but then, with shocking suddenness, he spotted his uncle's purple nose sticking up amid the flowers on the casket right in front of him, which "froze [him] with a|n absolutely ⏐ new sensation all through the rest of the funeral" (I.8).

After that, whenever his religious mother repeated that she would "rather see [him] in [his] grave," than smoke, drink, or gamble, he thought of his dead uncle but pictured himself in the casket (I.7–8). That she preferred her brother dead rather than alive-but-drinking and felt the same about her son struck Jake as "strange" and "prejudiced [him] against all her views and moral values," including the admonition against drinking (I.8). So he declares he will not judge the drinking of the group at Pamplona, and he will not say "that it would be better for Niño de la Palma to be in his grave than to train with a crowd like that" (I.8).

But then he immediately undermines this conclusion, stating that if Niño does "train with them he [will] be dead soon enough," and the grave "is no place for a nineteen year old kid" (I.8). Events from the fiesta have forced him to reexamine his assumption that drinking is "quite unimportant" (I.7). However unimportant drinking may be for the others, it could cost Niño his life, so despite Jake's statement about not judging the "gang who were at Pamplona," he has no choice but to judge both them and himself (I.8). Like Hem, Jake finds himself caught between two worlds, and, as Hemingway may have known by this time, Jake's attempt to live in both simultaneously would eventually lead him to the irrevocable loss of the world that mattered most to him.

Hemingway's transition into the world of fiction prompted him to pause to consider how he wanted to approach his novel. He expressed these concerns in two editorial paragraphs, one probably written at the end of one session and the other at the beginning of the next. He began the first by echoing what he had said at the close of the previous session: "Probably any amount of this does not seem to have any thing to do with the story and perhaps it has not" (I.9). He then declared, "I am sick of clear restrained writing," which he changed to read, "I am sick of ⎸these ones with their⎸ clear restrained writing" (I.9).[25] Since 1922, under the guidance of Ezra Pound and Gertrude Stein he had been learning to perfect precisely such restraint. But he had not yet gained the kind of control over his story that "clear restrained writing" required; moreover, he wanted

> to get in the whole business and to do that there ha[d] to be things that seem[ed] as though they [did] had nothing to do with it just as in life. In life people are not conscious of these special moments that novelists build [up] ⎸their whole structures⎸ on. That is most people are not.

Then, addressing himself as well as the reader, he concluded:

> That surely has nothing to do with the story but you can[t] not tell until you finish it because none of the significant things are going to have [a] any literary signs marking them. You have to figure them out by yourself. (I.9)

Although Hemingway was to use many literary signs throughout the text, especially in the second half of the book, he did in fact present a number of the most important lines—the kind that "novelists build their whole structures on," such as "Montoya did not come near us" or "while she kissed me I could feel she was thinking of something else"[26]—with nothing whatsoever marking their significance, thereby forcing us to "figure them out" by ourselves. Of course, another reason Hemingway declared that he would not offer authorial emphasis is that he may not have been at all sure what the significant things would be. First there was the matter of getting in "the whole business."

At the beginning of the next session, after a skipped line, Hemingway wrote the second editorial paragraph:

> Now when my friends read this they will say it is awful. [It is not what they had hoped or expected from me.] Gertrude Stein once told me that remarks are not literature. All right, let it go at that. Only this time all the remarks are going in and if it is not literature who claimed it was anyway. (I.9)

And the "remarks" did go in, at least for a while. On the whole, though, "clear restrained writing" characterizes the novel far more than remarks and observations do. That is, Hemingway eventually practiced the kind of restraint Stein advocated, but for the time being he had to distance himself from both Stein and the restraint she demanded in order to explore his story.

These two editorial paragraphs came at an important time as Hemingway was staking out his territory and committing himself to writing a novel. Sick of "clear restrained writing," feeling that he had to break away from mentors such as Stein, he declared his freedom "to get in the whole business," to avoid the use of literary signs, not to be limited by the literary theories of others, to write in his own way, and possibly, to fail.

Hemingway then continued the story by shifting the setting: "To understand this situation in Pamplona you have to understand Paris" (I.9). His decision to write about Paris freed the story from the "clear restrained writing" against which he was rebelling, for under the rubric of helping the reader "understand Paris" he could justify the inclusion of practically anything. On this particular day, for instance, he wrote a remark-filled description of expatriate life in Paris. By Paris, he meant the cafés and restaurants of Montparnasse on the Left Bank and Montmartre on the Right. "This Paris is a very sad and dull place" (I.10). He devoted nearly half of this 400-word session to a description of Paris's "fairies" (I.10). This material, combined with the earlier detail that among the painters Duff posed for were "a who[le] group of what [are] one called Fairies," was perhaps intended to set up the reintroduction of Duff, who shows up at Braddocks's dancing club accompanied by a group of homosexuals (I.3).

Then, as he had done at the end of previous sessions, Hemingway set up what he would do next: "There are other fairly permanent inhabitants" (I.10). But by the time he continued, he had decided to rewrite the description from the previous session. This time his purpose was not simply to describe the Quarter but to lead to the introduction of Gerald Cohn. After reiterating "To understand what happened in Pamplona you must understand the quarter in Paris," he wrote: "There is nothing romantic about the quarter and very little that is beautiful. . . . It is too sad and dull a place to write about. I have to put it in because Gerald [i.e., Robert Cohn] had spent two years in it. That accounts for a great many things" (I.11–12). Gerald lives "in an atmosphere of abortions . . . dirty rumors . . . and a constant fear and dread by his companion that he was going with other woman [sic] and was on the point of leaving her" (I.12). He has written a novel of which he is the hero and has only two friends, "[Bradox] ⏐ Braddocks ⏐ and myself" (I.12). The introduction of Braddocks triggers an anecdote (later included in *A Moveable Feast*) of how Braddocks (based on Ford Madox Ford) snubbed a "distinguished looking lantern jawed man" that he said was the writer Hilaire Belloc, who was "absolutely done for. Absolutely through. . . . ⏐ Not a review in England will touch him, I tell you⏐" (I.14–15). The next day Jake sees the same lantern-jawed man and repeats the insider gossip to the people at his table, only to be embarrassed when he is told, "Hell. That's not Belloc. . . . That's Allister Crawley"—that is, Aleister Crowley (I.15).

Hemingway then completed the final step in the transition process by establishing the hero of his novel: "So I have never felt the same about Braddocks since . . . ⏐ I would avoid, if it were possible putting him in ⏐. . . . this story except that he was a great friend of Cohn and Cohn is the hero" (I.15). The next sentence reads, "Gerald Cohn was middleweight boxing champion of Princeton."

IV

The shift to Paris and the choice of Cohn as ironic hero enabled Hemingway to present two stories simultaneously: the one Jake tells about the expatriates, particularly Duff and Gerald, and the one Jake gradually reveals about himself. Moreover, from this point on there is remarkably close correspondence between the manuscript and the published text. When Hemingway revised the manuscript, he improved the phrasing and added details, but with the exception of the opening he made few changes to either the story or its structure.

One reason for this correspondence is that the manuscript consists of a series of discrete daily units, each crafted and completed, yet integrated within the larger context. Though he was now writing a novel, Hemingway, the newspaperman and short-story writer, thought in terms of one-day tasks. "I always worked until I had something done," he later reminisced in *A Moveable Feast*, "and I always stopped when I knew what was going to happen next. That way I could be sure of going on the next day."[27] He worked hard to get the words right the first time, and he usually succeeded. Seventy-nine percent of the words in the published novel come unchanged from the manuscript, and more than half of the remaining 21 percent consist of minor revisions of a sentence or less.[28]

The writing proceeded steadily. He wrote what became chapter 1 in the published text on 20 July, chapter 2 on 29 July, the first half of chapter 3 on 30 July, the second half on 31 July, and so forth. By 3 August he had filled the notebook he had begun eleven days earlier. Appropriately, the last pages describe Jake's bus trip and walk to work. Despite his abysmal previous night with the prostitute Georgette and then Duff, over whom he cried himself to sleep, he feels good about work. So, apparently, did Hemingway. As he later said, "Going down the stairs when I had worked well, and that needed luck as well as discipline, was a wonderful feeling and I was free then to walk anywhere in Paris."[29] Hemingway had a right to feel good. He was well on his way to completing his first novel. Day by day Hemingway, the disciplined craftsman, had begun to create a first-rate book—and he knew it.

But there were still unresolved problems, such as the one he spent most of the second notebook pursuing, namely choosing a protagonist. Early in the notebook, after the scene in which Jake returns from lunch with Gerald, he wrote a comment intended to reaffirm Gerald's centrality:

> Now you can see. I looked as though I were trying to get to be the hero of this story. But that was all wrong. Gerald Cohn is the hero. When I bring myself in it is only to clear up something.

But the rest of this aside indicates that he was no longer altogether comfortable with Gerald as his protagonist:

> Or maybe Duff is the hero or Nino [*sic*] de la Palma. [But] He never really had a chance to be the hero. Or maybe there is not any hero at all. Maybe a story is better without any hero. (II.7)

In the session that followed he tried to return the focus to Gerald by setting up a date between him and Duff, thereby explaining why she did not show up at the Hotel Crillon to meet Jake. Between sessions, however, he altered the plot, a decision that led to the elimination of first Gerald and then Duff as potential heroes. Recasting the last part of the previous scene so that Gerald now had a date with Frances, he then wrote the scenes in which Frances lashes out so scornfully and Gerald responds so weakly that he loses whatever chance he may have had to be the hero, ironic or otherwise. As Jake later observes, Gerald "was the hero for a time but he has been dropped" (V.16).

Hemingway then turned his attention to Duff in scenes that would not have taken place if he had not altered the plot, for Duff would otherwise have been with Gerald instead of the count. In these scenes—which are longer in the manuscript than in the published text—Hemingway portrays Duff as charming but selfish and thoughtless, even cruel, incapable of sustained thought and primarily interested in getting drunk. Count Mippipopolous, by contrast, enjoys life and values quality. Having learned that the secret is "to know the values," he embodies many of the qualities that Jake admires. He lives deliberately and cannot be wrenched by events from one overwhelming emotion to another the way Jake can (II.34; SAR, 60).[30] They do, however, share an awareness that enables them to talk to one another as though Duff were not there. As she gradually suspects that she is being humored, she becomes defensive, even hostile. Controlled by things both outside and within herself—her senses usually dulled by alcohol, her mind often empty, her thoughts fragmented—she is unable to take responsibility, unable even to finish her sentences. The count—who was to have shown up in Pamplona (see outline, below)—is attracted to her, as are other men, by her "vitality" and charm, but she seems to have little else to recommend her, and not enough character to provide a main focus for the novel.

Thus, under the guise of presenting a story without heroes, Hemingway had annihilated the fictional representations of the lovers who had wounded his pride and whom he held most responsible for the fiasco of the 1925 fiesta. But he was not writing a heroless story, for by eliminating potential heroes, he was moving inexorably toward making Jake the hero. Yet because he was consciously trying *not* to do this, he was able to present Jake's story obliquely, thereby avoiding the indulgences that often marred his presentation of protagonists in subsequent novels.

In the printed text the negative portrayals of Gerald and Duff end Book 1, completing the section that had centered on the expatriate world of the Quarter. Book 2 traces the movement of Jake and Bill away from the Quarter, toward the good life, and then back into the Gerald-Duff milieu at Pamplona where things, including Jake, fall apart.

V

Notebook III is the men-without-women notebook. Not only does it center on the friendship between Jake and Bill, but it was also written primarily during the week that Hemingway spent without his wife, Hadley, who had gone ahead to Paris. But whereas Jake's world grew calmer without Duff, Hemingway's became more frantic without Hadley as he turned again and again to the manuscript, writing multiple, but shorter, daily sessions.[31]

Jake and Bill live the good life that the count and Jake had talked about in the previous section. Bill is "the best of the lot" (I.2). Twice Hemingway made him the first-person narrator, once at the Ledoux–Kid Francis fight (which is described in the manuscript) and again at Burguete. At the fight Jake and Bill shout until they are hoarse, moved by the courage and skill of Ledoux, a veteran fighter who has lost his punch and now lives solely on courage and skill. Significantly, Hemingway does not say who won the fight; it is *how* Ledoux fights that makes him special. Like the count, he serves as a model of how to live well, and at the end of the scene Jake transfers these qualities to Bill by telling him that in his own way he is as good a man as Ledoux.

Two days later, however, Hemingway made a change that may have reduced Bill's role considerably. Originally it was Bill, not Jake, who was Catholic, the insider who would be Jake's spiritual guide in Spain. But as Hemingway was writing about their ride on the train filled with other pilgrims, he reversed their religions.[32] By making Jake the Catholic, Hemingway had given him a system of values and beliefs that was historically grounded, and as James Michener has observed, "the first essential for anyone who wishes to understand Spain [is to realize that] in every manifestation of life Spain is a Catholic country."[33] Beneath the world of the Quarter, beneath the world of *afición*, is the world of Spanish Catholicism, which retains much of its medieval form and spirit and has survived numerous periods of disillusionment like the one that followed the Great War. Though Jake may be a "rotten Catholic" (*SAR*, 97), it is not for lack of trying. In addition to attending the fiesta he also undertakes a private pilgrimage that takes him to a number of stops along the medieval pilgrimage route to the shrine of Santiago de Compostela (that is, St. James, the apostle), including Tours, Rouncevalles, Pamplona, and—after the fiesta—San Sebastian. Jake may even have intended to continue along the route to the shrine of Santiago, whose French name—St. Jacques—may account for Hemingway's choice of the name "Jake."[34] So important was Santiago to Hemingway that he later chose this name for his protagonist in *The Old Man and the Sea*.

Hemingway then described Jake, Bill, and Gerald's car ride across the Pyrenees to Pamplona, and in the following session he wrote about Gerald and Bill's bet about whether Duff and Mike would arrive on the evening train. By this time he knew enough about his story to be able to outline the rest of it on the back of the third notebook:

Chap XIII– ⎰finishes with Gerald not going
Chap XIV   ⎱Ride to Burguete⎰
           Fishing return to Pamplona
Chap XV   Duff Gerald and Mike there
           ⎱Descencajonada—when we get in ⎰

	the party at the wine shop
	Mike's first out burst
Chap XVI	Encierro, first corrida
	brings back to point where book
	starts. goes on with that night—
	the South American. the dancing place.
	Noel Murphy. Count shows up.
XVII	Duff sleeps with Niño
	de la Palma. Gerald fights
	with Niño
XVIII	Corrida Duff goes off
	with Niño. Count refuses Mike
	job. Bill goes to Paris. Mike
	talks, ⎰ goes to Saint Jean de Luz to wait
	for Duff. ⎱ Gerald talks, ⎰ goes to [Saint
	Jean de Luz] ⎰San Sebastian⎱
	afterwards Paris⎱. I go
	on down to into Spain to bring
	Duff back. Get her letter. (III.53)

Because this outline corresponds closely to what Hemingway actually wrote, it indicates that before he returned to Paris he had his story firmly in hand. On 17 August, the last day of his Spanish summer, he wrote all of chapter 14 (*SAR*, chapter 11)—the bus ride to Burguete—in one sustained session, enabling him to return to Paris comfortable in the knowledge that he had gotten Jake and Bill to the mountains, thereby setting up the next section of the story.

About this time he also chose the working title, "Fiesta," that he maintained throughout the rest of the manuscript and that still designates the British edition of this novel.

VI

Back in Paris, having discovered his hero and worked out his plot, Hemingway began to experiment more with technique. Each day he chose a method or a theme to wrestle with, in effect writing a short story daily, each with its own physics, but integrated within the larger story. This resulted in a rich inner text, easily overlooked in the printed novel but readily apparent when the novel is divided into the daily stories.[35] For instance, on four successive days from 24 to 27 August he based each day's composition upon a metaphor associated with one of the main characters: *afición* for Jake, bankruptcy for Mike, the gored and segregated steer for Gerald, and the Circe myth for Duff—all this despite his earlier intention not to use such "literary signs." Then he paid tribute to James Joyce: on 28 August he wrote Jake's nighttime monologue (considerably longer in the manuscript), and on 30 August he filled the description of the first day and night of the fiesta with allusions to the *Odyssey*. Throughout the first half of September the self-contained daily units continued: Jake's betrayal of *afición*, the fight scene, Jake's walk back to his hotel where the water wouldn't flow, the story of the peasant killed during the running of the bulls, Duff's triumphant appearance after sleeping with Guerrita (Niño's fictionalized name in the manuscript), Belmonte in the ring, Guerrita in the ring, Jake's getting drunk on the last night of the fiesta, the ride back to France, Jake's recuperation in San Sebastian, and the arrival of Duff's telegrams. Then the pace slowed dramatically for several days before Hemingway finished the novel in a final burst on 21 September.

One of his experiments, though, was ongoing and concerned the calendar for the novel. If the dates in the Paris section are taken literally (for example, "Monday, 20 June"), they correspond to 1921. But in the Burguete section this calendar no longer fits. One morning after Jake and Bill have been fishing for "[three] Ι [four]ΙΙ five Ι days," Jake asks Wilson-Harris what day it is and is told, "Wednesday, I think. Yes, quite. Wednesday. Wonderful how one loses track of the days up here in the mountains" (IV.17; *SAR*, 127). Because they arrived on Monday and have been fishing at least three days, it cannot be Wednesday, yet Hemingway has gone out of his way to point out this discrepancy. The reason for this is made clear several chapters later: "At noon of Sunday the sixth of July the fiesta exploded" (IV.49; *SAR*, 152). Hemingway had adopted a different calendar for the Burguete-Pamplona section of the novel, one that corresponds to 1924, when both the fishing and the fiesta were wonderful. The 1925 fiesta was supposed to renew the physical and spiritual emotions of the 1924 fiesta, but day by day Hemingway was painfully aware of the differences between the fiestas, and it was this difference that he tried to put into his novel. He did this in two ways: by basing the Burguete section on the successful 1924 fishing trip, instead of the one in 1925 when logging had silted the streams and killed the fish; and by calling to mind the days of the 1924 fiesta, thereby creating a dual perspective that intensifies the fictionalized account of the 1925 fiesta. In this way, although he did not write about the 1924 fiesta, he made its presence felt. This is a good example of what he meant when he said: "If a writer of prose knows enough about what he is writing about he may omit things that he knows and the reader, if the writer is writing truly enough, will have a feeling of those things as strongly as though the writer had stated them. The dignity of movement of an ice-berg is due to only one-eighth of it being above water."[36]

Another of the issues Hemingway had been trying to answer

since the opening story is whether what happened at Pamplona was the result of the individuals involved or of the fiesta. In the fifth notebook, at the end of the description of the opening of the fiesta, he wrote: "The fiesta made every one a little crazy certainly but it had the effect of speeding up the natural tendencies through this insistence on the unimportance of consequences. Still I think it is only incidental to the story. If it had not been the fiesta it would have been something else" (V.3). This must have been a troubling conclusion for Hemingway to come to, for the difference between Hem's endangering of Niño and Jake's endangering of Pedro Romero is one of degree, not of kind.

At the end of August Hemingway caught up to the material from the opening story, but he neither inserted nor rewrote any of it, as he was still planning to begin the novel *in medias res*. Instead he simply referred to events already described and went on with the story: "It was when Bill and I went over to the hotel to get the ⌐ wine bag and the ⌐ glasses that we met Nino [*sic*] de la Palma that I started in this story telling about" (V.10). Eight pages later, having changed Niño's name, he wrote: "The next day Guerrita did not fight. . . . It was that day that the [United States senator] ⌐ ambassador ⌐ and his party came into town [and it was that evening that Guerrita was at the table with us. In the evening Mike started to curse Gerald]" (V.18). And on the following page he wrote: "We ate . . . fairly late and it was then I had my talk with Quintana and that Guerrita came over and talked with us. After dinner the town was fuller than it had ever been" (V.19). Sometime later, probably after he had begun to revise the novel and had decided against the *in medias res* beginning, Hemingway inserted several editorial instructions: "Insert ambassador and party" (V.18); "Put in dinner with Nino [*sic*]—drunk scene etc."; and "Insert Quintana talk. Insert Guerrita party at cafe [*sic*]" (V.19). Eventually Hemingway did insert several scenes from the opening story: Hem's first meeting with Niño (*SAR*, 162–64); Hem and Quintana's decision not to give Niño the invitation from the ambassador (*SAR*, 171–72); and the climactic scene in the café (*SAR*, 172–78). But he left out Mrs. Carleton, whose narrative function had been appropriated by Brett.

The manuscript also contains important clues for reading the end of the novel, which has troubled many readers who find themselves unsure whether Brett is at her best or worst, or whether Jake has learned anything, and if he has, why he drinks so much in the final scenes. In the last half of the novel Hemingway had become increasingly cryptic, having provided what he felt were sufficient clues for the reader to infer what the characters must have been thinking and feeling. However, he may have carried the compression too far when he deleted a 633-word passage that helps to make sense of the ending by providing a key to Jake's erratic behavior in Madrid. In that passage Jake reacts to the two telegrams from Duff. Her call for help destroys his fragile new beginning at San Sebastian, where he had gone to resume his pilgrimage and get "all straightened inside again" (VI.36). From this point to the end of the novel his emotions will vacillate wildly, sometimes from one line to the next. Jake is a man on the edge, like Nick in "Big Two-Hearted River," but unlike Nick, he cannot put off fishing the swamp for another day. So to protect himself he pretends to be "perfectly hard about it," reassuring himself that he "could have a good time. I had been having a good time for two days. I would get this Madrid thing over with. There was no use belly aching about it. That was not the way 'good people' acted" (VI.41–42). But the phrase "good people" suddenly triggers a tirade that starts with Braddocks ("that ass [who had] started the good people phrase") and goes on to include the aristocracy and finally his injury: "Besides you learned a lot about a woman by not sleeping with her. I ought to be glad I was the way I was. Oh yes very glad. Glad as hell. Nothing like recognizing your advantages. I went in to lunch" (VI.42–43). His reaction suggests just how difficult it is going to be for him to maintain his controlled, hard-boiled pose.

In the manuscript Jake sleeps well on the Sud Express to Madrid, but when Hemingway revised the passage he decided that if Jake were thoroughly upset, he would be unable to sleep. This one change, as Frederic Svoboda has pointed out, allowed him to eliminate the entire passage about Jake's response to Duff's telegrams, as Jake's inner state can be inferred from his sleepless night.[37] However, in eliminating the passage Hemingway also eliminated information that explains Jake's otherwise baffling behavior in the closing scenes of the novel.

For instance, when Jake arrives at the Hotel Montana, his conversation with the fat woman who apparently owns the *pension* is sarcastic and cynical. But the moment he sees Duff, he feels "all aching inside" (VI.45). Duff tells him, "I knew you would come," and then draws him back within her influence, first by kissing him "very suddenly and fiercely" and then by getting him to admit that he still loves her (VI.45–46). However, even as Jake confesses, "I love you. But I try so damn hard not to," he observes, "She was thinking of something else" (VI.46). Here he was, filled with pain, still in love with her, once again vulnerable despite his resolve not to be, and she is not even listening as he confesses his love. *This* may have been the moment she lost her control over him. Holding her, he comments, "She felt so small. I had always thought of us as about the same size" (VI.46). But though he pities her, he still feels hurt and angry. Throughout the final scenes flashes of anger and sarcasm break through his "good people" pose as she continually talks about her relationship with Guerrita, in spite of her protest that she "never [wants to] talk about it" (VI.47; SAR, 242). Despite her pain—or perhaps because of it—she glows with self-satisfaction at having done the right thing in breaking off with the bullfighter, and in her glowing she is oblivious to what Jake is feeling.

But it is not at all certain that she has done something noble. Perhaps she has simply made a virtue of necessity. Duff and Guerrita belong to different worlds and different generations. Though she could run away with him, she could never have stayed with him, regardless of her claim: "You know I'd have lived with him if I hadnt [sic] seen it was bad for him" (VI.47; SAR, 243). But because she was the one who sent him away, she can indulge in the illusion that she has nobly saved him from ruin. The fact is, however, that she cannot know for sure what effect she may have had on his career or his life, any more than Jake can know the ultimate effect of his bringing the two of them together.[38]

Jake's attempt to maintain his "good people" pose accounts for their excessive civility in the bar at the Palace Hotel. But as Duff continues to talk about Guerrita, other emotions arise. After leaning over the bar to sip her martini in order to steady her hand enough to pick up her drink, she tells him, "He was born in [1905] nineteen five. I was in school in Paris then. Think of that." Jake responds, "Any thing you want me to think about it?" After Duff's rebuke, "Dont [sic] be an ass," the civility returns, and they have another drink, but once again Duff talks about Guerrita (VI.49; SAR, 244). As Hemingway concludes the final completed notebook, Duff announces how "damned good" she feels for "deciding not to be a bitch" (VI.50; SAR, 245); when, however, she pontificates that being decent is "sort of what we have instead of God," Jake feels obliged to comment, "God's not too bad," to which Duff, not surprisingly, responds, "He never worked very well with me" (VI.53; SAR, 245).

They have a third martini before lunching at Botin's, where Jake has a huge meal and at least four bottles of wine, in marked contrast to the way he had been living in San Sebastian. At one point early in his retreat he had observed, "It was pleasant to be drinking slowly and tastingly" (VI.31; SAR, 232). Now he tries to adopt the same stance— "I'm not getting drunk. . . . I'm just drinking a little wine" (VI.54–55; SAR, 246)—but the quantity and the rapidity with which he drinks suggest that he is seeking to anesthetize his pain while outwardly trying to maintain his disciplined pose. Shortly before they leave the restaurant, his real feelings flash when Duff says, "Dont [sic] get drunk Jake. . . . You don't have to," to which he responds, "How do you know?" (VI.54; *SAR*, 246).

In the final scene Jake's mood again vacillates as he settles back in the taxi and puts his arm around Duff. However, when she leans against him and says, "We could have had such a damned good time together," an advance that at any other time would have drawn Jake into intimate conversation, Jake seems able for the first time to resist the old illusion: " 'Yes,' I said. 'It's nice as hell to think so' " (changed in revision to "Isn't it pretty to think so?") (VI.55; *SAR*, 247).

In this final scene there is the suggestion, symbolized by the policeman with the raised baton interposed between Duff's final statement and Jake's answer, that this time he is able to maintain control over his emotional response. If this is so, the ending offers promise for Jake, that physically and psychologically injured character who, while searching for a faith that will enable him to live his life, has unforgivably betrayed the code of perhaps his most promising hope because of his desperate love of a woman not worth loving. But even if the final scene is hopeful, it represents only a first step. Jake has achieved a transforming awareness, but he has yet to become transformed. That change, if it is to come, will be won slowly, day by day, as the sun rises and sets.

Beneath the last line Hemingway centered the words "The End" and dated it "Paris Sept 21, 1925" (VI.55).

VII

Hemingway had written the novel in eight and a half weeks, and he was exhausted. "Tired as hell inside," he was, like Jake, drinking a great deal and needed to get away.[39] The following weekend he went to Chartres to unwind, but he could not stop. Instead he wrote a foreword to his novel, which during the previous week he had decided to call "The Lost Generation," a phrase that ultimately became the book's epigraph.[40] In this foreword he explains that he got the title from Gertrude Stein. One day, when a young, capable mechanic fixed her car, Stein had expressed surprise because she thought that World War I had rendered a whole generation incapable of doing anything well. The garage owner told her that those too young to have fought in the war were fine; rather, "it is the ones between twenty two and thirty that are no good. C'est un generation [sic] perdu" (202c).[41] It is within this "lost generation" that Hemingway placed himself:

This is about something that is already finished. For whatever is going to happen to the generation of which I am a part has already happened. . . . There will be more entanglements, there will be more complications, there will be successes and failures. . . . [A few will learn to live perhaps. One or two may learn to write or to paint. . . .] But none of it will matter particularly to this generation because to them the things that are given to people to happen have already happened. (202c)

This foreword belies Hemingway's later statement that the Gertrude Stein epigraph was "splendid bombast," and it indicates that he took the "lost generation" phrase seriously.[42] But perhaps because he did not want to be indebted to Stein, Hemingway decided against using it as his title. He then considered other titles: "The Sun Also Rises," "Rivers to the Sea," "Two Lie Together," and "The Old Leaven" (202c). The fact that all of these quotations come from the Bible suggests that Hemingway intended to use his title to point to the religious dimensions of this apparently secular novel.

After the weekend in Chartres Hemingway put aside the manuscript for several months. Then in late November or early December he started to revise it. Three times he tried to rework the original opening—twice as a third-person narration (195, 197, 197a)[43]—but the task of reconciling the details of the opening story with those of the novel was proving difficult, and he eventually decided to begin instead with the portrait of Duff.

This change from *in medias res* to straight chronology altered the novel in a fundamental way. Hemingway had written the manuscript assuming that he did not have to explain things, as the reader already knew about Pamplona. But eliminating the beginning story removed the referent for much that followed. In effect Hemingway had created a different kind of *in medias res*, one that starts not in the middle of the plot, but in the middle of the text. This transformed the text into an impressive—if unplanned-for—example of his iceberg theory of writing. The year before he had done the same thing with "Indian Camp" when he cut the beginning because it explained too much about young Nick Adams.[44] Without the opening scene in Pamplona, the reader has to sense the importance of lines that have lost their context, to sense more than he knows, which is possible because the text appropriates and internalizes the significance of the opening material while omitting the story itself. The omission of this story also creates a compelling sense of inevitability about events in the novel, an inextricable movement toward *something*. The reader experiences the relentless working out of events already set in motion long before the fiesta. Eliminating the opening story transformed the novel into a tragedy, and the Paris section, originally intended as background to help the reader "understand what happened in Pamplona," now sets the tragic forces into motion.

Removing the opening story was the only major structural change Hemingway made while he was revising the manuscript. He did not add a single scene and cut only two (the Ledoux–Kid Francis fight and an alpine story Jake tells at Burguete). Yet he claimed that of all his books this one was the toughest to revise. Perhaps the explanation lies in the pressure he felt to produce something first-rate, but more probably it had to do with the conditions under which he revised the novel.

On 12 December he and his family arrived in Schruns, Austria. For the next three weeks he was sick, spending much of his time in bed reading and writing letters. More significantly, however, his emotional life was in turmoil. He was falling in love with Pauline Pfeiffer, who arrived for the holidays, and his relationship with Hadley was deteriorating.

In addition he was worried about relations with his publisher. On 8 December, against the advice of his wife—but with the approval of Pauline—he had sent *The Torrents of Spring*, his satire of Sherwood Anderson, to Boni and Liveright, with whom he had a three-book contract. He knew that they had little choice but to turn down a book that attacked their most successful author, and he was aware that their rejection would release him from his contract. Scribner's, Knopf, and Harcourt, Brace all had expressed interest in publishing his work. On 30 December he learned that the book had been rejected. Free to seek another publisher, he eventually decided to go to New York to take care of things personally, arriving on 9 February. There he met with Horace Liveright to terminate their contract and then with Max Perkins of Scribner's (the beginning of a lifelong friendship), to whom he showed the first half of his revised novel.

Hemingway was something of a celebrity in New York because of the publication of *In Our Time* the previous fall, and he enjoyed the attention. Staying longer than intended, he did not leave until about 20 February, arriving in France eight days later. Before returning to Schruns, however, he met Pauline Pfeiffer in Paris, where they apparently consummated their relationship, an event that, according to *A Moveable Feast*, consumed him with guilt and remorse.[45]

Back in Austria, he returned to his novel. A few days later Dos Passos and the Gerald Murphys arrived for a week of skiing. Somehow, despite the interruptions, he was able to tell Max Perkins on 10 March that he had "only five more chapters to do over and would then like to have another look through it before sending the Ms. over."[46] By 25 March—according to the date he listed on the cover of the setting copy that he sent to Scribner's—he had finished the revision. He then returned to Paris where he had the novel retyped professionally, using two typists to speed up the process, one typing through what became chapter 8 in the published text, the other typing the remainder. On 24 April he sent the completed typescript to Perkins.

These biographical details suggest that the time Hemingway actually spent revising the manuscript was far less than he later intimated. Nor, apparently, was he as close to his material as he claimed to be, for a number of inconsistencies in the manuscript—such as impossible time sequences or Jake's telling about events he could not possibly have witnessed—survived the revision.[47] Whatever the reason—marital problems, his concern about publishers, or an interrupted writing schedule—the revision lacks the detailed concentration that Hemingway later claimed to have brought to the task. If it is true that revising *The Sun Also Rises* was the most difficult job of writing he ever did, it was so primarily because of problems outside the text. Despite statements to the contrary—perhaps intended to stress the crafted nature of what appeared to many to be a roman à clef—Hemingway learned how to write a novel by writing the manuscript, not by revising it.

He also refused to show the manuscript to Scott Fitzgerald until he had sent it off to Scribner's. He wanted no help from the competition, especially Fitzgerald, who the previous fall had convinced Hemingway to cut the opening of "Fifty Grand," a decision Hemingway regretted the rest of his life (though the fact that he never restored the cut despite ample opportunity to do so suggests that what he really regretted was that Fitzgerald may have been right).[48] When Fitzgerald finally did read the novel, he objected vehemently to the "elephantine facetiousness" of the opening and urged Hemingway to cut it. "And my advice," he concluded, "is not to do it by mere pareing [sic] but to take out the worst of the *scenes*."[49] Once again Hemingway had to admit that Fitzgerald was right.

On 5 June, creating the impression that cutting the opening was his own idea, he told Maxwell Perkins: "I believe that, in the proofs, I will start the book at what is now page 16 in the Mss [sic]. There is nothing in those first sixteen pages that does not come out, or is explained, or re-stated in the rest of the book—or is unnecessary to state. I think it will move much faster from the start that way. Scott agrees with me."[50] However, perhaps to save face or to retain his sense of editorial control over the text, he chose to begin not where Fitzgerald had suggested—at the beginning of what is now chapter 3 as Jake is sitting on the terrace of the Café Napolitain—but rather where he himself had first felt in control of the story: with the portrait of Cohn that immediately followed the transitional material. As a result, when *The Sun Also Rises* was published in October 1926, it lacked both the opening story and the material written during the transitional period, but though the early stages of the novel are absent from the published text, they have been preserved in the manuscript, enabling us to retrace the steps Hemingway took on his way to his first novel.

Hemingway had written a tightly constructed, multileveled, and masterfully understated novel. It was a remarkable achievement, especially for a first novel. He had started with actual people who came with fully equipped personalities. This helped him create complex yet consistent characters, because what he wrote in the opening story had to ring true with what he knew; and later it helped him project a fiction that was as "true" as anything he had taken from actuality. He had good material to work with: an exotic festival, a fascinating mix of characters, a volatile emotional situation, and his own painful and intense emotions. He wrote with skill and exuberance, the young artist realizing his potential, playing with form and technique day by day. He took chances. He daringly left things out as he wrote. He deleted explanatory and speculative passages. He refused to interpret for the reader, presenting scenes without comment, offering minimal descriptions, and pointing to embedded symbols and clues only obscurely. And in revision he transformed the novel into a tragedy. By the time he was done, Hemingway emerged with a large, complex but tightly compressed story that more than sixty years after its publication we are still learning how to read.

Notes

1. Plimpton, "Interview with Hemingway," *Hemingway and His Critics*, 34.
2. Recently there have been a number of Hemingway biographies dealing with this material. See especially *The Young Hemingway*, Reynolds's thoroughly researched and lively written account of Hemingway's formative years and the world he lived in. Still useful is Baker's *Hemingway*, though the section on the composition of *The Sun Also Rises* is unfortunately marred by inaccuracies. Meyers's *Hemingway* briefly treats the story of the composition. Lynn's *Hemingway* offers an "explanation" of what happened at Pamplona that both oversimplifies and misrepresents the situation. Reynolds's *The Sun Also Rises: A Novel of the Twenties* is a wonderful introduction to the novel and its milieu. See also Svoboda's *Hemingway and The Sun Also Rises* and the special *Sun Also Rises* issue of *Hemingway Review* 6 (Fall 1986).
3. MacLeish, quoted in Introduction to Hemingway, *Selected Letters* (hereafter *SL*), xx.
4. Reynolds, *Hemingway's Reading*, 3.
5. To William B. Smith, Jr., 6 December 1924, *SL*, 136; to Dr. C. E. Hemingway, 7 November 1923, *SL*, 100; to Howell Jenkins, 9 November 1924, *SL*, 131; and to Ezra Pound, 19 July 1924, *SL*, 119.

6. To William D. Horne, 17–18 July 1923, *SL*, 88.

7. Chink Dorman-Smith, an Irish officer in the British army, had been a close friend since the war. John Dos Passos and Hemingway also met during the war and later became friends in Paris. Donald Ogden Stewart was a humorist and writer whose wit stimulated and challenged Hemingway. Bill Bird ran the continental branch of the Consolidated Press and published Hemingway's slim book of experimental prose, *in our time* (1924). George O'Neil was the teenaged son of a minor American poet. Sally Bird, wife of Bill Bird, was the only member of the group who disliked the bullfights; she did not, however, let this interfere with her enjoying the rest of the fiesta.

8. To Pound, 19 July 1924, *SL*, 119.

9. St. John, "Interview with Stewart," 191.

10. "Somehow I don't care about writing a novel and I like to write short stories and I like to work at the bull fight book" (to Maxwell Perkins, 15 April 1925, *SL*, 156). "I got a commission to write a book on bull fighting with Flechtheim," (to John Dos Passos, 22 April 1925, *SL*, 158). "I get something out of bulls and the men that fight them, I don't know what. Anyhow I've got it all, or a big part of it, into the next book" (to Sherwood Anderson, 23 May 1925, *SL*, 162).

11. Hemingway later claimed that he began the manuscript on his twenty-sixth birthday, 21 July 1925. He wrote the story on thirty-two looseleaf pages and then continued in a notebook dated 23 July.

12. Hemingway typically ended one session by setting up the next, sometimes even writing the first sentence of the following scene. He told George Plimpton, "You write until you come to a place where you still have your juice and know what will happen next and you stop and try to live through until the next day when you hit it again" ("Interview with Hemingway," *Hemingway and His Critics*, 22).

13. This title is crossed out, and squeezed in underneath is the two-line title "Fiesta / A Novel." However, this change was made with blue ink, which Hemingway did not begin using until 11 August.

14. Previously unpublished material in this essay is copyright 1989 by the Ernest Hemingway Foundation and is printed by permission. Parenthetical numbers refer to manuscript items in the Hemingway Collection at the John F. Kennedy Presidential Library in Boston. The thirty-two pages of the opening story constitute item 193; the seven 100-page notebooks containing the rest of the manuscript are designated item 194. Each notebook has an additional number, except the last, which is numbered as though it were a continuation of Notebook VI. Page numbers are based on photocopies, each photocopy containing two notebook pages—the verso and recto of an open notebook page. Thus, IV.25 refers to two pages halfway through Notebook IV. Item 202c refers to the foreword to "The Lost Generation: A Novel" that Hemingway wrote a week after finishing the manuscript. Items 195, 197, and 197a refer to three typescript revisions of the "Fiesta" manuscript, written at the end of November or the beginning of December 1925.

15. In the published novel all that remains of Mrs. Carleton is one unnamed reference; she is the American woman Jake refers to who collects bullfighters (*SAR*, 172).

16. That is, Duff Twysden, Donald Ogden Stewart, and Pat Guthrie, prototypes for Brett Ashley, Bill Gorton, and Mike Campbell; Bill Smith and Hadley Hemingway appear as characters only in the opening story.

17. Up and down arrows indicate added material.

18. Reynolds, "False Dawn," 185.

19. At first glance it would appear that there are six missing pages, the last unbound page having been designated 31, but this is not the case. When Hemingway returned to this opening material in Notebook V, he was still planning to begin *in medias res*, so he did not insert any of the opening story at that time. Later, however, he made the notation "Put in dinner with Nino [*sic*]—drunk scene etc" (V.19). If there were six missing manuscript pages, that material should have appeared in the revised novel immediately after the insertion of the opening story in chapters 15 and 16 of the published text (pp. 162–78). However, there is no evidence of any missing material; that is, in the published text, immediately following what had been the end of the opening story is the line that in the manuscript follows the directive "Put in dinner with Nino [*sic*]."

20. Angle brackets indicate deleted material. Roman numerals indicate notebook numbers (see note 14). The manuscript actually reads, "[Don] ↑Bill↓ was the best of the lot." However, because this change was made in blue ink, which Hemingway did not begin using until 11 August, it refers to the character "Bill Gorton," not to Bill Smith, and it does not indicate Hemingway's first use of a fictionalized name in the manuscript.

21. In a letter written shortly after the publication of *The Sun Also Rises* Hemingway told Maxwell Perkins that "Brett Ashley is a real person" and that "the only stuff in the book that was not imaginary" is "the Brett biography," the original of which he wrote during these two sessions (*SL*, 224).

22. Later in the manuscript Bill says that "when Duff took Mike up he was using dope or something. She cured him" (V.46).

23. About this time Hemingway decided to eliminate two characters: Bill Smith and Hadley Hemingway, the narrator's wife. Also about this time he decided upon the narrator's war wound. The idea of writing about a sexually maimed war veteran goes back at least to 1921, and he had discussed the idea with Fitzgerald just two months earlier. (I am grateful to Michael Reynolds for this information.) But the psychological impact may have come in part from his own situation. Apparently Hemingway wanted to sleep with Duff Twysden, but out of consideration for Hadley she refused. If this is so, then his situation paralleled that of Jake, who also felt a sexual desire that he could not fulfill. It may be that when Hemingway dropped Hadley from the story, he retained the sexual restriction that marriage to her represented. In a sense she became the wound. As Fitzgerald aptly observed, Jake "isn't *like an impotent man. He's like a man in a sort of moral chastity belt*" (to Hemingway, June 1926, *Correspondence of Fitzgerald*, 196, emphasis his).

24. See note 20.

25. I take it that here and in the following two paragraphs we are hearing Hemingway's voice rather than Jake's. However, whether Hemingway intended these paragraphs as part of the story or as commentary upon it, they all but certainly express his concerns about the task he had undertaken.

26. Hemingway, *The Sun Also Rises*, 228, 241.

27. Hemingway, *A Moveable Feast*, 12.

28. Balassi, "The Writing of the Manuscript of *The Sun Also Rises*," 65.

29. Hemingway, *A Moveable Feast*, 13.

30. *SAR* numbers refer to pages in the published edition of *The Sun Also Rises*.

31. He told Howell Jenkins that "he was working harder than he had ever worked in his life, often until three or four in the morning. Then he would fall

asleep, his head feeling like a frozen cabbage, only to jump awake again a few hours later, with the words already stringing themselves into sentences, clamoring to be set down" (Baker, *Hemingway*, 199).

32. After the man from Montana, referring to Jake and Bill's inability to get seated for lunch on the train of Lourdes-bound pilgrims, says, "It's a pity you boys ain't Catholics. You could eat in there all right," the manuscript reads, " 'I am,' said Bill. 'That's the trouble.' " Then Hemingway changed his mind and made Jake the Catholic so that by the next paragraph it is Bill who is saying, "When do us Protestants get a chance to eat, Father?" (III.18; *SAR*, 87–88).

33. Michener, *Iberia*, 44.

34. See Stoneback, "From the rue Saint-Jacques to the Pass of Roland to the 'Unfinished Church on the Edge of the Cliff.' "

35. See Balassi, "The Writing of the Manuscript of *The Sun Also Rises*," 73–78. This chart can be used to subdivide the Scribner's text and follow the session-by-session development of the novel.

36. Hemingway, *Death in the Afternoon*, 192.

37. Svoboda, *Hemingway and The Sun Also Rises*, 84–86.

38. In real life Niño was seriously gored not long after this. He lost his nerve and never fulfilled his potential. He spent his last years as a drunkard. One wonders, as Hemingway must have, what effect the 1925 fiesta and Hemingway's crowd had on him. See Adams, "The Sun Also Sets"; see also Hemingway, *Death in the Afternoon*, 87–90.

39. To Ernest Walsh, ca. 15 September 1925, *SL*, 169. (Baker's dating of this letter appears to be inaccurate; in it Hemingway refers to his novel as "finished," so the letter was apparently written after 21 September.)

40. In that foreword Hemingway says, "I did not hear this story [about the lost generation] until after I had written this book" (202c). If this is true, he must have heard the story and chosen his new title during the previous week.

41. See note 14 for an explanation of parenthetical numbers.

42. To Maxwell Perkins, 19 November 1926, *SL*, 229.

43. See note 14 for an explanation of parenthetical numbers.

44. The deleted beginning of "Indian Camp" is printed as "Three Shots" in *The Nick Adams Stories*, 3–5.

45. Hemingway, *A Moveable Feast*, 208.

46. To Maxwell Perkins, 10 March 1926, *SL*, 197.

47. For instance, Jake describes the funeral of Vicente Girones even though Jake left Pamplona before the funeral took place. Earlier in the book Hemingway forgot that the day Jake, Bill, and Gerald travel from Bayonne to Pamplona is a Sunday; businesses are open and the cathedral is nearly empty.

48. See Beegel, " 'Mutilated by Scott Fitzgerald?' "

49. To Hemingway, June 1926, *Correspondence of Fitzgerald*, 195.

50. *SL*, 208.

Works Cited

Adams, Sam. "The Sun Also Sets." In *Hemingway and The Sun Set*, edited by Bertram D. Sarason, 212–21. Washington, D.C.: NCR Microcard Editions, 1972.

Baker, Carlos. *Ernest Hemingway: A Life Story*. New York: Charles Scribner's Sons, 1968.

Balassi, William. "The Writing of the Manuscript of *The Sun Also Rises*, with a Chart of Its Session-by-Session Development." *Hemingway Review* 6 (Fall 1986): 65–78.

Beegel, Susan F. " 'Mutilated by Scott Fitzgerald?': The Revision of Hemingway's 'Fifty Grand.' " In *Hemingway's Craft of Omission: Four Manuscript Examples*, 13–30. Ann Arbor: UMI Research Press, 1988.

Fitzgerald, F. Scott. Letter to Ernest Hemingway. In *The Correspondence of F. Scott Fitzgerald*, edited by Matthew J. Bruccoli and Margaret M. Duggan, 193–96. New York: Random House, 1980. Reprinted in Svoboda, *Hemingway and The Sun Also Rises*, 137–40.

Hemingway, Ernest. *Death in the Afternoon*. New York: Charles Scribner's Sons, 1932.

———. *Ernest Hemingway: Selected Letters, 1917–1961*. Edited by Carlos Baker. New York: Charles Scribner's Sons, 1981.

———. "Fiesta" [draft of *The Sun Also Rises*]. 1925. Manuscript. Items 193–94, Hemingway Collection, John F. Kennedy Presidential Library, Boston.

———. "The Lost Generation." 1925. Manuscript. Item 202c, Hemingway Collection, John F. Kennedy Presidential Library, Boston.

———. *A Moveable Feast*. New York: Charles Scribner's Sons, 1964.

———. *The Nick Adams Stories*. Edited by Philip Young. New York: Charles Scribner's Sons, 1972.

———. "The Sun Also Rises" [fragments of draft]. 1925. Typescript. Items 195, 197, 197a, Hemingway Collection, John F. Kennedy Presidential Library, Boston.

———. *The Sun Also Rises*. New York: Charles Scribner's Sons, 1926.

———. "Three Shots." In *The Nick Adams Stories*, edited by Philip Young, 3–5. New York: Charles Scribner's Sons, 1972.

Hemingway Review 6 (Fall 1986). Special issue for the sixtieth anniversary of the publication of *The Sun Also Rises*.

Lynn, Kenneth S. *Hemingway*. New York: Simon & Schuster, 1987.

Meyers, Jeffrey. *Hemingway: A Biography*. New York: Harper & Row, 1985.

Michener, James. *Iberia: Spanish Travels and Reflections*. New York: Random House, 1968.

Plimpton, George. "An Interview with Ernest Hemingway." *Paris Review* 18 (Spring 1958): 61–82. Reprinted in *Hemingway and His Critics*, edited by Carlos Baker, 19–37. New York: Hill & Wang, 1961.

Reynolds, Michael. "False Dawn: *The Sun Also Rises* Manuscript." In *A Fair Day in the Affections: Literary Essays in Honor of Robert B. White, Jr.*, edited by Jack D. Durant and M. Thomas Hester, 171–86. Raleigh, N.C.: Winston Press, 1980. Reprinted in *Hemingway: A Revaluation*, edited by Donald R. Noble, 115–34. Troy, N.Y.: Whitson Publishing Co., 1983.

———. *Hemingway's Reading, 1910–1940*. Princeton: Princeton University Press, 1981.

———. *The Sun Also Rises: A Novel of the Twenties*. Boston: Twayne Publishers, 1988.

_____. *The Young Hemingway*. New York: Basil Blackwell, 1986.

St. John, Donald. "Interview with Donald Ogden Stewart." In *Hemingway and The Sun Set*, edited by Bertram D. Sarason, 189–206. Washington, D.C.: NCR Microcard Editions, 1972.

Stoneback, H. R. "From the rue Saint-Jacques to the Pass of Roland to the 'Unfinished Church on the Edge of the Cliff.'" *Hemingway Review* 6 (Fall 1986): 2–29.

Svoboda, Frederic J. *Hemingway and The Sun Also Rises: The Crafting of a Style*. Lawrence: University Press of Kansas, 1983.

SALLY WOLFF AND DAVID MINTER

A "Matchless Time": Faulkner and the
Writing of *The Sound and the Fury*

I

William Faulkner began writing *The Sound and the Fury*, his first great novel, in 1928, during a time of upheaval in his professional and personal life. In the decade preceding the dark period from which *The Sound and the Fury* emerged, he had launched his career as a writer of poetry. His first published poem, "L'Après-Midi d'un Faune," appeared in the *New Republic* in 1919. Over the next few years he completed *Vision in Spring*, which in 1984 became the sixth of his handmade books to be published since his death in 1962, and published "Portrait" (1922) and a few other poems in the *Double Dealer*. He also wrote a play entitled *The Marionettes*, another of the handmade books published since his death. On 15 December 1924 the Four Seas Company of Boston published his first book of poetry, *The Marble Faun*. Within five years' time, Faulkner had not only begun his career as a fiction writer but had published perhaps his finest novel. The events surrounding the composition of *The Sound and the Fury* proved to be among the most trying of the writer's life, and yet he always described the act of writing this novel as an experience unparalleled in exhilaration, joy, and surprise.

In Faulkner's early poetry, themes and motifs appear that reemerge significantly in later novels and stories. Both *The Marble Faun* and *The Marionettes* revolve around the figure of the unattainable woman. In a poem called "A Dead Dancer" the themes of love, betrayal, and death intermingle. As Judith Sensibar has noted, women in this poem represent "a bitter mix of impossible evil and equally impossible good."[1] Beginning in 1925, however, during the stay in New Orleans when he met and became friends with Sherwood Anderson, Faulkner began to turn toward fiction, first in a series of prose sketches, later published as the *New Orleans Sketches* (1957/1968), and then in a novel called *Soldiers' Pay* (1926). With help from Anderson, who put in a good word for Faulkner with his publisher, Boni and Liveright, *Soldiers' Pay* was published shortly after Faulkner finished it, by which time he was at work on his second novel, *Mosquitoes* (1927), which also grew out of his New Orleans experience. It too was published by Boni and Liveright. Later, looking back on this early period as one of mounting confidence, Faulkner recalled thinking that "writing novels is easy."[2]

On the whole, Faulkner's first two novels were well received. Reviewers described both of them as promising, particularly *Soldiers' Pay*, and predicted further artistic development. Faulkner too felt confident. Writing to Horace Liveright in October 1927, he announced the near completion of his third novel, *Flags in the Dust*, in exuberant terms. "At last and certainly," he wrote, "as El Orens' sheik said, I have written THE book, of which those other things were but foals. I believed it is the damdest [sic] best book you'll look at this year, and any other publisher."[3] Assuming that the manuscript would be accepted and published, Faulkner added a plea that Boni and Liveright stop making unauthorized changes in the manuscripts: "smooth the printer's fur, cajole him, some way. He's been punctuating my stuff to death; giving me gratis quotation marks and premiums of commas that I dont need."[4]

Just over a month later, in a letter dated 25 November 1927, Liveright wrote to Faulkner bluntly rejecting *Flags in the Dust*: "It is with sorrow in my heart," he wrote, "that I write to tell you that three of us have read Flags in the Dust and don't believe that Boni and Liveright should publish it. Furthermore, as a firm deeply interested in your work, we don't believe you should offer it for publication." The book, Liveright asserted, was so "diffuse and non-integral," lacking in "plot, dimension and projection," as to suggest that Faulkner did not even "have any story to tell." Embedded in Liveright's criticism was a view of Faulkner's development that directly challenged Faulkner's own. *Soldiers' Pay*, Liveright said, "was a very fine book and should have done better"; *Mosquitoes* showed little spiritual growth and no improvement in writing; and *Flags in the Dust* was not fit for publication.[5]

Faulkner's initial response to Liveright's letter came quickly. In a letter dated 30 November he veiled his shock and disappointment behind a show of confidence and indifference: "It's too bad you dont like Flags in the Dust. Unless you are holding it against that $200.00 you advanced me in the summer, I'd like for you to fire it on back to me, as I shall try it on someone else. I still believe it is the book which will make my name for me as a writer."[6] In fact, however, as weeks stretched into months and Faulkner's efforts to revise *Flags in the Dust* became frustrated and confused, his disappointment deepened. The following February he wrote Liveright a second time, in terms that reflect the confusion in which he was moving. "I have a belly full of writing, now," he said, "since you folks in the publishing business claim that a book like that last one I sent you is blah. I think now that I'll sell my typewriter and go to work." Even if he decided to "light in and bang you out a book to suit you," he added, he would not write anything "as youngly glamorous as 'Soldiers' Pay' nor as trashily smart as 'Mosquitoes.' "[7]

Liveright's rejection of *Flags in the Dust* initiated one of the darkest periods in Faulkner's life. In *Flags in the Dust* he had first conceived the imaginary kingdom, Yoknapatawpha County, that would later provide the setting of his greatest fiction. But even at the time it gave Faulkner a sense of great discovery that ill prepared him for criticism, let alone total rejection. In response to disappointment, so deep as to resemble grief, Faulkner reacted to having his discovery rejected by turning inward, in a move that would change his career, as we see in *The Sound and the Fury*, his first great experimental novel. Several years later he continued to describe the impact of Liveright's rejection in terms that are charged with emotion. He had felt so "shocked," he said, that he responded with "blind protest," with "consternation and despair, like a parent who is told that its child is a thief or an idiot or a leper." Yet despite the darkness initiated by rejection and self-doubt, fed by his own mixed and even tortured response, Faulkner clung to the "stubborn and fading hope" of salvaging his career, first by trying to revise *Flags in the Dust* and then by beginning a new novel.[8]

In a letter to his favorite aunt, Aunt Alabama (Mrs. Walter B. McLean), probably written in the spring of 1928, Faulkner described the difficult and confusing process of revision: "I have been trying to get the mss. in some sort of intelligible shape to send to you. . . . Every day or so I burn some of it up and rewrite it, and at present it is almost incoherent. So much so that I've got a little weary of it and think I shall put it away for a while and forget about it."[9] Wanting to be free of it but still hoping to find someone who would publish it, he decided to send the manuscript to Ben Wasson, a friend from Mississippi who was working in New York at the American Play Company. Wasson knew something about publishing circles, he admired Faulkner, and he was willing to help. Later Wasson reported that he tried about ten publishers before Hal Smith at Harcourt, Brace and Company persuaded Alfred Harcourt to publish *Flags in the Dust*, provided it was cut substantially. Later still, Wasson performed that task, without Faulkner's participation. Published in 1929 as *Sartoris*, the novel focuses on the Sartoris family and deletes large sections of material about the Snopes family and the Benbow family that were not restored until 1973, when Random House published *Flags in the Dust*. In the process some of the fullness that marked Faulkner's original discovery of his imaginary kingdom was lost.

While Wasson was turning *Flags in the Dust* into *Sartoris*, Faulkner persisted in his stubborn effort to save his career by pushing forward a new venture, one born of anguish he could find no other way of sharing. Soon he was writing stories about some children named Compson. One he called "The Evening Sun Go Down" and another "A Justice." Both deal with children who face dark and baffling experiences without adequate support. At the end of the second, we see the children moving through a "strange, faintly sinister suspension of twilight." As Faulkner continued to ponder the Compson children, he began more and more clearly to see them poised between the end of innocence and the beginning of divisive awareness. Soon he was at work on a manuscript entitled "Twilight," which became the novel called *The Sound and the Fury*. In March 1928 he wrote to Liveright in tones reminiscent of those of the preceding October, but with a new edge, too: "I have got going on a novel, which, if I continue as I am going now, I will finish within eight weeks. Maybe it'll please you."[10]

In ways still not wholly clear, the professional crisis triggered by Liveright's rejection of *Flags in the Dust* combined and interacted with a personal crisis that probably centered on Faulkner's childhood sweetheart, Estelle Oldham. In 1918 Estelle's marriage to the socially more acceptable Cornell Franklin had initiated one of Faulkner's earliest encounters with rejection. In 1927 Estelle had moved back to Oxford and, soon after, initiated divorce proceedings. During the intervening years Faulkner had courted other women and in New Orleans had fallen in love with at least one of them—Helen Baird. But he had also gone on seeing Estelle when she returned for visits with her family, and after her separation from Cornell Franklin, he and Estelle resumed their courtship almost as if the ten-year interruption caused by her marriage had never occurred.

Yet at the same time Faulkner was apparently involved with another woman whom he mentions, though not by name, in a letter to Aunt Bama in 1928: "We all wish you would [come down]. I have something—someone, I mean—to show you, if only you would. Of course it's a woman. I would like to see you taken with her utter charm, and intrigued by her utter shallowness. Like a lovely vase. . . . She gets the days past for me, though. Thank God I've no money, or I'd marry her. So you see, even Poverty looks after its own."[11] Several years later he spoke to Maurice Coindreau of the "severe strain" of this period as imposed by "difficulties of an intimate nature" ("des difficultés d'ordre intime").[12] These problems almost certainly involved grave concerns about his life as a writer and the fear that he "would never get published again."[13] But it seems probable that they included doubts about how both Estelle and the new woman who was filling his days were going to fit into his personal life.

It was from within this context of self-examination and uncertainty that Faulkner wrote *The Sound and the Fury*, his "dark story of madness and hatred."[14] In part, writing it was an act of reemergence, from which we can now date his arrival as one of the greatest of modern novelists. Years later he spoke of a "matchless time" in a writer's life when talent and energy perfectly converge:

> I think there's a period in a writer's life when he is, well, simply for lack of any other word, fertile and he just produces. Later on, his blood slows, his bones get a little more brittle, his muscles get a little stiff, he gets perhaps other interests, but I think there's one time in his life when he writes at the top of his talent plus his speed, too. Later the speed slows; the talent doesn't necessarily have to fade at the same time. But there's a time in his life, one matchless time, when they are matched completely. The speed, and the power and the talent, they're all there and then he is . . . "hot."[15]

For Faulkner that time began in 1928 with *Flags in the Dust*, which he later said carried "the germ of my apocrypha in it." And despite the pain and consternation of rejection, that matchless time continued with great force through the eight-year period between 1928 and 1936 in which he published not only *These 13* (1931) and *Doctor Martino and Other Stories* (1934), not only *Sartoris* (1929), *Sanctuary* (1931), and *Pylon* (1935), but also four great novels: *The Sound and the Fury* (1929), *As I Lay Dying* (1930), *Light in August* (1932), and *Absalom, Absalom!* (1936).

II

Looking back, we can see that Faulkner was justified in thinking of *Flags in the Dust* as a turning point. For it was then that he began to discover the rich possibilities of coming home. Having lived first in New Orleans and then abroad for several months, he had returned to his native Oxford to write about the country and the people he knew. "I learned that, to be a writer, one has first got to be what he is, what he was born," he said.[16] As early as 1925 in a piece published in the April issue of *Double Dealer* and written when he was living in New Orleans, he acknowledged his strong sense of place by thanking "whatever gods may be" that he was a provincial writer whose roots were planted in native soil.[17] During those same months Sherwood Anderson reinforced Faulkner's sense that his homeland was destined to play a special role in his art: "You're a country boy," he said. "All you know is that little patch up there in Mississippi where you started from."[18]

In *Flags in the Dust* Faulkner began mining the experiences and echoing the voices of the land he knew best. Drawn to explore both the past and the present as active forces in the lives of individuals as well as whole families and an entire region, he was able to draw not only on the traditions, customs, and folkways of his homeland but also on its myths and legends, the old tales and talking, that he had heard as a boy growing up. Soon he felt that he had tapped resources for his art that were limitless, and he began writing in ways that still strike readers as bold and original.

In coming home Faulkner had in a sense turned toward the "actual" as a source of inspiration for character and setting. Later he described his imaginative process as "sublimating the actual into the apocryphal." In fact, however, the resources he discovered in and around Oxford included not only the actualities—the present and past of his family, his society, and his culture—but also the legends and myths that had grown up around those actualities, in which the process of imaginatively taking possession of experience and transmuting it into art had already begun. In the old tales and talking that were his almost by right of birth, human imaginations brooded over and played with the facts of life; in them the actual and the apocryphal mingled. Throughout his life Faulkner's relations with both aspects of his heritage, its actualities and its apocryphal commentary on those actualities, remained intimate and yet strained. Having decided against exile, the chosen path of many writers of his generation, including Gertrude Stein, James Joyce, T. S. Eliot, Ezra Pound, and Ernest Hemingway, he decided to appropriate the land of his birth by making it his own. Yet he continued to think of himself as being at home without being at home. His return made possible rich discoveries, but it also evoked deep ambivalences that played a crucial role in the change that took place in his art, a change that was no less radical for now seeming almost inevitable.

In February 1927 Faulkner wrote to Liveright saying that he was writing "a collection of short stories of my townspeople."[19] From this experience came the stories and novels, beginning with *Flags in the Dust*, set in and around the imaginary town of Jefferson and the imaginary county of Yoknapatawpha. Nearly ten years later, for the publication of *Absalom, Absalom!* (1936), he drew a map of his creation that carries the following description:

> Jefferson,
> Yoknapatawpha Co.,
> Mississippi

Area, 2400 sq. Miles
Population, Whites, 6298
Negroes 9313

William Faulkner,
Sole Owner & Proprietor

Throughout the rest of his life he continued to speak casually of his fictional kingdom as if it were a place with a people and a history—a life—of its own. Asked many years later to trace the origin of the Yoknapatawpha fiction, he said:

With *Soldier's Pay* and *Mosquitoes* I wrote for the sake of writing because it was fun. Beginning with *Sartoris* I discovered that my own little postage stamp of native soil was worth writing about and that I would never live long enough to exhaust it, and by sublimating the actual into apocryphal I would have complete liberty to use whatever talent I might have to its absolute top. It opened up a gold mine of other peoples, so I created a cosmos of my own.[20]

The discovery Faulkner made in writing *Flags in the Dust* not only contained "the germ" of his "apocrypha" in it, giving his work a new direction; it also prepared for his emergence as a writer of marked originality.

In *Flags in the Dust* Faulkner focuses primarily on the external or public history of Yoknapatawpha. In it the story of a family named Sartoris becomes a story of the region in which they live. The central town of Jefferson, the outlying villages, the rivers, and the railroad emerge as important features of a largely preindustrial, agrarian world that is in many ways traditional. If, on one side, we recognize the region's abject sense of defeat, failure, and guilt as palpable, on the other we feel the presence of what Malcolm Cowley called Faulkner's "brooding love for the land where he was born and reared."[21] We know that in his creation he drew heavily on familiar places that were entangled with the lives of his family—the landscape, history, and demography of Tippah County and the village of Ripley as well as those of Lafayette County and the village of Oxford. We know too that he drew on the history of his family and his region, and on his family's and his region's keen sense of the force of history in shaping human lives. A part of his task is to pit the authority of fiction against the force of history, thus to limn the struggle of a solitary individual in a determined and even overdetermined world. He later described his characters as being composed "partly from what they were in actual life" but also "partly from what they should have been and were not."[22] In creating them he exercised what Sherwood Anderson called the "play of the imagination over the facts of life."[23] The Sartoris family carries heavy memories, and their burdens increase as their numbers dwindle. *Flags in the Dust* describes four generations, each more haunted by a sense of doom than the one before it. Isolated in the present, they are also held by the past.

III

Having tried to salvage *Flags in the Dust* only to become frustrated, Faulkner turned inward, as though to make yet another beginning. The strong sense of shared history and public event that we feel in *Flags in the Dust* is replaced by a deep, brooding internality in *The Sound and the Fury*. Over the years Faulkner talked a great deal about the conception and composition of *The Sound and the Fury*, and though his descriptions varied in details, they remained remarkably consistent. Writing *The Sound and the Fury* unfolded as a striking out against the harsh publishing world that had rejected his first Yoknapatawpha novel, but it also led him back into his own past and down into himself:

> One day I seemed to shut a door between me and all publishers' addresses and book lists. I said to myself, Now I can write. Now I can make myself a vase like that which the old Roman kept at his bedside and wore the rim slowly away with kissing it. So I, who had never had a sister and was fated to lose my daughter in infancy, set out to make myself a beautiful and tragic little girl.[24]

Writing for himself rather than his publishers, with a new focus on home and family, Faulkner created a story of lost innocence that evokes a sense of love that he seems to have desired but never experienced. He began, he said, with a story that he thought could be "done in about two pages," having "no plan at all" for a book, only to have the material develop quickly, first in expected and then in unexpected directions.[25] "Caddy had three brothers almost before I wrote her name on the paper," he later remarked. On several occasions he attributed the origin of the story to a clear image of "a brother and a sister splashing one another in the brook and the sister fell and wet her clothing and the smallest brother cried, thinking that the sister was conquered or perhaps hurt."[26] In a famous interview with Jean Stein vanden Heuvel he once described his initial impression of the heroine. "It began with a mental picture. I didn't realize at the time it was symbolical. The picture was of the muddy seat of a little girl's drawers in a pear tree where she could see through a window where her grandmother's funeral was taking place and report on what was happening to her brothers on the ground below."[27] Once begun, he said, "the entire story" seemed to "explode on the paper before me."[28]

The result is a passionate and moving story about four children who come of age amid the decay and dissolution of their family. Doomed by the "dark, harsh flowing of time," they seem almost already to have suffered the loss of all that they love. Faulkner's great achievement in telling their story derives in part from the deep emotional power of the story he weaves. But it also owes much to the complex stylistic and formal devices he discovered in the process of telling his story. Given the personal nature of the theme of his story, as well as the personal turmoil of the months in which he wrote, it is not surprising that he wrote with new intensity, or that the act of writing became an experience unlike any he had known before. But the terms in which he described the writing, having to do with ecstasy and grandeur as well as "splendid failure," remain striking. His creative power, what he termed "the force which drives a writer," seemed almost limitless. Sitting down to write each morning, it was as though he put drudgery, bitterness, and self-doubt behind him and experienced a sense both of anticipation and of joy that he would never again be able quite to match. "The Sound and the Fury had given me . . . that emotion definite and physical and yet nebulous to describe: that ecstasy, that eager and joyous faith and anticipation of surprise which the yet unmarred sheet beneath my hand held inviolate and unfailing, waiting for release."[29]

Faulkner later described himself as having tried several times to recapture the intensity and ecstasy he had discovered in writing *The Sound and the Fury*, and more specifically in creating Caddy Compson, only to fail. By comparison with *The Sound and the Fury*, writing *As I Lay Dying* seemed to him too "deliberate." "Before I ever put pen to paper and set down the first words," he said, "I knew what the last word would be." Having hoped again to "recapture it" in writing *Light in August*, he had finally to acquiesce "to the fact that it would not recur." As early as 1933 he had begun to fear that he would "never know it again." Later he pictured himself as viewing his books, "ranked in order on the shelf," not with pride or pleasure but with "flagging attention and distaste." And later still he seemed to live more in dread than in hope, holding out against the time when "not only the ecstasy of writing would be gone, but the unreluctance and the something worth saying too." Through it all *The Sound and the Fury*, "the one that failed the most tragically and the most splendidly," remained the novel for which he felt the most tenderness—the tenderness, we might add, of a mother as well as a father and of the beloved as well as the lover, a fact that helps to account for the always complex emotion that runs through the novel, waiting for us sleeplessly: "That was *The Sound and the Fury*—the one that I worked at the longest, the hardest, that was to me the most passionate and moving idea, and made the most splendid failure. That's the one that's my—I consider the best, not—well, best is the wrong word—that's the one that I love the most."[30] To this Faulkner added two things: first, that the novel had restored his sense of worth as a writer by giving him "something to get up to tomorrow morning" and "believe is valid"; and second, that the shadowy figure of Caddy Compson was the one that most forcibly captured his imagination.[31]

During the writing of *The Sound and the Fury* Faulkner remained so private about what he was doing that neither Estelle nor Phil Stone, an Oxford lawyer and early literary advisor, knew about the book until it was almost finished. After a period that Faulkner later set at about six months, as *The Sound and the Fury* neared completion, he began to disengage himself from it by introducing it to other people. Recalling his first acquaintance with the book, Stone later described a three- or four-month span during which he sat in "Bill's little room in the little tower of the old Delta Psi chapter house" while Faulkner "read *The Sound and the Fury* to me page by page." He added: "I could not make head nor tail of it . . . [until] we got into the part about Quentin [and] the whole thing began to unfold like a flower."[32] Later Stone claimed to have suggested the title, though Faulkner said simply that it grew "out of my unconscious. I adopted [the words] immediately, without considering then that the rest of the Shakesperean [*sic*] quotation was as well suited, and maybe better, to my dark story of madness and hatred."[33]

With some revising left to do, Faulkner journeyed to New York, where he revised his new manuscript and then offered it for publication. The completed manuscript carries the following information: "New York, N.Y. October, 1928." In a letter probably written in October from New York to his Aunt Alabama, he expressed pleasure that Harcourt, Brace had bought the rights to *Flags in the Dust*, which would be published as *Sartoris*, but he still felt doubtful about whether he would find a publisher for his new work: "Harcourt Brace & Co bought me from Liveright. Much, much nicer there. Book will be out in Feb. Also another one, the damndest book I ever read. I dont believe anyone will publish it for 10 years. Harcourt swear they will, but I dont believe it."[34] But to Ben Wasson, his friend and agent, he showed confidence that seemed almost independent of what publishers would think or say about his new novel. Wasson recalls Faulkner's coming to his room and tossing "a large obviously filled envelope on the bed. 'Read this one, Bud,' he said. 'It's a real son of a bitch. . . . This one's the greatest I'll ever write. Just read it.' "[35]

IV

The events immediately preceding the publication of *The Sound and the Fury* had, as Ben Wasson later stated, "a great bearing" on Faulkner's career as a writer.[36] Shortly after Faulkner submitted the novel to Harcourt, Brace and Company, Hal Smith decided to form a new firm called Jonathan Cape and Harrison Smith. He asked Harcourt for permission to take Faulkner's manuscript with him to his new publishing house—a request Harcourt granted at least in part because he had reservations about the novel: "You're the only damn fool in New York who would publish it," he replied.[37] Several literary editors of Smith's new publishing house recorded their first encounters with Faulkner's strange novel. Wasson, who had just been appointed an editor, was "enthralled" by it, but told Faulkner candidly that the "sheer technical outrageousness and freshness of the Benjy section made it hard to follow."[38] Lenore Marshall, another editor, found the novel dense: "Numerous readings were needed to fathom it. The manuscript was unclear and uncompromising, no concessions; time surged back and forth through mirrors; the inner chaotic truth of the mind took its place beside the truth of the surface; the author offered no help; an immense compulsive store of original energy poured out, scarcely to be contained within the sentence bounds." Despite these complexities, she recalls, "We accepted the novel."[39] Cape and Smith would publish Faulkner's fourth novel.

Part of the difficulty in reading the novel, for editors then and readers now, stems from the unconventional nature of Faulkner's writing. In composing *The Sound and the Fury* he began experimenting with narrative form as well as with punctuation and capitalization. The story as he first conceived it, he said, could be done in about two pages, but in the ensuing months he expanded that original idea into a long, complex novel. In his essay "The Composition of *The Sound and the Fury*" Leon Howard has suggested that by examining the chronological order of events in the novel and comparing them with the final version, we can discern Faulkner's process of composition. To discover Faulkner's original narrative line Howard cut up a copy of *The Sound and the Fury* "into the fragments of what were obviously its constituent parts and pasted them together again in order to re-create the separate parts and arrange them in a normal time sequence." Analyzing the holograph manuscript, now at the University of Virginia, he postulated that Faulkner began by creating "a frame story into which he could insert what he had already written as fragmentary flashbacks."[40]

Although it is virtually impossible to know precisely which sections of the novel Faulkner composed first, the marginal additions to the manuscript do suggest that Faulkner altered, revised, and transposed a good deal of material during the writing process. For example, although he originally numbered the beginning page of the Quentin section "34," he eventually added 92½ pages of material to precede this opening of the section. Howard suggests that Faulkner "started with thoughts of an orderly narrative and eventually decided to deal it out in parts—but with the shrewdness of someone who realized that he was devising a new game for an incomplete deck."[41]

Along with these compositional experiments Faulkner also began overturning typographical standards. When he felt it hindered the meaning or pace of his writing, he simply dropped traditional punctuation, including commas, periods, and apostrophes. With some simple words—"wont," "cant," "oclock," "Mr," "Mrs," and "Dr"—he almost never followed convention. But he also took liberties in order to suggest dialect inflections and to render the flow of a character's thoughts and feelings. In the first three parts of The Sound and the Fury, experience comes to us, not as a direct recounting of action, but as a given individual's—Benjy's, Quentin's, or Jason's—apprehension of it. Experience internalized—what we sometimes call interior monologue or stream of consciousness—is all that we have to work with in the first three sections of the novel. To denote shifts in time sequences and "thought transference," Faulkner used italics. A proud and meticulous craftsman, he knew that his idiosyncratic style made things difficult for editors and readers. But his patience sometimes wore thin when editors attempted to standardize his manuscripts by changing his punctuation, rearranging his sentence structure, or making additions to the text.[42] In a skirmish over The Sound and the Fury he asserted authorial privilege with what Ben Wasson remembered as "lightning bolts of wrath."[43]

Assigned to edit The Sound and the Fury for Cape and Smith, Wasson made many changes, deleting the italics in the Benjy section, replacing them with wider spacing to indicate changes in time from past to present, and even making a few additions to the text itself. When Faulkner received the galleys bearing Wasson's changes, he responded by insisting that his work be restored:

> the form in which you now have it is pretty tough. It presents a most dull and poorly articulated picture to my eye. . . . I think it is rotten, as is. . . . Also, the parts written in italics will all have to be punctuated again. You'd better see to that, since you're all for coherence. And dont make any more additions to the script, bud. I know you mean well, but so do I. I effaced the 2 or 3 you made.[44]

In this letter Faulkner also brought up the possibility of printing Benjy's section without italics but in different colors of ink, in order to record the flow of events for Benjy and at the same time differentiate among basic times and scenes in which the events occurred. Disappointed that the idea seemed unfeasible, he wrote Wasson, "I wish publishing was advanced enough to use colored ink for such, as I argued with you and Hal in the speak-easy that day. . . . But if you won't have it so, I'll just have to save the idea until publishing grows up to it."[45]

Later, for a proposed special edition of the novel, Faulkner resurrected this idea with Bennett Cerf, who wanted to reissue *The Sound and the Fury* in a limited edition with Grabhorn Press, which was known for its finely crafted work. Cerf wrote to Edwin Grabhorn that "Faulkner himself is marking this section so that the printer will know exactly what color each paragraph must appear in. Personally, I think the three colors should be black, maroon, and either dark blue or dark green." Subsequently Faulkner sent to Cerf his only copy of the novel marked in colors to indicate shifts in time. Later, after the project fell through, Faulkner wrote several times asking that the color-marked copy be returned to him. But Cerf never returned the book, and apparently it has been lost.[46]

Faulkner's use of italics in Benjy's section has always perplexed readers. To a group of students he explained his purpose: "I had to use some method to indicate to the reader that this idiot had no sense of time. That what happened to him ten years ago was just yesterday. The way I wanted to do it was to use different colored inks, but that would have cost so much, the publisher couldn't undertake it."[47] As a young man Faulkner had done several pen drawings that showed genuine talent, and he had also made color drawings and handsome hand-lettered and hand-illustrated books of his early poetry and his play, *The Marionettes*, for his friends, relatives, and lovers. Once or twice he designed covers for his novels, though none was ever used. Perhaps these interests in art inspired his unusual proposal to print *The Sound and the Fury* in several colors. By 1955, however, he said in another interview that his "original fear that the reader might need such a device seems not to have been valid" and that he no longer had the "desire to see the novel so printed."[48]

Problems with printing *The Sound and the Fury* resolved, Wasson next began thinking about effective ways of publicizing it. He took the galley proofs of the novel to Evelyn Scott, a young Tennessee writer whose new novel about the Civil War, *The Wave* (1929), had just been published by Cape and Smith. Scott wrote a laudatory and perceptive commentary on Faulkner's novel, which Cape and Smith published as a handsome prepublication pamphlet and distributed to critics, book dealers, and salesmen. It was, as Wasson remarked, the first clear sign of a reader "that seemed to give a serious damn" about Faulkner's work.[49] In her response to Faulkner's complex work Scott anticipated the special role that fellow artists—Conrad Aiken, Jean-Paul Sartre, Albert Camus, Ralph Ellison, Eudora Welty, and Robert Penn Warren—would play in making Faulkner's greatness visible to us.

In Benjy, Scott saw a "simplicity. . . untried by the standards of a conscious and calculating humanity"; in Quentin, a protest against dishonor; in Dilsey, self-respect and the recovery of "the spirit of tragedy which the pattern of cynicism has often made seem lost"; and in Jason, a set of "emotional barriers against reflection and self-investigation" that characterized a "young South" that was scornful of its traditions. *The Sound and the Fury*, she concluded, was an "important contribution to the permanent literature of fiction" with "all the spacious proportions of Greek art." While acknowledging the "monstrous" tragedy, suffering, and terror in the novel, she insisted that it possessed "a novel essence" and reflected the same faith in mankind "which has always lived in the most ultimate expression of the human spirit."[50]

Accompanied by the pamphlet carrying Scott's praise, *The Sound and the Fury* was published on 7 October 1929. Over the next several months, as the stock market lurched toward panic and then collapse, reviewers responded to the novel's strange surface and structure with puzzlement as well as scorn and praise. Edward Crickmay, in the *Sunday Referee*, called it a "strange and disturbing novel" that gave him the feeling that he had "passed through one of the strangest experiences of my life—an experience which can only be paralleled in actual life by walking through a darkness which is lit fitfully by an electric storm and from which isolated figures emerge for a moment and then disappear."[51]

Other reviews were less favorable. Writing for *Nation*, Clifton Fadiman described Faulkner's themes and characters as too "trivial" to justify "the enormous and complex craftsmanship expended on them." Writing for *Hound and Horn*, Dudley Fitts criticized Faulkner for using "deliberate obscurity" and "considerable incoherence" to shroud "melodrama." He proclaimed the novel "almost unreadable." On 30 November Howard Rockey warned readers of the *Philadelphia Inquirer* that *The Sound and the Fury* might drive them "to apply for admission to the nearest insane asylum." A month earlier Winfield Townley Scott had assured readers of the *Providence Sunday Journal* that they had nothing to worry about; it was a "tiresome" novel, full of "sound and fury—signifying nothing."[52]

On balance, however, the reviews were favorable. Writing for the *New York Herald Tribune*, Lyle Saxon called *The Sound and the Fury* "a great book." In the *Saturday Review* Basil Davenport described the novel as "original and impressive" and the author as "the man to watch." Henry Nash Smith, for *Southwest Review*, declared that "no matter how universal the standard, there are certain pages in this novel which are very near great literature." Noting that Faulkner was a "provincial writer," Smith went on to praise the "unusual scope" of his work. By disclosing "unguessed possibilities in the treatment of provincial life without loss of universality," *The Sound and the Fury* established Faulkner as a writer who "refused to be tyrannized by conventions, even the conventions of revolt."[53]

Unlike the reviews, sales of *The Sound and the Fury* spoke with a single voice. The first printing of nearly 1,800 copies was supplemented by two smaller printings, triggered mainly by the brief notoriety of *Sanctuary* (1931), Faulkner's sixth novel. A total of just over 3,300 copies satisfied American readers for fifteen years. By the time the novel was reprinted in 1946, it had been out of print for several years, as had all of Faulkner's books. Over the succeeding decades, however, a remarkable revival of interest has established Faulkner as a major literary figure and *The Sound and the Fury*, the most written-about of all his novels, as a classic of modern literature.

V

Given the technical brilliance of *The Sound and the Fury*, it is easy to forget how simple and moving its basic story is. We observe the Compson children as they move toward the threshold of adulthood to confront an uncertain future. The resemblance between the Compson family and Faulkner's own family is implicit in Faulkner's own remark that he knew Caddy would have three brothers before he "wrote her name on paper." Several central events of the novel bear resemblance to the death of Faulkner's maternal grandmother, whom he and his brothers called "Damuddy," after whose lingering illness and funeral the boys were sent away so that the house could be fumigated. The terrible inadequacy of Mr. and Mrs. Compson as parents draws on Faulkner's own early experiences with a mother who was often harsh, demanding, and overbearing, and a father who moved back and forth between resignation and bitterness, drinking heavily. In the figure of Dilsey, Faulkner memorialized Mammy Callie, the black woman who raised him and his brothers, and to whom he dedicated *Go Down Moses*:

To MAMMY
CAROLINE BARR
Mississippi
[1840–1940]
Who was born in slavery and who
gave to my family a fidelity without
stint or calculation of recompense
and to my childhood an immeasur-
able devotion and love

Faulkner was fond of remarking that *The Sound and the Fury* was a story that required four tellings. In the last of these the story comes to us in a more detached voice. But in each of the first three sections the story is told by one of the three brothers. From the remote and strange world of Benjy's idiocy and innocence, we move through the intensely subjective and private world of Quentin's bizarre idealism, to the more familiar and practical meanness of Jason's materialism, rage, prejudice, and self-pity. The narrative reflects each brother's mental state: Benjy's perceptions revolve around basic needs, sensations, and responses; Quentin's convoluted thoughts shape his feelings, especially those that he finds least acceptable, into a decadent poetic prose, full of idiosyncratic allusions and patterns; and Jason's callous self-centeredness finds expression in colloquialisms and clichés that somehow seem all the more terrifying for being both familiar and funny. Jason is American both in the prejudices he harbors against blacks, women, and Jews and in the poorly repressed hostility he directs toward all people who are vulnerable. But he is also American in his insatiable desire to incorporate—to own and possess and control everything. He mirrors modern capitalism's indiscriminate and insatiable drives. From Jason's story we move to a fourth telling, one informed by traditional and even specifically Christian values. Though felt as something terribly weakened if not wholly lost, these values, and the ordering principles that go with them, are also felt as having once been powerfully present and as still being residually so.

If in the story of Jason we observe the near triumph of all that is terrible, in the stories of Caddy and Miss Quentin we observe the degradation of all that is beautiful. Deserted by her mother, Miss Quentin is left with no one from whom to learn love, and so repeats her mother's dishonor and flight without ever finding appropriate objects for her tenderness. Together Caddy's and Miss Quentin's stories, particularly when juxtaposed to Jason's, do as much as any stories in modern literature to illustrate W. B. Yeats's vision of modernity in "The Second Coming," where "The best lack all conviction, while the worst / Are full of passionate intensity."

Given the power of her presence and even more the power of her illusiveness, Caddy, Faulkner's "beautiful and tragic little girl," plays a central role in making the force of *The Sound and the Fury* felt. It was Faulkner's need to tell Caddy's story adequately that led him to transform a short story called "Twilight" into a long and rich novel. "I loved her so much," he said, "I couldn't decide to give her life just for the duration of a short story. She deserved more than that. So my novel was created almost in spite of myself." Later he said that he had simply "written the same story four times," only to find that each telling of the tale left him unsatisfied.

> I tried to tell it again, the same story through the eyes of another brother. That was still not it. I told it for the third time through the eyes of the third brother. That was still not it. I tried to gather the pieces together and fill in the gaps by making myself the spokesman. It was still not complete. . . . I never could tell it right, though I tried hard and would like to try again, though I'd probably fail again.[54]

He considered the novel "not a deliberate *tour de force*," but a story that "just grew that way. . . . I was still trying to tell one story which moved me very much and each time I failed." Unable finally to render Caddy as fully or as beautifully as he imagined her, he called *The Sound and the Fury* the book that "failed four times."[55]

To the end of his life Faulkner spoke of Caddy with deep devotion. Yet it was not until he had finished writing that he discovered how deeply she answered his own needs: "I did not realize then that I was trying to manufacture the sister which I did not have."[56] Looking back, he also came to associate her with the daughter he was fated to lose, whom he had named for his Aunt Alabama. Beyond that, Caddy seems to embody the lover he had always imagined. Certainly she was, in complex ways, the imaginative creation he most adored. Late in his life, in an interview at the University of Virginia, he said, "To me she was the beautiful one, she was my heart's darling."[57]

Yet despite her centrality Faulkner seems to have discovered Caddy essentially as he presented her—through the felt needs of her brothers. To Benjy, whom Faulkner described as "something eyeless and voiceless which . . . existed merely because of its ability to suffer," Caddy offers a kind of love and tenderness that he can find nowhere else.[58] Losing her, Benjy endures meaningless and nameless suffering. For Quentin, losing Caddy means unrelieved despair. Unable either to accept Caddy's sexuality—which he associates with "the ditches the dark woods hot hidden furious in the dark woods" or to protect, save, or redeem her from it ("Did you ever have a sister? Did you? Did you?")—Quentin lets his grief carry him to suicide. He associates Caddy first with the oversweet scent of honeysuckle, then with the passion of dark woods, and then with the image of Little Sister Death, to whom he finally gives himself. Having failed both as a forbidden lover and as chivalric deliverer, he completes with his death the only remaining role he can play in Caddy's story—that of the despairing lover.

One result of Faulkner's narrative approach to Caddy is that she emerges very slowly, in scattered glimpses. Where Caddy is concerned, Faulkner's art is an art of concealment and avoidance before it is an art of disclosure and engagement. He approaches Caddy as he might a desirable woman; memory and desire, passion and evasion intermingle. In part this stems from an aesthetic notion that Faulkner shared with Mallarmé and others, which holds not only that beauty is difficult and illusive and, therefore, not easily attained, but also that indirection is more passionate because it draws the reader or viewer into an active imaginative role through which the process of creation is completed. For Faulkner both desire and hesitation touched almost everything, making his imagination allusive as well as illusive, and his art an art of surmise and conjecture. One of the rewards of his difficult art derives, then, from its deepest logic, which creates an enlarged role for the reader, and even imposes it. In *The Sound and the Fury* even the most private and personal of stories must become collaborative before they can become great art.

In *Flags in the Dust* Faulkner turned to his heritage for artistic inspiration. In *The Sound and the Fury* he confronted the mixed pain, loss, and joy of his childhood. In it we observe the passing of innocence, as it gives way to the dark forces of madness and hatred. In the figure of Caddy we observe the passing of childhood and youth before the "dark, harsh flowing of time." Caddy plays several roles. She is maternal, especially in the tenderness with which she cares for Benjy; she is a loving sister; and she becomes a desirable, maturing woman and lover. She thus evokes for us emotions that are close to those Faulkner felt in writing *The Sound and the Fury*, which he described as "definite and physical and yet nebulous to describe." Fearing her even as (and all the more because) he desired her, concealing her even as he disclosed her, Faulkner created a heroine who comes into being within the decaying world that surrounds her, and so experiences a fate of "dishonor and shame," only to emerge as a beautiful and compelling woman, standing at the center of one of the classics of modern American literature.

Notes

1. Sensibar, *Origins of Faulkner's Art*, 92.

2. "Faulkner's Introduction to *The Sound and the Fury*" (*Southern Review*), 710.

3. See Meriwether, "Faulkner and El Orens." Faulkner refers to *Revolt in the Desert*, by T. E. Lawrence, "whom the Arabs called El Orens." The passage describes Arabs admiring a fighter plane at Um el Surab: "Indeed and at last they have sent us THE aeroplane, of which these things were foals."

4. *Selected Letters*, 38.

5. Liveright to Faulkner, 25 November 1927, quoted in Blotner, *Faulkner*, 559–60.

6. *Selected Letters*, 39.

7. Ibid., 39–40.

8. Blotner, "Faulkner's Essay on the Composition of *Sartoris*," 123.

9. *Selected Letters*, 40–41.

10. Ibid., 40.

11. Faulkner to Mrs. Walter B. McLean, probably in the first half of 1928, quoted in Minter, *Faulkner*, 92.

12. Quoted in Minter, *Faulkner*, 94.

13. "Introduction to the Modern Library Edition of *Sanctuary* (New York, 1932)," 177.

14. Faulkner, quoted in Coindreau, "Preface to *The Sound and the Fury*," 109.

15. Interview in the Nagano Seminar, Japan, 1955, in *Lion in the Garden*, 149–50.

16. "A Note on Sherwood Anderson," 8.

17. "Verse Old and Nascent," 116.

18. Quoted in "A Note on Sherwood Anderson," 8.

19. *Selected Letters*, 34.

20. Interview with Jean Stein vanden Heuvel, 1956, in *Lion in the Garden*, 255.

21. Cowley, "Introduction," in Faulkner, *The Portable Faulkner*, 19.

22. Quoted in Minter, *Faulkner*, 77–78.

23. Ibid., 75.

24. "Faulkner's Introduction to *The Sound and the Fury*" (*Southern Review*), 710.

25. *Faulkner in the University*, 32.

26. "Faulkner's Introduction to *The Sound and the Fury*" (*Mississippi Quarterly*), 413.

27. Interview with Jean Stein vanden Heuvel, 1956, in *Lion in the Garden*, 245.

28. "Faulkner's Introduction to *The Sound and the Fury*" (*Mississippi Quarterly*), 413.

29. "Faulkner's Introduction to *The Sound and the Fury*" (*Southern Review*), 709.

30. *Faulkner in the University*, 77.

31. Ibid., 67.

32. Quoted in Blotner, *Faulkner*, 219–20.

33. Quoted in Coindreau, "Preface to *The Sound and the Fury*," 109. The spelling error may be the author's, the translator's, or the editor's.

34. *Selected Letters*, 41.
35. Wasson, *Count No Count*, 89.
36. Ibid., 26.
37. Quoted in Blotner, *Faulkner*, 241.
38. Wasson, *Count No Count*, 90.
39. Marshall, "The Power of Words," 16.
40. Howard, "The Composition of *The Sound and the Fury*," 114, 116.
41. Ibid., 125.
42. See editorial comments by Blotner and Polk in Faulkner, *Novels 1930–1935*, 1019–27.
43. Wasson, *Count No Count*, 97.
44. *Selected Letters*, 44–45.
45. Ibid.
46. Blotner, *Faulkner*, 318.
47. *Faulkner in the University*, 94.
48. Quoted in Meriwether, "Textual History of *The Sound and the Fury*," 298.
49. Wasson, *Count No Count*, 97.
50. From the text reprinted in Bassett, *Faulkner: The Critical Heritage*, 76–81.
51. Ibid., 90–91.
52. Ibid., 81–82, 88; Rockey, "Fiction, Largely European."
53. Bassett, *Faulkner: The Critical Heritage*, 85–87; Saxon, "A Family Breaks Up."
54. Interview with Jean Stein vanden Heuvel, 1956, in *Lion in the Garden*, 245.
55. Interview in the Nagano Seminar, Japan, 1955, in *Lion in the Garden*, 147.
56. "Faulkner's Introduction to *The Sound and the Fury*" (*Mississippi Quarterly*), 413.
57. *Faulkner in the University*, 6.
58. "Faulkner's Introduction to *The Sound and the Fury*" (*Mississippi Quarterly*), 414.

Works Cited

Bassett, John, ed. *William Faulkner: The Critical Heritage*. The Critical Heritage Series. London: Routledge & Kegan Paul, 1975.

Blotner, Joseph. *Faulkner: A Biography*. One-volume edition. New York: Random House, 1977.

———. "William Faulkner's Essay on the Composition of *Sartoris*." *Yale University Library Gazette* 47 (January 1973): 121–24.

Coindreau, Maurice. "Preface to *The Sound and the Fury*." Translated by George M. Reeves. *Mississippi Quarterly* 19 (Summer 1966): 107–15.

Faulkner, William. *Faulkner in the University: Conferences at the University of Virginia, 1957–1958*. Edited by Frederick L. Gwynn and Joseph Blotner. Charlottesville: University Press of Virginia, 1959.

———. "Introduction to the Modern Library Edition of *Sanctuary*, (New York, 1932)." In *Essays, Speeches, and Public Letters*, 176–78. Edited by

James B. Meriwether. New York: Random House, 1965.

_____. *Lion in the Garden: Interviews with William Faulkner, 1926–1962*. Edited by James B. Meriwether and Michael Millgate. New York: Random House, 1968.

_____. "A Note on Sherwood Anderson." In *Essays, Speeches and Public Letters*, 3–10. Edited by James B. Meriwether. New York: Random House, 1965.

_____. *Novels 1930–1935*. Edited by Joseph Blotner and Noel Polk. The Library of America. New York: Literary Classics of the United States, 1985.

_____. *The Portable Faulkner*. Edited by Malcolm Cowley. New York: Viking Press, 1946.

_____. *Selected Letters of William Faulkner*. Edited by Joseph Blotner. New York: Random House, 1977.

_____. "Verse Old and Nascent: A Pilgrimage." In *Early Prose and Poetry*. Edited by Carvel Collins. Boston: Little, Brown, 1962, 114–18.

_____. "William Faulkner's Introduction to *The Sound and the Fury*." Edited by James B. Meriwether. *Mississippi Quarterly* 26 (Summer 1973): 410–15.

_____. "William Faulkner's Introduction to *The Sound and the Fury*." Edited by James B. Meriwether. *Southern Review* 8 (Autumn 1972): 705–10.

Howard, Leon. "The Composition of *The Sound and the Fury*." *Missouri Review* 5 (Winter 1981–82): 111–28.

Marshall, Lenore. "The Power of Words." *Saturday Review*, 28 July 1962, 16–17.

Meriwether, James B. "Faulkner and El Orens." *Faulkner Newsletter and Yoknapatawpha Review* 1 (April–June 1981): 2.

_____. "Notes on the Textual History of *The Sound and the Fury*." *Papers of the Bibliographical Society of America* 56, no. 3 (1962): 285–316.

Minter, David. *William Faulkner: His Life and Work*. Baltimore: The Johns Hopkins University Press, 1980.

Rockey, Howard. "Fiction Largely European and Very Good in the Average." *Philadelphia Inquirer*, 30 November 1929, 18.

Saxon, Lyle. "A Family Breaks Up." *New York Herald Tribune*, 13 October 1929, 3.

Sensibar, Judith L. *The Origins of Faulkner's Art*. Austin: University of Texas Press, 1984.

Wasson, Ben. *Count No Count: Flashbacks to Faulkner*. Jackson: University Press of Mississippi, 1983.

SCOTT DONALDSON

A Short History of *Tender Is the Night*

I

   As F. Scott Fitzgerald said of himself, the man who started *Tender Is the Night* was not the one who finished it.[1] It could hardly have been otherwise, for the years from 1925 to 1934 saw the author's private universe fall apart, while the world outside descended into decadence and depression. Fitzgerald had an affair—or said he did—with the young actress Lois Moran, to balance out the affair Zelda had—or said she did—with the French aviator Edouard Jozan. During drinking bouts he alienated friends, got into fights with strangers, and landed in jail several times. Zelda suffered through spells of ill health and at least one abortion. Living in a series of rented apartments and rented houses, the Fitzgeralds became estranged. Zelda threw herself into the dance with a fervency bordering on madness, then slipped over the line in the most severe of her recurrent mental breakdowns. The stock market collapsed. Scott's father died. Zelda's father died. All the fathers died, and with them went the assurance and the solidity of the prewar era. Anyone could see that Spengler was right, that Yeats was right: the west was in decline, the center could not hold, the old values did not obtain. It even began to seem that Marx was right. Certainly he spoke to the troubled times, as did Freud and Jung. *Tender Is the Night* reflected all those changes, even as it told the story of one talented and charming man dwindling from early promise into middle-aged oblivion. Like almost everything Fitzgerald wrote, the novel makes a deeply personal statement. It also stands as his testimony to modernism.
   The book did not start out so ambitiously. As he originally conceived the idea for his novel during the cold, rainy months of the fall and winter of 1924–25, Fitzgerald had no more than a glimmer of such a sweeping scheme in mind. On 1 May 1925, to be sure, he wrote Maxwell Perkins that his next novel would be "something really NEW in form, idea, structure—the model for the age that Joyce and Stein are searching for, that Conrad didn't find."[2] But that amazing (and never-defined) envelope was to contain a rather unpromising plot. The

protagonist of Fitzgerald's earliest draft toward *Tender Is the Night* is a twenty-one-year-old Southerner named Francis Melarky who has been kicked out of West Point and worked as a technician in Hollywood, where he became emotionally involved with a young actress. Francis, a hot-tempered youth, is now traveling in Europe with his domineering mother. On the Riviera they meet a group of charming American expatriates, including Seth and Dinah Roreback (or Rorebeck, or Piper), and Abe Herkimer (or Grant, or North), an alcoholic composer. Abe and Francis serve as seconds in a duel between Gabriel Brugerol (later Tommy Barban) and Albert McKisco, a writer who retains his name and integrity as a character throughout. Francis goes to Paris with the Rorebacks, where he falls in love with Dinah. Fitzgerald's narrative broke off here, but he planned to follow Francis through a process of degeneration. Eventually, he was to murder his mother in a drunken rage.[3] Fitzgerald worked on this basic version—stage one in the three-stage, twelve-draft history of the book's composition—from 1925 until 1929. He called it variously *Our Type*, *The World's Fair*, *The Melarky Case*, and *The Boy Who Killed His Mother*,[4] and got about a fourth of it down on paper.

Fitzgerald projected this new novel—and exaggerated its progress toward completion—in the wake of the financial disappointment of *The Great Gatsby*. He had hoped that *Gatsby* would sell 75,000 or 80,000 copies, enough to wipe out his debt to Scribner's and stake him to a block of time for the new book. He had written and revised *Gatsby* under firm, self-imposed discipline and felt that he had earned a respite from his labors. But *Gatsby* sold only 20,000 copies, and he was forced to turn out stories for the *Saturday Evening Post* (at $2,000 a crack, as of late 1924) to make ends meet. Resenting this necessity, he denigrated the results. As soon as he was far enough ahead on "trash," he wrote Perkins, he would devote full time to his next novel. If that one did not sell, he might as well give up and go to Hollywood.[5]

So it was a discouraged writer who set down the first drafts of *Our Type*—professionally discouraged and personally humiliated. Zelda's affair with Jozan in the summer of 1924, at the very time when he was tearing along on the last stretches of *Gatsby*, hit Fitzgerald hard. He was shattered, as Andrew Turnbull put it, because "he really believed in love, and in what two people [could] build against the world's cheap skepticism."[6] And the apparent sexual success of the dark, strong naval aviator with his wife called his very manhood into question. Then there was the disastrous stay in Rome. Late in October 1924 Fitzgerald mailed the typescript of *The Great Gatsby* to Perkins. Two weeks later he and Zelda and Scottie journeyed to Italy for five months in Rome and Capri that left him with an abiding hatred of the

Italians and a nagging memory of "just about the rottenest thing that ever happened in my life."[7]

They went to Rome for no better reason than that Zelda had been reading Henry James's *Roderick Hudson*. They knew no one, and for social companionship briefly attached themselves to the cast of *Ben Hur*, then being filmed in "papier-mâché arenas" grander than the real ones. Aside from this diversion, Fitzgerald disliked everything he encountered. The weather was execrable. He was drinking far too much and was often angry. He was furious when he was displaced from a restaurant table in favor of an Italian who possessed or pretended to a title. After one evening of revelry, he started a brawl in a nightclub. After another, he got into an altercation with a cabdriver who insisted on overcharging him; blows were struck, and Fitzgerald was summarily taken to jail. These incidents precipitated a magazine article, "The High Cost of Macaroni," that was never published, and Fitzgerald then rewrote the fight with the cabdriver as the first chapter of the Melarky version of his novel. This fight was later relocated to the seventh chapter of the Melarky version, and finally to the end of Book 2 of *Tender Is the Night*, by which time Dick Diver had replaced the young Hollywood technician as the novel's protagonist.

Fitzgerald could hardly have known in 1925 how absolutely appropriate the setting would be to the decline and fall of Dick Diver, a character he had not yet invented. In "The High Cost of Macaroni" he characterized Italy as "a dead land where everything that could be done or said was done long ago, for whoever is deceived by the pseudo activity under Mussolini is deceived by the spasmodic last jerk of a corpse."[8] The language was extravagant, but in fact Rome offered "a perfect microcosm" of what had once been great and had now become debased in Western civilization. It was the one city in the world where Diver might most appropriately suffer through his own process of abasement and degradation. In this way, what might otherwise have seemed merely his private downfall was linked to a more general malaise.[9]

The cabdriver-fight scene in Rome, written originally for stage one, the Melarky version, was eventually transplanted to stage three, and that was true of almost everything he wrote during 1926–29. Different though it may have been in initial conception, Fitzgerald was able to lift characters and scenes from this version, polish them up, move them around, and use them to his purpose in the novel he published in 1934. Though he was to circulate the myth that he wrote and scrapped hundreds of thousands of words, the fact is—as Matthew Bruccoli has shown—that very little he wrote, even during stage one, had to be wholly discarded.

II

Fitzgerald's correspondence with the agent Harold Ober and the editor Maxwell Perkins from 1925 to 1934 tells a repetitive tale of promises made and promises broken. Again and again Fitzgerald assured both men that he would soon complete his novel in progress. Yet he refused despite their urging to settle on a title or even to reveal much of what he had in mind. He would say only that his novel was to be based in part on the famous Leopold-Loeb murder case of 1924, on the January 1925 murder of her mother by a sixteen-year-old San Francisco girl named Dorothy Ellingson, and on "Zelda & me & the hysteria of last May & June in Paris. (Confidential)."[10] On the strength of no more information than that, in June 1926 Ober sold serial rights to *Liberty* magazine for $35,000.[11] Here was a bonanza well within reach. All Fitzgerald needed to do was to finish the novel and put it in the mail. He could not bring it off.

The initial deadline Fitzgerald set himself was fall 1926, gradually extended to the end of the year, to March 1927, to June 1927, and so on and on. In the beginning he projected a book of about 75,000 words, slightly longer than *Gatsby* though only half the length of the eventual *Tender*. In letters to Ober and Perkins he radiated confidence that he could finish the novel at or close to his original deadline. So *Liberty* advertised the serial in its 11 December 1926 issue, and Scribner's made plans for book publication soon after the last magazine installment.

From the start in mid-1925, Fitzgerald had been celebrating the quality of his work in progress to Perkins (he did not do so to Ober). The book was "going to be great," he insisted. It was "wonderful." It would establish him as "the best American novelist." In February 1926, after reporting T. S. Eliot's praise of *Gatsby* as "the 1st step forward American fiction had taken since Henry James," Fitzgerald added in exultation, "Wait till they see the new novel!"[12] Naturally Perkins was eager to publish the book. When nothing was forthcoming from Fitzgerald during the early months of 1927, he twice attempted to spur him into action.

The World's Fair sounded like a fine title, Perkins wrote on 20 January 1927. Why didn't they announce it now? That would give Fitzgerald "a sort of proprietorship" over the title and generate interest in the novel. At that time Fitzgerald was in Hollywood, where he spent six weeks working on a Constance Talmadge movie called *Lipstick* (his script was not used). He also became seriously interested in the young actress Lois Moran, the model for Rosemary Hoyt. Don't give out the title yet, he wired Perkins from California; he'd deliver the novel to *Liberty* in June. In early April, after the Fitzgeralds moved to a rented mansion called Ellerslie outside Wilmington, Delaware, Perkins tried again. If Fitzgerald would send the title, and some text, and "enough of an idea to make an effective wrap," Scribner's could put out a dummy. But, Perkins added, the important thing was to finish the novel, after all, and he certainly didn't mean to harass his author.[13]

Neither of these overtures stimulated progress on the novel. Fitzgerald's private life was in such disorder as to prevent him from doing any sustained work. What energy he could summon up went into short stories, for these could generate income rapidly and did not demand the effort of concentration a novel required. As Fitzgerald later described the problem in a letter of 11 March 1935 to Perkins, you could write a short story on a bottle, but not a novel. A novel required organizational skill, fine judgment, and mental speed—all of which deserted him under the influence of alcohol. "If I had one more crack at [Tender Is the Night] cold sober I believe it might have made a great difference."[14]

According to Bruccoli, Fitzgerald made "no progress at all" on the book during 1927, 1928, and half of 1929. That was not what he told Perkins, however. As the new year of 1928 came around the corner, he pleaded for "Patience yet a little while" from his publisher. Scribner's investment, he said, was not at risk. In reply, Perkins assured him that the firm felt "no anxiety whatever" about the book. The only thing was, the editor observed in his letter of 3 January 1928, that he worried about the time that was elapsing between Gatsby and the new novel. Perkins anticipated no extended delay, of course. "We can count on your novel for the fall, can't we?" he asked Fitzgerald on 24 January 1928. "It must be very nearly finished now."[15] These well-meaning comments from an eager and supportive editor must have rankled in Fitzgerald's breast as the days and weeks and months slid away during the long period of procrastination ahead.

Liquor eased the passage of time, or seemed to, as is manifest in Edmund Wilson's account of "A Weekend at Ellerslie" in late February 1928. Thornton Wilder attended the Fitzgeralds' house party, as did Gilbert and Amanda Seldes, John and Anna Biggs, Esther Strachey (Gerald Murphy's sister), and the cast of Zoë Akin's The Furies, then playing Wilmington. The carousing soon turned frantic, and Wilson decided to escape a day early. Before he left, Fitzgerald read him and Seldes one of the Riviera chapters from his novel in progress. It was impressive work, but Wilson knew better than to ask when the book would be completed. Any inquiry along that line, he had learned, was liable to produce "a sharp retort." Wilson understood that it was Fitzgerald's conscience that lashed out at him, but that did not make the situation any more comfortable.

Another subject much on Fitzgerald's mind during that Delaware weekend was World War I. In inviting Wilson to the party, he referred to the "slaughter of Paschendale" and to the troops "shivering in the lagoons at Ypres." On the wall of his study at Ellerslie he hung the trench helmet he had been issued but never worn in action, for he had not gone overseas. He also seemed fascinated with an album of photographs showing mutilated soldiers. Wilson would not know what to make of this until *Tender Is the Night* emerged, with its characterization of the war as a watershed in western history and as a parallel to hostilities between the sexes.[16]

Throughout 1928 Fitzgerald continued to promise delivery of the Melarky-matricide version he had in fact virtually abandoned. "ALL COMPLETED AUGUST," he wired Ober's office in June, by way of asking for a deposit to his bank account. "[D]one *sure* in September," he wrote Perkins late in July.[17] Finally, on 28 November, he sent Perkins "the first fourth of the book (2 chapters, 18,000 words)." In addition he wrote that he was patching up chapters 3 and 4 and would deliver those soon. But he sailed for Europe in March 1929 without delivering any more of the manuscript, even though—in stage one, fourth draft—he had in fact finished four chapters. "I hate to leave without seeing you," he wrote Perkins, "and I hate to leave without the ability to put the finished ms in your hands."[18] The two chapters he mailed on 28 November 1928 were the only ones that either Perkins or Ober would see until another five years had elapsed.

By the middle of 1929, Fitzgerald seems to have decided at last that the Melarky version was not going to work out. For one thing, matricide was a subject—as Wilson remarked—that "might well have taxed Dostoevsky."[19] Secondly, he must have sensed that his protagonist was not sufficiently interesting or attractive to command the attention of readers. Even his name was all wrong, for while Francis echoed Fitzgerald's given name, Melarky suggested both a degree of discomfort with the material and a measure of authorial self-disgust.

A new approach was called for, and Fitzgerald began to uncover it during his March 1929 journey across the Atlantic. In his story called "The Rough Crossing," written shortly after the boat docked in France, cracks begin to develop in the marriage of Adrian and Eva Smith. Adrian, a thirtyish playwright who has lately become a celebrity, pairs off during their Atlantic crossing with a lovely young girl named Betsy D'Amido. Her very youth, Fitzgerald writes, "seemed to flow into him, bearing him up into a delicate romantic ecstasy that transcended passion." Here (as once earlier, in a 1927 story called "Jacob's Ladder") he was transmuting his feeling for Lois Moran into fiction, and laying the groundwork for the Dick Diver–Rosemary Hoyt affair. "One Trip Abroad," a story published in 1930, went still further into the dissolution-of-a-marriage theme. Nicole and Nelson Kelly inherit some money and go to Europe, where they succumb to the dissipation of expatriate society. Like the Smiths, the Kellys drink too much and quarrel with each other. They also are unfaithful to each other. Wherever they travel in Europe, they meet another couple, still younger than they, who are obviously going through a process of steady deterioration. At the end, Nicole comes to understand that the other couple serve as their doubles. "They're us! They're us!" she tells her husband. "Don't you see?"

Both of these stories functioned as trial runs for stage two of *Tender Is the Night*, "the Kelly-shipboard version" in Bruccoli's terminology. "I am working night & day on novel from new angle that I think will solve previous difficulties," Fitzgerald wrote Perkins in mid-summer 1929.[20] The "new angle," the surviving drafts reveal, involved the transatlantic voyage of Lew and Nicole Kelly, a successful young film director and his wife. During the trip Lew is attracted to an aspiring young actress named Rosemary, who sneaks into first class in order to meet and make an impression on him. Later, presumably, the film director was to undergo much the same pattern of degeneration as Francis Melarky. Fitzgerald finished only two chapters of this version; it did not solve his "previous difficulties" with the novel. But stage two wove another major theme into the thickening tapestry of his novel in progress.

Armed with the Kelly-shipboard material, Fitzgerald once again projected an early completion of his book. "SENDING THREE FOURTH OF NOVEL SEPT 30TH STARTING NEW STORY NEXT WEEK CAN YOU DEPOSIT THREEFIFTY," he cabled his agent on 29 August 1929. All he needed, he thought, was a little free time, a clear month here, a couple of months there, but it was the middle of November before, as he wrote both Perkins and Ober, he could contemplate "two uninterrupted months" ahead for the novel. Meanwhile, Ober was importuning him to mail half the manuscript, or even a smaller portion, to keep *Liberty* interested. He asked in October, in December, and, rather plaintively, in March 1930, "Couldn't you send over a few chapters of the novel. . . . Otherwise it means 1931." This last request inspired Fitzgerald to a rationalization. It would be "ruinous" to let *Liberty* start serializing an uncompleted novel, he pointed out. Besides, what if they didn't like the first part? The ever-patient Ober replied that he had talked to *Liberty*, that they wouldn't think of beginning the story until they had the complete manuscript, and that there was "not the least likelihood" of their turning it down.

After that, the subject of the novel faded out of the Fitzgerald–Ober correspondence until 19 May 1931, when the agent sent a mes-

sage designed to boost the author's ego and, with luck, produce results. "I believe," Ober began, "and others, who are much more
competent judges than I, believe that you ought to go further than any
American writer and I think now is the time for you to get down to
hard work and finish the novel."[21]

Though he subjected them to repeated delays and disappointments, neither Ober nor Perkins was ready to give up on Fitzgerald or
his book. The more time and money they invested in their author, the
less they were willing to contemplate his failure. It was a psychology
that Fitzgerald well understood—and wittily illustrated in his 1938
story "Financing Finnegan." Finnegan, a figure based on Fitzgerald
himself, is a wastrel with talent, forever on the verge of a brilliant book
that fails to materialize. But his publisher and agent refuse to write
him off. Instead they enter into "a silent conspiracy to cheer each
other up about Finnegan. . . . They could not bear to hear a word
against him—even from themselves."

Patience is not invariably rewarded, but in the case of *Tender Is the
Night*, it was. The novel could not possibly have achieved the power
of its final form without the passage of nine years between inception
and completion. Fitzgerald began in 1925 with a melodramatic plot,
an admiration for Gerald and Sara Murphy, and a devotion to the
apocalyptic ideas of Oswald Spengler. An extraordinary couple, the
Murphys moved easily among the expatriate rich and formed lasting
friendships with the great artists of the day—Picasso and Léger, Dos
Passos and Hemingway among them. Afflicted with acute sensitivity,
Fitzgerald envied the Murphys their social ease with both groups. As
a consequence he often behaved badly in their company, particularly
during the liquid summer of 1925. In stage one of his novel the characters of Seth and Dinah Piper were fashioned after the Murphys. Like
their originals, the Pipers knew how to make the world brighter for
everyone around them. In other words, they had charm. He had
spent almost five years, Fitzgerald commented in September 1929, on
a novel dealing with "the insoluble problems of personal charm."[22]
Seth Piper–Gerald Murphy personified that quality. The picture of
Dick Diver in the early Cap d'Antibes scenes of *Tender Is the Night*,
raking the sand, supervising the revels, and giving too much of himself to others, closely resembles the Piper-Murphy of stage one. Later
in the published novel, however, the Divers were to become composite characters, modeled more closely on the Fitzgeralds than on the
Murphys.

III

At every stage of composition *Tender Is the Night* depicted the decline of its principal character. And in each version Fitzgerald located this personal tragedy within the context of a wider cultural malaise. Underlying this pattern was the influence of Oswald Spengler's *Decline of the West*. Fitzgerald had read Spengler the same summer (1924) he was writing *Gatsby*, he later maintained in a letter to Perkins. That seems improbable, as Spengler's magnum opus was not translated into English until 1926. In any event, by 1927 Fitzgerald had become a disciple of the German philosopher. "He and Marx are the only modern philosophers that still manage to make sense in this horrible mess," he wrote Perkins. He was especially impressed by Spengler's "dominant supercessive idea" that the West was in the throes of a fatal malady. In the final deterioration of the West, Spengler believed, money would replace aristocracy, and "monied thugs" and "new Caesars" would take control. Fitzgerald superimposed this concept on the framework of his novel: Spengler provided him with an intellectually impressive rationale for his own conviction that something was terribly wrong at the very heart of Western civilization.[23]

In *Tender Is the Night* sexual degeneration is the most powerful metaphor for this cancerous decline. Devereux Warren's incestuous relationship with his daughter Nicole clearly exemplifies this moral corruption, but it is only the most obvious of a number of examples in Fitzgerald's novel. In addition to echoes of incest in the Dick Diver–Rosemary Hoyt relationship and elsewhere, other forms of sexual deviance penetrate every corner of the book's expatriate society. Campion, Dumphry, and the Chilean youth Francisco are overtly homosexual. Mary North Minghetti and Lady Caroline Sibly-Biers are almost certainly lesbians, as are the cobra-headed women at the party on the rue Monsieur. Moreover, Fitzgerald cut still other passages portraying what he regarded as sexual perversion, presumably to avoid offending public taste. One example is the "Wanda Breasted" episode, which Malcolm Cowley printed as an appendix to his 1951 revised edition of the novel. This scene forcefully conveys the disgust of Francis Melarky (and the author) at discovering that Wanda, a girl he has desired, was "a hysterical Lesbian." "God damn these women!" he thinks.

Fitzgerald might have written a first-rate novel by weaving his rhetorical and storytelling magic around such materials as the Jozan–Lois Moran adulteries, his relationship with the Murphys, and Spengler's notion of a dying culture. But he could not have written the novel that became *Tender Is the Night* without living through the tragedy of Zelda's breakdown on 23 April 1930 and her subsequent unsuccessful attempts to regain her health. Her collapse fit perfectly into his Spenglerian world view: the world had proved too much for her—or more specifically, a postwar world that invited women to compete against men.

Here Fitzgerald grafted onto Spengler the basic argument of D. H. Lawrence's *Fantasia of the Unconscious*: that modern men and women were engaged in a struggle for dominance, and that women were winning. Lawrence's book, which Fitzgerald read in the spring of 1930, inveighed against a reversal of sex roles in contemporary society. As Lawrence saw it, contemporary man was losing sight of his principal objective in life—a "disinterested craving . . . to make something wonderful out of his own head and his own self"—as a consequence of his sexual desire. Trying to please the female, Lawrence felt, led to male weakness, and women naturally proceeded to fill the vacuum of leadership. The generic modern woman, he wrote, "becomes the fearless inwardly relentless, determined positive party. . . . She is now a queen of the earth, and inwardly a fearsome tyrant." These ideas appealed to Fitzgerald, and logically so, because they so nearly reflected his own. "I believe," he wrote Mrs. Bayard Turnbull as stage three of *Tender* was taking shape in September 1932, "that if one is interested in the world into which willy-nilly one's children will grow up the most accurate data can be found in the European leaders, such as Lawrence, Jung, and Spengler."[24]

Fitzgerald overtly wrote Lawrence into *Tender* in his account of the visit to the battlefield at Amiens. A less obvious borrowing involves Dick Diver, who is defeated by the sexual as well as the monetary power of his wife. He would not have abandoned his profession—his drive to build "something wonderful" out of himself—but for the exigencies of his passion for Nicole. And Zelda's collapse is also interpreted in Lawrentian terms. The character most closely modeled on Zelda in the novel is not Nicole but the nameless, desperately ill woman artist, tortured by eczema, whom Dick Diver attempts to cure. Though he cannot save her, in a long discussion doctor and patient explore the crucial theme of the war between the sexes. She has been driven to her plight, Diver tells the dying woman, because she has insisted on doing battle against men in a deadly competition. Unlike Nicole Diver and Mary North and Rosemary Hoyt, she has been unwilling to feign conceding dominance to men while turning that apparent concession to her advantage.

In almost everything he wrote Fitzgerald focused on the competition between the sexes. In his early fiction the contest is more a game than a battle; Amory Blaine and the girls he courts only play at love. But soon the competition takes on mortal consequences, as for Myrtle Wilson and Jay Gatsby. In *Tender Is the Night* the sexes battle in open warfare, and it is significant that—except for Diver's unfortunate female patient—the women emerge as the winners, while the men either die, like Abe North and the Englishman Maria Wallis shoots in the Gare St. Lazare, or fade away like Diver himself. There can be little doubt that the author regarded his marriage with Zelda Sayre Fitzgerald as just such a struggle for survival. In *Tender Is the Night* he imagines how it might have been were he, like Diver, to lose while Zelda-Nicole emerged from the field triumphant. And the battleground on which they fight it out, in a novel that is full of references to warfare, is that of psychiatry.

Opinions vary as to the accuracy and validity of Fitzgerald's understanding of psychology. Though he did a considerable amount of reading and research on the subject—and profited from extended conversations with Zelda's Jungian doctors and with Margaret Egloff, a young divorcee studying with Jung in Switzerland—Henry Dan Piper was probably right that the author "really did not know enough about psychiatry to treat it authoritatively." Fitzgerald's central character, for example, seems too much an amalgam of charm and vulnerability, of Murphy and himself, to be convincing as a scientist and doctor. Dr. Diver's method of treatment consists of little more than telling his patients to control themselves. Moreover, Fitzgerald converted Freud's concept of transference from a stage in the psychoanalytic process to a vampiresque exchange of energy in which the patient gains strength by draining the vitality of the healer. This interpretation of "transference" manifestly had more to do with Fitzgerald's own life than with the psychoanalytical model. He saw himself undergoing "emotional bankruptcy," with much of his diminishing store of resources having evaporated in the course of his marriage. But *Tender Is the Night* is a novel, not a scientific treatise, and should be assessed on those grounds. Fitzgerald was interested in showing how men and women in postwar times had become locked in mortal combat. On that basis, as the *Journal of Nervous and Mental Disease* commented in 1935, the novel succeeds splendidly. "For the psychiatrist and psychoanalyst," the review observed, "the book is of special value as a probing story of some of the major dynamic interlockings in marriage."[25]

By the fall of 1931 Zelda was thought to be well enough to leave institutional care, and the Fitzgeralds returned to the United States. Zelda stayed in Montgomery while Scott went to Hollywood in search of funds to finance an extended period of work on the novel. Now, at last, he was very nearly ready to launch into stage three, rescuing what was usable from the first two stages—about 35,000 words—and adding another 115,000 words to the script that became *Tender Is the Night*. There remained but to add a Marxist plank to the intellectual substructure provided by Spengler, Lawrence, and Jung. On arrival in Alabama Fitzgerald told a newspaper interviewer that he was "somewhat of a Communist in ideals." He not only read *New Russia's Primer*, a simplified account of the Five Year Plan circulated by the Book-of-the-Month Club, but was enough impressed by it to insist that Zelda read it also and discuss it with Scottie. Anticipating the drumbeat of revolution, he suggested she take their money out of the bank in Montgomery, against the chance of economic collapse.[26] When he formulated his "General Plan" for stage three early in 1932, he couched much of it in Marxist terms. The protagonist was to have been "brought up in a family sunk from haute burgeosie to petit burgeoisie." Though himself "a communist-liberal-idealist, a moralist in revolt," he was to suffer his decline as a consequence of "living under patronage ect. & among the burgeoise." In the end, having cured his homicidal wife, he is a mere shell of his former self. Yet he does manage to fulfill his ideals in one way, by sending "his neglected son into soviet Russia to educate him."[27]

Obviously Fitzgerald did not follow much of this plan. Diver has no discernible political position, nor does he send a son to Russia. Yet *Tender Is the Night* does contain a strong political component. In the opening section, for example, the White Russians who once frequented the hotels of the Riviera are glimpsed driving taxicabs. At the Divers' party McKisco's socialism meets its match in Barban's anarchic strength; later the soldier of fortune Barban is employed to rescue Russian aristocrats. In a large measure, though, the novel makes its statement not through any overt commentary but by depicting the corruption and callousness of the haute bourgeoisie, with Baby Warren as the prime example, and by delineating the downfall of an older, better time. As John Dos Passos was to remark, "the whole conception of the book is enormous—and so carefully understated that—so far as I know—not a single reviewer discovered it." *Tender Is the Night*, he told Fitzgerald, demonstrated "the collapse of one of the great afterwar imperial delusions. . . . The way you first lay in the pretty picture and then start digging under the surface is immense."[28]

In no way were Americans more deluded, Fitzgerald thought, than in the pages of the books their children read. With Zelda more or less incapacitated, he increasingly assumed the role of mentor to their daughter Scottie; and it is clear, from the evidence of *Tender Is the Night*, that he was appalled by what he discovered in the standard reading material for preadolescents. Rosemary, for example, is initially described as lacking in judgment, for she comes to the Riviera "as dewy with belief as a child from one of Mrs. Burnett's vicious tracts." Frances Hodgson Burnett's popular *Little Lord Fauntleroy* (1886) and *The Secret Garden* (1911) presented a falsely idealized picture of existence, leaving young readers ill-equipped to confront stern reality. Moreover, Fitzgerald characterizes the lesbians at the rue Monsieur party as "all fashioned by Louisa M. Alcott or Madame de Ségur." In other words, the treacly confections of Louisa May Alcott and her French counterpart, Sophie (Rostopchine), Comtesse de Ségur, led not merely to ignorance but to moral degradation. Fairy tales adversely affected Dick Diver as well. He would have been much better off, we are told, had the Fairy Blackstick in Thackeray's anti–fairy tale granted him "a little misfortune" in his youth to steel him for the rigors ahead.[29]

IV

In January 1932 Zelda Fitzgerald, who had begun working on a novel of her own, suffered a relapse and was taken to Baltimore for treatment. At about the same time her husband set down his extended "General Plan" for stage three of his novel. The plan included a plot outline and descriptive details about major characters such as Dick, Nicole, "the actress" (Rosemary Hoyt), and "The Friend" (Tommy Barban). Fitzgerald's model for this plan came from Emile Zola's notes for *L'Assommoir*, as recorded in Matthew Josephson's *Zola and His Time*. He acknowledged the indebtedness in a note to Josephson and recommended a similar procedure to John O'Hara.[30] With this preliminary task accomplished, Fitzgerald was confident as never before. Characteristically, though, he underestimated the difficulty and duration of the job ahead of him. On 15 January 1932 he wrote Perkins that he was $6,000 ahead and was going to spend "five consecutive months on the novel. . . . Am replanning it to include what's good in what I have, adding 41,000 new words & publishing."[31] It was to require another two years and more than 100,000 "new words" before *Tender Is the Night* was ready for publication.

The most immediate roadblock to progress was Zelda's illness and the threat posed by *her* novel. Despite being institutionalized at Phipps Clinic and limited to two hours a day of concentrated work, over a six-week period she finished the novel she had begun in Alabama. Then, not altogether disingenuously, she sent the typescript first to Max Perkins and to her husband second. When Fitzgerald read this draft of *Save Me the Waltz*, he was outraged. "PLEASE DO NOT JUDGE OR IF NOT ALREADY DONE EVEN CONSIDER ZELDAS BOOK UNTIL YOU GET

REVISED VERSION," he wired Perkins on 16 March. The same day, he wrote an angry letter to Dr. Mildred Squires, the psychiatrist who had been treating his wife (and to whom her novel was dedicated). Therein he spelled out his two major objections to her book. In the first place, she had used the name "Amory Blaine" for her male protagonist, "a somewhat anemic portrait painter." And of course Amory Blaine is the autobiographical hero of Fitzgerald's *This Side of Paradise*. He did not like the borrowing, and he assuredly did not like being made a fool of. Secondly, he thought that Zelda was preempting his turf and appropriating his subject matter. Then too, he must have felt a measure of shame that Zelda had completed a novel in a few short months, despite a severe breakdown, while his had been seven years in preparation, so far. Most of all he considered himself betrayed. Zelda had written her book, he maintained, "under a greenhouse which is my money, my name, and my love."[32] Yet she felt no responsibility toward the greenhouse, knocking glass out of the roof whenever she chose.

In explaining why she had delayed sending him the script, Zelda wrote Scott that she wanted to avoid the kind of "scathing criticism" he'd recently given her stories. And, she confessed, "I was also afraid we might have touched on the same material." Basically her letter was one of apology, placing her husband in control of the family literary productions. From that time on he took over, guiding Zelda's revisions, keeping Perkins informed, and even telling the editor how much (and how little) to praise his wife's work. By the middle of May he sent the rewritten *Save Me the Waltz* to Scribner's with his evaluation that the novel was now a good one, perhaps very good. The book was published on 7 October and sold about 1,400 copies. The reviews were indifferent.[33]

It is easy to understand how Zelda Fitzgerald's fevered prose—full of improbable metaphors, linking apparently inappropriate nouns and adjectives—might have blinded reviewers to her novel's merits. Like *This Side of Paradise*, her husband's first novel, *Save Me the Waltz* commits any number of sins against literary art, yet it does not fail in the most fundamental way of all: it does not fail to live. Alabama Beggs and her sisters come vividly to life in the opening sections, as does her sexual attraction to the Frenchman Jacques Chevre-Feuille and her frantic pursuit of excellence in ballet. Her husband, the successful painter David Knight, is a much less successfully realized character and verges on villainy in his casual willingness to be seduced by the actress Gabriele Gibbs in Paris. The novel draws substantially on the Fitzgeralds' recent experience for its subject matter—more so than does *Tender Is the Night*. There are also striking similarities between the two novels.

A number of episodes in *Save Me the Waltz* prefigure parallel ones in *Tender Is the Night*. In Zelda's novel Alabama Beggs Knight is forced to give up her engagement as a ballet dancer in Naples to return to the bedside of her dying father. In *Tender* Dick Diver is called back to the United States by the death of his father. The Knights' child Bonnie is given a bath in dirty water, much like the one the Divers' children take at the Minghettis'. David Knight is cursed with the same sort of compulsion to please others that helps to undermine Dick Diver; both of them muse on the matter in precisely the same language. "So easy to be loved—so hard to love." Alabama assumes a Nicole-like toughness in reflecting on her attraction to Jacques: "You took what you wanted from life, if you could get it, and you did without the rest." *Waltz*'s Miss Dickie Axton shoots her lover in the Gare de l'Est; *Tender*'s Maria Wallis shoots hers in the Gare St. Lazare.

The Fitzgeralds' novels also share a number of common themes. One is the importance of work and the way it can be compromised by possession of wealth. Dick Diver succumbs to the lure of leisure his wife's money provides; Nicole occupies much of her time in fabulous spending sprees. Spending money "played a big part" in Alabama's life as well, until she lost, through her work in the ballet, "the necessity for material possessions." Both Zelda and Scott deplored the illusions American children are brought up on, through fairy tales and the blandishments of commercial advertising. Lumbered with such Pollyannaish expectations, they are ill equipped to confront harsh reality. And *Waltz*, like *Tender*, included at least one section in which socialism is regarded with some sympathy.[34]

None of these resemblances troubled Fitzgerald unduly. *Save Me the Waltz* remained after all the story of Zelda Sayre—the narrative of an attractive and willful Southern belle who marries a successful Northern artist, sees her marriage collapse through infidelity during a long period of expatriation in France, and recovers her dignity through immersion in the ballet. The novel told almost all of Zelda's story, omitting only the crucial fact of her mental illness. This was a subject her doctors warned her against writing about, but she turned to it nonetheless after the disappointment of *Save Me the Waltz*'s reception. In the spring of 1933 Scott found out about it and immediately tried to stop her. His novel in progress was going to deal with Nicole Diver's schizophrenia. To have Zelda exploring the same subject in her writing seemed intolerable—and it was on this specific issue that the famous literary battle between them was joined. Fitzgerald took the position that whatever happened to either of them belonged to him to use in his fiction, as he was the professional writer whose work paid the bills. On these grounds he sometimes signed stories and articles (or signed them jointly, as "by F. Scott and Zelda Fitzgerald") that were substantially written by her. On the same grounds he took excerpts from Zelda's mentally troubled letters and reassigned them to Nicole.

In a long and exceedingly bitter confrontation witnessed by Dr. Thomas Rennie on 28 May 1933, the Fitzgeralds debated this issue. "What is the matter with Scott," she said by way of retaliation to his claims of professional privilege, "is that he has not written that book and if he will ever get it written, why, he won't feel so miserable and suspicious and mean towards everybody else." It was characteristic of Fitzgerald that he took that remark, obviously intended to wound, and refashioned it for *Tender*. "You're a coward!" Nicole Diver tells her husband. "You've made a failure of your life, and you want to blame it on me." Zelda reluctantly agreed not to write about insanity until Scott finally finished his novel. After that, she said, she would insist on her artistic independence, even if it meant divorce.[35]

V

Throughout the summer and early fall of 1933 Fitzgerald worked hard to ready stage three for the presses. "The novel has gone ahead faster than I thought, he wrote Perkins on 25 September. In about a month he would "appear in person" in his publisher's office, "carrying the manuscript and wearing a spiked helmet. . . . *Please do not have a band as I do not care for music.*"[36]

By this time it had been decided to serialize the book in *Scribner's* magazine. *Scribner's* paid $10,000 for the rights, with $6,000 of that applied to his debt at the book publishers. It is hard to say exactly what motivated this decision; the original *Liberty* contract—secured by a healthy advance—was for several times that sum. It may be that Fitzgerald opted for *Scribner's* largely out of loyalty to Perkins, who had been supportive throughout the long hiatus between novels. It may be that he regarded *Scribner's*, a respected monthly, as a more fitting medium for a serious novel than either *Liberty*, a weekly that had (in Perkins's phrase) recently become "horribly cheap" or the rather less literary monthly *Cosmopolitan*. In addition, as Ober suggested, a weekly like *Liberty* would be hard put to find space for a novel as long as Fitzgerald's. In any event serial publication would be a good thing, Fitzgerald felt, because he had written "a book that only gives its full effect on second reading."[37] He was right about his novel—*Tender* does profit from second (or third, or many) readings—but rather naive to expect that critics or the general public would actually read both the magazine serial and the book.

Scribner's printed the novel in four installments, beginning in

January 1934. Fitzgerald delivered his manuscript late in October 1933, but he was by no means finished with it at that stage. He was an inveterate reviser of his own prose, who constantly made changes up to the last possible moment. In this instance he did extensive rewriting on the serial galleys before magazine publication and then again on the book galleys which are set from the *Scribner's* serial. In the end he ran out of time to revise, because book publication was scheduled for 12 April 1934, only a few weeks after the appearance of the final installment in the April 1934 *Scribner's*. As long as he could, Fitzgerald retouched for felicity of expression, but neither he nor Perkins gave the book the kind of scrupulous editorial attention it deserved. As a result *Tender Is the Night* has never appeared in a well-edited text. The book is full of misspellings, particularly of foreign words, and is further flawed by errors in chronology. As Bruccoli points out, it is "scandalous" that so important a novel should exist only in bad texts.[38]

Once he had his general plan for this novel firmly in mind, Fitzgerald completed the book in little more than a year. Rather remarkably, he was able to salvage most of stage one by reassigning much of the material about Francis Melarky either to Rosemary Hoyt or to Dick Diver. But this copy was not merely lifted from one draft and plunked down in another. Fitzgerald substantially reworked the old Melarky material and added new dialogue and incident to flesh out his portraits, especially that of his protagonist. Then, of course, he had the tale of Nicole's violation and madness to tell afresh, and the ruin of the Divers' marriage.

Stage three of the novel had several titles, but each of them focused clearly on Dick Diver. The first draft was called *The Drunkard's Holiday*, the second draft *Doctor Diver's Holiday*, and as late as 29 October 1933 he wrote the editor Alfred Dashiell of *Scribner's* magazine that his title would be, simply, *Richard Diver*. The final change to *Tender Is the Night*, made over Perkins's objections, seems in retrospect a masterstroke, for this title, with its echo of Keats's romantic and melancholy "Ode to a Nightingale," admirably captures the spirit of the novel. Keats's famous ode, Fitzgerald said, was a poem he read often, and always with tears in his eyes. In addition he thought of the phrase in connection with love, and with love as a battle. The word *night* "does a great deal for the title," he told Archibald MacLeish. "Women are different by day and by night and night has its own particular relationship to love. . . . There is a difference in depth of a woman's face when she's defending herself in full light and in the dark, when she's not defending herself."[39]

Having fixed on a title, Fitzgerald labored over the serial galleys, altering word order here, making emendations for the ear there. Besides these stylistic distinctions he made significant deletions and additions in moving from magazine to book copy. Some of these were dictated by standards of taste at the time: he could treat the subject of incest far more openly for Scribner's the book publishers than for *Scribner's* magazine, for example. Yet he cut more material than he added in revising. He omitted six scenes from the serial, totaling about thirty pages, and added only a few new pages. Two of the deleted scenes describe Abe North's adventures in the Ritz Hotel bar. One has to do with a rather messy affair between Dick Diver and a governess in Innsbruck. Three take place on shipboard during Diver's return from his father's funeral.[40]

In one of these shipboard scenes the now-successful novelist Albert McKisco brings his typewriter on deck each day to work in public, hence becoming "the most noticeable figure on the ship." Moreover, McKisco is annoyed when a female novelist, also on board, sets up her typewriter on deck to compete with him. This scene obviously denigrated McKisco and hence detracted from the effect of his function as an opposite to Diver. Abe North's alcoholism and failure foreshadow what will happen to Fitzgerald's protagonist, as many readers have noticed. But the reversal between McKisco and Diver—his rise nicely contrasts with Diver's decline—has largely escaped critical notice.[41] Among the additions perhaps the most significant is a conversation between Dick and Rosemary as they part in Rome. "I guess I'm the Black Death," Diver tells her. "I don't seem to bring people happiness any more." And in fact after Rome he is seen only once more in his former role as one who bestows "carnivals of affection" on others.

This, of course, is the scene at the jail in Antibes, where Diver talks the chief of police into releasing Mary Minghetti and Lady Caroline after the transvestite episode. Though Diver is not proud of himself for fixing "this thing he didn't give a damn about," the incident shows him as capable of helping others even though Nicole no longer requires his services. An editorial problem arose at *Scribner's* magazine in connection with the jail scene. The final installment of the novel ran overlong, and Perkins wired Fitzgerald, asking him to cut the episode from 1,250 words to 800. In response, the author pointed out that the rescue was absolutely necessary: "OTHERWISE DICKS CHARACTER WEAKENS . . . IT IS NEEDED AND WAS WRITTEN TO BOLSTER HIM UP IN INEVITABLY UNDIGNIFIED CUCKOLD SITUATION." Instead of cutting, he actually lengthened the scene to 1,400 words in final serial galleys. "It is legitimate to ruin Dick," he pointed out, "but it is by no means legitimate to make him ineffectual."[42]

Clearly Fitzgerald wanted to preserve some trace of the "dignified and responsible" protagonist he had depicted in the first part of the book. This determination probably accounted for the extremely important deletion he made in the semifinal draft for the serial. Both in *The Drunkard's Holiday* and in *Doctor Diver's Holiday* the book ends with Diver drunk. In the one version he falls on his face after making the sign of the cross; in the other he is helped away by a waiter Baby Warren sends to his aid. In the actual ending Fitzgerald softened this motif. Even here, admittedly, Diver takes "a big drink" of brandy after bidding his children good-bye and drinks anisette with Mary Minghetti on Gausse's terrace; though it is still morning, he is "already well in advance of the day . . . where a man should be at the end of a good dinner." Undoubtedly it is the liquor that persuaded him to make Mary feel that he cares about her. Yet when that charade is over and he stands up to bless the beach, he sways a little but does not need assistance.[43] It would have been too great an indignity, Fitzgerald must have decided, to let Diver exit staggering.

From the beginning of his career Fitzgerald thought of himself as something of an advertising expert. (He had worked briefly in a New York advertising agency in 1919.) So he was liberal with advice to Perkins about the proper way to introduce *Tender Is the Night*. The novel had been a long time in progress, but that should be played down, he said. "No exclamatory 'At last, the long awaited ect,'" he advised, for people would only say, "Oh yeah" to that. Above all he wanted to avoid any suggestion of frivolity. This was "a horse of a different color" from his *Saturday Evening Post* stories. "Please do not use the phrase 'Riviera' or 'gay resorts,'" he cautioned Perkins. In fact it might be appropriate to include a suggestion that "after a romantic start, a serious story unfolds." He was also "absolutely dead" on any kind of ballyhoo or personal publicity. "The reputation of a book must grow from within upward, must be a natural growth," he insisted.[44] In this respect he could not have been righter, and *Tender Is the Night* was to illustrate the point precisely. It is a novel whose reputation has developed over the decades, a novel that was undervalued in its own time.

VI

When at last *Tender Is the Night* was published, Fitzgerald had high hopes for it. "It's good, good, good," he told another writer,[45] and confidently awaited confirmation of that view from the book-buying public, from the critics, and from his literary colleagues. Financially the novel's sales may have been hurt by its serialization in *Scribner's*, and book sales generally were poor in that rock-bottom Depression year. Under the circumstances *Tender* sold well, though not nearly so well as Fitzgerald had anticipated. There were three printings totaling about 15,000 copies during the spring of 1934. During April and May the book ranked tenth on the *Publisher's Weekly* best-seller lists. The Literary Guild made it an alternate selection and apparently considered it for a more prominent place in its offerings. (It had been a mistake "to refuse the Literary Guild subsidy," Fitzgerald wrote Perkins a year after publication.) In all, sales earned him royalties of about $5,000, less than enough to pay his debts.[46]

The reviews varied widely. Gilbert Seldes, who knew both Fitzgerald and the Riviera well, chose to demolish a cliché of the book-reviewing trade in praising *Tender*. It was not a book he could not put down, Seldes said. It was a book he *had* to put down because it evoked life with such intensity that he had "to stop, to think and to feel." At the opposite end of the range of opinion were those who tarred the author with the brush of the Jazz Age writer; no matter what he wrote, some reviewers were unwilling to give him thoughtful attention. The most typical attitude, perhaps, was struck by Fanny Butcher in the *Chicago Tribune*, who relied upon yet another catch phrase in classifying the novel. It was, she concluded, "a brilliant failure."[47]

To the extent that the reviews were unfavorable, it was not so much a consequence of their subject matter as Fitzgerald had feared and subsequent literary historians have assumed. *Tender* was published, after all, in the trough of the Depression, and it might have been anticipated that his depiction of the life of rich expatriates on the Riviera would rub politically sensitive readers the wrong way. In fact at least one such left-wing critic—Philip Rahv in *The Daily Worker*—criticized the author for writing about such characters at all. Rahv recognized that the novel portrayed the imminent collapse of the leisure class, "dying in hospitals for the mentally diseased, in swanky Paris hotels and on the Riviera beaches." Yet, he maintained, Fitzgerald discerned "a certain grace" in the last contortions of this class, and this apparent sympathy drove Rahv to a patently wrong-headed diatribe at the conclusion of his review: "Dear Mr. Fitzgerald, you can't hide from a hurricane under a beach umbrella."[48] This reaction, however, was the exception and not the rule. Mostly the criticism of *Tender* focused not on political issues but on technical literary grounds.

A number of reviewers thought the book was poorly structured, that its having begun with Rosemary's adoring point of view on the Riviera aroused a "categorical expectancy" that was violated as she faded out of the book and it concentrated instead on Dick Diver's downfall. Fitzgerald was enough disturbed about this charge to rec-ommend to novelist Joseph Hergesheimer that he open the book in the middle and read on from there. Hergesheimer had earlier told Fitzgerald that it was "almost impossible to write a book about an actress," and he was not the only one—Fitzgerald's letter pointed out—to be "repelled by the apparent triviality of the opening."[49]

A still more common objection—one that cropped up often in the early reviews—was that Diver's disintegration was insufficiently pre-pared for. Even Fitzgerald's former mentor at Princeton, Dean Chris-tian Gauss, paused at the end of a laudatory letter to remind the author that he had had the feeling, while reading Part 3 of the maga-zine serial, "that Dick went haywire too fast." Part of the difficulty stemmed from that romantic beginning, in which Diver was bodied forth in such glowing terms. Many readers, then and now, did not *want* to see him suffer and decline. Others, rather simplistically, ob-jected that there was no one reason to account for his degeneration, as if so complex a matter as the breakup of a personality under stress could be reduced to a single cause or to one traumatic event. Diver's crack-up, as Bruccoli observes, "is deeply rooted in his character—in his desire to please, in his egotism, and in his romantic view of life."[50] Or, it might be said, he sacrifices himself to restore his wife's health. But he is also victimized by her wealth and the casual brutality of the rich, and by the moral corruption festering everywhere around him. If Fitzgerald learned anything from Zelda's illness, it was that human beings could not be labeled and accounted for. So Diver is not Charm, any more than Macbeth is Ambition.

Unlike the reviewers, most of Fitzgerald's fellow authors immedi-ately saw the virtues of the novel. "It's so tightly knit together that it can't be read in pieces," John Dos Passos perceptively remarked. He had been "enormously thrown off by the beginning" but later realized how well it worked. *Tender Is the Night* surpassed *The Great Gatsby*, John Peale Bishop wrote Fitzgerald. It established him as "a true, a beautiful and a tragic novelist." It was "one of the great books of the world," John O'Hara decided at once.[51] And there were encomiums from James Branch Cabell, Archibald MacLeish, and others. Yet one crucial colleague remained to be heard from during the first weeks after publication.

"Do you like the book?" Fitzgerald finally wrote Hemingway on 10 May 1934. "For God's sake drop me a line and tell me one way or another." Ernest could not hurt his feelings, either way, Scott assured him. Hemingway took his friend at his word and replied with his "old charming frankness." He found fault with the composite characters in the novel (Murphy-Fitzgerald-Diver, for instance), a subject which led to further correspondence between the two writers. In addition he lectured Fitzgerald severely. It was true, he conceded, that *Tender Is the Night* proved Fitzgerald could think. Yet aside from that it was flawed because "a long time ago you stopped listening except to the answers to your own questions," and not listening had a way of drying writers up. Most of all, Hemingway disapproved of Fitzgerald's exploring his own troubles in fiction (he was to have the same reaction, except more so, when Fitzgerald published his "Crack-Up" essays in *Esquire*). "Forget your personal tragedy," Hemingway instructed him. "We are all bitched from the start and you especially have to be hurt like hell before you can write seriously. But when you get the damned hurt use it—don't cheat with it. . . . You see, Bo, you're not a tragic character. Neither am I. All we are is writers and what we should do is write." It was too bad that he'd married someone who "wants to compete with you and ruins you" and too bad also that he was "a rummy," though no more a rummy than James Joyce or most good writers. After this much by way of faultfinding, Hemingway ended with encouragement for the future: "You can write twice as well now as you ever could. All you need to do is write truly and not care about what the fate of it is."[52]

In effect Hemingway's letter had less to do with the novel than with what he regarded as Fitzgerald's waste of his talent. And within a year he had amended his judgment in favor of *Tender*. "A strange thing," he wrote Perkins on 15 April 1935, "is that in retrospect his Tender is the Night gets better and better. I wish you would tell him I said so."[53] Fitzgerald was happy to get the news, for by that time he was occupied in doing exactly what Hemingway had warned him against: worrying about the fate of his book.

The appearance of *Tender Is the Night* found Fitzgerald in the same financial position he had occupied after *Gatsby* emerged nine years earlier. In debt, he could not afford even a brief period of "filling up" before returning to work on *Saturday Evening Post* stories. But at least he now had a property that might be sold to Hollywood or Broadway, or so he assumed. *Gatsby* had brought him $15,000 for screen rights, and the play based on the novel earned him another $18,000; naturally he hoped for a similar return from *Tender*. Even before publication Harold Ober was negotiating with the studios for screen rights. RKO showed the most interest, he wrote Fitzgerald on 8 March 1934, and between them author and agent speculated about possible casting. Fitzgerald proposed the actress Ann Harding for Nicole, but RKO and Ober thought Katharine Hepburn might be better. All agreed that Fredric March would make an effective Dick Diver. This remained idle speculation, however, for RKO's nibble did not become a bite. Nonetheless, in April and May Fitzgerald and his young Baltimore protégé,

Charles Marquis (Bill) Warren, turned out a treatment for the films. Fitzgerald then sent Warren to Hollywood to peddle their adulterated version (in a melodramatically upbeat ending, Dick operates to save Nicole's life).[54]

Warren had no luck, but by January 1935 United Artists was considering another treatment of the novel for its star Miriam Hopkins. United Artists was unlikely to buy the book outright, Ober reported, but the producer Samuel Goldwyn might want to take an option on the rights and then pay Fitzgerald to work on the screenplay. In response Fitzgerald said he hated Hollywood "like poison" but might be persuaded to spend six weeks there at a guaranty of $2,000 a week.[55] Nothing came of that lead, either. *Tender Is the Night* was not made into a film—a bad film, as it turned out—until 1961.

Fitzgerald pursued Broadway much as he had Hollywood. By December 1934 he had lined up yet another young would-be author, Robert Spafford, to fashion a play based on the novel. Ober was not enthusiastic about this arrangement, as Spafford was so inexperienced. Far more promising were the options that the producer Sam H. Grisman took in 1935 and 1936, with veteran theater hands Jack Kirkland and Austin Parker to write the dramatization. Neither Spafford nor the Grisman-Kirkland-Parker team came up with anything salable, however. So it was with some desperation that Fitzgerald welcomed an overture from the dramatists Cora Jarrett and Kate Oglebay in October 1937. "[S]omething must be done within the next two years to keep the book alive," he wrote Ober. By January 1938 a contract was signed with Jarrett and Oglebay, with the dramatists and the novelist to split potential royalties and receipts down the middle. Within a few weeks Jarrett produced a script that Fitzgerald thought was excellent, if almost too faithful to the original. In a surge of optimism he once again speculated about possible actors for the roles. Margaret Rawlings seemed a very good choice for Nicole; Beulah Bondi did not. Moreover, Robert Montgomery had often spoken to him about playing Dick Diver. But the Jarrett-Oglebay team could not secure backing for their script, and no one else has since.[56] *Tender Is the Night* has yet to be seen in a major theatrical production.

In addition to angling for a film or play based on *Tender* Fitzgerald sought to keep his book alive through republication. The original Scribner's edition seemed to have run its course by May 1936, when the author wired Donald Klopfer and Bennett Cerf proposing that *Tender* be published in the inexpensive and popular Modern Library format. *Gatsby* had come out in the Modern Library in 1934, and Fitzgerald thought it would be beneficial both to the publishers and to himself to have two of his books represented in the series. Despite some initial encouragement and discussions by mail over several months, Klopfer and Cerf—especially Cerf—decided against the suggestion.[57]

Another two years passed without any action on *Tender*. Then, in March 1938, Perkins revealed his "secret hope that we could some day—after a big success with a new novel—make an omnibus book of 'This Side of Paradise,' 'The Great Gatsby,' and 'Tender Is the Night.' . . . But," he added, "we must forget that plan for the moment." Ignoring Perkins's comment about the need for a new novel first, Fitzgerald leaped at the suggestion. He was in Hollywood for an extended stay, and an omnibus volume would be a way of keeping his name before the reading public. "How remote is that idea," he asked, "and why must we forget it[?]" Economics was one reason, Perkins responded. The Depression was bottoming out again, and Scribner's was selling only about a third as many copies as during prosperous times. Besides, he doubted that *Tender* had yet taken on the patina of "romantic glamour" that books from the past sometimes acquired.[58] Though neither the Modern Library edition nor the omnibus volume had come to pass, Fitzgerald continued to plot for the future of his novel. *Tender* was, he felt confident, a book that people would not forget if only they had a chance to read it. And despite its brief appearance on the best-seller charts, he thought it had not really had its chance. Hard times had militated against sales, but perhaps the fault had been his as well. What if he were to do some rearranging?

As early as his correspondence with the Modern Library in mid-1936, Fitzgerald contemplated making alterations in *Tender*. His initial telegram to Cerf, on 16 May 1936, broached the subject thus: "IF I MADE CERTAIN CHANGES TOWARD THE END WHICH I SEE NOW ARE ESSENTIAL COMMA IT WOULD MAKE ALL THE DIFFERENCE IN THE SPLIT UP OF THE TWO PRINCIPAL CHARACTERS." Three months later, now mindful that the inexpensiveness of the series depended on printing from the original plates, he reassured Cerf that any revisions would take the form of *inserted* pages with "terse and graceful" headings as a guide to the reader, or at worst minor rewritings that conformed to "equivalent line lengths." The idea was to revise while avoiding expensive typesetting and printing costs. "DO YOU THINK THAT ONCE PUBLISHED A BOOK IS FOREVER CRYSTALIZED," Fitzgerald had telegraphed Cerf. Whatever the reply, it is clear that for him the answer was no.[59]

VII

By 24 December 1938 Fitzgerald had become convinced that *Tender* needed restructuring. "It's great fault is that the *true* beginning—the young psychiatrist in Switzerland—is tucked away in the middle of the book."[60] Reshaping the book to begin with Diver in his young manhood would, he estimated, "require changes in half a dozen other pages." Soon thereafter, presumably, he set about making such an alteration in his personal copy of the novel, cutting pages loose from the binding and reassembling them to conform to this scheme:

Analysis of *Tender*:
    I   Case History 151–212 61 pps (change moon) p. 212
   II Rosemary's Angle 3–104 101 pps. p. 3
 III Casualties 104–148, 213–224 55 pps. (–2) (120 & 121)
 IV Escape 225–306 82 pps.
  V The Way Home 306–408 103 pps. (–8) (332–341)

In his private copy, now located in the Firestone Library at Princeton, he followed almost all of this plan, which besides rearranging the text involved eliminating the two-page and eight-page sections noted in parentheses: the first appearance of the materialistic newspaper vendor (120–21) and the visit to the Minghettis (332–41). On the inside front cover of this copy he wrote in pencil: "This is the *final* version of the book as I would like it."

"Final version" he may have called it, yet there are indications that Fitzgerald died without finishing his revisions. In fact he obviously intended to do more than merely rearrange the narrative and delete a few scenes. He also planned to go through the entire novel one last time. He did just that in the first two chapters of the copy at Princeton, where he made a number of brief but important revisions: cutting some phrases entirely, improving others, catching some spelling errors, changing punctuation. Then, next to a penciled asterisk near the end of chapter 2, he wrote, "This is my mark to say that I have made final corrections up to this point."[61] Obviously the rest of the novel did not benefit from these emendations. In addition Fitzgerald may have had still more extensive alterations in mind. According to a passage in his notebooks,

> *Tender* is less interesting toward the climax because of the absence of conversation. The eye flies for it and skips essential stuff for they don't want their characters resolved in dessication and analysis but like me in action that results from the previous. All the more reason for *emotional* planning.[62]

This note, with its fascinating insight into reader psychology (the eye "flies" for conversation amid gray pages and wants characterization acted out), suggests that Fitzgerald might have worked for more dialogue toward the end of the novel—for more scene and picture, in Jamesian terms—had he been able to complete his "final corrections."

Though Fitzgerald had not completed fine-tuning his novel, his notes planning the revision and his chopped-up copy of the book warranted the publication in 1951 of what its editor, Malcolm Cowley, called "the author's final version." For a few years Scribner's circulated this version of the novel, before reverting to the original. The publishers elected to use the original text in their Scribner Library paperback, published in 1960, and that is the version of the novel read in most college classes. Yet an error by an employee of the publishers resulted, in the early 1970s, in a large paperback run of the 1951 version, and students of that period are likely to have been issued copies of the Cowley version.

Which version is better continues to form the subject of a lively debate. Basically, Cowley argued in his introduction, the 1951 version was an improvement over the 1934 one because it focused on Dick Diver from the very start and traced his downfall chronologically, avoiding the flashback necessitated by beginning with Rosemary's point of view on the Riviera. (Cowley also corrected some of the novel's errors.) Any clarity that might have been gained in this way, critics objected, could hardly make up for the elements of mystery and suspense that were sacrificed. "It seemed to take the magic out" of the novel, Hemingway commented. Besides, it was more realistic to introduce Diver in midcareer. That was after all the way, Ford Madox Ford maintained, that we became acquainted with most people in real life. We meet them, become interested in them, and subsequently find out what we can about them. In fiction also, it made more sense to "get [one's protagonist] in with a strong impression, and then work backwards and forwards over his past." [63]

The most thorough and effective argument against the 1951 version has been made by Brian Higgins and Hershel Parker in a long essay. Of their many points, two carry the most weight. First, Higgins and Parker maintain that by not beginning with Rosemary's adoring picture of Diver, the novel fails to provide him with the kind of status that could render his ultimate defeat truly significant. We can hardly feel tragic about his collapse, they observed, "because we have scarcely been allowed to think well of him." Their second, and more telling, objection has to do with the way the novel was written. Complicated as the composition of *Tender* certainly was, it seems clear that Fitzgerald wrote his novel in the order it originally appeared, starting with the Riviera material, shifting back to Diver's early career, then coming forward into the future. It follows that the author, as he sat down to work on Book 2, must have had what he had written in Book 1 more or less in mind, and so on through the book. As John Dewey asserted, "the artist is controlled in the process of his work by his grasp of the connection between what he has already done and what he is to do next." The order of composition matters a great deal, and artists are apt to underestimate the damage they may do, in retroactive attempts at revision, by restructuring their fiction.[64]

The Cowley version has its defenders as well as its detractors. Among these are Wayne Booth, in his *Rhetoric of Fiction*, and Milton R. Stern in his fine introduction to *Critical Essays on "Tender Is the Night."* In this essay Stern takes up (and attempts to dispose of) the various grounds for objection and ends by calling for well-edited printing of *both* versions. That may be too much to hope for. In any event the 1934 version is now clearly in the ascendancy. Yet all scholars would surely agree with Stern that "a carefully edited fair edition" of *Tender Is the Night* is badly needed. To this date Scribner's has shown no inclination to produce such an edition. Because the novel will pass into the public domain in 1990, however, those who care about Fitzgerald's work and his reputation may not have many more years to wait.[65]

In arriving at an ultimate assessment of the merits of *Tender*, few have been unable to resist comparing it to Fitzgerald's other great novel. In several ways it stands at the opposite end of the spectrum from *Gatsby*. Fitzgerald himself drew the lines of distinction in a letter to John Peale Bishop on 7 April 1934, a few days before the novel was published. His intention was "entirely different" this time, he explained. "The dramatic novel has canons quite different from the philosophical, now called psychological, novel. One is a kind of *tour de force* and the other a confession of faith. It would be like comparing a sonnet sequence with an epic."[66] *Gatsby* was his dramatic novel and *Tender* his psychological one. *Gatsby* was his sonnet sequence, brief, emotionally charged, and tightly knit. *Tender* was his epic, large if not sprawling in theme and scope, at once concerned with the downfall of its protagonist and a wider social context.

The contrast between the two books is underlined by their endings. *Gatsby* in effect ends with Jay Gatsby floating mortally wounded on a pneumatic mattress in the pool of his grotesque mansion. Nick Carraway is around to tell us about the funeral, about his chance meeting with Tom Buchanan in New York, about the carelessness of the rich, above all about the wonder of Gatsby's capacity to dream. But the novel is, as Fitzgerald said, a dramatic one and reaches its climax when George Wilson shoots Gatsby dead. It is much more difficult to fix on one particular scene as the climax of *Tender*. As Alan Trachtenberg has pointed out, the novel is best regarded as one of "process," whose "movements are more elaborately and calculatedly subtle and complex" than was true of *Gatsby*. To grasp the implications of *Tender* one must allow "feelings and hints to accumulate" episode by episode.[67] So it is appropriate to end with a "dying fall," Diver's fading out of Cap d'Antibes sunshine into a lackluster future in upstate New York. Significantly, no authorial voice, no Carraway standing in for Fitzgerald, is around to point the moral and generalize. At the end of an epic there is too much to think about to be encapsulated by any narrator.

Notes

1. Quoted in Bruccoli, *Some Sort of Epic Grandeur*, 369.
2. Fitzgerald to Perkins, 1 May 1925, *Letters of Fitzgerald*, 182.
3. For this plot summary of the Melarky version, as for most of the textual information in this essay, I am indebted to Bruccoli's valuable and thorough *Composition of "Tender Is the Night,"* 26–27.
4. Ibid., 23.
5. Fitzgerald to Perkins, ca. 24 April 1925, *Dear Scott/Dear Max*, 102.
6. Turnbull, *Fitzgerald*, 145.
7. Quoted by Malcolm Cowley in an endnote to *Tender Is the Night*, 354.
8. Quoted in Turnbull, *Fitzgerald*, 148.
9. For an extended treatment of this theme see Roulston, "Dick Diver's Plunge."
10. See the correspondence between Fitzgerald and Perkins in July and August 1925, *Dear Scott/Dear Max*, 117–20, and Bruccoli, *Composition of "Tender Is the Night,"* 18.
11. Fitzgerald to Ober, May–July 1926, *As Ever, Scott Fitz*, 89–92; to Perkins, ca. 25 June 1926, *Dear Scott/Dear Max*, 144.
12. Fitzgerald to Perkins, ca. 10 September, ca. 27 December, ca. 30 December 1925, 20 February 1926, *Dear Scott/Dear Max*, 121, 125, 128, 134.
13. Perkins to Fitzgerald, 20 January, 7 April 1927, *Dear Scott/Dear Max*, 146–47; telegram quoted in Bruccoli, *Composition of "Tender Is the Night,"* 50.
14. Fitzgerald to Perkins, 11 March 1935, *Dear Scott/Dear Max*, 218–19.
15. Fitzgerald to Perkins, ca. 1 January 1928, and Perkins to Fitzgerald, 3 January, 24 January 1928, *Dear Scott/Dear Max*, 149–50.
16. Edmund Wilson, "A Weekend at Ellerslie."
17. Fitzgerald to Ober, 3 June 1928, *As Ever, Scott Fitz*, 113; to Perkins, ca. 21 July 1928, *Dear Scott/Dear Max*, 152.
18. Quoted in Bruccoli, *Composition of "Tender Is the Night,"* 56–58.
19. Wilson, "A Weekend at Ellerslie," 375.
20. Fitzgerald to Perkins, ca. June 1929, *Dear Scott/Dear Max*, 156.
21. Fitzgerald to Ober, 29 August, received 16 November 1929, received 13 May 1930, and Ober to Fitzgerald, 2 July, 23 October, 5 December 1929, 5 March 1930, 19 May 1931, *As Ever, Scott Fitz*, 144, 153–54, 158, 162, 165, 167–68, 177.
22. Fitzgerald to Betty Markell, 16 September 1929, *Letters of Fitzgerald*, 495.
23. For an excellent summary of the Spenglerian elements in Fitzgerald's novel see Lehan, *Fitzgerald and the Craft of Fiction*, 30–35.
24. For the best discussion of Lawrence's influence see Sklar, *Fitzgerald*, 260–63, who quotes the letter to Mrs. Turnbull. Wexelblatt, "Fitzgerald and Lawrence," suggests still deeper resonances between the two writers.
25. Piper, *Fitzgerald*, 222–23; Steinberg, "Hardness, Light, and Psychia-

try"; Berman, "*Tender Is the Night:* Fitzgerald's *A Psychology for Psychiatrists*"; review of *Tender Is the Night* in *Journal of Nervous and Mental Disease* (July 1935).

26. See Donaldson, "Political Development of Fitzgerald."

27. The "General Plan" is reprinted in Bruccoli, *Composition of "Tender Is the Night,"* 76–82. Fitzgerald's spelling is used throughout.

28. Dos Passos to Fitzgerald, April 1934, *Correspondence of Fitzgerald,* 358.

29. See Donaldson, " 'No, I Am Not Prince Charming.' "

30. Bruccoli, *Composition of "Tender Is the Night,"* 86; Fitzgerald to O'Hara, 25 July 1936, *Letters of Fitzgerald,* 539.

31. Fitzgerald to Perkins, ca. 15 January 1932, *Dear Scott/Dear Max,* 173.

32. See the discussion of this dispute in Mayfield, *Exiles from Paradise,* 181–87, and in Bruccoli, *Epic Grandeur,* 322–25.

33. Bruccoli, *Epic Grandeur,* 326–29.

34. Zelda Fitzgerald, *Save Me the Waltz,* 190–91, 177–78, 35, 204, 98, 104, 210, 138–39, 206, 86.

35. Bruccoli, *Epic Grandeur,* 348–55, reproduces part of the transcript Dr. Rennie made of this debate.

36. Fitzgerald to Perkins, 25 September 1933, *Dear Scott/Dear Max,* 181–83.

37. Ober to Fitzgerald, 3 October 1933, *As Ever, Scott Fitz,* 199–201; Fitzgerald to Perkins, 29 September 1933, 13 January 1934, and Perkins to Fitzgerald, 30 September 1933, *Dear Scott/Dear Max,* 183–85, 188–89.

38. Bruccoli, *Composition of "Tender Is the Night,"* 206, 214, 218.

39. Fitzgerald to Dashiell, 29 October 1933, *Correspondence of Fitzgerald,* 318; Bruccoli, *Composition of "Tender Is the Night,"* xxiii, 174–75, 180; MacLeish, *Reflections,* 90.

40. Bruccoli, *Composition of "Tender Is the Night,"* xxi, 191, 198–99, 202.

41. Terry, "Albert McKisco's Role," calls attention to the omission of the shipboard scene and its effect.

42. Fitzgerald to Perkins, 5 February 1934: two telegrams, *Correspondence of Fitzgerald,* 329; letter, *Dear Scott/Dear Max,* 191.

43. Bruccoli, *Composition of "Tender Is the Night,"* 173; Cowley, endnote to *Tender Is the Night,* 356; Fitzgerald, *Tender Is the Night,* Scribner's, April 1934, 310.

44. Fitzgerald to Perkins, 19 October, 20 October 1933, 5 February, 4 March 1934, *Dear Scott/Dear Max,* 186–87, 192–94.

45. Cowley, Introduction to *Tender Is the Night,* x.

46. Bruccoli, *Epic Grandeur,* 367.

47. Seldes, "True to Type"; Butcher, "New Fitzgerald Book."

48. Rahv, "You Can't Duck Hurricane."

49. Chamberlain, "Books of the Times," 294–96; Fitzgerald to Hergesheimer, probably fall 1935, *Letters of Fitzgerald,* 532–33.

50. Chamberlain, "Books of the Times," 311–12; Bruccoli, *Composition of "Tender Is the Night,"* 109, 198.

51. Dos Passos to Fitzgerald, April 1934, and Bishop to Fitzgerald, 3 April 1934, *Correspondence of Fitzgerald,* 358–59; John O'Hara to Thomas O'Hara, 9 April 1934, *Selected Letters of O'Hara,* 90.

52. Fitzgerald to Hemingway, 10 May, 1 June 1934, *Letters of Fitzgerald,* 307–8; Hemingway, quoted in Bruccoli, *Epic Grandeur,* 375–76.

53. Hemingway, quoted in Perkins to Fitzgerald, 8 April 1935, *Dear Scott/Dear Max,* 219.

54. Fitzgerald to Ober, 21 February, 8 December 1934, and Ober to Fitz-

gerald, 8 March 1934, *As Ever, Scott Fitz*, 203–4, 209; Bruccoli, *Composition of "Tender Is the Night,"* 25; Bruccoli, *Epic Grandeur*, 380–81.

55. Ober to Fitzgerald, 8 January 1935, and Fitzgerald to Ober, 10 January 1935, *As Ever, Scott Fitz*, 215–17.

56. Fitzgerald to Ober, 26 December 1934, 1 February, ca. 5 September, 6 November, 18 November 1935, 8 October 1937, ca. Christmas 1937, 9 February, 17 February 1938 (enclosing letter to Mrs. Edwin S. Jarrett), and Ober to Fitzgerald, 3 September, 12 November, 20 November 1935, 2 March 1936, 11 January, 7 February 1938, *As Ever, Scott Fitz*, 211–12, 218–19, 225, 227, 228, 230–31, 256–57, 341, 345–54; Fitzgerald to Mrs. Mary Leonard Pritchett, 4 March 1938, *Letters of Fitzgerald*, 570.

57. Fitzgerald to Perkins, 13 June 1936, *Dear Scott/Dear Max*, 230, 277; to Cerf, 23 July 1936, *Letters of Fitzgerald*, 536–37.

58. Perkins to Fitzgerald, 9 March, 24 May 1938, and Fitzgerald to Perkins, 23 April 1938, *Dear Scott/Dear Max*, 242–47.

59. Fitzgerald to Cerf, 16 May 1936, *Correspondence of Fitzgerald*, 432; to Cerf, 13 August 1936, *Letters of Fitzgerald*, 540–41.

60. Fitzgerald to Perkins, 24 December 1938, *Dear Scott/Dear Max*, 250–51.

61. Cowley, Introduction to *Tender Is the Night*, xii–xiii.

62. Note quoted in "Appendix" to Bruccoli, *"The Last of the Novelists,"* 155.

63. Cowley, Introduction to *Tender Is the Night*, xiv–xvi (in addition to his corrections, Cowley decided not to omit one of the two passages Fitzgerald had planned to eliminate, the scene at the Minghettis' involving the dirty bathwater); Hemingway to Edmund Wilson, 28 November 1951, *Hemingway: Selected Letters*, 743; Bruccoli, *Composition of "Tender Is the Night,"* 10–11, 15 (citing Ford).

64. Higgins and Parker, "Sober Second Thoughts." Parker expands on these points in *Flawed Texts and Verbal Icons*, 72–79 (citing Dewey, 76), 219.

65. Booth, *Rhetoric of Fiction*, 190–95; Stern, introduction to *Critical Essays*, 25–30.

66. Fitzgerald to Bishop, 7 April 1934, *Letters of Fitzgerald*, 363.

67. Trachtenberg, "The Journey Back."

Works Cited

Berman, Jeffrey. *"Tender Is the Night*: Fitzgerald's *A Psychology for Psychiatrists." Literature and Psychology* 29, no. 1–2 (1979): 34–48.

Booth, Wayne C. *The Rhetoric of Fiction*. Chicago: University of Chicago Press, 1961.

Bruccoli, Matthew J. *The Composition of "Tender Is the Night": A Study of the Manuscripts*. Pittsburgh: University of Pittsburgh Press, 1963.

————. *"The Last of the Novelists": F. Scott Fitzgerald and "The Last Tycoon."* Carbondale: Southern Illinois University Press, 1977.

————. *Some Sort of Epic Grandeur: The Life of F. Scott Fitzgerald*. New York: Harcourt Brace Jovanovich, 1981.

Bryer, Jackson R., ed. *F. Scott Fitzgerald: The Critical Reception*. New York: Burt Franklin, 1978.

Butcher, Fanny. "New Fitzgerald Book Brilliant; Fails as Novel." *Chicago Tribune*, 14 April 1934. Reprinted in Bryer, *Fitzgerald: The Critical Reception*, 298–99.

Chamberlain, John. "Books of the Times." *New York Times*, 13 April, 16 April 1934. Reprinted in Bryer, *Fitzgerald: The Critical Reception*, 294–96, 311–12.

Cowley, Malcolm. "Introduction" and "Note" to F. Scott Fitzgerald, *Tender Is the Night*, ix–xviii, 349–56. New York: Scribner's, 1951.

Donaldson, Scott. " 'No, I Am Not Prince Charming': Fairy Tales in *Tender Is the Night*." In *Fitzgerald/Hemingway Annual 1973*, edited by Matthew J. Bruccoli and C. E. Frazer Clark, Jr., 105–12. Washington, D.C.: Microcard Editions, 1974.

————. "The Political Development of F. Scott Fitzgerald." In *Prospects 6*, 322–24. New York: Burt Franklin, 1981.

Fitzgerald, F. Scott. *As Ever, Scott Fitz: Letters between F. Scott Fitzgerald and His Literary Agent Harold Ober, 1919–1940*. Edited by Matthew J. Bruccoli. Philadelphia: Lippincott, 1972.

————. *Correspondence of F. Scott Fitzgerald*. Edited by Matthew J. Bruccoli and Margaret M. Duggan. New York: Random House, 1980.

————. *Dear Scott/Dear Max: The Fitzgerald–Perkins Correspondence*. Edited by John Kuehl and Jackson R. Bryer. New York: Scribner's, 1971.

————. *The Letters of F. Scott Fitzgerald*. Edited by Andrew Turnbull. New York: Scribner's, 1963.

————. *Tender Is the Night*. Serial version. *Scribner's Magazine*, January 1934, 1–8, 60–80; February 1934, 88–95, 139–60; March 1934, 168–74, 207–29; April 1934, 252–58, 292–310.

————. *Tender Is the Night*. New York: Scribner's, 1934.

————. *Tender Is the Night*. With two appendices from the manuscripts. Preface and endnotes by Malcolm Cowley. New York: Scribner's, 1951.

Fitzgerald, Zelda. *Save Me the Waltz*. London: Jonathan Cape, 1969.

Hemingway, Ernest. *Ernest Hemingway: Selected Letters, 1917–1961*. Edited by Carlos Baker. New York: Scribner's, 1981.

Higgins, Brian, and Hershel Parker. "Sober Second Thoughts: Fitzgerald's 'Final Version' of *Tender Is the Night*." In *Proof 4*, edited by Joseph Katz, 129–52. Columbia, S.C.: Faust, 1975.

Lehan, Richard D. *F. Scott Fitzgerald and the Craft of Fiction*. Carbondale: Southern Illinois University Press, 1966.

MacLeish, Archibald. *Reflections*. Edited by Bernard A. Drabeck and Helen E. Ellis. Amherst: University of Massachusetts Press, 1986.

Mayfield, Sara. *Exiles from Paradise: Zelda and Scott Fitzgerald*. New York: Delacorte, 1971.

O'Hara, John. *Selected Letters of John O'Hara*. Edited by Matthew J. Bruccoli. New York: Random House, 1978.

Parker, Hershel. *Flawed Texts and Verbal Icons*. Evanston: Northwestern University Press, 1984.

Piper, Henry Dan. *F. Scott Fitzgerald: A Critical Biography*. New York: Holt, Rinehart & Winston, 1965.

Rahv, Philip. "You Can't Duck Hurricane under a Beach Umbrella." *Daily Worker*, 5 May 1934. Reprinted in Bryer, *Fitzgerald: The Critical Reception*, 315–17.

Review of *Tender Is the Night*. *Journal of Nervous and Mental Diseases* 82 (July 1935): 115–17.

Roulston, Robert. "Dick Diver's Plunge into the Roman Void: The Setting of *Tender Is the Night*." *South Atlantic Quarterly* 77 (Winter 1978): 85–97.

Seldes, Gilbert. "True to Type: Scott Fitzgerald Writes Superb Tragic Novel." *New York Evening Journal*, 12 April 1934. Reprinted in Bryer, *Fitzgerald: The Critical Reception*, 292–93.

Sklar, Robert. *F. Scott Fitzgerald: The Last Laocoön*. New York: Oxford University Press, 1967.

Steinberg, A. H. "Hardness, Light, and Psychiatry in *Tender Is the Night*." *Literature and Psychology* 3 (February 1953): 3–8.

Stern, Milton R. "Introduction." In *Critical Essays on "Tender Is the Night*," edited by Milton R. Stern, 25–30. Boston: G. K. Hall, 1986.

Terry, Laura. "Albert McKisco's Role in Dick Diver's 'Intricate Destiny.' " M.A. thesis, College of William and Mary, 1987.

Trachtenberg, Alan. "The Journey Back: Myth and History in *Tender Is the Night*." In *Experiences in the Novel: Selected Papers from the English Institute*, edited by Roy Harvey Pearce, 138–43, 152. New York: Columbia University Press, 1968.

Turnbull, Andrew. *Scott Fitzgerald*. New York: Scribner's, 1962.

Wexelblatt, Robert. "F. Scott Fitzgerald and D. H. Lawrence: Bicycles and Incest." *American Literature* 59 (October 1987): 378–88.

Wilson, Edmund. "A Weekend at Ellerslie." In Edmund Wilson, *The Shores of Light*, 373–83. New York: Farrar, Straus & Young, 1952.

KENETH KINNAMON

How *Native Son* Was Born

I

Like Henry James and Thomas Wolfe, Richard Wright is his own best critic, at least on matters pertaining to the conception and composition of his greatest novel. In person and on paper he was ready to explain the genesis of *Native Son* (1940), analyze its personal and political significance, and defend it from racist attack. As a militant black Communist writer, winner of the *Story* magazine contest for employees of the Federal Writers Project for *Uncle Tom's Children* (1938) as well as second prize for "Fire and Cloud" in the *O. Henry Memorial Award Prize Stories of 1938*, he was already an experienced lecturer as he was completing his novel in the late winter and spring of 1939. In February of that year he lectured at the Harlem Community Center on "Negro Children in New York," in May he spoke at the Brooklyn YMCA on "The Cultural Contributions of the Negro in America," and in September he appeared with Langston Hughes and the Communist politician James W. Ford at the Festival of Negro Culture in Chicago. He may not have discussed his forthcoming work on these occasions, but he probably did so back in New York in a guest appearance in his friend Edwin Seaver's writing class at the New School for Social Research on 8 December 1939, in a lecture entitled "The Problems of the Fiction Writer Today" at the Dalcroze School of Music on 26 January 1940 under the auspices of the League of American Writers, and in a talk the following month in Chicago at the Woodlawn AME Church.[1]

Native Son was published on 1 March 1940 to great critical acclaim. Within two weeks of this date Wright had spoken at Columbia University and at the 135th Street Branch of the New York Public Library on "How 'Bigger' Was Born," a lecture he repeated in July at the Church of the Good Shepherd in Chicago and at the White Rock Baptist Church in Durham, North Carolina, and on 6 September at a gala fund-raiser for the Negro Playwrights Company at the Golden Gate

Ballroom in Harlem.[2] A condensed version appeared in print in the *Saturday Review* of 1 June, followed by a more drastic condensation in the September–October issue of *Negro Digest*. Sales figures on *Native Son* were excellent in March and April, but when they began to fade in May, Wright's editor at Harper's, Edward Aswell, proposed a "documentary edition" (later called "author's edition") of the novel with an appendix containing the full text of "How 'Bigger' Was Born," David L. Cohn's hostile review of *Native Son* in the May issue of *Atlantic Monthly*, and Wright's rebuttal of Cohn.[3] When Cohn understandably refused to go along with this scheme, Harper's published the complete *How "Bigger" Was Born* as a pamphlet. Grosset & Dunlap included the pamphlet version as a preface to its inexpensive reprint of *Native Son* in 1942, and it has been reprinted several times since then.

In *How "Bigger" Was Born* Wright recalls and analyzes the long gestation of *Native Son* in the experiences of his childhood in the South. Restless and rebellious, the Bigger type Wright observed (and to a degree himself embodied) both defied the racist order and withdrew from the black culture that provided nurture and compensation to those who could accommodate their lives to the system of white supremacy. The first example Wright cites appears to be merely a schoolyard bully, but as other examples unfold, his violent, aggressive personality comes to seem generic, his sadism the only means of his self-realization. The other four Southern Biggers described by Wright turn from brutalizing other blacks to direct confrontation with the white world. Bigger No. 2 declined to pay his rent or his debts for food and clothing, refusing to recognize the legitimacy of the racist economic system that denied an adequate supply of these essentials to black people. The third Bigger moved a step farther by taking his recreation without paying the white man for it, habitually walking into a motion picture theater without a ticket. Bigger No. 4, a more intellectual type with a manic-depressive personality, violated racial taboos of all kinds, refused to work, brooded and joked about racial injustice, and ended up in an insane asylum. The fifth Bigger specialized in boarding street cars without paying and sitting in the white section, defying with knife in hand the white conductor's orders to move. These exhilarating gestures of rebellion were necessarily of brief duration in a Jim Crow society: "Eventually, the whites who restricted their lives made them pay a terrible price. They were shot, hanged, maimed, lynched, and generally hounded until they were either dead or their spirits broken."[4]

For historical reasons, Wright explains, black reaction to the conditions of Southern life tended toward the extremes of rebellion and submission, the latter category including both drunks and strivers,

Uncle Toms and blues men. The rebellious Bigger type, though, was both estranged from the folk culture and attracted to the promise and glamour of the white life to which he was denied access. First understanding the Bigger phenomenon only in these racial terms, Wright added the dimension of class to caste through his contact with Communism, somewhat euphemistically called in How "Bigger" Was Born "the labor movement and its ideology." Bigger could be white as well as black, and his rebellious personality held a revolutionary potentiality that could seek either Communist or fascist fulfillment. Although Wright had already encountered problems with party functionaries and was to denounce his former comrades bitterly in The Outsider (1953), he could hardly have been more emphatic in declaring the importance of that deepened understanding of the Bigger type made possible by Marxist thought: "The extension of my sense of the personality of Bigger was the pivot of my life; it altered the complexion of my existence. . . . It was as though I had put on a pair of spectacles whose power was that of an x-ray enabling me to see deeper into the lives of men."[5] Critics who read Native Son as a black nationalist repudiation of Marxism—Bigger's instinctive black triumph over Boris Max's arid white theorizing—would do well to ponder these words. Wright's effort in the novel is to reconcile his sense of black life with the intellectual clarity and the possibility of social action provided by Communism, to interpret each group to the other. What he would soon be writing in explanation of his revolutionary verse of the mid-1930s applies equally well to Native Son, though his audience for the novel was much larger: "I would address my words to two groups: I would tell Communists how common people felt, and I would tell common people of the self-sacrifice of Communists who strove for unity among them."[6]

Further exposure to the urban Biggers of Chicago, more explosive even than the Biggers of the South, deepened Wright's understanding of the type, as did his further reading in white literature reflecting the frenetic life of cities and his close study of Biggers in prerevolutionary Russia and in Nazi Germany. "Tense, afraid, nervous, hysterical, and restless," Wright explains, the Bigger Thomas of his novel is the "product of a dislocated society; he is a dispossessed and disinherited man; he is all of this, and he lives amid the greatest plenty on earth and he is looking and feeling for a way out." Obstacles to telling the truth about such a character were formidable, but Bigger had so captivated Wright's imagination that he resolved to portray him, determined to do justice to all the dimensions of his complex character and significance: his individual consciousness in all its subjectivity; his ambivalent feelings as a black native son toward the country that excludes him; the existential qualities of "primal fear and dread"[7] that are the psychological basis of all our lives, underlying and conditioning our social experience; the political meaning of Bigger's life; his relationship with other blacks; his raw Chicago environment.

In *How "Bigger" Was Born* Wright states that his exposure to urban Biggers while working in the South Side Boys' Club coalesced the years of brooding about the type and prompted him to begin the actual writing of the novel. The year was 1935. Probably he only sketched preliminary notes, for at this time he was busy writing poetry and the posthumously published *Lawd Today* (1963). More sustained work began in New York early in 1938. The first reviews of *Uncle Tom's Children* persuaded him that an even more unflinching confrontation with the full dimensions of racism was necessary: "I found that I had written a book which even bankers' daughters could read and feel good about. I swore to myself that if I ever wrote another book, no one would weep over it; that it would be so hard and deep that they would have to face it without the consolation of tears. It was this that made me get to work in dead earnest."[8] Moving to Brooklyn on 13 April to live with his Chicago friends Jane and Herbert Newton, Wright worked intensely through the spring, summer, and early fall, completing a first draft of 576 pages by 24 October.[9]

The rebellious young black men Wright had himself observed South and North became collectively the prototype of his protagonist, but as if to validate the literary character another Bigger, whom Wright never saw, emerged from obscurity late in May and affected the novel even more directly than his earlier counterparts. As Wright was nearing the midway point of his first draft, two young black men, Robert Nixon and Earl Hicks, were arrested in Chicago and charged with the murder of a white woman. Nixon became the central figure in the case, which received sensationalized coverage in the Chicago press, especially the openly racist *Tribune*. Without adducing any evidence of rape, this newspaper began its extensive coverage by calling Nixon "a colored sex criminal" and continued to use such epithets as "sex moron," "rapist slayer," "brick moron," and "jungle beast." The *Tribune* exploited fully the racial as well as sexual angle, a volatile combination. Today's reader of *Native Son* might well regard the racism of the newspaper article presented early in Book 3 as highly exaggerated, but in point of fact it is adapted from an actual *Tribune* piece on the Nixon case:

Comes from a Little Town.

The Negro youth is Robert Nixon. He is 18 years old and comes from a pretty little town in the old south—Tallulah, La. But there is nothing pretty about Robert Nixon. He has none of the charm of speech or manner that is characteristic of so many southern darkies.

That charm is a mark of civilization, and so far as manner and appearance go, civilization has left Nixon practically untouched. His hunched shoulders and long, sinewy arms that dangle almost to his knees; his outthrust head and catlike tread all suggest the animal.

He is very black—almost pure Negro. His physical characteristics suggest an earlier link in the species.

Ferocious Type.

Mississippi river steamboat mates, who hire and fire roustabouts by the hundreds, would classify Nixon as a jungle Negro. They would hire him only if they were sorely in need of rousters. And they would keep close watch on him. This type is known to be ferocious and relentless in a fight. Though docile enough under ordinary circumstances, they are easily aroused. And when this happens the veneer of civilization disappears. . . .

As he talked yesterday Nixon's dull eyes lighted only when he spoke of food. They feed him well at the detective bureau, he said. He likes cocoanut pie and strawberry pop. It was after a generous meal of these refreshments that he confessed two of his most shocking murders. . . . These killings were accomplished with a ferocity suggestive of Poe's "Murders in the Rue Morgue"—the work of a giant ape.

Again the comparison was drawn between Nixon and the jungle man. Last week when he was taken . . . to demonstrate how he had slain Mrs. Florence Johnson, mother of two small children, a crowd gathered and there were cries of: "Lynch him! Kill him!"

Nixon backed against a wall and bared his teeth. He showed no fear, just as he has shown no remorse. He stood in a snarling attitude until police took him indoors and the crowd was ordered away.

The article ends by quoting Sheriff Sevier of Nixon's native parish: "It has been demonstrated here that nothing can be done with Robert Nixon. Only death can cure him."[10] As soon as Wright heard about this case, early in June, he wrote his friend Margaret Walker in Chicago, asking her for newspaper clippings on the Nixon case. Walker complied, collecting all the clippings from all the Chicago dailies. So assiduous was she that "he had enough to spread all over his nine by twelve bed room floor and he was using them in the same way Dreiser had done in *American Tragedy*. He would spread them all out and read them over and over again and then take off from there in his own imagination."[11]

Not content with press coverage of the Nixon case, Wright traveled to Chicago in November to gather additional information. A typed agenda for this trip shows how thorough and meticulous

Wright was in accumulating naturalistic details to assure the verisimilitude of his Chicago setting.[12] The Nixon case both stimulated his imagination and provided him material, but he shaped the material to his thematic purpose. Newspaper coverage of Bigger Thomas, the inquest, and the trial corresponds in many details to the Nixon case, but elsewhere Wright makes significant changes to develop his ideological points. Nixon's first attorney was Joseph Roth of the International Labor Defense, but he was soon replaced by black lawyers of the National Negro Congress, who represented him at the trial. By eliminating black legal representatives and magnifying the role of the white radical Boris Max, Wright accomplishes two purposes. As a Communist Max can articulate a Marxist analysis of Bigger's situation that clearly derives from Wright's own conceptual analysis of the effects of racism on the Bigger type.[13] At the same time, in the final scene Wright can contrast Bigger's black emotional apprehension of the meaning of his ordeal with Max's white intellectual interpretation of it, a contrast of complementary understandings not possible if Wright had followed the Nixon case and provided Bigger with black lawyers. Another change also shows Wright's Communist perspective in *Native Son*. After Nixon was arrested for the murder of Mrs. Florence Johnson, Chicago police used third-degree methods to extract from him confessions, later withdrawn, of other crimes, including the murder of another woman a year earlier, in which he was alleged to have written the words "Black Legion" with his victim's lipstick on her bedroom mirror. The Black Legion, as Humphrey Bogart fans will recall from a film about the group, was an extremist right-wing organization in Detroit and other Midwestern cities, a kind of Northern urban version of the Ku Klux Klan. When Bigger thinks of diverting suspicion from himself, he signs the ransom "Red" and draws a hammer and sickle. By changing from fascists to Communists, Wright implies that the latter share with Bigger the role of social outcast, a point Max emphasizes later in the novel.[14]

Most of *How "Bigger" Was Born* is devoted to Bigger himself, but at the end of the essay Wright turns to the actual process of writing the novel, concentrating on the tensions between truth and plausibility, the varieties of narrative technique used while maintaining and projecting Bigger's perspective, the opening and closing scenes written after the first draft, and, briefly, the process of revision. This remarkable exercise in literary autoanalysis concludes by placing *Native Son* and its subject in the context of the American tradition in fiction: "We do have in the Negro the embodiment of a past tragic enough to appease the spiritual hunger of even a James; and we have in the oppression of the Negro a shadow athwart our national life dense and heavy enough to satisfy even the gloomy broodings of a Hawthorne. And if Poe were alive, he would not have to invent horror; horror would invent him."[15]

II

As revealing as *How "Bigger" Was Born* is, it does not tell us everything about the composition of *Native Son*. An examination of letters, notes, manuscripts, and galley and page proofs at Yale University, Princeton University, the Schomburg Collection of the New York Public Library, and the Fales Collection of New York University supplements the essay in rewarding ways. These materials show in detail Wright's evolving conception of his novel and the artistry with which he articulated, shaped, and refined it. They also show how others seem to have participated in this creative process, notably his literary agent, Paul Reynolds, his editor, Edward Aswell, and his introducer, Dorothy Canfield Fisher. My somewhat cursory examination of these materials allows me to make some preliminary observations and reach some tentative conclusions, but they await and require more thorough and detailed investigation.

After completing his first draft, Wright began to revise his book, a process that continued for over a year.[16] Large and small changes were made, most on Wright's own initiative but some suggested by others. Stylistic revision usually moved toward clarity, more precise diction, or greater economy of expression. For example, the Schomburg version's "another cigarette in his lips" becomes the more vivid "another cigarette slanting across his chin" in the published novel. The prolix "Bigger took a deep breath and looked from face to face, as though it seemed to him the heighth [*sic*] of foolishness that he should have to explain" is compressed to "Bigger took a deep breath and looked from face to face. It seemed to him that he should not have to explain" (*NS*, 11, 21).[17] The word *ofays*, unintelligible to most white readers, is changed to *white folks* in the novel as published.[18] In addition to authorial revisions on almost every page of the Schomburg typescript of the first draft, several inserts in Wright's hand make more extensive changes.

As the manuscript evolved, Wright altered his representation of dialogue in various ways. The phrase "said Bigger" and the like is changed to "Bigger said."[19] The intermediate version's representation of Jan and Mary's drunken speech ("Goshbye, shoney" and "shome") is softened in the novel ("Goo'bye, honey" and "some") to avoid an inappropriate comic quality shortly before Mary is killed. Wright's rendering of black dialect in *Native Son* contrasts in a significant way to his earlier practice. In an early draft of his short story "Down by the Riverside," probably completed in 1935, he writes dialect as dialect whether using a typewriter or pencil: "Naw, Lawd. Ah cant break down like this. . . . They'll know somethings wrong if Ah ack like this" or "Ah wan some watah."[20] In *Native Son* Wright's usual method is to write standard English speech and then change the spelling to produce dialect, as in the speech of Reverend Hammond: "L~~or~~d Jesus, [aw] turn ~~y~~our eyes ~~and look with mercy upon us sinners.~~ Look int~~o~~ the [Y] [l] [er] heart of this po~~o~~r lost boy. ~~You~~ said that mercy w~~as~~ a~~lw~~ays Y~~ou~~rs" [Yuh] [uz] [w] or "F~~or~~get everything but yo~~ur~~ fate, son."[21] [e] [i] In his broad dialect as well as his submissive Christianity, Reverend Hammond is an anachronistic survival of black Southern culture rapidly being changed by the altered conditions of Northern urban life. None of the other black characters, not even Mrs. Thomas, speaks as he does. Wright's new method of creating such dialect surely results from his own estrangement from his Southern past.

On a much larger scale Wright made important changes that greatly improved the opening and closing episodes of the novel. In the original version of the opening scene Bigger is not awakened by the clanging alarm clock that also wakes the reader up to the squalid realities of life in a black slum, but by knocking on the door of the Thomas family's kitchenette apartment in Chicago. The caller is Sister Mosley, a church friend of Mrs. Thomas, who has dropped by on her way to work to leave tickets to be sold for an Easter rally. The long and tedious dialogue between Bigger, his mother, and Sister Mosley occupies most of sixteen typed pages. Bigger's street friend Jack arrives shortly after the departure of Sister Mosley, but Mrs. Thomas refuses to let him in. Filled with disgust by Sister Mosley's importunate solicitude for the state of his soul and his mother's incessant scolding and nagging, Bigger clearly prefers the secular street to the sacred storefront. Deriving from Wright's own rejection of religion as the opiate of the black people, the scene does prepare the way for Bigger's later rejection of Reverend Hammond (here first called Temple), but the scene lacks any drama except verbal bickering and fails to emphasize the squalor of the South Side environment.[22] In *How "Bigger" Was Born* Wright explains that one night while drinking he thought of a battle with a rat: "At first I rejected the idea . . . I was afraid that the rat would 'hog' the scene. But the rat would not leave me. . . . So, cautioning myself to allow the rat scene to disclose *only* Bigger, his family, their little room, and their relationships, I let the rat walk in, and he did his stuff."[23] The rat's stuff was powerful stuff indeed, creating some of the most effective opening pages in American fiction. Economically and above all dramatically, the scene deftly establishes the relationship between all four members of the Thomas household (not just between Bigger and his mother), exposes the sordid and crowded conditions of their existence, shows the incipient violence of Bigger's personality, and, additionally, symbolically foreshadows Bigger's fate as a black "rat" hunted down by a remorseless and powerful foe. The importance of the change can hardly be overestimated. The excitement of the rat scene rivets the reader's attention to a tense narrative. If the novel had been published with the omitted original opening, many bored readers would have put the book down after perusing the first few pages.

The original conclusion to *Native Son* was also changed, but by deletion rather than substitution. Wright's explanation in *How "Bigger" Was Born* is incomplete: "In the first draft I had Bigger going smack to the electric chair; but I felt that two murders were enough for one novel. I cut the final scene."[24] The problem, however, seems not so much another violent death as overwriting for a self-conscious poetic effect. In Wright's developmental notes for the novel is a typed sheet headed "POETIC MOTIFS TO BE WOVEN INTO FINAL SCENE," consisting of seven items, the last of which reads "Most important of all poetic motifs is that of life being a deep. [*sic*] exciting and entralling [*sic*] adventure; that is the note on which the book should end to carry over the promise and feeling of something which must happen in the future I MUST SPEAK IN POETIC TERMS OF THIS."[25] To do so he drew upon a central metaphor of his creative imagination—fire. Fire figures prominently in such early poems as "Between the World and Me," "Everywhere Burning Waters Rise," and "Obsession," as well as in three of the four stories of *Uncle Tom's Children*. In the final story of the collection, "Fire and Cloud," the protagonist tells his followers: "Ah *know* now! Ah done seen the *sign*! We's gotta git together. Ah know whut you life is! Ah done felt it! It's *fire*!"[26] *Black Boy* begins its narrative of Wright's early life with the episode of his setting fire to his house at the age of four. The central event in the plot of *The Long Dream* is a terrible fire in a black night club based on the actual holocaust of the Rhythm Nite Club in Natchez in 1940.[27]

Unlike most of these instances, however, the metaphorical dimension of fire in the original conclusion of *Native Son* does not proceed from an actual conflagration but exists only in a vague and implausible dream world of Bigger's imagination: "The picture enclosed him about, shutting the world out from him, making it a dream of restless shadows, and giving him a sense of being near an invisible but glowing center of fire, at the border of a land filled with a strange stillness." As the time for execution arrives, a guard comes to his cell and orders him to "*sit up kid*." Bigger struggles to maintain the purity of his vision by rejecting this demand of the actual world: "The voice came to him from faraway, and instead of calling him from his vision of many men who were sparks and all men who were a flame of life, instead of making him recede from the boundaries of that silent land where his senses felt a new and strange peace, the voice drew him closer. The heat of that flame, invisible but strong with its heat, and the silence and stillness of that land were so deep that he could heat [*sic*] it." As the legs of his pants are being slit for placement of the electrodes, he thinks: "A short time and then he would be englufed [*sic*] in that ever widening yellow flame of fire leaping from a ball of fire. A short time and then he would walk into that new and strange land, with its still silence." In the brief space of the final page and a half of the first draft, the "fiercely glowing flame of fire and the silence of that new and still land" recur seven times, culminating in the moment of death in the electric chair: "In a split second he knew that death was near and the flame became a huge fiery sun suspended just above him, in front of his eyes, and his arms were open to embrace it and walk into that land beyond the sun and then he sprang forward to it, his dry lips kissing the hot fire; he felt a dark silent explosion and he was in the blinding light of a new and unseen day, enwrapped in the silence of a land beyond the sun." Thus metaphor becomes metonymy.

How much more effective the ending became when Wright cut this repetitious and overblown rhetoric, chastened his propensity for poeticizing, and avoided the sensationalism of an attempt to render the moment of electrocution. Having affirmed the terrible knowledge of his self-realization through murder; having parted from Max, who understands him as a social symbol but only imperfectly as a human being; and having won through to a sense of equality by calling Jan simply by his first name rather than referring to him as Mister Jan, thus speaking to a white as whites speak to blacks—having accomplished these things Bigger is left in existential solitude as the simple, monosyllabic concluding sentences sound the knell of the fate that inexorably follows his fear and flight: "He still held on to the bars. Then he smiled a faint, wry, bitter smile. He heard the ring of steel against steel as a far door clanged shut" (*NS*, 359).

III

Suggestions about revising the opening and closing scenes may have been made by such friends as Jane Newton, Theodore Ward, and Ralph Ellison, but the changes, essentially Wright's, were in place by the time he showed the novel to his agent, Paul Reynolds, in February 1939. In a letter on the last day of that month Reynolds wrote that he found the first part "very impressive" but wished that "it had a little more humor." After completing his reading of the entire manuscript, he reported to Wright on 2 and 8 March with praise of Bigger, the other black characters, and Max. He found the other white characters implausible, however, and also suggested cutting the "Fate" section, especially the courtroom scenes and newspaper material. Six weeks later Reynolds wrote that Edward Aswell, the editor at Harper's, "has nearly finished your novel and he asks if you could come in to see him next Tuesday. . . . I think he has in mind certain revision [sic], if you agree." By 11 May Reynolds was wishing "all power . . . with the revision," and on 16 June he reported that Aswell "is very keen about the book and thinks you did a swell job of the revision. He said there were two or three minor points he would like to discuss with you."[28]

Wright followed the suggestion of his agent to cut the last section of the novel, but we do not know exactly what revisions were agreed to in conference with Aswell. Nevertheless it seems likely that discussion focused on the controversial subjects of sex and politics, for much of the latter revision of the manuscript consisted of deletion of passages concerning these matters.

An attentive reader must pause in Book 3 over a point State's Attorney Buckley makes while grilling Bigger. Attempting to implicate him in various unsolved crimes and to break him down for confession, Buckley mentions the planned robbery of Blum's delicatessen and then goes on: "You didn't think I knew about that, did you? I know a lot more, boy. I know about that dirty trick you and your friend Jack pulled off in the Regal Theatre, too. You wonder how I know it? The manager told us when we were checking up. I know what boys like you do, Bigger" (NS, 260). What dirty trick? The reader going back to Book 1 finds none. The solution to this puzzle is that the quoted passage, which Wright neglected to delete for consistency, refers to an episode of masturbation by Bigger and Jack in the darkened theater that went through the various drafts all the way to galley proof before it was crossed out. Hardly are Bigger and Jack seated when the graphic description begins: " 'I'm polishing my nightstick,' Bigger said."[29] Seen by a passing woman, Bigger and Jack are reported to the manager.[30] The masturbation scene continues for a full page, ending when the two change seats because of the mess they have made.

As the original version of the episode in the Regal Theatre continues, the movie begins with a newsreel showing wealthy young white women on a Florida beach. One of these is Mary Dalton, who is shown in a close-up embracing Jan Erlone as the narrator comments: *"Mary Dalton, daughter of Chicago's Henry Dalton, 4605 Drexel Boulevard, shocks society by spurning the boys of La Salle Street and the Gold Coast and accepting the attentions of a well-known radical while on her recent winter vacation in Florida."* Other sexy scenes with mildly lewd comments by the narrator follow. Recognizing the address as the one at which he will make application for employment that very afternoon, Bigger and Jack discuss the sexual possibilities with Mary. With this deleted passage in mind, it is easy to understand Bigger's otherwise implausible speculation in the novel as published: "Maybe he [Mr. Dalton] had a daughter who was a hot kind of girl" (*NS*, 29).

Before the changes in galley proof, then, Wright was presenting Bigger as a typically highly sexed nineteen-year-old who had been titillated by a newsreel showing the scantily clad Mary kissing and embracing her lover. He is soon to witness such scenes in person, for that night he chauffeurs Mary and Jan, who make love in the back seat while Bigger drives them around Washington Park.

> He looked at the mirror. Mary was lying flat on her back in the rear seat and Jan was bent over her. He saw a faint sweep of white thigh. They plastered all right, he thought. He pulled the car softly round the curves, looking at the road before him one second and up at the mirror the next. He heard Jan whispering; then he heard them both sigh. Filled with a sense of them, his muscles grew gradually taut. He sighed and sat up straight, fighting off the stiffening feeling in his loins. But soon he slouched again. His lips were numb. I'm almost drunk, he thought. His sense of the city and park fell away; he was floating in the car and Jan and Mary were in back kissing, spooning. A long time passed. Jan sat up and pulled Mary with him.

After expurgations in galley proof, the passage as published deleted all mention of Bigger's arousal:

> He looked at the mirror; they were drinking again. They plastered, all right, he thought. He pulled the car softly round the curves, looking at the road before him one second and up at the mirror the next. He heard Jan whispering; then he heard them both sigh. His lips were numb. I'm almost drunk, he thought. His sense of the city and park fell away; he was floating in the car and Jan and Mary were in back, kissing. A long time passed. (*NS*, 67–68)

Similar deletions are made in the subsequent scene in the Dalton house when Bigger carries the drunken Mary to her room and puts her to bed. In the published version Bigger kisses Mary and "she swayed against him" (*NS*, 73), but the deleted galley passage continues more explicitly: "He tightened his arms as his lips pressed tightly against hers and he felt her body moving strongly. The thought and conviction that Jan had had her a lot flashed through his mind. He kissed her again and felt the sharp bones of her hips move in a hard and veritable grind. Her mouth was open and her breath came slow and deep." A marginal note by this passage in an editor's hand, probably Aswell's, reads "suggest cutting this."[31] Later, as Bigger is having sex with his girl friend Bessie Mears, he fantasizes that she is Mary. This scene was retained in the galleys and changed only in page proof.

Because explicit interracial sexual scenes had never before appeared in serious American fiction, Wright's conception of Bigger as a highly sexed, poor young black man with a physical interest in a wild, rich young white woman was daring indeed. Bankers' daughters reading such a story would be titillated or shocked, but they would certainly not be moved to tears of compassion for Bigger. As Aswell knew, and as he must have argued to Wright, to retain such highly charged sexual scenes would risk censorship and thus prevent the larger political message from being conveyed, or at best undercut that message by diverting the salacious reader's attention. For whatever reason, the changes were made, resulting in a softened, less threatening, more victimized Bigger, one over whom bankers' daughters might weep after all.

The other significant category of changes from manuscript and proof to published novel is political. Here it is more difficult to separate Wright's artistic imperatives from thematic changes suggested by others. Many readers of *Native Son* have been bothered by the prolixity of Book 3, especially the long speeches of both attorneys. Wright himself was quite aware of the problem, for his developmental notes contain such self-admonitions as the following: "How much of Max's examination of Bigger can be transferred to early pages. . . . Compress Buckley's speech. . . . Cut or compress newspaper articles where they can be don [*sic*] so."[32] Buckley's speech was compressed by half a page, but more extensive cuts were made in Boris Max's plea to the court. The published version (*NS*, 324–39), which, as Dr. Johnson said of *Paradise Lost*, none ever wished longer than it is, was in fact five pages longer in galley proof. It would be difficult to argue that the longer version is more effective, but some interesting material was cut.

Early in the galley version Max emphasizes the public hysteria accompanying Bigger's trial: "the low, angry muttering of that mob which the state troops are holding back . . . the hungry yelping of hounds on the hunt." The implicit comparison of Bigger to a fugitive slave adds historical resonance, but Wright must have realized—or Aswell may have reminded him—that the threat of a lynch mob storming a courthouse was not plausible in the city of Chicago, however many times it had happened in the South. Other cuts involved such topics as anti-Semitism, naive white liberalism, the social barriers between Bigger and Mary, and the analogy—a familiar one in Afro-American literature—between black rebelliousness and the American Revolution. Cumulatively these deletions have the effect of toning down slightly the political message of Book 3, though they also mitigate the artistic tedium their inclusion would exacerbate.

Other cuts in Max's speech are necessary for consistency. Having dropped the original ending of the novel, Wright omits from the galleys passages about "life, new and strange" and passages invoking fire imagery: "Bigger Thomas is part of a furious blaze of liquid life energy which once blazed and is still blazing in our land. He is a hot jet of life that spattered itself in futility against a cold wall." Here Wright may have been uneasy with the orgasmic hyperbole of such a metaphor. Certainly other cuts deemphasize Bigger's sexuality, such as the deletion of a reference to masturbation as a trope for Bigger's entire life. In Buckley's speech, too, Wright cuts a reference to the Florida newsreel and "the obnoxious sexual perversions practiced by these boys in darkened theatres."

Still other deletions may have occurred to Wright independently or have been suggested by Aswell or others. At one point Max is considering the paradoxes of racism. A white chauffeur arriving with the drunken daughter of his employer, he argues, would have informed him of her condition, but racist treatment of Bigger "made him do the *very* thing we did not want." Max goes farther: "Or, am I wrong? Maybe we *wanted* him to do it! Maybe we would have had no chance or justification to stage attacks against hundreds of thousands of people if he had acted sanely and normally! Maybe we would have had to go to the expensive length of inventing theories to justify our attacks if we had treated him fairly!" Such implausible and involuted speculation justifies deletion, but the cumulative effect of cuts involving racial politics, like that of those concerning Bigger's sexuality, is to lower the stridency of Wright's message, to soften the characterization, perhaps even to dilute the theme. One can maintain plausibly that deletions enhanced the literary value of Book 3, or even that more cuts would have improved it further, but the fact remains that Wright finally decided or was persuaded to let Max say less than he said through the drafts and unrevised galleys. In the case of *Native Son*, Edward Aswell, a white liberal from Tennessee and Harvard who had been Thomas Wolfe's editor and was to become Wright's valued friend, may even be regarded as standing in relation to Wright as Max stands in relation to Bigger: sympathetic, loyal, analytical, understanding to a point, but not quite ready to accept the full and uncut expression of a sensibility so radically different from his own.

Moreover, Aswell decided at the last minute not to let *Native Son* go unmediated into the world. In early summer of 1939 the Book-of-the-Month Club had expressed interest in the novel. On 23 September his literary agent wrote Wright optimistically: "We have always understood that Dorothy Canfield has as much or more influence in the Book-of-the-Month Club than anyone else so I am really quite hopeful though I don't know anything about it." Fisher, a productive and well-known writer, was a member of the board of selection. The matter dragged on for the rest of the year, delaying publication by several months. Never before had the Book-of-the-Month Club selected a novel by a black writer. Finally, early in the new year, Aswell wrote with the good news that the book had been selected as a March alternate. Furthermore, he noted that "Dorothy Canfield Fisher has written a brief Introduction." Nine days later he expressed satisfaction with Fisher's effort and his regret that Wright had not had an opportunity to see it: "Under ordinary circumstances, if there had been more time, we should have wanted to consult you before deciding to put in it [*sic*]. Pressed as we were, I took the responsibility of saying that I felt pretty sure you would approve. I hope I have not guessed wrong." Presented with a fait accompli and the likelihood that the Book-of-the-Month Club would not accept the novel as a selection without the introduction, Wright could do little but assent with as much grace as he could muster. After another week Aswell wrote: "I am glad you liked Dorothy Canfield's Introduction."[33]

What we have here is a latter-day example of the process of white authentication that Robert Stepto has shown to be so characteristic a feature of slave narratives.[34] In this process a well-known white abolitionist would provide a preface, guarantee, or letter attesting to the veracity or historicity of the narrative and the genuineness of the author's credentials. Only with such a seal of approval, the feeling was, would a predominantly white audience be receptive to a black story. The difficulty was that the authenticator's white perspective inevitably distorted as it mediated the necessarily different black perspective of the author. Max and Bigger again—or Aswell and Wright.

Dorothy Canfield Fisher of Arlington, Vermont, was an influential and energetic white liberal with a steady stream of books to her credit since the first decade of the century. Nevertheless her credentials as a commentator on black life and letters were minimal: membership on the board of trustees of Howard University and treatment of a light family passing for white in the subplot of an early novel (*The Bent Twig*, 1915). But her most recent novel, *Seasoned Timber* (1939), was an attack on anti-Semitism. It must have seemed to Aswell that her heart was in the right place, and there could be little doubt that her endorsement would help sales. Her brief introduction is accurately characterized by Robert Stepto as "innocently vapid,"[35] but it is also confused, offering two opposed interpretations of Bigger. First, he is compared to a laboratory rat or sheep frustrated by the denial of fulfillment in American society. Then, as if to compensate for this emphasis on environmental determinism, she describes the theme of *Native Son* as "the Dostoievski subject—a human soul in hell because it is sick with a deadly spiritual sickness" (*NS*, x). She raises two points that many reviewers and readers seized upon, but she makes no effort to reconcile them. Steering the reader in advance in opposite directions, Fisher's introduction does the novel a disservice. Writing to Aswell several years later about a preface to *Black Boy* (the proposed title at the time was *American Hunger*), Wright commented: "I'm wondering if the reader himself will not make up his mind as to what I'm trying to do when he is wading into the book?"[36] The question is equally relevant to *Native Son*.

IV

Wright's novel was born, then, with the assistance of various white midwives, male and female. However much domesticated by white assistance at its delivery, it was still a robust infant whose loud cries reverberated through the literary atmosphere as the 1940s began. By presenting Bigger as he was—"resentful toward whites, sullen, angry, ignorant, emotionally unstable, depressed and unaccountably elated at times, and unable even, because of his own lack of inner organization which American oppression has fostered in him, to unite with members of his own race"[37]—Wright knew that he risked confirming in white minds a racist stereotype, that his own comrades in the Communist party might reject his complex emotional and artistic honesty, and that the black bourgeoisie would be shamed by his frankness and would urge him to accentuate the positive in his racial portrayal. In a real sense, then, Wright was not so much appealing to his audiences as he was confronting them with a harsh and unpalatable truth, forcing them to undergo such emotional turmoil as to reexamine their attitudes and expand their awareness of the meaning, universally existential and politically revolutionary as well as racially revealing, of Bigger Thomas. Wright would assault his readers' sensibilities, not curry their favor or indulge their sentimentality.

How well did he succeed? If there is one common denominator to the 423 reviews, notices, essays, lectures, sermons, editorials, letters to the editor, and poems that appeared in the two years after the publication of the novel, it is their testimonial to the *power* of the work, the searing emotional force that gripped readers with or against their will. "Shock our sensibilities," "tremendous wallop," "power and drama and truth," "throbs from the opening line, with a wallop propelled to the end," "tremendous power," "a terrible story, a horrible story," "its frank brutalities . . . will horrify many readers," "powerful story," "powerful novel," "engrossing, terrible story," "a supershocker," "grim and frightening," "one of the most powerful novels of all time"—such phrases recurred many scores of times in the reviews of *Native Son*.[38] So powerful was its impact that one reviewer could only describe it as "a book which takes you by the ears and gives you a good shaking, whirls you on your toes and slaps you dizzy against the wall."[39] When the reader regained full consciousness, one supposes, he or she could then ponder the message Wright had conveyed with such overpowering force.

Doing so, the reader was likely to note the thematic issues of race and politics and the literary qualities of narration and characterization. Whatever its universal dimensions, *Native Son* is first of all a novel about the American racial situation, and this aspect of its theme elicited comment from almost all of its reviewers. For most, regardless of race or region, Wright made a cogent as well as a moving case against white racism. As far north as Maine an anonymous reviewer noted that Bigger was a victim of environmental determinism: "a mean Negro who might have been a solid asset in another environment." As far south as Houston another claimed that "Wright makes a masterful, unrelenting appeal" for racial understanding, however much other Southerners may object to the novel's theme. In the Midwest a reviewer judged that "the picture of the Negro, against the white world, as presented by Wright, is the most illuminating I have ever read," and in California students emphasized its importance as a revelation of social injustice and a demand for change.[40]

Concerning the strictly literary qualities of the novel, discussion centered around narration and characterization, with only a few perceptive observers noting Wright's symbolism. A clear consensus of praise for the work's literary artistry emerged, even from many who objected to its themes. Repeatedly the driving narrative momentum with its strong dramatic quality was singled out for favorable comment: "for the first two-thirds of the book," an influential Midwestern reviewer wrote, "no tale of pursuit and capture has rivaled it."[41] Likewise Wright's characterization, especially of Bigger, was widely admired, many reviewers agreeing with Henry Seidel Canby's early comment that "only a Negro could have written" such a psychologically penetrating book.[42] Canby and a few others, indeed, seemed to emphasize the psychological dimension of Wright's story as a way of evading the social message. But more often reviewers considered characterization as well as narrative pace and structure as a means of realizing the author's theme. Many agreed with a reviewer in Albany, New York: "He has proven with this vigorous novel that for psychological imagination, for power of dramatic construction, for the convincingness and reality of his characters, he has few equals."[43] Reviewers who noted Wright's symbolism, his crisp dialogue, his "prose . . . as firm as steel,"[44] and his satiric touches helped to amplify the artistic particulars of the craft that had produced such a powerful effect.

In assessing this achievement reviewers inevitably compared Wright to other writers, most frequently to Steinbeck, whose *Grapes of Wrath* had appeared the year before; to Dostoevski, author of another psychologically acute story of crime and punishment; and to Dreiser, author of another American tragedy. Several reviewers likened Wright to the socially conscious novelists Erskine Caldwell, Charles Dickens, James T. Farrell, Maxim Gorky, and Harriet Beecher Stowe. Other writers, religious leaders, and a single filmmaker mentioned a time or two included Arna Bontemps, Millen Brand, Joyce Cary, Humphrey Cobb, Pietro di Donato, Thomas Dixon, Dos Passos, Dumas, Faulkner, Jessie Fauset, the Greek tragedians, D. W. Griffith, Hemingway, Victor Hugo, George Lee, Richard Llewellyn, Malraux, Albert Maltz, Claude McKay, Margaret Mitchell, Conrad Richter, Shakespeare, Upton Sinclair, Gertrude Stein, Tolstoy, Jean Toomer, Turgenev, Waters E. Turpin, Carl Van Vechten, Len Zinberg, Zola, Abraham Lincoln, the Biblical Samson, and Jesus Christ. However singular Wright's novelistic vision may have been, it was immediately placed by reviewers in various literary traditions, most notably that of social protest.

Native Son very quickly became a popular as well as critical success. Advance sales, Book-of-the-Month distribution, and first-week sales totaled 215,000 copies, an extremely large printing for a first novel. In its issue of 16 March 1940, two weeks after publication, *Publisher's Weekly* alerted the book trade to high rates of reorders from bookstores and to Harper's heavy advertising campaign. An advertisement entitled "Public Stampedes for 'Native Son' " that appeared in various black newspapers was only mildly hyperbolical.[45] On the national best-seller charts the novel first appeared in the second week of March, ranked very high though never in first place (a position then held by Richard Llewellyn's *How Green Was My Valley*) for two months thereafter, began to fade in late spring, wilted in July, and did not appear in August or thereafter. In particular cities in particular weeks—New York, Chicago, Philadelphia, San Francisco, St. Louis— *Native Son* did rise to the top of the best-seller list.[46] Moreover, library copies were circulated briskly, although at least one library in a major Southern city refused to purchase the book.[47]

Literary America was not yet ready to award a black writer a major prize in fiction, but the frequency with which Wright was nominated was another indication of the strong impact of *Native Son*. Only a few days after publication F. P. A. (Franklin P. Adams) penned the following versified "Book Review" in his widely read column: "All the prizes should be won / By Richard Wright's 'Native Son.' " Soon afterward black journalists expressed similar sentiments, Frank Marshall Davis predicting a Pulitzer Prize and Arthur Huff Fauset an eventual Nobel Prize for Wright. By May such diverse voices as Walter Winchell and an editorial writer for *New Masses* had joined the chorus, though ultimately to no avail.[48] Still, *Native Son* was a serious contender for a Pulitzer Prize.

Another measure of the novel's effect is the way it was used in discussions of the actual social conditions reflected so graphically in the fictional work. Several journalists and sociologists cited *Native Son* in discussions of poor housing in Chicago and elsewhere.[49] Others drew parallels between Bigger Thomas and actual living individuals.[50] A writer in the denominational organ of the Disciples of Christ suggested that *Native Son* "would be a good book for all judges, police officers, and prosecutors who have to do with the Negro to read."[51]

It is always difficult to gauge precisely the effect of a problem novel on the future of the problem it treats, but from the available evidence it seems safe to claim that Wright's intention to shock his readers into a new awareness of the terrible dimensions of American racism was to a large degree accomplished. Irving Howe once wrote that "the day *Native Son* appeared, American culture was changed forever."[52] The change was not basic or profound, but it was real. The several hundred thousand readers of the work could no longer see racial issues in quite the same way. *Native Son* did not start a war, as Lincoln claimed *Uncle Tom's Cabin* did, or directly effect legislation, as *The Jungle* did, but it did alter the social as well as literary sensibilities of many of its readers.

Although interest in *Native Son* declined during the McCarthyist hysteria and the racial complacency of the late 1940s and the 1950s, it revived in the 1960s and continues to the present. The novel has been widely translated and reviewed abroad. Along with his fourteen other books, *Native Son* brought its author global recognition and a permanent place in American literature. Whatever we may think of the changes Edward Aswell persuaded Wright to make, we must honor this editor for his prophetic confidence in the stature of *Native Son*. On 29 February 1940, the day before its publication, he wrote these words to Richard Wright: "I hope that this will reach you tomorrow, because I should like to be among the first to congratulate you once more on *Native Son*. You know what I think of it, and I have always thought it, but let me be a little more explicit. It is not only a good book, a sincere, straight, and honest book, a courageous book, a powerful and eternally moving book, but in addition to all this, I truly believe, a great book. It is my conviction that its publication will be remembered in years to come as a monumental event."[53]

Notes

I am grateful to Ellen Wright for granting me permission to use and quote from restricted material in her late husband's papers at Yale University. Without her generous cooperation this essay would not have been possible.

1. For notices of the lectures cited see "Symposium on Negro Culture Today"; "Wright Speaks Tonight on Negro Culture"; "Ford, Wright, Hughes to Speak at Savoy"; "You are cordially invited . . ."; and "Wright Shows New Book."

2. "Book Marks for Today"; "Richard Wright Tells Library Forum How He Wrote 'Native Son' "; " 'Native Son' Author to Relate Birth of 'Bigger' "; " 'Native Son' Author Says Slump Wrecked Illusions"; Hansen, "The First Reader."

3. Aswell to Wright, 29 May, 13 June, 18 June, 21 June 1940, Wright Archive, Beinecke Library, Yale University (hereafter cited as Wright Archive); Cohn, "The Negro Novel."

4. Wright, *How "Bigger" Was Born*, 6.

5. Ibid., 11–12.

6. Wright, *American Hunger*, 66. Originally the final third of the autobiographical manuscript completed late in 1943, this account of Wright's Chicago period was omitted when *Black Boy* was published in 1945, though portions had appeared in periodicals.

7. Wright, *How "Bigger" Was Born*, 18, 26.

8. Ibid., 29–30.

9. Wright to his literary agent, Paul R. Reynolds, 24 October 1938, quoted in Fabre, *The Unfinished Quest*, 556. Fabre's valuable treatment (169–77) of the composition of *Native Son* is based mainly on his correspondence with Jane Newton, who witnessed it at first hand.

10. Leavelle, "Brick Slayer Is Likened to Jungle Beast." Cf. *Native Son* (hereafter cited as *NS*), 238–40.

11. Margaret Walker Alexander, "Richard Wright," 60. In this important essay she also relates Wright's visit to Chicago in November.

12. The complete agenda (Wright Archive, JWJ Wright 813):

1. Get detail map of the South Side. Street Car grades & maps
II. Pick out site for Dalton's home.
3. Get a good street layout for Dalton's home.

4. Select empty house for Bigger's murder of Bessie.

5. Trace with ample notes the legal route whch [sic] was taken in trying Nixon.

6. Go through Cook County Jail; get some dope from the project about it.

7. Get picture, if possible, and go through court where trial took place.

8. Select site for Blum's delicatessen.

9. Select area of Bigger's capture.

10. See, visit, death house at Stateville and talk to Nixon if possible.

11. Give Bessie's home a definite address.

12. (Detail execution, if possible (SEE).

13. Talk to ILD heads about pleas, court procedure. (Ira Silber)

14. Get from Chicago Public Library *Maureen's* book on Loeb and Leopold trial.

15. Get location of Loeb and Leopold and Franks old home

16. Get other books from library pertaining to trial

17. Investigate House of Correction for Boys.

18. Get complete dope on inquest.

19. Get a copy of inquest return verdict.

20. Get copy of indictments.

21. Get form in which judges [sic] sentence is rendered.

22. From what station would one go to Milwaukee on train?

23. Get "Old Rugged Cross" song for use in preacher's talk with Bigger.

24. Select site for Bigger's home (3700 block on Indiana). Investigate Indiana from 43 to 39 for scene of Bigger's capture.

13. For a different view of Max's politics see Siegel, "The Conclusion of *Native Son*."

14. I have also treated the Nixon case and its relation to *Native Son* in "*Native Son*: The Personal, Social, and Political Background," 68–71, and *The Emergence of Wright*, 121–25.

15. Wright, How *"Bigger"* Was Born, 39.

16. The revised page proofs at the Fales Collection of the New York University Library carry the date 1 December 1939.

17. Davis and Fabre's *Wright: A Primary Bibliography* is an invaluable guide to the study of Wright's texts, but it errs in calling the Schomburg version a "setting typescript" (27). It is the first typed draft of 576 pages, for it contains opening and closing scenes dropped when the novel was set for galley proofs.

18. See the intermediate version in the Wright Archive (JWJ Wright 814). The passage appears on 61 of the novel.

19. Wright Archive, JWJ Wright 814.

20. Wright Archive, JWJ Wright 954.

21. Wright Archive, JWJ Wright 813. Cf. Wright, *Native Son*, 240, 241. Apostrophes were added by an editor, not by Wright.

22. This scene and the original closing scene are in the Schomburg typescript of the first draft.

23. Wright, How *"Bigger"* Was Born, 38.

24. Ibid., 37.

25. Wright Archive, JWJ Wright 813.

26. Wright, *Uncle Tom's Children*, 314.

27. Winslow's "Nightmare Experiences" is a review of *The Long Dream* containing a pioneering discussion of fire imagery in Wright.

28. Reynolds's letters are in the Wright Archive.

29. Wright Archive, JWJ Wright 818.

30. The following deleted passage would have appeared in the first paragraph on 322: "A man whom Bigger recognized as the manager of the Regal Theatre told how Bigger and boys like him masturbated in the theatre, and of how he had been afraid to speak to them about it, for fear they might start a fight and cut him."

31. It could also be the hand of Frances Bauman, who, according to Fabre, helped Wright go over the galleys. See Fabre, *The Unfinished Quest*, 177.

32. Wright Archive, JWJ Wright 813.

33. Aswell to Wright, 2 January, 11 January, 18 January 1940, Wright Archive.

34. Stepto, *From behind the Veil*, 3–31.

35. Ibid., 129.

36. Wright to Aswell, 14 January 1944, Box 34, Harper & Brothers Collection, Princeton University Library. Fisher was chosen instead of Wright to provide the introduction to *Black Boy* as well!

37. Wright, *How "Bigger" Was Born*, 21.

38. See "*Afro* Readers Write about 'Native Son'"; "Among Books Reviewed in March"; "Highlights in New Books"; "'Native Son' Delves Into Race Problems"; "Negro's Answer"; "A Remarkable Book by Negro"; "Wright, Richard" (*Booklist*); "Wright, Richard" (*Pratt Booklist*); "A Powerful Novel of Negro's Struggle in a White World"; Fairall, "An Engrossing, Terrible Story"; Gannett, "Books and Things"; Gray, "A Disturbing View"; "Another 'American Tragedy.'"

39. Davis, "Books of the Week in Review."

40. "Books and Bookfolk"; "Negro's Novel Is Overwhelming"; "Powerful Plea for Negro Race"; Ball, "The Vicarious World"; Dalton, "First Novel Wins Acclaim."

41. Butcher, "Negro Writes Brilliant Novel."

42. Canby, "*Native Son* by Richard Wright."

43. L[ewis], "Between the Book Covers."

44. Berry, "The World of Books."

45. "Book Marks for Today"; "'Native Son' Sells Rapidly"; "Public Stampedes for 'Native Son.'"

46. I base this information on charts in the *Brooklyn Eagle*, *New York Times*, *New York Herald Tribune Books*, and *Publisher's Weekly*.

47. "News of Books and Authors"; Herndon, "Books Read at Harlem Library." On the banning in Birmingham see "Dixie Library Bans 'Native Son'"; letters to the editor of the *Birmingham News*, 17 March, 22 March, 30 March, 31 March, 5 April, 12 April, 14 April 1940; "Banning Books Indirectly"; letters to the editor of the *Birmingham Post*, 16 March, 20 March, 2 April, 10 April 1940; "Throwing No Stone"; and Smith, "Dope with Lime."

48. A[dams], "The Conning Tower"; Davis, "'Native Son' Greatest Novel Yet by American Negro"; Fauset, "I Write as I See"; Winchell, "On Broadway"; "Pulitzer Awards."

49. "Chicago Slum Shown"; Cayton, "Negro Housing in Chicago"; Holt, "The Wrath of the Native Son"; Hayes, "Murder Motive Traced to Housing Evil"; Carter, "244,000 Native Sons"; Harkness, "Some Notable Comment"; Stone, "The Rat and Res Judicata."

50. "Native Son Used to Halt an Eviction"; Lacy, "Wright's Novel Comes True"; "Conditions Breed 'Bigger Thomas.' "
51. Lemon, "Book Chat."
52. Howe, "Black Boys and Native Sons."
53. Aswell to Wright, 29 February 1940, Wright Archive.

Works Cited

A[dams], F[ranklin] P. "The Conning Tower." *New York Post*, 4 March 1940, 14.
"*Afro* Readers Write about 'Native Son.' " *Baltimore Afro-American*, 1 June 1940, 13.
Alexander, Margaret Walker. "Richard Wright." In *Richard Wright: Impressions and Perspectives*, edited by David Ray and Robert M. Farnsworth, 47–67. Ann Arbor: University of Michigan Press, 1973.
"Among Books Reviewed in March *Boston Evening Transcript* Especially Recommends." *Boston Evening Transcript*, 13 April 1940, 5:1.
"Another 'American Tragedy.' " By W. L. *Raleigh News and Observer*, 24 March 1940, M:5.
Aswell, Edward. Letters to Richard Wright. Wright Archive, Beinecke Library, Yale University, New Haven, Connecticut.
Ball, Barbara. "The Vicarious World." *Berkeley Daily Californian*, 26 March 1940, 4.
"Banning Books Indirectly." *Birmingham News*, 5 April 1940, 16.
Berry, Lee. "The World of Books." *Toledo Blade*, 9 March 1940, 5.
"Book Marks for Today." *New York World-Telegram*, 12 March 1940, 17.
"Books and Bookfolk." *Portland Press Herald*, 9 March 1940, 13.
Butcher, Fanny. "Negro Writes Brilliant Novel, Remarkable Both as Thriller and as Psychological Record." *Chicago Daily Tribune*, 6 March 1940, 19.
Canby, Henry Seidel. "*Native Son* by Richard Wright." *Book-of-the-Month Club News*, February 1940, 2–3.
Carter, Michael. "244,000 Native Sons." *Look*, 21 May 1940, 8–13.
Cayton, Horace R. "Negro Housing in Chicago." *Social Action* 6 (1940): 4–38.
"Chicago Slum Shown in Negro Writer's Novel." *Public Housing Weekly News*, 9 April 1940, 2.
Cohn, David L. "The Negro Novel: Richard Wright." *Atlantic Monthly* 165 (1940): 659–61.
"Conditions Breed 'Bigger Thomas,' Bring Terror and Violence to Community." *New York Amsterdam News*, 14 September 1940, 1.
Dalton. "First Novel Wins Acclaim for Young Negro Writer." *Stanford Daily*, 10 April 1940, 4.
Davis, Bennett. "Books of the Week in Review." *Buffalo Courier-Express*, 3 March 1940, 6:2.
Davis, Charles T., and Michel Fabre. *Richard Wright: A Primary Bibliography*. Boston: G. K. Hall, 1982.

Davis, Frank Marshall. " 'Native Son' Greatest Novel Yet by American Negro." *Nashville Defender*, 9 March 1940.

"Dixie Library Bans 'Native Son': Alabama Library Won't Place 'Native Son' on Its Shelves." *Pittsburgh Courier*, 20 April 1940, 1, 4.

Fabre, Michel. *The Unfinished Quest of Richard Wright*. New York: William Morrow, 1973.

Fairall, Helen K. "An Engrossing, Terrible Story Is This Novel about a Negro by a Negro." *Des Moines Register*, 3 March 1940, 9.

Fauset, Arthur Huff. "I Write as I See: A Negro Renaissance?" *Philadelphia Tribune*, 4 April 1940, 4.

"Ford, Wright, Hughes to Speak at Savoy Sept. 2." *Chicago Defender*, 2 September 1939, 5.

Gannett, Lewis. "Books and Things." *New York Herald Tribune*, 1 March 1940, 17.

Gray, James. "A Disturbing View of Our Unsolved Race Problem." *St. Paul Dispatch*, 8 March 1940, 10.

Hansen, Harry. "The First Reader." *New York World-Telegram*, 9 September 1940, 17.

Harkness, Samuel. "Some Notable Comment on *Native Son*." In Wright, *Native Son*, "Seventh Edition" [7th printing] (1940), 363–64.

Hayes, Frank L. "Murder Motive in Book Traced to Housing Evil." *Chicago Daily News*, 6 May 1940, 11.

Herndon, Angelo. "Books Read at Harlem Library Show People Seek a Way out of Poverty." *Sunday Worker*, 7 April 1940, 5.

"Highlights in New Books." *Bakersfield Californian*, 26 March 1940, 18.

Holt, Arthur E. "The Wrath of the Native Son." *Christian Century* 57 (1940): 570–72.

Howe, Irving. "Black Boys and Native Sons." *Dissent* 10 (1963): 353–68.

Kinnamon, Keneth. *The Emergence of Richard Wright: A Study in Literature and Society*. Urbana: University of Illinois Press, 1972.

———. "*Native Son*: The Personal, Social, and Political Background." *Phylon* 30 (Spring 1969): 66–72.

Lacy, Sam. "Wright's Novel Comes True: Washington's 'Native Son' Blames Poverty for Life of Crime." *Washington Afro-American*, 1 June 1940, 5.

Leavelle, Charles. "Brick Slayer Is Likened to Jungle Beast." *Chicago Sunday Tribune*, 5 June 1938, 1:6.

Lemon, C. W. "Book Chat." *World Call*, May 1940, 23, 46.

L[ewis], R. J., Jr. "Between the Book Covers." *Albany Times-Union*, 3 March 1940, 10A.

" 'Native Son' Author Says Slump Wrecked Illusions." *Durham Morning Herald*, 29 July 1940, 3.

" 'Native Son' Author to Relate Birth of 'Bigger.' " *Chicago Defender*, 6 July 1940, 6.

" 'Native Son' Delves into Race Problems." *Bloomington [Illinois] Sunday Pantagraph*, 10 March 1940, 9. [An Associated Press review, it appeared in several other newspapers.]

" 'Native Son' Sells Rapidly." *Publisher's Weekly*, 137 (1940): 1161.

"Native Son Used to Halt an Eviction." *Chicago Defender*, 11 May 1940, national edition, 1–2.

"Negro's Answer." *Newsweek*, 4 March 1940, 40–41.

"Negro's Novel Is Overwhelming, Bitter, Profound." *Houston Press*, 22 March 1940, 27.

"News of Books and Authors." *Daily Worker*, 15 July 1940, 7.

"A Powerful Novel of Negro's Struggle in a White World." By A. M. F. *Milwaukee Journal*, 3 March 1940, 5:3.

"Powerful Plea for Negro Race." *Akron Beacon Journal*, 10 March 1940, 8D.

"Public Stampedes for 'Native Son.'" Publisher's advertisement. *New York Age*, 16 March 1940, 2. *New York Amsterdam News*, 9 March 1940, 2. *Pittsburgh Courier*, 23 March 1940, 4, and several subsequent issues through 11 May.

"Pulitzer Awards." *New Masses*, 14 May 1940, 26.

"A Remarkable Book by Negro." *Hartford Courant*, 3 March 1940, magazine section, 6.

Reynolds, Paul. Letters to Richard Wright. Wright Archive, Beinecke Library, Yale University, New Haven, Connecticut.

"Richard Wright Tells Library Forum How He Wrote 'Native Son.'" *New York Age*, 16 March 1940, 2.

Siegel, Paul N. "The Conclusion of Richard Wright's *Native Son*." *PMLA* 89 (1974): 517–23.

Smith, Lillian E. "Dope with Lime." *North Georgia Review*, Spring 1940 (mimeographed letter), 1.

Stepto, Robert B. *From behind the Veil: A Study of Afro-American Narrative*. Urbana: University of Illinois Press, 1979.

Stone, I. F. "The Rat and Res Judicata." *Nation*, 23 November 1940, 495–96.

"Symposium on Negro Culture Today." *Daily Worker*, 11 February 1939, 7.

"Throwing No Stone." *Raleigh News and Observer*, 1 April 1940, 4.

Winchell, Walter. "On Broadway." *New York Sunday Mirror*, 5 May 1940, 10.

Winslow, Henry F. "Nightmare Experiences." *Crisis* 66 (February 1959): 120–22.

Wright, Richard. *American Hunger*. New York: Harper, 1977.

———. *Black Boy*. New York: Harper, 1945.

———. Chicago agenda. Wright Archive, Beinecke Library, Yale University, New Haven, Connecticut.

———. "Down by the Riverside." Typescript. Wright Archive, Beinecke Library, Yale University, New Haven, Connecticut.

———. *How "Bigger" Was Born*. New York: Harper, 1940.

———. Letters to Edward Aswell. Harper & Brothers Collection, Princeton University Library, Princeton, New Jersey.

———. *The Long Dream*. Garden City, N.Y.: Doubleday, 1958.

———. *Native Son*. New York: Harper, 1940.

———. "Native Son." Typescript. Schomburg Collection, New York Public Library, New York.

_____. "Native Son." Typescript. Wright Archive, Beinecke Library, Yale University, New Haven, Connecticut.

_____. *Native Son*. Galley proofs. Wright Archive, Beinecke Library, Yale University, New Haven, Connecticut.

_____. *Native Son*. Revised page proofs. Fales Collection, New York University Library, New York.

_____. *Uncle Tom's Children: Four Novellas*. New York: Harper, 1938.

"Wright, Richard. Native Son." *Booklist* 36 (1 April 1940): 307.

"Wright, Richard. Native Son." *Pratt Institute Library Quarterly Booklist* 6 (October 1940): 24.

"Wright Shows New Book." *Chicago Defender*, 24 February 1940, 22.

"Wright Speaks Tonight on Negro Culture." *Daily Worker*, 12 May 1939, 3.

"You are cordially invited to come to the regular Reunion of the Writers' School." Printed invitation to a lecture by Wright on "The Problems of the Fiction Writer Today." Wright Archive, Beinecke Library, Yale University, New Haven, Connecticut.

LOUIS OWENS

The Mirror and the Vamp:
Invention, Reflection, and Bad,
Bad Cathy Trask in *East of Eden*

I

For John Steinbeck *East of Eden* was "the book," the one he had been practicing for all of his life. "I have written each book as an exercise," he told his publisher, Pascal Covici, "as practice for the one to come. And this is the one to come. There is nothing beyond this book—nothing follows it. It must contain all in the world I know and it must have everything in it of which I am capable."[1] In *East of Eden* Steinbeck attempted to come finally to terms with the two central concerns of his career: the delusive American myth and the magic of the creative imagination out of which fiction evolves. In this novel he would map a twofold exploration, one into his artistic self and one into the psychic heart of his country, and his terrain would be the people and places he knew best: the microcosmic Salinas Valley, where he grew up, and the family out of which he sprang—culminating in the author himself.

As a testament to this search for both the source of the American idea and the fiction-making impulse, Steinbeck created his *Journal of a Novel*, a collection of "letters" compiled daily as he composed this sprawling novel. Written ostensibly to Covici, his friend and editor at Viking Press, the letters chart the novel's creation, replete with signposts of intense self-consciousness found in an almost daily obsession with the objects and conditions of literary creation: pencils and pencil sharpeners, desks and angles of desks, isolation and intrusion. So pervasive does the author's concern for the mechanics of fiction making become, in fact, that one feels a Beckettian impulse surfacing through the journal letters, letters written surely for the writing rather than the reading and not to be read by Covici himself until, after the novel's completion, they were delivered to the editor in a talismanic box hand-carved by the author. Together with *East of Eden*, Steinbeck's *Journal of a Novel* allows us to slip through the looking glass of self-reflection into the process beyond the product.

This large, epic novel had been long aborning. As early as 1944 Steinbeck had written to his close friend Carlton Sheffield to say, "Within a year or so I want to get to work on a very large book I've been thinking about for at least two years and a half. Everything else is kind of marking time."[2] Given Steinbeck's repeated declaration that all of his career had been in preparation for *East of Eden*, there can be little doubt that even this early the author's mind was on the "big book" that he would conceive of first under the title of "The Salinas Valley." Major events would intervene, however, before Steinbeck could begin his great book.

II

In March 1943 Steinbeck, just divorced from his first wife, Carol, who had offered such crucial support in his early years as a struggling novelist, married his second wife, Gwyn Conger, a marriage destined for a rather quick and unhappy end. Immediately he moved with his new wife to New York, where he would spend most of the remaining years of his life, a move that would cut him off irretrievably from northern California and what has since come to be known as "Steinbeck country." Once located on the East Coast, too old for active duty in the Second World War, he accepted a position as correspondent for the *New York Herald Tribune* and set out for the European war zone, where he spent several months writing the dispatches that would later be collected in *Once There Was a War*.

In the year following his return from the bloody Italian campaign his first son, Thom, was born and another publicly successful and critically misunderstood novel, *Cannery Row*, was published, to be followed in the next two years by the birth of a second son, John, and the publication of *The Pearl*, *A Russian Journal*, and the Book-of-the-Month Club selection *The Wayward Bus*. But just as life seemed to be favoring John Steinbeck, two major shocks sent the author reeling. The first and most devastating was the death of Edward Ricketts in May 1948, a tragedy followed three months later by Gwyn's announcement that she wanted a divorce.

If he consciously fought against romanticism and sentimentality in his prose, Steinbeck celebrated it in his relationships with women. When Gwyn, the woman he had loved through the murky lens of romance, began to attack him, he was knocked off balance, confused. When Ed Ricketts, the marine biologist who had for years been his closest friend and model for the "Doc" figure in "The Snake," *Cannery Row*, *In Dubious Battle*, and *Sweet Thursday*, was struck by a train and killed, the author's sense of loss and confusion was enormous.

The year in which his second marriage turned into a quite nasty nightmare and in which he lost Ed Ricketts was the year Steinbeck began to work on *East of Eden*. In January 1948 he wrote to Paul Caswell, editor of the *Salinas-Californian* in Steinbeck's hometown:

> I am gathering material for a novel, the setting of which is to be the region between San Luis Obispo and Santa Cruz, particularly the Salinas valley; the time, between 1900 and the present.
>
> An exceedingly important part of the research necessary will involve the files of the Salinas papers; will it be possible for me to consult these files? Do you know what has happened to the files of the INDEX-JOURNAL and would it be possible for you to arrange my access to them?[3]

A month later he had settled briefly in Monterey, on the coast a few miles from Salinas, and was negotiating with Caswell for copies of the Salinas newspaper's front pages:

> Your letter this morning and its news was very good. With this base cost of five hundred dollars for the front pages we could have perhaps . . . for about two hundred and fifty dollars more a selection from the rest of the paper, for instance the editorials on subjects of either momentary or permanent interest, advertising of foods, clothing at intervals of say every six months. Personals and back page county news. A sampling of this sort of thing would be very valuable to me and perhaps to you.
>
> . . . I can't tell you how grateful I am to you for your cooperation in this matter. It will not only make my work much easier but will greatly increase its accuracy and perhaps its sound of reality and verisimilitude.[4]

Back in New York a month later, Steinbeck wrote to Caswell on 16 March: "This is going to be a huge job but I think increasingly that it is a very important one for me to do. . . . Am going to spend the whole summer on these papers and I hope at the end of that time to be the best informed person in the world on Salinas Valley as it was, not as it is remembered by old timers."[5]

In May he wrote again to Caswell:

> The death of Ed Ricketts changed many things. My timing is changed about completely. It is my hope now that I may be able to do the research out there and my self. This of course would be much better than the sampling on film. . . . I am having to do a reorganization job with myself. . . . A death only happens quickly to the person dying. The living take a long time to realize and to make adjustments.[6]

Earlier in the same month his obsession with verisimilitude in this big novel had been underscored in a letter to Caswell asking for "modern detail maps of the county—maps with place names as well as contours. . . . The fine old map is very good for the over all picture of the county but it hasn't the detail I need."[7]

By September 1948, wrenched badly by the divorce and death, he was back in California, living in seclusion in the family cottage in Pacific Grove, where, supported by a $25-a-month stipend from his father, he had begun his writing career with his first wife, Carol. On 1 September he wrote to Pat Covici to describe his life as a "full circle with 20 years inside of it." Financially and emotionally shattered by the divorce, stunned by the loss of Ricketts, he spent his time working on a script for Elia Kazan's film *Viva Zapata!* and traveling somewhat frantically back and forth between Pacific Grove, Hollywood, and Mexico. All the while, however, he continued to think about and make notes for "The Salinas Valley," writing to a new romantic interest, Wanda Van Brunt: "I don't know what I will do when I finish the script. I may go to Europe for a little while but not for long. Then I will start on my long novel for which I have been practicing so long. And in that time I'm going to put on the crown of my life and no one is going to take it off until that work is done. And god help anyone who gets in the way of it."[8] To fellow author John O'Hara he wrote in June 1949: "I've been practicing for a book for 35 years and this is it. I don't see how it can be popular because I am inventing method and form and tone and context."[9]

Before committing himself fully to what he thought would be the crowning work of a lifetime, however, Steinbeck met, romanced, and married Elaine Scott, moving from Monterey and the home of his childhood and major fiction back to New York to live out his life on the East Coast. It was in New York, in a comfortable house on Seventy-second Street, secure in a new marriage, that he actually began, on 29 January 1951, to write the novel that would evolve into *East of Eden*. One month before the writing began, he declared in a letter to his long-time friend George Albee: "Of course I want the new book to be good. I have wanted all of them to be good. But with the others—all of them—I had a personal out. I could say—it is just really practice for 'the book.' If you can't do this one, the practice was not worth it."[10]

As if *East of Eden* had been too long gestating to be allowed simply to appear on the page, Steinbeck conceived of the companion to his novel, the accompanying letters to Covici that would much later be published as *Journal of a Novel: The East of Eden Letters*. Written daily before each stint of work on the novel, the letters allowed Steinbeck an opportunity to reflect upon the fiction he was creating, work out the problems of the novel, try out ideas, clarify purpose. The result is a volume that displays the daily workings of a writer's mind in a way unique in literature, for the *East of Eden* letters are not simply notes, drafts, or trial runs at fiction. As Steinbeck's biographer Jackson J. Benson has pointed out, the collection of "letters" is not precisely a record of the writing of the novel, but "a semipublic rather than private journal that seldom discusses writing techniques or problems very specifically and that only dimly suggests the terrible struggle he had with the novel."[11]

East of Eden took a long time to jell. Contemplated at one time by its author as simply a nonfiction family history, and later as a Dos Passos–like counterpointing of history and fiction, the novel was slow to evolve. On the ruled pages of a large notebook provided by Covici, Steinbeck began with the first letter. "Dear Pat," he wrote, "How did the time pass and how did it grow so late. Have we learned anything from the passage of time? . . . We come now to the book. It has been planned a long time. I planned it when I didn't know what it was about. . . . The last few years have been painful. . . . Certainly they have changed me."[12]

From the novel's beginning on 29 January 1951 until the end of the first draft on 1 November, there would be a letter for each working day, the letter written in Steinbeck's minute, crabbed hand on the left side of the notebook with the novel itself taking shape on the right-hand page, the novelist's reflections on the writing of the novel and the novel itself mirroring one another on opposing pages. And like another book about the American myth—Benjamin Franklin's *Auto-biography*—this novel began as an address to the author's sons. "I am choosing to write this book to my sons," Steinbeck states early in the journal letters. "They are little boys now and they will never know what they came from through me, unless I tell them." What he intended to tell was "one of the greatest, perhaps the greatest story of all—the story of good and evil, strength and weakness, of love and hate, of beauty and ugliness." What he would try to show, he declared, was "how these doubles are inseparable—how neither can exist without the other and how out of the groupings creativeness is born. . . . The craft or art of writing is the clumsy attempt to find symbols for the wordlessness. In utter loneliness a writer tries to explain the inexplicable."[13] The boys would determine the shape of the first chapter:

> Before too long I am going to have to write Chapter I. And it must have its design made in advance. What is it that I want to say in my opening? First I want to establish the boys—what they are and what they are like. Then I would like to indicate my reason for writing this book to them. Then I would like in general terms to tell them what their blood is. Next I want to describe the Salinas Valley in detail.[14]

As we all know, of course, the plan changed and the published novel begins with a lyrical description of the literal and symbolic

Salinas Valley, a long paragraph that does complex duty in this difficult novel. The direct address to his boys had served to set the novel in motion, but John and Thom would appear in the novel only in the fictionalized versions of the Trask twins, Caleb and Aron, Steinbeck's deep concern for his own troubled sons, especially Thom, reflected in the novel's problematic twins. Still, the author clung briefly to his initial plan: "as the book progresses, it is my intention, every other chapter, to continue the letter to the boys with all the thinking and the detail necessary for one to understand the main story of three generations of Trasks."[15] In the course of creation, the letter to the boys would evolve into the narrative intrusions of John Steinbeck, the implied author who enters the story as both writer and character with a resulting narrative complexity that, while giving rise to much misgiving on the part of critics, has yet to be fully appreciated.

Steinbeck was correct when he wrote, "This is my most complicated and at the same time, my most simple sounding book." And, he claimed, "you will have to look closely to see its innovations even though there are many." Anticipating quite accurately the kind of critical misreading he had experienced throughout his career, he prophesied: "But oh! Jesus am I going to catch critical hell for it. My carefully worked out method will be jumped on by the not too careful critic as slipshod. For it is not an easy form to come on quickly nor to understand immediately."[16] Much earlier, while still working on the *Zapata* script, he had written to Covici, "My critics . . . are still waiting for me. They are going to be very angry with The Salinas Valley because it will be even more unlike Mice and Men."[17]

Naming the novel became a difficult task. From the working title that he had held in mind for years, "The Salinas Valley," he shifted toward other possibilities, contemplating briefly and fortunately dismissing the title "Canable." "No," he wrote Covici, "that has a double or rather a triple meaning I don't want. The name is so important that I want to think about it." From the novel's title he went on in the same letter to discuss the Trask family name: "I remember a friend of my father's—a whaling master named Captain Trask. I have always loved the name. It meant great romance to me. Anyway, the last part of the first chapter will refer to the Trasks and their place."[18] From a romantic whaling captain named Trask it was but a short leap of imagination to a Calvinistic captain named Ahab, and behind *East of Eden* lurks that other, earlier exploration of the nature of good and evil, *Moby-Dick*, a novel referred to repeatedly in the *East of Eden* letters. "I believe that Moby Dick," Steinbeck declares at one point, "so much admired now, did not sell its first small edition in ten years. And it will be worse than that with this book."[19] Finally, the myth of an American Eden, that battleground where the Garden would be wrested from evil, gave rise, on 11 June 1951, to the novel's ultimate title: "And I think I have a title at last," Steinbeck wrote in the journal letters, "a beautiful title, EAST OF EDEN. And read the 16th verse to find it. . . . the Salinas Valley is surely East of Eden."[20]

As he got deeper into the writing of this long-planned novel, Steinbeck's perception of his work underwent inevitable change. He became obsessed not only with his own family history as it came to life in the novel's Hamilton clan, but with the Trask family as well. "These Trasks now," he wrote in the journal. "They fascinate me. . . . All about the natures of the Trasks and their symbol meanings I leave you to find out for yourself. There is a key and there are many leads. I think you will discover the story rather quickly for all of its innocent sound on these pages. Now the innocent sound and the slight concealment are not done as tricks but simply so that a man can take from this book as much as he can bring to it."[21]

Samuel Hamilton, the novel's epic-sized hero, was modeled directly upon Steinbeck's grandfather of the same name, a hardscrabble farmer, storyteller, and ingenious inventor who had homesteaded a ranch close to King City amidst the rolling Gabilan Mountains an hour's drive south of Salinas. Samuel, who drills wells and dreams of blasting through the valley's hardpan to free the trapped waters, is the novel's fisher king and artist, a Daedalian artificer who stands at his anvil forging art from words as well as wood and metal. In the course of writing the novel, in the process of inventing his fictional grandfather, Steinbeck came to identify closely with Samuel. In a telling declaration, he wrote Covici that "I know you make fun of my inventions and my designs. But they are the same thing as writing. *I come from a long line of inventors.* This is in my blood. We are improvisors and will continue to be."[22]

It should be obvious here that in addition to the numerous gadgets he took delight in "inventing" around the house—a new paperweight, for example, or an angled writing desk—Steinbeck was undoubtedly thinking at this moment of the novel itself, his supreme invention and improvisation. From the simple "history" it seemed in its original conception, *East of Eden* was evolving into an investigation of the creative imagination and, concomitantly, of the fiction-making process itself. And as if to counterbalance the increasingly complex threads of allegory (the obvious Biblical framework) and fictional self-consciousness, Steinbeck worked with growing concern to ensure that his "facts" would be correct. Not only did he go directly to Salinas to negotiate for extensive samplings of local newspapers throughout the years covered by the novel, he also began in April 1951 to subscribe to the Salinas newspaper, declaring that reading it gave him "a sense of closeness with the region." He corresponded with the sister he was closest to, Beth, and urged her to talk with his older sister, Esther, in order to clarify points concerning family history. He hired the city editor of the Salinas paper, W. Max Gordon, to research and cross-check historical details for the novel, stating that "in writing this book there are many matters of exact fact which must be accurate." Concerning Steinbeck's obsession with accuracy, Benson notes that "he made a prodigious effort to be precise about dozens of small things that hardly anyone knew about; even the smallest references in passing to people and events went back to the real thing."[23]

In the middle of June 1951 Steinbeck and his new wife, Elaine, moved to Nantucket Island, where he bought a small sailboat and continued to work long hours on the novel, writing to his agent, Elizabeth Otis, to say, "I stay fascinated with *East of Eden*. Never has a book so intrigued me."[24] The same month, he was writing in the journal: "I know it is the best book I have ever done."[25]

A writer who had always worked alone, avoiding the public and keeping unfinished drafts to himself, Steinbeck began during this time to do the unusual: to show the novel a piece at a time to his publisher, Covici. Each week Covici would come to collect the latest material, or Steinbeck would mail that section to Covici at Viking Press. Covici would have Steinbeck's almost illegible handwriting transcribed into type, send one copy back to the author, and keep a second copy, a process that soon wore on the author. "Steinbeck developed very mixed feelings about this procedure," Benson writes in his biography. "Pat . . . took the opportunity of his visits to the writer to discuss the work-in-progress and make suggestions. This John found intolerable."[26] Finally, in the journal letters to Covici, which Covici was to read only after the novel was completed, Steinbeck wrote, almost as if talking to himself, "I want to ask and even beg one thing of you—that we do not discuss the book any more when you come over. No matter how delicately we go about it, it confuses me and throws me off the story. So from now on let's do the weather or fleas or something else but let's leave the book alone."[27] Paradoxically, Steinbeck added a second reader when he started sending the typescript to Elizabeth Otis in a futile hope that the novel might be serialized.

From beginning to end of the first draft Steinbeck used the letters to Covici, the journal of the novel, to test ideas and work out plot elements. Lee Chong's conclusions concerning the Cain and Abel story central to *East of Eden* are first developed in the journal and then transferred almost verbatim to a critical moment in the novel. The obsession with the Hebrew word *timshel*, upon which the theme of free will in the novel turns, comes to light, on the other hand, in an exchange of actual letters between Steinbeck and Covici. In response to Steinbeck's customary enthusiasm about such a find, Covici responded: "Your scholarly discourse I found fascinating but I am a little afraid that you are getting into deep waters. I just heard from Dr. H. L. Ginsberg of the Jewish Theological Seminary, one of our outstanding rabbinical scholars, and he told me that the word *tinshel* [sic], a pure future tense, means 'shall.' He translates the line as follows: 'Thou shalt prevail over it.' "[28] Later Covici wrote to Steinbeck to tell of the discovery of a note in an 1812 edition of the Bible, which, he said, was "a clear proof of free will."[29] Steinbeck, ever the craftsman, asked Covici for the Hebrew characters so that he could carve them into the wooden box he was secretly making, the box into which the completed novel would go as a gift.

A great deal more changed as the novel moved toward completion. One month into the novel Steinbeck was calling Charles Trask by the name of Carl and planning to move that character to California. Carl would have in succession two wives and would be a "mover and shaper." Two weeks later he found he was "forced to change the name of Carl Trask" because the character had "changed his symbolic nature."[30] In the course of the revision the twice-married character destined for California would become the lonely and set-apart bachelor Charles, who would live and die in isolation on the Connecticut farm. These early elements of Charles's character would be transferred to his brother, Adam, who would become the American Adam questing after Eden.

Another significant change involved the Salinas River, which was to have greater structural significance early in the novel's conception. "Now as you well know," Steinbeck wrote to Covici in the journal letters, "Adam and his family must move down river toward the mouth. They will stop at Salinas for this generation. The last part will be at Moss Landing where the river enters the sea. This was the plan from the beginning and it is going to be followed so that my physical design remains intact and clear."[31] The novel ends in the town of Salinas, however, not at Moss Landing, where the Salinas River empties into the Pacific; but that Steinbeck continued to think of the river as a key structural device is suggested in his declaration near the work's end that he had gone over the novel again "to see whether it is fulfilling its purpose and staying within the banks of its design."[32]

A few weeks before completing the first draft, Steinbeck began to despair, complaining to Covici that "it has things in it which will probably never come out because readers do not inspect very closely.

. . . The hell with it."[33] After so many months contriving what he felt to be the greatest of his fictions, he said,

> Writing is a very silly business at best. There is a certain ridiculousness about putting down a picture of life. And to add to the joke—one must withdraw for a time from life in order to set down that picture. And third one must distort one's own way of life in order in some sense to simulate the normal in other lives. Having gone through all this nonsense, what emerges may well be the palest of reflections. Oh! it's a real horse's ass business.[34]

Still, he held to his belief that this was the great work of his career, writing in the journal, "This is the Book still as far as I am concerned."[35]

During the final week of writing he began to work in a panicked rush, staying up all night thinking and getting up at dawn to sit at his writing table, dreading the end and writing: "The book is more important than the finish. I'll try to re-establish in my mind the fact that the book is never going to be done. That way it will move smoothly to the finish. God knows how to do this. But yesterday's work was way off." He complained of having to throw that day's work away.[36]

He completed the novel on 1 November and on 16 November wrote to a friend, the Scandinavian artist Bo Beskow: "I finished my book a week ago. Just short of a thousand pages—265,000 words. Much the longest and surely the most difficult work I have ever done. . . . I have put all the things I have wanted to write all my life. This is 'the book.' If it is not good I have fooled myself all the time. I don't mean I will stop but this is a definite milestone and I feel released. Having done this I can do anything. Always I had this book waiting to be written."[37]

Six months later he was writing to Elizabeth Otis from Europe with a sigh of relief: "Last night I read from the galleys of East of Eden and it is better than I thought."[38] By November 1952, much to his surprise, *East of Eden* was heading the best-seller list in the United States.

III

Much of Steinbeck's life and family history went into *East of Eden*, not merely in the Hamilton episodes taken from "true" ancestral stories but also in the anguished attempt to come to terms with the nature of good and evil, the painful investigation of fathers and sons, and the exploration of place. It would be difficult not to see the very painful break with Gwyn and Steinbeck's feelings of shock and betrayal in response to his wife's actions and accusations as a wellspring for a character such as Cathy/Kate in the novel. Benson states that "in the pain of the aftermath of his separation from his second wife, he spent a great deal of time brooding over questions that preoccupied him: why did she seem to work for the destruction of herself and others, and why did she seem to prefer deceptions, even while it accomplished nothing? Predictably, the answer he came up with was that 'Why?' was the wrong question—she had no motive. She did what she did because that was the way she was."[39]

Of his monstrous character Cathy Ames Trask, Steinbeck wrote in the journal, "And Cathy is going to worry a lot of children and a lot of parents about their children but I have been perfectly honest about her and I certainly have her prototype."[40] Though the critic must resist myriad temptations to blur fiction and biography, in this case it is difficult not to locate this "prototype" in Gwyn Conger and to see Cathy as a device through which Steinbeck was coming to terms with his own devastating emotional experience. When he wrote to Bo Beskow a few months after the split with Gwyn, declaring that American women were "part man, part politician—they have the minds of whores and the vaginas of Presbyterians . . . American married life is the doormat to the whore house," a pattern of thought that might lead to such a character as Cathy seems obvious.[41]

That *East of Eden* took form in part out of Steinbeck's attempts to come to terms with personal trauma was suggested by John Ditsky in his seminal study of the novel, *Essays on East of Eden*, in which he wrote that the novel might be "an act of exorcism of private poisons." Ditsky also leads us toward a much more crucial element in the composition of *East of Eden* when he declares that "it takes no stretching of the point to conclude that for Steinbeck, this most planned of his novels is most genuinely his portrait of the artist as a mature man."[42] For beyond Steinbeck's allegorical worrying of the Cain and Abel myth, beyond his lifelong fascination with the American myth, beyond his lengthy laying to rest of private ghosts is a much more intriguing dimension to this novel, that of invention. More than anything else, *East of Eden* is a novel about its own creation.

Reading the *East of Eden* letters, one is struck again and again with the novelist's fascination with the process of invention. First the mechanics, the daily worrying over tools of the trade. "The writing table is perfect," he declares. "I have never been so content with anything. And the blue wing-back chair is wonderfully comfortable."[43] More important is the choice of pencil—would it be the "black Calculator stolen from Fox Films" or the "Mongol 23/8F which is quite black and holds its point well"?[44] Day after day the author worries the question of pencils:

A pencil that is all right some days is no good another day. For example, yesterday I used a special pencil soft and fine and it floated over the paper just wonderfully. So this morning I try the same kind. And they crack on me. Points break and all hell is let loose. . . . I have my plastic tray you know and in it three kinds of pencils for hard writing days and soft writing days. Only sometimes it changes in the middle of the day, but at least I am equipped for it. I have also some super soft pencils. . . . Pencils are a great expense to me.[45]

On 23 March, Good Friday, Steinbeck goes on for a full page like this, discussing to a point of almost hilarious absurdity—like a character from a Samuel Beckett novel—the selection of pencils, the problems of pencils, until the pencil seems a metaphor for the very act of creation. Months later, near the end of the novel, he is still writing in his letters to Covici: "When I get home I am going to put new blotters on my writing table and sharpen absolutely new pencils . . . and I'll be going into the last part of the book."[46]

It takes no stretching of the critical imagination to see that as he increasingly used the letters as mirrors for the daily process of creation, Steinbeck, a novelist who never had much use for realism and who experimented ceaselessly with the forms of his fiction, became more and more interested not in the conventional process of plot and character generation but in the workings of the creative fiction-making mind reflected back from the pages *facing* the novel. Benson argues that when Steinbeck tries "to use a strong plot, as in *East of Eden*, the novel becomes very labored and one has the feeling constantly that he is following a plot reluctantly."[47] The labored feeling that Benson and others have reacted to may well arise from the fact that the plot of the novel came to exist for Steinbeck as little more than a device through which the fictionalizing impulse might be exposed. The insistence throughout the *East of Eden* letters that this would be his "most complicated and at the same time . . . most simple sounding book" and that "you have to look closely to see the innovations even though there are many" and that it "took three years of puzzled thinking to work out this plan for a book" all suggest that much more is at stake in this novel than a mere allegorical rendering of a too obvious moral. The "great covered thing" and the "carefully worked out method" that Steinbeck predicted critics would miss, that would not be "an easy form to come on quickly nor to understand immediately," may well be this self-reflective element.

It is profitable, I think, to read *East of Eden* as another of the large number of novels that are to a significant extent concerned with their own creation—to read it to a certain degree, that is, as a self-conscious novel. That Steinbeck would arrive at such a work in the early 1950s should not be surprising, given his eagerness to experiment with form throughout his career and his self-expressed doubts concerning the limitations of both the conventional novel and realism itself. It should be remembered that as early as 1933 he was confessing, "I never had much ability for nor faith nor belief in realism."[48]

East of Eden is, I believe, Steinbeck's greatest experiment, and one that succeeds more than some of us have thus far suspected. A key to this reading of *East of Eden* can be found in the opening paragraphs of the novel, in which he begins with his usual method of carefully establishing his setting before introducing his characters, but in which he quickly and deftly goes beyond such a mechanical formula to move from geography to symbol:

> I remember that the Gabilan Mountains to the east of the valley were light gay mountains full of sun and loveliness and a kind of invitation, so that you wanted to climb into their warm foothills almost as you want to climb into the lap of a beloved mother. They were beckoning mountains with a brown grass love. The Santa Lucias stood up against the sky to the west and kept the valley from the open sea, and they were dark and brooding—unfriendly and dangerous. I always found in myself a dread of west and a love of east. Where I ever got such an idea I cannot say, unless it could be that the morning came over the peaks of the Gabilans and the night drifted back from the ridges of the Santa Lucias. It may be that the birth and death of the day had some part in my feeling about the two ranges of mountains.

In this paragraph Steinbeck illustrates the way in which a kind of psychic topography grows out of an untutored, intuitive response to natural symbols: the rising and setting sun. We find here a delineation of the symbolic landscape that dominates Steinbeck's writing, from early to late, and we find a hint of what Clifford Lewis has termed the split in the American consciousness—the almost Manichaean sense of opposed absolutes: good and evil, life and death.[49] Here the dualism is introduced that will quickly become the structural center of the novel, and the focus is not merely upon the landscape but upon the consciousness responding to that landscape: the developing consciousness of the artist.

As perhaps every reader has discovered, *East of Eden* is about man's struggle for full knowledge, for the freedom of will implied in Steinbeck's interpretation of *timshel*: "thou mayest." He who accepts his fallen state—the Ishmael who embraces full knowledge—has the potential to survive in this world and, perhaps, to grow to greatness. Samuel Hamilton is such a man, and Cal Trask is becoming one—the everyman, Steinbeck's "sorry" man. He (or she) who does not attain this fullness of vision will perish, literally and/or spiritually. Adam,

Aron, Charles, and Cathy represent two sides of the American consciousness at war, and in these doomed characters the twain never meet.

What Steinbeck is suggesting in the opening paragraphs is the way in which this sense of opposed absolutes rises from deep within man, represents something profound and inevitable in human consciousness. The central theme of *East of Eden* appears to grow naturally and quickly out of a child's—little Johnny Steinbeck's—response to his environment, and out of the effect of that remembered response upon the mind of the mature creative artist. Steinbeck is demonstrating the way fiction itself is created, how it rises out of the deepest feelings for place, and how what the artist knows—place, family—can become transformed into a fictional structure. In the opening chapter of *East of Eden*, the so-called American myth, so powerfully embedded in the American psyche, the myth of the new garden in which the American Adam squares off against evil, seems to emerge out of a convergence of feelings for place, and out of this intuition comes a structure.

From place, the microcosmic Salinas Valley, Steinbeck moves rapidly in the opening pages of the novel to introduce his family, the Hamiltons, out of whom the creative source of the novel—John Steinbeck—springs. He tells us that "once, fifty miles down the valley, my father bored a well," and he recounts his wonder at what was found beneath the fertile valley, adding, "and it seemed to me sometimes at night that I could feel both the sea and the redwood forest in it [the valley]."[50] In these lines he lays bare the creative process again, for out of this "real" memory will come Samuel Hamilton's fictional discovery of the fallen star that precedes the Trask twins' birth and symbolizes the merger of "dark violence" and great beauty deep in the valley. As the long-vanished sea beneath the valley floor, with its rich, dark strata, must, like all Steinbeckian seas, bring to mind the unconscious, the fallen star may also suggest a plunge into his unconscious.

Whereas the conventional novelistic method is to allow imaginative sources to disappear behind the text, Steinbeck brings his sources into full light in these opening pages, allowing the reader a rare glimpse of the raw materials of fiction. Like his inventive, storytelling grandfather, Steinbeck bores into the wellsprings of the self to bring forth his fiction, and in the process of that search he discovers the star of creation, or cosmos, which represents a compelling act of imagination. He makes his world, re-membering in the act of creation.

A few paragraphs after we have been told of his father's well and his own dark thoughts concerning the valley, Steinbeck introduces his grandfather, Samuel Hamilton, followed by the introduction of another *fact* about the valley: the cycles of flood and drought, the latter of which "put a terror on the valley" reminiscent of the violence Samuel intuits when he looks down on the Edenic bottomland. Steinbeck declares that "it never failed that during the dry years the people forgot about the rich years, and during the wet years they lost all memory of the dry years" (*EoE*, 3). In this passage Steinbeck is simply remembering the way it was, and *is*, in the valley, and he is simultaneously underscoring the dangerous inability of the valley's inhabitants to hold in mind seemingly contradictory realities. The man who can accept the reality of both the rich years and the terror of drought will be the "balanced man" of Melville's *Moby-Dick*, the man with a Catskill eagle in his soul. Steinbeck continues in this first chapter to remember in a casual, lyrical tone what the valley was like, offering a list of place names with easy-paced commentary in keeping with the tone and style of this introductory chapter. The list of place names ends casually with "Corral de Tierra for a fence of earth; Paraiso because it was like Heaven." Those who have read *The Pastures of Heaven* may recall that Pastures of Heaven is Steinbeck's ironic name in that novel for the actual valley called Corral de Tierra, and that the inhabitants of this paradisaical valley suffer from dangerous delusions. These casually juxtaposed place names underscore in *East of Eden* the duality of vision already introduced: the same plot of earth may fence in earthly imperfections or may, through another peephole, seem paradise.

Once the dualism at the heart of *East of Eden* has been deftly introduced in this opening, reminiscent chapter, Steinbeck brings in the whole Hamilton clan in chapter 2, beginning with the autobiographical statement: "I must depend upon hearsay, old photographs . . ." (*EoE*, 5). Conveniently, the Hamilton ranch nestles in the Gabilan Mountains to the east of the valley, the mountains of life described in the opening paragraphs, and, also conveniently, "From their barren hills the Hamiltons could look down to the west and see the richness of the bottom land and the greenness around the Salinas River" (7). Obviously Steinbeck is again simply telling us what *is*—the Hamilton Ranch, now known by another name, really is there in the Gabilan Mountains, a bone-dry ranch of hardscrabble rounded hills, and from these hills one *can* look down on the richness of the river valley and across the valley to the dark wall of the Santa Lucias, where the sun descends into blackness. Because of their location, however, the Hamiltons become strongly identified with the life force in this novel, the life force associated with the eastern mountains in the opening paragraphs of the book. Samuel Hamilton becomes a force for good, a kind of savior, water-witch, grail knight, and nonteleological visionary all rolled into one, and when he bends to grasp a handful of the dry, seemingly barren earth, Samuel is demonstrating his bond with these hills.

With the introduction of the Hamiltons Steinbeck has introduced the soil from which the artistic consciousness of the novel will grow. What remains is for him to create the fictional structure necessary to make this the story of America, and out of this need grows the Trask narrative. And as if the beginnings of the Hamilton narrative have indeed prepared the way for the allegorical Trasks, chapter 2, the first Hamilton chapter, ends with the introduction of Adam Trask in a single line: "Such a man was Adam Trask."

In conjoining the Trask and Hamilton narratives, Steinbeck was fully aware of the risks he was taking. Critics would complain, he predicted, putting the words in the mouth of a hypothetical editor: "The book is out of balance. The reader expects one thing and you give him something else. You have written two books and stuck them together." Steinbeck's well-known answer is, "No, sir. It goes together. I have written about one family and used stories about another family as well as counterpoint, as rest, as contrast in pace and color." The same editor laments: "Right in the middle you throw in a story about your mother and an airplane ride. The reader wants to know where it ties in and, by God, it doesn't tie in at all. That disappoints a reader." Finally, Steinbeck responds coyly to his invented editor, saying, "Yes sir. I guess you're right. Shall I cut out the story of my mother and the airplane?"[51]

Steinbeck foresaw correctly. Again and again critics have lamented the structural outrage of this novel, focusing particularly upon the episode of Olive Hamilton's airplane ride. Typical is my own earlier reaction: "Completely out of place in whatever thematic unity the novel possesses, this episode is reminiscent of the most damaging of Steinbeck's sentimental writing in the war dispatches later published as *Once There Was a War*."[52]

If Steinbeck knew with such certainty that this would be labeled a structural flaw, why did he do it? And why, since chapters focusing exclusively upon the Hamiltons constitute less than 10 percent of the entire novel, did he insist upon including the Hamiltons? The contrast in pace and color offered by the Hamilton narrative is minimal and disappears entirely in the fourth book of the novel. Whatever contrast in pace and color exists in the final book comes only through Steinbeck's authorial intrusion to tell us what he believes, what the collective "we" felt about the war, and how "we" responded to it along with the Trasks. That such a small portion of the novel as the Hamilton narrative could appear to have such an impact is remarkable and is to be explained largely by the fact that the Hamiltons are the novel's round, human characters, the characters that transcend the role of "symbol people" Steinbeck assigned to the Trasks. Thus the story of Tom and Dessie, a poignant tale of two cases of arrested emotional development coming together in their loneliness, overbalances the Trask drama, steals its thunder.

It may also be that Steinbeck took the risk he did with the Hamiltons out of a desire, in this novel, to keep the reader fully aware of the "real" world out of which fiction grows. "In fact," Steinbeck told Covici in the *East of Eden* letters, "all of the Hamilton stories are true."[53] The one Hamilton who slips away from the "real," however, is Samuel. In Samuel the Hamiltons produce their one figure of suspect reality, a larger-than-life patriarch with shining aura, a freer of waters and restorer of wasted lands, a flawed man so good that he tips the scale.

The reason for Samuel's growth toward Trask-like symbolhood is precisely Samuel's growing involvement in the Trask narrative, in which Steinbeck is operating in the realm of idea, of allegory, with little concern for making his symbol-people believable. What, in an earlier reference to his short fiction, Steinbeck had called the "stream underneath" is all that counts, and with the Trasks—the story of the prelapsarian Adam and very fallen Eve—the stream flows rapidly above the surface of the story itself. Once involved with Adam Trask, Samuel immediately begins to grow beyond the dimensions of Steinbeck's remembered grandfather to fill a vacuum in the larger story— he grows into the heroic dimensions required to fill the need for a nonteleological visionary, a balanced man. One could say that Samuel is stolen from the Hamilton narrative and transfers his allegiance as a fictional construct to the allegorical realm of Trask. And it seems very likely that Steinbeck wants us to be aware of this transference.

Samuel's transformation from remembered grandfather to fictional creation is highlighted for the reader in Steinbeck's treatment of Samuel's supposed long-lost love back in Ireland. In the beginning pages of the novel Steinbeck tells us of Samuel's past, saying, "There was a whisper—not even a rumor but rather an unsaid feeling—in my family that it was love drove him out [of Ireland], and not love of the wife he married. But whether it was too successful love or whether he left in pique at unsuccessful love, *I do not know*" (*EoE*, 6; emphasis mine). Steinbeck follows this with the declaration, "I think there must have been some other girl printed somewhere in his heart, for he was a man of love and his wife was not a woman to show her feelings" (6). By chapter 24, more than 250 pages later, Steinbeck has allowed that early conjecture and the character called Samuel to grow to the point that Samuel is able to tell Adam of the vision of love that has come to him "night after night, month after year, right to the very now," adding, "And I think I should have double-bolted my mind and sealed off my heart against her, but I did not. All of these years I've cheated Liza" (263).

Samuel is the point of contact between "real" and fictional worlds in the novel, the bridge. How much of Samuel is created and how much remembered? Near midpoint in the novel Steinbeck breaks in to state, "And Samuel was wise, but I think he knew only one side of Tom" (*EoE*, 245). Given his obvious freedom to invent Samuel, why doesn't Steinbeck know everything Samuel knows? Of Uncle Tom, Steinbeck intones, "What I set down about him will be the result of memory plus what I know to be true plus conjecture built on the combination. Who knows whether it will be correct?" (245–46). And to impress upon us this limited, autobiographical approach to Tom Hamilton, Steinbeck uses the expression "I remember" or a slight variation of that expression eleven times in three brief paragraphs as he begins to tell us about Tom. Similarly, of Dessie's tragedy, he writes, "I do not know any details of her love affair. . . . All I know is . . ." (251).

Steinbeck is obviously deciding when and where to disguise his fiction making within the hidey-hole of autobiography, a great freedom that his presence in the novel, and the presence of the Hamilton narrative, allows him. However, in the character of Samuel, Steinbeck is, more importantly, demonstrating the way in which fiction grows out of the real. What happens to Samuel is that he is contaminated by the fictional Trask narrative and its demands in a way the other Hamiltons are not. And Steinbeck, by repeatedly entering the novel to remind us of the creative process, attempts to ensure that we see this process taking place. We are allowed behind the curtain of the author's workshop to watch Samuel's transformation.

Just before he introduces Samuel to Adam Trask, Steinbeck begins his chapter with a sermon on the freedom essential to the creative mind: "And this I believe: that the free, exploring mind of the individual human is the most valuable thing in the world. And this I would fight for: the freedom of the mind to take any direction it wishes, undirected" (*EoE*, 114). Here he may be anticipating the new direction the character of Samuel will take as the author's "free, exploring mind" illuminates the conflict between good and evil, between self-imposed blindness and the human need to attain full knowledge. Very quickly, Samuel will spin out of his Hamilton orbit and into that of the Trasks, and with this declaration Steinbeck may well be preparing the reader for this new creative freedom.

Throughout the novel Steinbeck breaks into his narrative to remind us of his authorial presence, addressing his reader directly, as when he writes, "You can see how this book has reached a great boundary that was called 1900" (*EoE*, 111); or ruminating upon those beliefs he holds most dear; or mimicking the collective voice of the nation; or even analyzing his characters and then coming back to qualify and contradict himself. To introduce Horace Quinn's role in the Trask narrative, for example, Steinbeck enters the story, saying, "We could not imagine anyone else being sheriff," and later, as Cal prepares to take Abra on their important picnic, Steinbeck adds, "We knew—or at least we were confident—that on May Day, when all the Sunday School picnics took place in Alisal, the wild azaleas that grew in the skirts of the streams would be in bloom" (520). By this point, near the end of the novel, autobiography and fictional narrative have merged completely, with the authorial voice joining the authorial constructs as a participant—a character—within the fiction.

IV

A consideration of *East of Eden* as a self-conscious fiction may also allow us to come to terms with one of the major problems often cited by critics: Cathy Ames Trask. Is Cathy the C.A.T. a genetically misshapen monster who simply is predetermined to be evil because of something she lacks? (Is she, as Benson suggests, a product of Steinbeck's pondering upon the evils of his second wife?) Or is she more psychologically complex than this, as her early and late obsessions with the Wonderland Alice seem to suggest? Why, if *timshel* must apply to all of us, does it seem not to apply to Cathy or Adam, or even Charles, who is incapable of feeling sorry? If this novel is designed to mark the end of an era—naturalism with its emphasis upon pessimistic determinism—as Ditsky has persuasively suggested, why does Steinbeck create absolutists such as Adam and Cathy, who seem, for most of the novel, incapable of free will?

An answer may be that in the course of this long novel the implied author—the voice creating the characters and plot—changes, grows, and learns, as Steinbeck suggests in the opening line in *The Log from the Sea of Cortez* when he declares that "The design of a book is the pattern of a reality controlled and shaped by the mind of the writer." At first he states that Cathy is a monster, declaring simply, "I believe there are monsters born in the world" (*EoE*, 62). Later he qualifies: "It doesn't matter that Cathy was what I have called a monster" (114). Finally he writes: "When I said Cathy was a monster it seemed to me that it was so. Now I have bent close with a glass over the small print of her and reread the footnotes, and I wonder if it was true" (162). He is reminding us that to create is to learn, and furthermore, with his allusion to the "small print" of his character, reminding us that as readers we too are involved in the process of fiction making, that Cathy has existence only on the page.

Very subtly, in his introduction of Cathy, Steinbeck also illustrates for us the way in which a fictional creation takes form. At the beginning of chapter 8 the authorial voice declares its belief that not only are "monsters born in the world" but "Cathy Ames was born with the tendencies[,] or lack of them, which drove her all her life. . . . She was not like other people." Following the clear statement of the author's conception of his character, we are given a description of that character: "Her nose was delicate and thin, and her cheekbones high and wide, sweeping down to a small chin so that her face was heart-shaped. Her mouth was well shaped and well lipped but abnormally small. . . . Her ears very very little, without lobes, and they pressed so close to her head that even with her hair combed up they made no silhouette. They were thin flaps sealed against her head." Cathy's resemblance to a serpent must be obvious to anyone reading such a description, and to ensure that we do not miss the satanic suggestion, Steinbeck adds: "Her feet were small and round and stubby, with fat insteps almost like little hoofs" (*EoE*, 63–64).

If we pay close attention to the process taking place here, we should become aware that we are being allowed to watch as the character's form rises quite clearly out of the artist's conception of that character. The Cathy we begin to see conforms to the author's idea of Cathy defined for us a few lines earlier. Because at this point in the novel the implied author conceives of Cathy as predetermined to evil, inherently depraved, she takes a snake-like form. Later Cathy's form will change as the author's conception of her changes.

In *East of Eden* Steinbeck first illustrates the way the sense of opposed absolutes at the heart of the American myth grows out of an intuitive response to environment. Then he demonstrates the way in which this dualism is manifested in everyday life—the flood-drought cycle, the Fence of Earth–Paradise juxtaposition. Next he introduces the Hamiltons and bares the autobiographical sources of his fiction: his father's well-drilling, for example. At this point he brings in the Trask narrative, overlaying the autobiographical narrative with the allegorical fiction. He gradually allows Samuel to be drawn into the fiction, leaving the remaining Hamiltons firmly fixed in the realm of autobiography. Samuel thus becomes the highly charged point of contact between autobiography and fiction, a role most appropriate to the eloquent artificer and teller of tales at his forge. In this role Samuel becomes a proto-Daedalus, from whom John Steinbeck, the artificer of this amazing novel, will descend.

And finally Steinbeck, or the implied author called John Steinbeck, enters the novel as not simply the "recording consciousness" of such an earlier work as *In Dubious Battle*, but as interpreter and creator, one who creates the "reality" of the novel as he records it, learning as he records and changing as he learns. As he comes to know more about the idea called Cathy/Kate, his feelings change. He qualifies and contradicts his earlier self. The disclosure process of conventional novels is altered so that the novel discloses itself to the author as well as the reader in the process of its creation. What the reader, what America itself, must learn in the course of this novel is what the author learns: a belief in absolutes, an Ahabian monomania, is dangerously delusive; the pursuit of Eden leads to the destruction of whatever earthly paradise may be possible. The author too must learn the necessity for balance, the danger of staring too long into the fire.

Steinbeck's method resembles that described by Austin Wright as the creation of a "narrator-controlled world," one in which "the autonomy of the fictional world breaks down the inventive/narrative distinction: in effect, the inventor's manipulations have become the teller's, implicitly seeming to reflect the latter's creative, expressive, or rhetorical needs."[54]

In the *East of Eden* letters Steinbeck lamented in frustration, "I don't know why writers are never given credit for knowing their craft."[55] Given the general failure of early reviewers to comprehend the carefully worked out methods of such simple-seeming works as *The Pastures of Heaven*, *To a God Unknown*, *Tortilla Flat*, and *Cannery Row*, Steinbeck's frustration is more than understandable.

In 1979, in his *Fabulation and Metafiction*, Robert Scholes made this surprising observation about Steinbeck: "For the last decade of his life, one of America's finest writers in the realistic/naturalistic tradition was engaged in a serious artistic struggle through which he sought to come to terms with fabulation." Scholes was speaking here specifically of *The Acts of King Arthur and His Noble Nights*, but he went on to ponder, "What moved Steinbeck toward fabulation? What but the same impulse that was moving younger writers in the same direction—the sense that the positivistic basis for traditional realism had been eroded, and that reality, if it could be caught at all, would require a whole new set of fictional skills."[56]

The struggle Scholes defined had been going on in Steinbeck for much more than one decade: it was a lifelong quest. *East of Eden*, long viewed as problematic, stands as sharp evidence of both Steinbeck's dissatisfaction with the tradition Scholes names and his desire to experiment and in so doing to explore a kind of metaphysics of fiction making. Like that other great book in the deep heart of the American myth, Benjamin Franklin's *Autobiography*, *East of Eden* is as much about the creating consciousness at the source of the text as it is about character and event. And like Franklin's *Autobiography* and many of Steinbeck's other works, *East of Eden* is a more subtle and complex construction than we are at first prepared to believe. The *East of Eden* letters, mirroring day by day the novel forming on the facing pages, may well offer a key to a fascinating understanding of Steinbeck's one large work of self-reflection.

Notes

1. Steinbeck, *Journal of a Novel*, 9.
2. Quoted in Benson, *True Adventures of Steinbeck*, 552. Like all others interested in Steinbeck's life and writing I am indebted to Jackson Benson for his invaluable work in this biography and elsewhere.
3. Steinbeck to Caswell, 2 January 1948, John Steinbeck Research Center, San Jose State University, San Jose, California (hereafter JSRC).
4. Steinbeck to Caswell, 22 February 1948, JSRC.
5. Steinbeck to Caswell, 16 March 1948, JSRC.
6. Steinbeck to Caswell, 27 May 1948, JSRC.
7. Steinbeck to Caswell, 3 May 1948, JSRC.
8. Steinbeck to Wanda Van Brunt, 22 February 1959, JSRC.
9. Quoted in Benson, *True Adventures of Steinbeck*, 697.
10. Quoted in Ibid., 665.
11. Ibid., 150. Accepting to a large extent the popular critical view that *East of Eden* is a seriously flawed novel, in his biography Benson goes as far as to say, "of the two books written at the same time, one consciously and the other, in a sense, unconsciously, it may be that the *Journal* will prove in the long run the greater of the two" (ibid., 691).
12. Steinbeck, *Journal of a Novel*, 3.
13. Ibid., 4.
14. Ibid., 7.
15. Ibid.
16. Ibid., 14, 29, 31.
17. Quoted in Benson, *True Adventures of Steinbeck*, 627.
18. Steinbeck, *Journal of a Novel*, 7.
19. Ibid., 29. James Barbour's essay, in this volume, gives a more precise account of the sales of *Moby-Dick*.
20. Ibid., 104. Steinbeck is referring to Genesis 4:16, "And Cain went out from the presence of the Lord, and dwelt in the land of Nod, on the east of Eden."
21. Ibid., 16–17.
22. Quoted in Benson, *True Adventures of Steinbeck*, 679 (emphasis mine).
23. Ibid., 682.
24. Quoted in ibid., 683.
25. Steinbeck, *Journal of a Novel*, 112.
26. Benson, *True Adventures of Steinbeck*, 679.
27. Steinbeck, *Journal of a Novel*, 58.

28. Covici, quoted in Benson, *True Adventures of Steinbeck*, 686.
29. Ibid.
30. Steinbeck, *Journal of a Novel*, 18, 27.
31. Ibid., 134.
32. Benson, *True Adventures of Steinbeck*, 687.
33. Ibid., 691.
34. Ibid., 692.
35. Steinbeck, *Journal of a Novel*, 157.
36. Benson, *True Adventures of Steinbeck*, 693.
37. Ibid., 697.
38. Ibid., 716.
39. Ibid., 666.
40. Steinbeck, *Journal of a Novel*, 46.
41. Quoted in Benson, *True Adventures of Steinbeck*, 627.
42. Ditsky, *Essays on East of Eden*, 9, 11.
43. Steinbeck, *Journal of a Novel*, 8.
44. Ibid., 9.
45. Ibid., 35–36.
46. Ibid., 160.
47. Benson, *True Adventures of Steinbeck*, 181.
48. Steinbeck, *Steinbeck: A Life in Letters*, 87.
49. Lewis, "Steinbeck," 261.
50. Steinbeck, *East of Eden* (Bantam edition), 2. Cited hereafter as *EoE*.
51. Steinbeck, *Journal of a Novel*, 180–81.
52. Owens, *Steinbeck's Re-Vision of America*, 145.
53. Steinbeck, *Journal of a Novel*, 63.
54. Wright, *The Formal Principle in the Novel*, 70–71.
55. Steinbeck, *Journal of a Novel*, 14.
56. Scholes, *Fabulation and Metafiction*, 3–4.

Works Cited

Benson, Jackson J. *The True Adventures of John Steinbeck, Writer*. New York: Viking Press, 1984.

Ditsky, John. *Essays on East of Eden*. Steinbeck Monograph Series, no. 7. Muncie, Ind.: Ball State University, 1977.

Lewis, Clifford Lawrence. "John Steinbeck: Architect of the Unconscious." Ph.D. dissertation, University of Texas at Austin, 1972.

Owens, Louis D. *John Steinbeck's Re-Vision of America*. Athens: University of Georgia Press, 1985.

Scholes, Robert. *Fabulation and Metafiction*. Urbana: University of Illinois Press, 1979.

Steinbeck, John. *East of Eden*. New York: Bantam Press, 1955. First published New York, 1952.

———. *Journal of a Novel: The East of Eden Letters*. New York: Viking Press, 1969.

———. *Steinbeck: A Life in Letters*. Edited by Elaine Steinbeck and Robert Wallsten. New York: Viking Press, 1975.

Wright, Austin. *The Formal Principle in the Novel*. Ithaca: Cornell University Press, 1982.

TOM QUIRK

Afterword

The essays gathered here tell the stories of how certain classic works in American literature came to be, works that have exceptionally interesting compositional histories. By using the term "classic" we do not mean to be exclusionary or insistent. The subjects of these essays have claimed and reclaimed, generation after generation, the attention and respect of a considerable number of readers. A "classic" is accepted, in a word. That, in a certain sense, is its liability. In her essay "Composition as Explanation," Gertrude Stein identifies the loss quite precisely:

> Those who are creating the modern composition authentically are naturally only of importance when they are dead because by that time the modern composition having become past is classified and the description of it is classical. That is the reason why the creator of the new composition in the arts is an outlaw until he is a classic, there is hardly a moment in between and it is really too bad very much too bad for the enjoyer, they all really would enjoy the created so much better just after it has been made than when it is already a classic.[1]

In tracing the genesis of certain American classics, the contributors to this collection have gone even farther than Stein in attending to the "outlaw" qualities of literary composition. For it is not merely the newly composed but the not yet composed that claims their attention and begins their inquiry. At a time when earnest and urgent appeals to attach oneself to critical doctrine resemble the Puritan appeal for a second or "adult" baptism, one feels compelled to give testimony (as private and as public, as minutely scrutinized and, perhaps, as politically advantageous as the Puritan proclamation). In such a stormy climate of opinion it is unthinkable that we should speak for all of the contributors to this volume. Nevertheless it seems that the genetic method is a natural if unsuspected ally to literary interpretation and critical theory, though it attaches itself to no particular version of either. At any rate we are confident that all of the contributors to this volume share the common conviction that, to adapt the language of Stein, enjoyers really would enjoy the created so much better by knowing something about how it came to be before it became a classic.

Geneticism is a methodology, not an ideology, and its methods are typically inductive and empirical, sometimes radically so. Geneticism is a way of proceeding, leading often and inevitably to literary interpretation and making its appearance and claiming its methodological portion of such literary pursuits as textual and biographical criticism and literary history. The essays in this volume illustrate only a more restricted form of the generally genetic method, taking as their object elaboration of the genesis of particular texts rather than of whole historical periods or the entire corpus of a particular author. As such, they are subject to the limitation inherent in all forms of genetic criticism, which Alex Preminger has identified in the *Encyclopedia of Poetry and Poetics*: namely, that genetic inquiry can never make convincing statements about the "intrinsic" values of a literary work. However, if we are to believe some contemporary critical theorists, neither can other forms of criticism. Nor is it clear that such value statements are even desirable.

René Wellek and Austin Warren, speaking specifically about the relation of literature and biography, claimed some years ago in their *Theory of Literature* that biographical evidence cannot change or influence critical evaluation and that to ascribe to it "specifically *critical* importance" is a dangerous thing.[2] William K. Wimsatt and Monroe C. Beardsley, together and separately, have taken pretty much the same tack, but with particular reference to matters of literary intention and genesis. They jointly published "Intention" and the more familiar "The Intentional Fallacy," and Beardsley later elaborated upon some of the claims set forth there in his *Aesthetics*, as did Wimsatt, later still, in "Genesis: A Fallacy Revisited." The conclusions they drew were explicit. As Wimsatt put it, for the "objective critic" "the intention of a literary artist qua intention is neither a valid ground for arguing the presence of a quality or a meaning in a given instance of his literary work nor a valid criterion for judging the value of that work."[3] But more and more, the so-called autonomy of a literary work and the critic's objectivity have been called into question, and many now believe that a work of art cannot, and perhaps should not, be bracketed off from a reader's prepossessions and associations or from the biographical and historical circumstances that were the occasion of its creation.

Jacques Barzun once questioned the "misalliance" of biography and criticism and noted that the "extraneous" evidence of history and biography constitutes a kind of knowledge that cannot be evaded in critical endeavor; it, like other kinds of knowledge, is subject to whims of association and the tangents of personal interest. The best one can hope for is a methical mustering of such knowledge in the service of interpretation: "The duty of the critic or connoisseur is to fuse his knowledge with his perceptions and dismiss what is not apposite. If he succeeds, he will find that nothing he knows in this fashion is 'extraneous.' "[4] Sharing as they do a certain antipathy to the assumptions of the New Criticism, perhaps it is now time for literary scholars and contemporary theorists to reexamine the normally prickly relation that has existed between them. Perhaps the methodology of biographical and genetic criticism may be of service to the ideology of theorists, and perhaps the interests and idiom of theory will likewise prove useful to the scholar.

It is a truism of phenomenology that all consciousness is *consciousness-of*. The scholar, and particularly the scholar who would trace the contours of the compositional history of any given text, recognizes this but is more interested, generally, in the object of the preposition. For the genetic critic is bound and limited by evidence of the most conventional, even legalistic sort: letters, journals, manuscript drafts, sources, influences, and of course the printed texts themselves. In the absence of physical evidence regarding the genesis of a particular text, the genetic critic is forced to rely upon testimony, variant published texts, or perhaps other imaginative works by the same writer that indicate, sometimes only provisionally, the direction an author's work is taking. These and such other kinds of evidence as one may acquire provide access to a human awareness and ambition located in the author, the author as person perhaps, certainly as creative cause. And quite often the investigation of how a given work was written discloses not a single, unified intention but several sometimes contradictory intentions. At times it discloses unrealized ambitions, flawed texts, and carelessness or flagging interest, as well as sudden inspiration and passionate commitment.

It is not a method for the too exclusive lover of the beautiful. The characteristic quality of the classic, remarked Stein, is that it is beautiful. But a composition can be stimulating, annoying, irritating: "Of course it [the classic] is beautiful but first all beauty in it is denied and then all the beauty of it is accepted. If every one were not so indolent they would realise that beauty is beauty even when it is irritating and stimulating not only when it is accepted and classic."[5] Unless one is susceptible to the attractions of the all too human efforts of the imagination, the annoyances and irritations may prove neither stimulating nor beautiful. But the disclosures of the history of the composition of imaginative literature invite without restricting critical interpretation. Rather, they prove enabling to all sorts of theoretical discourse and critical assertion.

The history and theory of the genetic approach to literary study has not yet been written, but it is a time-honored method, if simple persistence of practice and interest confers any honor. Were such a history to be written, however, it would show that geneticism owes its origins to diverse and various sources: to the efforts of early biblical exegesis, perhaps; to the romantic organicism of Goethe, Schlegel, and Coleridge, certainly; to attention to textual controversies, particularly those surrounding Shakespeare that were debated throughout the nineteenth century; to the late nineteenth- and early twentieth-century evolutionary criticism that often took its cues from Darwin and Spencer; or, by contrast, to the anti-Spencerian metaphysics of William James, Henri Bergson, or John Dewey; or to later process philosophers such as Whitehead. These and other precursors to geneticism, perhaps as various and mutually repellent as those named above, provide a historical and intellectual foundation, haphazard though it may be, for the genetic method. Equally diverse are the forms such inquiry may take when it contemplates the growth of any given text.

Source and influence study is one such form, and John Livingston Lowes's *Road to Xanadu* stands as a magisterial monument to that sort of inquiry, even if finally insufficient to explain literary creation and authority. The sources, literary or other, that contributed to the formation of certain texts constitute an important form of evidence for the genetic critic, but they are not to be confused with the "causes" of imaginative creation. They are rather the stuff the imaginative writer borrows from, improves upon, reacts against. For genetic inquiry they often provide a factual basis for plotting the composition of a given work (particularly when the acquisition of or acquaintance with such sources is datable), and they offer indispensable clues to the mysteries of the creative imagination itself.

The same may be said for literary influences, though the investigation of this sort of evidence is problematic, for the reaction of creative writers (as readers) to works of the imagination may be idiosyncratic and impressionistic. The implications of this kind of study are vast and complicated. The artistic ambitions of a given writer to write a "novel," for example, might be based on what that writer takes a novel to be, and that in turn derives from the determination and careful inspection of a writer's reading. For those who take more than a merely taxonomic interest in genre as a theoretical issue, it is a question worth pursuing. The answer, as it happens, may or may not result in demonstrating that such and such a work belongs to a certain genre. More often it tends to subvert the generic understanding, what Kenneth Burke somewhere sardonically refers to as the "philosophy of the bin." Whether genre be understood as a culturally and historically conditioned mode of discourse or as a form of mind, when a literary work is examined with reference to the author's reading and defined in terms of imitation, emulation, or resistance to a given genre, the text often proves itself to be sui generis. Leo Lemay, for example, in his essay in this volume, remarks that Franklin's *Autobiography* belongs to that large class of conduct books so popular in the eighteenth century, but he also shows Franklin's radical and deliberate departure from that genre.

Unless the critic or the theorist is able to find interest in the rich particularity and uniqueness of literary discovery, rather than hankering after general assertion or critical axiom, the genetic method will prove a perpetual frustration. But until one knows in what ways a gifted writer is being derivative, how can one possibly know how the writer is being original? The study of sources and influences is essential to such understanding. But the study of literary influence is additionally complicated by the "intertextual" interests that any writer-as-reader is apt to have. Melville, for instance, may have taken some inspiration for his masterpiece from the popular romantic novelist Bulwer-Lytton, but the nonnovelistic influences of Byron, Carlyle, and Shakespeare had profounder effects upon the shaping of *Moby-Dick*. Willa Cather wished to emulate the style of *The Golden Legend* in *Death Comes for the Archbishop* and, in *The Professor's House*, the effects achieved in certain Dutch paintings she admired.

Genetic investigation differs from conventional literary criticism in its tendency to work on the other side of the cloth, so to speak. It reasons and reaches backward, always searching for the antecedents, the historical and biographical circumstance, the creative ambitions and inspirations for a given text. Its methods are conventionally empirical and inductive, and its test is scholarly accuracy. Nevertheless I see no reason why the efforts of both camps (and the dispositions of both groups have typically divided critics from scholars) might not have a cross-pollinating and mutually informative effect, one upon the other. "The demise of source-influence studies," writes Owen Miller, "corresponds to the need to replace the author as the 'authenticating source of identity' [of a text] . . . by the reader as the agent who confers identity on the text by locating it within the co-ordinates of his own literary repertoire of texts."[6] The casual and cavalier announcement of the "demise" of source and influence study (without consulting those who still interest themselves in such matters) and the equally casual identification of the "need" to replace the author in literary interpretation are calculated to aggravate rather than persuade a considerable number of literary historians, scholars, and biographers, not to mention those nonprofessional students of literature (in the classroom and out) who take a lively interest and pleasure in referring literary effects to historical contexts and human occasions.

If we are as Maine and Texas linked by the telegraph, to borrow the language of Thoreau, might we not discover, to quite reverse the intent of Thoreau's figure, that we actually have something to say to one another? For example, Herman Melville believed *The Anatomy of Melancholy* to be an "atheistical" document—an unusual reading to say the least. Is it not possible that the procedures and vocabulary of reader response criticism (properly informed about Melville's state of mind and his "literary repertoire") might be enlisted to account for this reading of a text, not the critic's but Melville's? And would not such a reading provide, in turn, clues for assessing Melville as a reader of texts, as well as a writer of them?

Still another manifestation of the genetic method is observable in the efforts and highly technical procedures of textual scholars. The importance of establishing authoritative and reliable texts ought not be undervalued. Some years ago, in an address to the American literature section of the Modern Language Association, C. Hugh Holman reminded us of the significance of sound historical scholarship. He also remarked that "the importance of the tradition of American literary scholarship appears a diminished thing—except when it is ignored, and then its centrality becomes embarrassingly obvious."[7] One such embarrassment is illustrative and famous, famous not because it is unusual but because it happened to so sensitive a literary intelligence as F. O. Matthiessen. Matthiessen had discovered in *White-Jacket*, in the image of the "soiled fish of the sea," an emblem for a deep-diving intelligence and originating power that could only be Herman Melville's. Unfortunately Matthiessen's critical eloquence had been expended in the service of a corrupt text; the editions printed in Melville's lifetime published—correctly—"the coiled fish of the sea." Interpretation relies upon texts, and plausible interpretation relies upon authoritative texts. Matthiessen, through no fault of his own, was put in the embarrassing position of an Emily Litella (as she was portrayed by Gilda Radner on *Saturday Night Live*): The profuse and impassioned utterance of a conviction, no matter how captivating or profound, if it is based on a false reading of the signs, calls forth the same sort of apologia, the only sort Emily Litella could give, "Oh! Why, that's very different. . . Never mind."

In part Holman's address was a plea, albeit an aggressive one, that critics exploit the resources, bibliographies, and texts to whatever critical purposes they wish, but that they learn as well to use what was bequeathed to them with "a sense of accuracy and a respect for fact." More recently, and no less aggressively, Hershel Parker has issued a similar plea in his *Flawed Texts and Verbal Icons*. He describes his book as "an insider's history of recent American editorial and textual theory and practice" and "an outsider's critique of recent literary criticism and theory,"[8] and with considerable zest he calls into question the procedures of both. Of the several provocative observations he makes, only two need concern us here: that, no less than the New Critics whom they seek to repudiate, contemporary theorists tend to treat the text as a verbal icon; and that the establishment of an authoritative text requires both a full account of the genesis of a manuscript and, concomitantly, a theory of the creative process.

As Parker demonstrates, Wimsatt and Beardsley's "Intentional Fallacy" still casts a long shadow over literary criticism and theory. Critics and theorists still tend to treat the literary text as a "given"; whether its givenness is regarded as the data of consciousness, an encoded linguistic construct, or a cultural artifact makes little difference. The performances of literary theorists, so often designed to destabilize or decenter texts, fail to take into account the fact that any given text may already be an unstable construct of meanings and signs. What is given to them is itself often the result of considerable textual debate; the texts they seek to problematize, before they ever see them, are often the results of scrupulous and difficult problem solving based upon what can be learned about an author's intention and the genesis of a manuscript.

However easily the critic may discount authorial intention, textual unity and wholeness are sometimes provisional and contingent upon an exacting determination of authorial intent. Before one attempts, for example, to "deconstruct" Jonathan Edwards's essay "The Mind" (in the University of California edition) or "Billy Budd, Sailor" (in the University of Chicago edition) it is well to remember that these are "reconstructed" texts (the first by Leon Howard, the second by Harrison Hayford and Merton Sealts), designed to resolve internal contradictions and satisfy the requirements of external evidence. However many meanings might be teased out of either, the efforts of Howard, Hayford, and Sealts coaxed coherent meanings out of the manuscripts and other evidence in order to provide a readable and authoritative text to begin with.

The preparation of reliable texts requires the minute inspection of manuscripts, letters, journals, diaries, and the like, and a thorough acquaintance with the publishing history of a text. But in order to decide upon a copy-text, in which may be inserted such variants as editorial rationale and external evidence warrant, some decision must be made about the author's intention. An author's intentions may be of several sorts. Parker, citing Michael Hancher, notes three such intentions: "programmatic intentions" (the author's intentions to write something—an epic, for example); "active intentions" (those at the time the author is completing the work); and "final intentions" (the author's intentions to "cause" certain effects, that is, "whatever the author wishes to accomplish *by means of* his completed work"). The editorial practice of relying upon an author's "final intentions" as the basis for preparation of an authoritative text is something Parker calls into question, preferring instead, and borrowing the term from John Searle, "intentions in action." The work is infused with the author's intention "during the process of composition, not before and not afterwards."[9]

Without entering into the complicated debates that thrive among textual editors, I want only to note how centrally the genetic method figures in the establishment of literary texts. Parker wishes, quite properly I believe, to install a notion of the creative process into the procedures of textual editing. (And, it should be mentioned, so does Steven Mailloux, who in his *Interpreting Conventions* finds such a notion entirely congenial to the interests of reader response criticism.) Whether one decides to give preemptive authority to the act of creation in the full flush of the moment and in the thrall of some compelling but indefinite inspiration, or to the uninspired and perhaps uninterested final intentions of an author separated from the motive impulse that gave birth to literary creation (sometimes by several decades), is a difficult question.

The first view tends to be a romantic/expressive one, inviting biographical and psychological speculation. The second is a classical/cultural one, treating the text as a cultural commodity, over which the writer has full authority during his or her lifetime and that sometimes reaches the public through the writer's willful accommodation to public taste and the commercial judgment of editors and publishers. This latter view has been provocatively explored by Jerome McGann in *A Critique of Modern Textual Criticism*. McGann locates his interest not so much in the author as creative cause, as Parker does, as in the historically conditioned manifold and shifting social relationships a text acquires in the course of printing, publishing, and reception. In any event the critic cannot blink the fact that, for example, *Pudd'nhead Wilson* is a haphazard affair, hastily slapped together, as Twain himself said, by a "jack-leg novelist," or that Twain deleted several of his more venomous anti-Southern sentiments from *Life on the Mississippi* because he wanted his book to sell in the South.

Parker's view of the creative process, and one that fully supports his views about literary authority and textual editing, is an aggregate of the views of John Searle, John Dewey, and the Cornell cognitive psychologists. But genetic criticism may appropriate any of several theories of the creative process to "explain" or confirm what may be learned about the genesis of a text. Notions of the creative imagination as "mental illness," a form of "healthful play," or magical "incantation" may do little or nothing to establish literary authority in a text, but they may go a long way in explaining how a certain imaginative project developed into the work it became. Were one to contemplate the work of art as an "analogue" of both the writer's and the reader's experience and fund of memories, as Bergson does according to his biological metaphysics and as Sartre does according to phenomenological reduction, one would have not only to abandon the text as verbal icon but to go beyond the notion of the verbality of literature itself. And were one to credit fully the comments of imaginative writers themselves about the creative process, still other cogent theories of creation might ensue, ones with particular value in interpreting the growth and imbedded meanings of specific texts.

Literary biography, in which genetic inquiry often plays an instrumental part, typically takes into account the announced ambitions of imaginative writers and links them to the growth of particular manuscripts into works of art. Too often, literary biography treats the works of imagination as something that merely "happened" to an author, and the story of a writer's life is frequently approached with a theory of personality, literary history, or political circumstance that the actual facts of that writer's life and the artistic achievement of the writer's works cannot finally corroborate. But biographers who approach their subjects in the interests of scholarly accuracy and genuine curiosity often disclose and dramatize the processes of the creative imagination in ways that are fully as provocative and convincing as their more theoretical counterparts.

The private or public "self" of an author may or may not be identical with the composing self that creates memorable literature. In either case the biographical circumstance of an author is the context out of which creation arises and into which, thanks to the biographer, we may place ourselves to better understand that creation. For Faulkner, as Sally Wolff and David Minter demonstrate, a "matchless" time proved to be the enabling circumstance for the creation of *The Sound and the Fury*. Steinbeck approached the writing of *East of Eden* with a leisure and financial security that promoted the high artistic ambitions he had for that novel. For Melville, damned as he was by dollars, *Moby-Dick* was an absorbing and self-consuming project, and he sometimes felt "pulled hither and thither by circumstance" as though he would at last be "worn out and perish." For Mark Twain, Porlockian interruptions may actually have proved not the impediment but the impetus to return, once again, to the manuscript of *Huckleberry Finn*. Without such aggravations and demands on his time he might never have sought escape in the creation of that book.

The literary biographer's efforts to tell the story of a life may never provide any overarching theory of the imagination, and the generalizations one may make about writers on the basis of the observation or re-creation of their writing habits may finally yield such merely commonplace and commonsensical observations as Malcolm Cowley made in his "Natural History of the Writer." Still they are not to be ignored. In describing the what and why of writers, Cowley defined the writer in vocational, social, functional, and psychological terms. In vocational terms "the writer is a person for whom writing is the central activity." In social terms "the writer is a person *with readers*." In functional terms "the writer is a craftsman whose medium is written language. . . . Like every good craftsman, he wants to make objects, or artifacts, that will have an independent existence and will play a part in the lives of people he has never seen." In psychological terms the writer is a person "who talks to himself, or better, who talks *in* himself."[10] In all these terms the biographer gives us a privileged glimpse into the purely human, if exceptionally devoted, occupation and habits of the creative temperament. And biographical statements may be converted into critical statements. A writer's preoccupations may become the themes and motifs of a text; the emotional coherence a writer achieves in any given work may provide the formal unity and structure of a work of art, and the lack of such coherence may point to the flaws and gaps in a text; a writer's private symbols or petty annoyances may become the myths of the tribe or a shared cultural grievance. In any case, by describing the contours of a writer's life as writer, and by relating that life to the imaginative growth of particular works or a whole corpus, the biographer provides access to a kind of genetic understanding that cannot quite be got in any other way.

The histories of composition offered in this volume often provoke critical conclusions quite in keeping with contemporary critical concerns. For example, Leo Lemay discusses the fascinating and perhaps deliberate lack of closure in Franklin's *Autobiography*; Robert Sattelmeyer traces in the development of *Walden* the sum of the author's histories "simultaneously present in a text at once fabular, mythic, scientific, and even scriptural in its dimensions"; and Louis Owens in giving careful attention to the circumstance of the composition of *East of Eden* reveals Steinbeck's interest in the metaphysics of fiction-making and claims that that novel may well be the author's "one great work of self-reflection."

Current critical discourse may in turn provide the genetic critic with a vocabulary that permits more intelligible statements about the sorts of disclosures the genetic method has routinely offered up for several generations. By the same token, may not the genetic method offer to theorists an available means to root their interests in a conventional scholarly engagement?

Still, if the study of the composition of a literary text is a "humanistic" enterprise (and it is), it may be guilty of any number of recent objections made against it. To the degree that Terry Eagleton's "humanist fallacy" applies to genetic studies, perhaps all the contributors to this volume stand accused. The humanist tendency is, according to Eagleton, to reduce all literature to some form of "interpersonal relations," an improbable dialogue between author and reader. But such a notion assumes a simplistic concept of "person."[11] It is a matter of record, at any rate, that Melville's best work came out of some "unmanageable thing" working within him, that Twain considered himself the "amanuensis" of his own art, and that Cather's chief delight in writing fiction was the freedom and interest of getting inside another person's skin.

Roland Barthes's announcement of the "death of the author" is not likely to convince those interested in biographical and genetic inquiry. But even if it did, perhaps it is worthwhile to point out the rather obvious fact that the first "reader" of any text is its author, and that that text (existing as it does in its becoming as a for-itself, not an in-itself) really does possess for the author/reader all the polysemic indeterminacy one could wish for. And the "intertextual" requirements of interpretation ought not to exclude from consideration journal entries, manuscript revisions and excisions, letters, diaries, and so forth.

Literary deconstruction has shown us the infinite regress of language, the constant deferral of meanings as they recede before our inquiry. But despite that we need not assume the writer did not know what he or she was about. The human mind, as Paul Valéry observed, can never "finish" anything, it is doomed to incompletion and fragment. Ishmael laments his inability to "express" the whale's tail: "Dissect him how I may, then, I but go skin deep; I know him not, and never will. But if I know not even the tail of this whale, how understand his head, much more, how comprehend his face, when face he has none?" Melville recognized the impossibility of expressing his whale, but, as James Barbour has shown, it was not until Melville committed himself to the "failure" of his book that he could deliver to the world the success that is *Moby-Dick*.

Willa Cather made the impossibility of expression an aesthetic principle: "Whatever is felt upon the page without being specifically named there—that, one might say, is created. It is the inexplicable presence of the thing not named, of the overtone divined by the ear but not heard by it, the verbal mood, the emotional aura of the fact of the thing or the deed, that gives high quality to the novel or the drama, as well as to poetry itself."[12] So did Wallace Stevens: "There is always an analogy between nature and the imagination, and possibly poetry is merely the strange rhetoric of that parallel: a rhetoric in which the feeling of one man is communicated to another in words of the exquisite appositeness that takes away all their verbality."[13] Such also was the aesthetic principle that, as William Balassi argues in his essay, governed the complicated genesis of Hemingway's The Sun Also Rises. Might not the deconstructionist use authorial statement and biographical resource to illuminate and corroborate critical perceptions, rather than being anxious to dismiss the authority of the author?

Nor does the biographer or the literary historian need to be told that biography and history are "fictions"—the very experience of having written either would have taught that. Experience taught Emerson that "man is a golden impossibility," but it also taught him that life is "sturdy" and that the mind "goes agonizing on" nevertheless. And James Harvey Robinson and Randolph Bourne observed that history is a useful fiction some eighty years ago. Fictions or not, biographer and historian alike also realize that facts are "brutes." It is well for the critic to remember that circumstances alter cases. For the genetic critic those circumstances are defined (not confined) by the factual record.

The genetic critic takes the name of an author very seriously. Nothing is more common in critical discourse than statements such as these: "Hawthorne anticipated Freud by seventy years"; "Sterne is the progenitor of meta-fiction"; "Dickens was the phenomenologist of nineteenth-century urban life." What is disturbing is not that these are nonsense statements (which from a certain point of view they are), but that a cluster of untested critical and theoretical postulates are smuggled into the argument under the author's name. The genetic critic appropriates critical author-ity by examining the very human circumstances that clarify a given writer's intentions, preoccupations, and motivations.

Such a critic does not need to assume that an author's literary intention must to be single or "pure," E. D. Hirsch notwithstanding. For the purposes of scholarly inquiry at least, one might posit, along with James or Sartre, that an empirical ego can and does account for and explain everything that the transcendental ego of Kant or Husserl may explain. Literary "meaning" need not be monolithic; it may be as diverse as a given writer's interests and ambitions. And an author may or may not be engaged in an act of communication in any given text. Imaginative writers may write "inside narratives" and conduct "private campaigns" intended as much to disguise as to disclose meanings, and to solve through the resources of literary art the real intellectual, ethical, or emotional dilemmas of the artist by entertaining fictional possibilities.

A more serious objection to geneticism, perhaps, is Kenneth Burke's, all the more serious for the jocular way in which he delivers it. The genetic critic, he claims, attempts to "restore" value and meaning to a text by reclaiming its linguistic, cultural, and economic context:

> The point is irrefutable. Insofar as a social context changes, the work of art erected upon it is likely to change in evaluation (though the genetic critic does not tell us whether we should also apply his method to an artist whose reputation has risen with the years—whether we should, by placing Melville in his times, "restore" to him the inferior position he held among his contemporaries).[14]

A reply to this kind of complaint may be found in Wallace Stevens's observation that, more often than not, the imagination is not identical to the reality (social, political, or personal) that impinges upon it. The whole effort of the imagination is a "violence from within that protects us from a violence from without. It is the imagination pressing back against the pressure of reality."[15] Surely, as Keneth Kinnamon demonstrates, *Native Son* is the vivid complaint of a black, Communist writer to a political reality imposed upon him. Perhaps more surprisingly, Scott Donaldson reveals a similar imaginative motivation in F. Scott Fitzgerald.

Because this collection is dedicated to the memory of Leon Howard, it is fitting to quote his own apology for his biography of Herman Melville, a biography that gave more than customary attention to how an imaginative writer's novels were composed:

> An account of the actual motives affecting Melville's composition and of the methods by which he put his books together may distress some of his admirers, but, in the long run, it may be well to recognize the fact that memorable literature is something which has risen above the frailties of its human origin rather than descended from some perfect inspiration. To those critics who insist that a work of literature makes its most admirable appearance as an independent object of aesthetic experience, I can only suggest that the arts which we call the humanities are, as a matter of fact, unavoidably human. Of them, literature is the most comprehensive and illuminating in its humanity; and, for my part, the knowledge of human beings, in all their complex relationships, which can be gained from literary study is one of the greatest incentives to its pursuit. I cannot, in short,

share the apparently widespread feeling that a rereadable book is so delicate a plant that it needs to be removed from its natural environment
before it can attract the imagination.[16]

These remarks were made more than thirty-five years ago, when
formalist criticism was very much in the saddle. Today, we are told,
critical theory has moved well beyond formalistic considerations. Indeed, John Sutherland recently identified the doctrines of contemporary critical theory as constituting a "New Pragmatism."[17] If that is so,
perhaps it can lay claim to the sort of rich and expansive interest in
human possibility we find in William James, who was thus hospitable
and receptive not because he was a pragmatist but because he was
loath to forfeit the productive tensions of discourse and the fruitful
claims we might make upon a very human future. We trust, at any
rate, that current theorizing has likewise moved toward broader toler-
ance of a critical method that interests itself in the imperfect and
human dimensions of the composition of memorable literature. Perhaps it may come to participate in that interest.

Notes

1. Stein, "Composition as Explanation," 514.
2. Wellek and Warren, *Theory of Literature*, 80.
3. Wimsatt, "Genesis: A Fallacy Revisited," 195.
4. Barzun, "Biography and Criticism," 496.
5. Stein, "Composition as Explanation," 515.
6. Miller, "Preface" to *Identity of the Literary Text*, xviii.
7. Holman, "American Literature," 456.
8. Parker, *Flawed Texts and Verbal Icons*, xi.
9. Ibid., 22–23; the term is from Searle's *Intentionality: An Essay in the Philosophy of Mind* (1983).
10. Cowley, "A Natural History of the Writer," 138–43.
11. Eagleton, *Literary Theory: An Introduction*, 120–21.
12. Cather, "The Novel Démeublé," 41.
13. Stevens, "Effects of Analogy," 118.
14. Burke, *Counter-Statement*, 77.
15. Stevens, "The Noble Rider and the Sound of Words," 36.
16. Howard, *Melville*, viii.
17. Sutherland, "Ivory Institutes."

Works Cited

Barzun, Jacques. "Biography and Criticism—A Misalliance Disputed."
     Critical Inquiry 1, no. 3 (March 1975): 479–96.
Beardsley, Monroe C. *Aesthetics: Problems in the Philosophy of Criticism.*
     New York: Harcourt, Brace, 1958.

Burke, Kenneth. *Counter-Statement*. Berkeley and Los Angeles: University of California Press, 1968.

Cather, Willa. "The Novel Démeublé." In *Willa Cather on Writing: Critical Studies on Writing as an Art*, 35–43. New York: Alfred A. Knopf, 1949.

Cowley, Malcolm. "A Natural History of the Writer." In *The Literary Situation*, 132–228. New York: Viking Press, 1958.

Eagleton, Terry. *Literary Theory: An Introduction*. Minneapolis: University of Minnesota Press, 1983.

Hayford, Harrison, and Merton M. Sealts, Jr., eds. *Billy Budd, Sailor: An Inside Narrative*. Chicago: University of Chicago Press, 1962.

Hirsch, E. D. *Validity in Interpretation*. New Haven: Yale University Press, 1967.

Holman, C. Hugh. "American Literature: The State of the Art." *American Literature* 52 (November 1980): 449–56.

Howard, Leon. *Herman Melville: A Biography*. Berkeley and Los Angeles: University of California Press, 1951.

––––––. *"The Mind" of Jonathan Edwards: A Reconstructed Text*. Berkeley and Los Angeles: University of California Press, 1963.

Lowes, John Livingston. *The Road to Xanadu: A Study in the Ways of the Imagination*. Boston and New York: Houghton Mifflin, 1927.

McGann, Jerome J. *A Critique of Modern Textual Criticism*. Chicago: University of Chicago Press, 1983.

Mailloux, Steven. *Interpreting Conventions: The Reader in the Study of American Fiction*. Ithaca: Cornell University Press, 1982.

Miller, Owen. "Preface" to *Identity of the Literary Text*. Edited by Mario J. Valdés and Owen Miller. Toronto: University of Toronto Press, 1985.

Parker, Hershel. *Flawed Texts and Verbal Icons*. Evanston, Ill.: Northwestern University Press, 1984.

Stein, Gertrude. "Composition as Explanation." In *Selected Writings of Gertrude Stein*, 511–23. Edited by Carl Van Vechten. New York: Random House, 1946.

Stevens, Wallace. "Effects of Analogy." In *The Necessary Angel: Essays on Reality and the Imagination*, 105–30. New York: Random House, 1951.

––––––. "The Noble Rider and the Sound of Words." In *The Necessary Angel*, 1–36.

Sutherland, John. "Ivory Institutes." *Times Literary Supplement*, 18–24 December 1987, 1402.

Wellek, René, and Austin Warren. *Theory of Literature*. 3d ed. New York: Harcourt, Brace & World, 1956.

Wimsatt, William K., Jr. "Genesis: A Fallacy Revisited." In *The Disciplines of Criticism: Essays in Literary Theory, Interpretation, and History*, edited by Peter Demetz, Thomas Greene, and Lowry Nelson, Jr., 193–225. New Haven: Yale University Press, 1968.

Wimsatt, William K., Jr., and Monroe C. Beardsley. "The Intentional Fallacy." *Sewanee Review* 54 (Summer 1946): 468–88.

Contributors

WILLIAM BALASSI is a Visiting Lecturer at the University of New Mexico. In addition to the book he is currently writing on the composition of *The Sun Also Rises*, he has coedited a book of interviews with Southwestern writers (forthcoming, 1990). His work has appeared both in scholarly journals, such as *The Hemingway Review*, and in popular magazines, such as *The Mother Earth News*.

JAMES BARBOUR is professor of English at the University of New Mexico, coeditor of *American Literary Realism*, and author of a number of essays on American literature. With Tom Quirk he has coedited Leon Howard's *Essays on Puritans and Puritanism* (1986) and *The Unfolding of "Moby-Dick"* (1987), and is currently editing the uncollected boxing essays of A. J. Liebling.

SCOTT DONALDSON is the Louise G. T. Cooley Professor of English at the College of William and Mary. He has written half a dozen books, edited several others, and published numerous articles on American literature and culture. He is best known for his literary biographies, which include *Poet in America: Winfield Townley Scott* (1972), *By Force of Will: The Life and Art of Ernest Hemingway* (1977), and *Fool for Love, F. Scott Fitzgerald* (1983). His most recent work is *John Cheever: A Biography* (1988). He is currently at work on a biography of the poet and patriot Archibald MacLeish.

KENETH KINNAMON is the Ethel Pumphrey Stephens Professor of English and chairman of the department at the University of Arkansas, Fayetteville. He is the author of *The Emergence of Richard Wright* (1972) and the compiler of *A Richard Wright Bibliography* (with the help of Joseph Benson, Michel Fabre, and Craig Werner). He has edited collections of essays on James Baldwin and *Native Son* and has coedited *Black Writers of America*.

J. A. LEO LEMAY is the H. F. du Pont Winterthur Professor of English at the University of Delaware. A specialist in early American literature, he has published widely on colonial and nineteenth-century American writers. He has recently written *The Canon of Benjamin Franklin, 1722–1776: New Attributions and Reconsiderations* (1985) and *"New En-*

gland's Annoyances": America's First Folk Song (1986) and edited *Benjamin Franklin: Writings* (1987), *Deism, Masonry, and the Enlightenment: Essays Honoring Alfred Owen Aldridge* (1987), and *An Early American Reader* (1988).

DAVID MINTER is professor of English at Emory University, dean of Emory College, and university vice-president for arts and sciences. He is the author of *William Faulkner: His Life and Work* (1980) and numerous essays on American literature. He is also editor of the Norton Critical Edition of *The Sound and the Fury* (1987) and coeditor of *The Harper American Literature* (1986) and *The Columbia Literary History of the United States* (1987).

LOUIS OWENS is a professor of English at the University of California at Santa Cruz. In addition to numerous essays his publications on Steinbeck include *John Steinbeck's Re-Vision of America* (1985) and *The Grapes of Wrath: Trouble in the Promised Land* (1989). He is a member of the editorial board of the *Steinbeck Quarterly* and coeditor of *American Literary Scholarship: An Annual*.

TOM QUIRK is professor of English at the University of Missouri at Columbia. He has written essays on a variety of American writers and is the author of *Melville's Confidence-Man: From Knight to Knave* (1982) and *Bergson and American Culture: The Worlds of Willa Cather and Wallace Stevens* (1990). With James Barbour he has coedited *Romanticism: Critical Essays in American Literature* (1986) and two books by Leon Howard, *Essays on Puritans and Puritanism* (1986) and *The Un-folding of "Moby-Dick"* (1987).

ROBERT SATTELMEYER is professor of English at Georgia State University. He is the coeditor of three volumes of Thoreau's *Journal* in the Princeton Edition of *The Writings of Henry D. Thoreau* and a member of the edition's editorial board. He has written *Thoreau's Reading: A Study in Intellectual History* (1988) and a number of articles on Thoreau and other nineteenth- and twentieth-century American authors.

SALLY WOLFF is assistant dean of Emory College at Emory University. She collaborated with David Minter on the Norton Critical Edition of *The Sound and the Fury* (1987); her other works include "Companion Collections: The Short Stories of Eudora Welty and Elizabeth Spencer" and "Eudora Welty's Nostalgic Imagination."

JAMES WOODRESS is professor emeritus at the University of California at Davis, author of *Howells and Italy* (1952) and of biographies of Booth Tarkington (1955), Joel Barlow (1958), and Willa Cather (1970, 1987). He is the founder and editor of *American Literary Scholarship* and recipient of the Jay B. Hubbell Medal in 1985 for service to the study and teaching of American literature.

Index